THE FRAMEWORK
OF PRICE THEORY

THE FRAMEWORK
OF PRICE THEORY

Clark Lee Allen

Southern Illinois University

Wadsworth Publishing Company, Inc., Belmont, California

L.C. Cat. Card No.: 67–12817
Printed in the United States of America

PREFACE

A recent advertisement for a well-known encyclopedia stated that man's knowledge of the world has doubled during the last twenty-five years. The "information explosion" through which we are living has, it seems to me, significant implications for college professors and those who design courses and curricula. There is so much to be taught and to be learned that the temptation may be to expect students to undertake work which in point of difficulty and in sheer quantity is well beyond their capacities. It becomes increasingly important for instructors and textbook writers to determine what is essential and what can be omitted or treated superficially. Emphasis, it seems to me, must increasingly be on basic tools first, with applications to particular problems to come in due course. This, at any rate, has been the objective in the preparation of this text. Lack of precise understanding of basic concepts has sometimes constituted a serious handicap for students in advanced courses in microeconomics, and I am convinced that this deficiency could have been prevented by appropriate instruction at lower levels. For the student for whom this will be the terminal course in economics, this text should provide insights into the problems that interest price theorists and into the ways they work out solutions.

Different professors teaching the same subject even with the same textbook are likely to offer quite different courses—so different, in fact, that a student might profitably take the same course under more than one professor. It seems to me that at least three quite different kinds of courses might make effective use of this text. First, some teachers may find that the topics covered and the emphasis given are essentially the same as those they want to develop in their courses. Second, some professors may want to develop many topics more fully than does the text. This may be done by class lectures or by assigning additional readings in other sources. The references at the close of each chapter include many discussions suitable for this purpose. Finally, some instructors may not want to push the theoretical analysis further than the text goes on most points, but rather may want to use a part of the class time to explore the applications and implications of the theory with their students. Questions such as the following should stimulate meaningful student responses: "Would you anticipate that the elasticity of demand for spark plugs would be greater or less than for new cars?" "What are the reasons for postulating a U-shaped long-run average-cost curve as the typical case?" "Trace through the process by which equilibrium would tend to be restored in a purely competitive market after an increase in demand." My undergraduate biology teacher used to reserve the last half hour of each laboratory period to eliciting responses from each student to the question, "What are you getting out of all of this?" Perhaps the technique should be more widely employed.

Much of the analysis in this text is demonstrated geometrically and algebraically. Since it is largely concerned with quantities and their relationships, price theory is essentially mathematical in nature, whether or not conventional mathematical symbols are employed. This text assumes no mathematical background for the student or the teacher beyond elementary high-school algebra and geometry. The concept of the derivative of a function is frequently used, but this is explained in the text, and any undergraduate can master the mechanics of taking derivatives of simple functions in a matter of minutes. The insights gained and the time saved are ample compensations for this small effort.

At the close of each chapter we will attempt to discuss, often in an informal and relaxed fashion, certain matters suggested by the earlier analysis but not developed as fully as they seem to deserve. Or we may introduce new materials pertinent to the subject at hand but not included in the main discussion. From time to time we may attempt applications of the abstract analysis to the real world. In this section anything goes. But in general it is hoped that the atmosphere will be similar to conversation among friends after dinner, sometimes light and perhaps amusing, occasionally serious and possibly profound —in short, *postprandial* (from Latin *post,* after, and *prandium,* dinner).

The author owes a debt of gratitude to many whose influence may be seen in many subtle ways. My colleagues have frequently been patient and helpful when I have encountered snags. I appreciate particularly the counsel of Professor Thomas A. Martinsek, Professor Kanji Haitani, and Professor Bernard J. Marks. My wife served in the role of intelligent-layman critic. She has read all of the manuscript and demonstrated a remarkable ability to spot errors in analyses which she did not understand. Miss Sharolyn Sharknas typed the manuscript. Southern Illinois University granted me sabbatical leave to work on the manuscript during the first two quarters of the academic year 1965–66. The following men read the manuscript in its entirety, and their suggestions and criticisms have made it a much-improved product: Professor Vincent Boland of the University of Arizona, Professor Pan Yotopoulas of the University of Wisconsin, Milwaukee, and Professor J. Thomas Romans of the State University of New York, Buffalo. Perhaps most of all I am indebted to my departmental chairman, Professor Robert G. Layer, who has permitted me to hold a local monopoly for the last eight years in the teaching of intermediate price theory.

Clark Lee Allen

CONTENTS

1. INTRODUCTION   *1*

    Wants, Goods, and Resources   2
    Consumption, Production, Distribution, Exchange   5
    Allocation of Resources   8
    Microeconomics and Macroeconomics   10
    Scope and Method of Price Theory   10
    Markets Classified   11
    The Profit-Maximizing Assumption   14
    Postprandium   15
    Selected References   20

2. THE ELEMENTS OF PURELY COMPETITIVE MARKET
   PRICE DETERMINATION   21

    The Nature of Demand   21
    The Nature of Supply   25
    Equilibrium Price   27
    The Ceteris-Paribus Assumption   31
    Postprandium   33
    Selected References   40
    Problems   41

3. THE PRICE ELASTICITY OF DEMAND   45

    Elasticity of Demand and Total Expenditure   46
    Point Elasticity of Demand   48
    Elasticity and Slope   55
    Postprandium   59
    Selected References   62
    Problems   63

4. ARC ELASTICITY OF DEMAND AND SUPPLY   68

    Arc Elasticity Formulas   69
    Arc Elasticity and Total Expenditure   71
    Cross Elasticity of Demand   74
    Income Elasticity of Demand   76

Elasticity of Supply   77
Postprandium   81
Selected References   83
Problems   83

5. MARGINAL UTILITY AND CONSUMER DEMAND   88

Diminishing Marginal Utility   89
Marginal Utility Curves and Demand Curves   92
Marginal Utility of Expenditure   93
Consumer Equilibrium   95
Measurement of Marginal Utility   97
Postprandium   98
Selected References   105
Problems   106

6. THEORY OF DEMAND: INDIFFERENCE CURVES   111

Properties of Indifference Curves   113
The Price Line   115
Consumer Equilibrium   117
Limiting Cases   118
Changes in Income and Prices   121
Deriving Demand Curves from Indifference Curves   123
Income and Substitution Effects   124
Effect of a Consumer Subsidy   127
Negative Income and Price Effects   128
Indifference Curves and Elasticity of Demand   130
Postprandium   133
Selected References   137
Problems   137

7. AVERAGE, TOTAL, AND MARGINAL REVENUE   145

Average Revenue and Marginal Revenue   148
Price, Quantity, Slope, and Marginal Revenue   151
Continuous and Discrete Marginal Revenue   153
Total Revenue and Average Revenue   156
Total Revenue and Marginal Revenue   158
Summary   159
Postprandium   160
Selected References   163
Problems   163

8. AVERAGE, TOTAL, AND MARGINAL COST   170

Total and Average Costs   172
Total and Marginal Costs   178
Average and Marginal Costs   180

Postprandium   *182*
Selected References   *186*
Problems   *187*

9. PRICES AND OUTPUT UNDER PURE COMPETITION   193

Competitive Firm's Most Profitable Output   *194*
Marginal Cost and the Firm's Supply Curve   *198*
Elasticity of Supply   *199*
Equilibrium Price   *201*
Long-Run Supply   *202*
Market and Firm Equilibrium   *203*
Decreasing-Cost Industries   *208*
Long-Run Average Costs   *209*
Postprandium   *211*
Selected References   *213*
Problems   *214*

10. PRICES AND OUTPUT UNDER PURE MONOPOLY   220

Profit-Maximizing Output and Price   *222*
Long-Run Costs   *226*
Taxation of Monopolies   *230*
Regulation of Natural Monopolies   *232*
Price Discrimination   *234*
Competition and Monopoly Contrasted   *238*
Postprandium   *242*
Selected References   *245*
Problems   *246*

11. PRICES AND OUTPUT UNDER MONOPOLISTIC COM-
PETITION   253

Monopolistic Competition   *255*
Monopolistic Competition as a Theory of the Firm   *256*
Monopolistic Competition and Selling Costs   *258*
Monopolistic Competition and Long-Run Equilibrium   *262*
Monopolistic Competition and Pure Competition Compared   *264*
Postprandium   *266*
Selected References   *267*
Problems   *268*

12. PRICES AND OUTPUT UNDER OLIGOPOLY   272

The Cournot Case   *274*
Rival's Price Assumed Constant   *278*
Mutual Dependence Recognized   *279*
The Kinked Demand Curve   *280*

Price Leadership   282
Sales Maximization   283
Alternative Solution to the Oligopoly Problem   285
Postprandium   287
Selected References   289
Problems   289

13. AVERAGE, TOTAL, AND MARGINAL PRODUCT   293

Total, Average, and Marginal Product   294
Geometry of Total-Average and Total-Marginal Product   295
Returns to Scale   299
Law of Variable Proportions   300
Production Functions and Cost Functions   304
Postprandium   305
Selected References   307
Problems   307

14. ISOQUANTS AND THE PRODUCTION FUNCTION   312

Marginal Rate of Substitution   313
The Isocost Curve   314
The Factor-Price Line   315
Relevant Range of the Isoquant   316
Changes in Factor Prices and Output   319
The Expansion Path   320
Isoquants and the Total Product Curve   322
Postprandium   324
Selected References   329
Problems   330

15. THE FIRM AS BUYER OF INPUTS AND SELLER OF OUT-
    PUTS   334

The Determination of Factor Prices   335
Input-Output and Cost-Revenue Relationships   338
Demand for a Factor   342
Equilibrium with Many Inputs   343
The Monopolistic Seller   344
The Monopsonistic Buyer   346
The Adding-up Problem   348
Postprandium   352
Selected References   355
Problems   356

16. POST-POSTPRANDIUM   362

Price Theory and Other Areas of Economics   366

INDEX   369

1

Introduction

The term *economics* is not easy to define. In this respect economics is unlike a number of other disciplines which can be defined concisely and meaningfully. The term *astronomy*, for example, is derived from the Greek words *astron*, meaning star, and *nomos*, meaning law, and astronomy may be defined as the science which treats of the stars, their motions, magnitudes, distances, and physical constituents. Or, the term *biology* is derived from the Greek *bios*, meaning life, and *logos*, meaning discourse; biology is the science of life, consisting of two main divisions, botany, the science of plant life, and zoology, the science of animal life. Or, if one had never encountered the term *ichthyology* but was told that this is the branch of natural history which treats of fish, he would have a pretty good idea of the subject matter of that discipline. No comparable brief definition of economics is available. The etymology of the term offers little insight. The word *economics* is derived from the Greek *oikos*, for house, and *nomos*, for law, which makes economics the science of household management. This comes close to what we today call home economics, but it provides little hint as to the sorts of things which interest professional economists.

Alfred Marshall, the distinguished English nineteenth-century economist, began his classic *Principles of Economics* with the statement, "Political Economy or Economics is a study of mankind in the ordinary business of life; it examines that part of individual and social action which is most closely connected with the attainment and with the use of the material requisites of wellbeing."[1] This statement may be valid, but it fails to convey incisively what contemporary economics is about.

The inability to formulate a precise definition of economics has not, however, been a source of embarrassment to most economists. Jacob Viner, a distinguished American economist, observed a number of years ago, "I find it difficult to conceive what useful purposes the formal definition of the scope of a discipline can serve, except the purposes of editors of encyclopedias and administrators of educational institutions, whose responsibility it may be to prevent overlapping, to obtain full coverage, and to arbitrate jurisdictional disputes."[2] Since we are students of price theory, not encyclopedia editors or university administrators, we will not attempt to compare various definitions of economics or try to invent a new one. We will be content with the notion that economics is what economists as such are concerned with.

Wants, Goods, and Resources

However, in order to see later in this chapter how price theory fits into the broad spectrum of economics, we might consider a general statement (not a definition) about economics. We may say that *economics is concerned with man's use of resources to produce goods to satisfy wants.* This statement says little more than does Marshall's definition of economics, but in this form it sets up three key words, *resources, goods,* and *wants,* which we will consider in inverse order.

The term *wants* as used in economics means essentially what it means in ordinary speech. A want is a desire for something; it implies a lack or deficiency. In general, the economist makes no distinction between wants and needs. If a man wants something and is able and willing to pay for it, that is an economic fact whether he needs the good or not. The distinction between want and need is essentially ethical and not economic in nature. In some areas, however, even the economist must consider needs *versus* wants. An underdeveloped country may want to borrow money from the United States to construct swimming pools and recreational facilities for its workers, but the American government officials might feel that although the want is real, the construction of swimming pools is well down the priority list of the underdeveloped country's needs, and an economic adviser to either the borrowing or

---

[1] Alfred Marshall, *Principles of Economics,* 8th ed. (London: Macmillan & Co., 1920), p. 1.

[2] Jacob Viner, *Studies in the Theory of International Trade* (New York: Harper & Row, Publishers, 1937), p. 594.

the lending country would certainly take such considerations into account. The central point is, however, that wants represent the basis of economic activity. If everyone's wants were fully satisfied without effort, there would be no economic process and, of course, no science of economics. But the essential nature of wants is that they are, in fact, never completely satisfied. Frequently, the satisfaction of one want creates new wants which did not exist before the first one was satisfied. If an undergraduate receives an automobile from his wealthy father, that gift almost certainly satisfies a want of considerable intensity. But now the student wants gasoline for his new car, and a spending allowance previously adequate is now insufficient. Universities sometimes find themselves on the brink of bankruptcy because of the generosity of their affluent alumni; money is given for new buildings, which satisfies wants of the college administrators, but now they need additional funds for janitorial and maintenance services which they did not require before. When a man becomes wealthy he is likely to have as many unsatisfied wants as he had as a poor man. He eats better; he lives in a better home and drives a better car; but now he wants a polo pony, for which he had no desire as a poor man. We may assume in general that man's wants are without limit. The more wants he is able to satisfy, the more new wants emerge. But the means for satisfying wants are limited, whether we consider the individual consumer or the entire economy. The United States has a remarkable ability to produce, but even it cannot produce all of everything that everyone would like to have. It accordingly becomes necessary to *economize;* choices must be made as to what and how much will be produced; decisions must be made as to which wants will be fully satisfied and which will be only partially satisfied or not at all. This is the essence of economics.

Those commodities and services which have the power to satisfy wants are called *goods,* and this is the second key word in our general statement about economics. The ability of a good to satisfy a want is called *utility.* All goods, accordingly, possess utility. Some goods, in addition, possess *scarcity.* Goods which possess utility but are not scarce are called *free goods;* those which possess both utility and scarcity are called *economic goods.* The term *scarcity* is frequently misused in popular speech. Scarcity is not synonymous with fewness or smallness of amount. It is a relative term; it refers to a limited supply in relation to the demand. The old saw, "as scarce as hens' teeth," misuses the word *scarce.* For the benefit of the urban student it may be pointed out that hens have no teeth; but they need no teeth, and hence hens' teeth, though nonexistent, are not scarce. But bread *is* scarce. There are in the world at any moment of time millions of loaves of bread, but the supply in relation to the demand is limited, and bread, therefore, possesses the quality of scarcity. If one has to give up something of value to acquire a good, that good is scarce. Free goods do not require a payment for their acquisition, but economic goods do. The number of free goods in a modern complex society is limited; fresh air and sunshine are frequently cited as examples of free goods, but an urban dweller in the Midwest in midwinter may find that it requires considerable expenditure to acquire either of them in adequate amounts. The economist is concerned only with economic goods, which in the aggregate are known as *wealth*. Economics has, indeed, been defined as the science of wealth. While it may be true that the best things in life are free, most people find it necessary to devote a considerable part of their energies in acquiring the next-best things, and these are the human activities which interest the economist.

The third key word in our general statement about economics is *resources*. In all economies resources are limited, and it is the combination of limited resources face-to-face with unlimited wants that brings about the economic problem. Differences in standards of living among the various countries of the world exist because of differences in resources and in the effectiveness with which they are exploited. The average annual per capita income in an underdeveloped country like Indonesia is less than the average weekly per capita income in the United States, and this reflects differences in resources and their use. The American Indian had a much lower standard of living than do Americans occupying the same geographical areas today because we now make more effective use of our resources.

The quantity and quality of resources and the uses to which they are put are so important that we will do well to pursue this matter a bit further. Below is a simple outline showing the several aspects of resources that are significant in economic analysis:

I. Resources
    A. Human
    B. Nonhuman
        1. Natural
        2. Man-made

It will be noted that all resources have been divided into two categories: human and nonhuman. Human resources are, of course, the people. Both the quantity and quality of people are important in determining the rate of economic growth achieved by a given economy. Demographers, as students of population are called, have much to say about the optimum population. The number of people in relation to nonhuman resources may be too large or too small. India and China are nations where the sheer numbers of people act to restrain economic growth, and Australia appears to have too few people to exploit her nonhuman resources with maximum efficiency. The current widespread concern about the "population explosion" in many parts of the world is a concern that the ratio between human and nonhuman resources is becoming less favorable to the maintenance of high standards of living, and, if this development goes unchecked, living standards will decline, perhaps to a calamitous degree. A twenty-first-century Black Death which decimates the population may become necessary to the maintenance of reasonably high living standards.

But perhaps even more important than the number of people as a factor affecting their economic development is their quality. Much has been said in recent years about the basic similarity of all people regardless of race or nationality, and the emphasis on the similarities may tend to obscure important differences among peoples. If an economy is to make rapid economic growth, there must be at least a significant minority who have imagination, ambition, energy, determination, and a love of power. For purposes other than economic growth these people may be unattractive if not positively objectionable. The typical business tycoon of the nineteenth century in the United States was scarcely an admirable character. He was likely to be vain, greedy, conniving, and ruthless, but he played an important and necessary role in the industrial advancement of the country, and without him economic progress in this country would undoubtedly have been retarded. A nation of lovable people, content with things as they are, and unwilling to take action which would harm some of their fellowmen, is not likely to be a wealthy nation. The quality of the population is also important insofar as it affects the kinds of political and economic institutions it maintains. Property arrangements which provide strong inducements for people to work hard and accumulate wealth contribute much to the rate at which economic development takes place. Inquisitiveness of mind and high regard for education contribute to the development of technology, and this in turn facilitates the effective exploitation of nonhuman resources.

Nonhuman resources include natural resources and man-made resources. Nature has been more generous in bestowing fertile lands, streams and lakes, mineral deposits, favorable climate, good harbors, and other natural resources in some parts of the world than in others, and this accounts in large part for differences in rates of economic development. Even the location of resources within a country may have an effect on economic progress. In Russia, for example, there are ample deposits of both iron ore and coal, but they are located many miles apart, and this is a serious handicap in developing a steel industry. The United States is more fortunate in that coal and iron are found in close proximity. The nonhuman resources include such things as machinery and tools and goods in process, all of which the economist calls *capital goods*. The quantity and quality of capital which a country has accumulated vitally affect its ability to produce goods and are determined by the quantity and quality of its people and the abundance and accessibility of its natural resources.

Consumption, Production, Distribution, Exchange

A topic as broad as man's use of resources to produce goods should be broken down into manageable divisions and subdivisions for careful analysis. An early French economist, Jean Baptiste Say, in his book *Traité d'Écono-*

mie Politique, first published in 1803, divided the subject of economics into the trilogy of production, distribution, and consumption, considering exchange as a part of production. This division of economics was used by economics textbook writers for over a century, and, in fact, only in relatively recent years have elementary textbooks followed a different pattern.

Although contemporary elementary economics textbooks no longer follow the consumption-production-distribution-exchange pattern, these terms are important in the economist's vocabulary, and the somewhat specialized meanings attached to them need to be understood by the modern student of economics. We shall, accordingly, briefly discuss each of them in turn.

We begin with *consumption.* Consumption is the use of economic goods in satisfying human wants. The act of consumption may result in the destruction of the object being consumed, as when one eats an apple, or it may in no way affect the thing being consumed, as when one looks at a painting on the wall. Consumption is, of course, the ultimate reason for the whole economic process; if it were not necessary to consume, there would be no economic activity. The effect of a proposed public policy on the consumer is a prime criterion for judging the merits or demerits of that policy,[3] but the body of economic theory relating to consumption is less well developed than are other aspects of economic theory. Largely neglected though he may have been by economic theorists, the consumer is always the *raison d'être* for the whole economic process and, accordingly, for all economic analysis.

Economists have had much more to say about *production.* Production is the creation of utilities. As we have seen, utility is the power to satisfy a want. Among the utilities created in the production process are *form* utility, where the shape of goods is changed, giving them added power to satisfy wants, as in manufacturing industries; *time* utility, where goods are taken when they are relatively abundant and held until they are more scarce, as in warehousing and storage industries; and *place* utility, where goods are moved from locations where they are relatively abundant to places where they are more scarce, as in transportation industries. In the production process a number of *factors* or *agents of production* are employed to transform primary goods into finished products. Traditionally four factors of production were recognized: land, labor, capital, and the entrepreneur. *Land* is a kind of short-hand expression for all natural resources. It includes the Mississippi river and coal still in the ground as well as urban and farm land. *Labor* is, of course, the human resource discussed earlier in this chapter. *Capital,* which is sometimes defined as man-made goods used to produce other goods, is the man-made nonhuman resource listed earlier under "I. Resources." And the *entrepreneur*

---

[3] *Cf.* Adam Smith, *The Wealth of Nations,* Modern Library ed. (New York: Random House, Inc., 1937), p. 625: "Consumption is the sole end and purpose of all production; and the interest of the producer ought to be attended to, only so far as it may be necessary for promoting that of the consumer. The maxim is so perfectly self-evident, that it would be absurd to attempt to prove it."

is the factor which coordinates and organizes the activities of the other factors; he is the decision maker and risk taker.

These terms, land, labor, capital, and entrepreneur, remain among the most common words in the economist's vocabulary, but contemporary writers find this classification of factors of production deficient for purposes of economic analysis. If all factors used in the economic process are to be classified under four heads, it is inevitable that differences within a category will sometimes be more significant than differences between categories. A ditch digger and a brain surgeon are, on the basis of the classical divisions of the factors of production, both classified as labor. But about all that they have in common is that they are human beings; they are not competitive with each other and are scarcely substitutable for one another. On the other hand, a ditch-digging machine is capital; but from the strictly economic point of view, the human ditch digger and the mechanical ditch digger have more in common than the human ditch digger and the brain surgeon have. Some contemporary writers, accordingly, say that instead of there being only four factors of production, there are, in fact, many: anything which a firm buys is a factor of production, and anything which a firm sells is a *product*. The product of one firm, therefore, may be a factor of another firm on the basis of this classification; sheet steel is a product of the steel industry but a factor of the automobile industry. Other modern writers have taken a different tack. These men divide all factors of production into two categories: capital and labor. On the basis of this classification no distinction is made between man-made and natural resources; land and capital are grouped together as a single factor of production, and the entrepreneur is considered as a specialized kind of labor. As in all cases, that classification is best which best serves the purposes at hand, and it is no more accurate to speak of a single "proper" or "correct" classification than it is to speak of a single "proper" or "correct" definition.

The third division of economics in the classical scheme was distribution. *Distribution* is the allocation of income among the factors of production. Note that as the term is used here we are speaking of the distribution of income and not the distribution of goods. The distribution of goods is a matter of transportation, and transportation, as we have seen, is a part of production since it creates place utility. The argument is that the factors of production have worked together to produce goods; these goods are sold, producing an income; the income belongs to the factors of production who have produced it. But how much of the aggregate income belongs to labor? how much to land? to capital? to the entrepreneur? These are the questions which belong to the division of economics called distribution, and it is in this area that many of the conflicts in economic society, disputes between labor and management and between owners and tenants, occur. The distributive share going to each of the factors of production is given a name; the share earned by land is called *rent*; that earned by labor is called *wages*; that earned by capital is called *interest;* and that earned by the entrepreneur is called *profit.* Distribution, then, is the study of rent, wages, interest, and profit.

The last of the divisions of economics in the classical scheme was called exchange. *Exchange* is the transfer of title or ownership. In very primitive societies exchange is effected directly by barter, but a modern industrial society employs a number of institutions designed to facilitate exchange; among these are money, banking, and credit.

Some of the earlier writers included as a fifth division of economics a section called *public finance,* which was concerned with the income and expenditures of the state. Other writers included *government* as a fifth factor of production with its distributive share called *taxes.* It is interesting to note that most of these writers had a good deal to say about the influence of government even though by present-day standards the economic role of the state was small.

Allocation of Resources

One of the most famous definitions of economics is the one set forth by Lionel Robbins, an eminent British economist: "Economics is the science which studies human behaviour as a relationship between ends and scarce means which have alternative uses."[4] This definition has been criticized by some as being too narrow,[5] but that is a debate in which we do not need to participate at the moment. What is significant for our purposes is that economics is basically concerned with the allocation of scarce resources. In language which we have used in this chapter, Robbins' definition might be restated as follows: Economics is concerned with the allocation of scarce resources which have alternative uses. Every economy has a limited supply of human and nonhuman resources, and in each economy the people have unlimited wants. By some means it must be determined how those resources are to be used, what goods will be produced, and who will get them. The basic economic problem has been described as consisting of these questions: What is to be produced? How is it to be produced? For whom is it to be produced?

There are essentially two methods for allocating scarce resources among competing uses, and both methods are used in varying proportions by all modern industrial societies. First, resources might be allocated deliberately by some central agency, probably the state. To the extent that this method is employed, it becomes necessary to prepare a list of wants in order of priority, determine what resources will be needed to produce each of the goods in the

---

[4] Lionel Robbins, *An Essay on the Nature and Significance of Economic Science,* 2nd ed. (London: Macmillan & Co., 1949), p. 16.

[5] This definition would seem, for example, to exclude the study of welfare from economics since welfare is an "end."

quantities required, and then assign human and nonhuman resources to the predetermined uses until all resources are as nearly fully employed as is feasible. The second method is to allocate resources through the price mechanism. If a good is not available in quantities desired by consumers, the price of that good will tend to rise. The increase in price will have two effects: it will curtail consumption by those consumers who have the smallest desire for the good or have the least ability to pay for it, and it will stimulate additional production of the good by firms who are seeking to increase their profits. When resources are allocated in this way, it is the consumer who, in the final analysis, determines what is produced, and this has been called the principle of *consumer sovereignty*.

A communist economy places chief reliance for the allocation of resources on public authority, and allocation by price plays only a secondary role. In the Soviet Union following the Russian Revolution the leaders of the state wanted to build up the industrial and military strength of the state, and they allocated resources to those ends. If they had permitted consumer sovereignty to prevail, it seems likely that standards of living would have risen in the short run, but the rapid economic and military development of the country might have then been rendered impossible. In recent years reports have come out of Russia indicating that they may be considering reducing the amount of government planning and placing greater reliance on the allocation of resources through the price system and depending to a somewhat greater extent on the profit motive to stimulate industrial production.[6]

A private-enterprise or capitalist economy places chief reliance for the allocation of resources on the price system, and allocation by public authority plays only a secondary role. Even in those areas where resources are allocated by public authority in a private-enterprise economy such as that of the United States, prices are frequently employed as the most effective device for accomplishing the purposes of the government. During periods of national emergency, consumer goods may be rationed by the government and resources may be directly allocated by the state, but in general the government resorts to indirect rather than direct controls. Taxes may be raised, for example, to reduce consumer purchasing power and relieve inflationary pressures, but such income as the consumer has after taxes may be spent without further government restraint. The public authorities may influence the interest rate through purchase and sale of government securities, and the change in interest rates may affect resource allocation, but the price system continues to function. The government may stockpile goods to prevent prices from falling or sell or threaten to sell from their stockpile to prevent prices from rising, but, although prices are affected by government action, resources continue to be allocated through the pricing mechanism. So even though in

---

[6] See, for example, "Long Live Libermanism," *Saturday Evening Post*, 238 (July 3, 1965), 92.

the United States the role of government in allocating resources has increased greatly in recent decades, the basic distinction between private enterprise as practiced in this country and socialism as worked out in Soviet Russia remains clear and unambiguous.

Microeconomics and Macroeconomics

Instead of following the classical divisions of consumption, production, distribution, and exchange, contemporary economics is usually divided into two major parts: microeconomics and macroeconomics. Microeconomics, as the name indicates, is the economics of small units, and the principal unit in this part of economics is the business firm. Microeconomics is primarily concerned with the forces which determine market prices and is essentially a synonym for price theory. Macroeconomics is concerned with the economics of large units, and the principal unit in this branch of economics is the state. Macroeconomics is concerned with the forces which affect national income and what can be done to increase and stabilize national income. Macroeconomics is the economics of national income and full employment. A less conventional view, but one which seems to have much to commend it, is that microeconomics is concerned with the allocation of resources through the pricing mechanism, while macroeconomics is concerned with the allocation of resources through public authority. But, as we have just seen, at least in the United States, efforts by the government to affect resource allocation are normally exercised by indirect controls which work through the price mechanism. The theory of prices, accordingly, although usually associated with microeconomics, is actually central to all of economics, including macroeconomics.

Scope and Method of Price Theory

The scope of price theory, and hence the scope of this book, is of course much narrower than the scope of all economics. We are, in the first place, concerned here only with economic analysis or economic theory. This excludes from our immediate sphere of interest other significant aspects of economics such as the study of economic institutions, economic history, and economic statistics. We limit our study of theoretical economics, furthermore, to an analysis of the forces which affect the price-formation process through which resources are allocated in a free-enterprise economy. Even significant aspects of prices are omitted from this study. We will not, for example, concern ourselves with the effects of rapid changes in prices on the economy, or methods for preventing inflation or deflation, or policies for recovering from periods of excessively high or low prices. Our concern will be limited to a consideration of the forces which affect the prices of individual commodities. The focus of our attention will be the market place.

Our approach to price theory will be static rather than dynamic. Static theory assumes prompt adjustments to changes, and it is not concerned with the time required for changes to take place or the paths in which economic variables move. These are the tasks of economic dynamics, and our knowledge of these matters remains limited. Static theory is concerned with determining the direction in which economic variables move in response to other variables. It attempts to explain the equilibrium position in a particular case on the assumption that the data do not change; tastes, resources, and technology are assumed to remain constant. The method of comparative statics has proven to be very useful to the economist. We begin with the economy in static equilibrium, then introduce a disturbance to the equilibrium and permit the economy to reach a new equilibrium without allowing other disturbances to enter. The comparison of the original equilibrium with the new one provides the economist with one of the most powerful tools at his disposal.[7] This is the method of intellectual experimentation. Seldom is the economist or the businessman or the politician able actually to manipulate economic variables and observe the effects of the changes. The economist must ask himself: what would happen if I could change A but hold B, C, D, . . . , N constant? Accurate answers to questions of this sort require that the economist have at his disposal a kit of intellectual tools which will help him think straight and to the point. Price theory is designed to provide some of the tools which will assist the economist in his analysis of economic variables.[8]

Markets Classified

Since the focus of price theory is on the market place, it is well from the beginning to have in mind the classification of markets which economists have found useful in their analysis of the price-forming processes. The following outline indicates the several market categories which will be described in some detail in later chapters of this book:

[7] See Kenneth E. Boulding, "In Defense of Statics," *Quarterly Journal of Economics*, 69 (November 1955), 485–502.

[8] *Cf.* John Maynard Keynes, "Introduction to the Series," in Hubert D. Henderson, *Supply and Demand* (New York: Harcourt, Brace & World, Inc., 1922), p. v: "The theory of economics does not furnish a body of settled conclusions immediately applicable to policy. It is a method rather than a doctrine, an apparatus of the mind, a technique of thinking, which helps its possessor to draw correct conclusions."

I. Competitive Markets
   A. Perfect competition
   B. Pure competition
II. Monopolistic Markets
   A. Monopolistic competition
   B. Oligopoly
   C. Pure monopoly

For many purposes we may distinguish only two categories of markets: markets perfectly competitive, and markets less than perfectly competitive. Perfect competition represents an ideal situation, both in the sense that it is considered the optimum or best type of market in that it results in the most efficient possible allocation of resources, and also in the sense that it exists largely in fancy since the number of instances of perfect competition in the real world are few indeed. Perfectly competitive prices are often used as the norm. It is a common belief that monopoly prices are high prices; but they are high compared to what? The answer is that monopoly price is usually higher than competitive price. The study of the perfectly competitive market, accordingly, occupies much more of the economist's time than the extent of its existence in the real world would on the face of it seem to warrant. Perfect competition plays much the same role in economics that the perfectly frictionless world plays in physics, the perfect fluid in hydrodynamics, and the perfect gas in thermodynamics. If we understand the world of perfect competition, we can by making appropriate modifications gain significant insights into the workings of the real world.

For some purposes it is helpful to distinguish between perfect competition and pure competition. A purely competitive market has the following characteristics:

1. The number of buyers and sellers in the market is so large that no single seller can affect the price of the commodity he sells. In geometric terms, the demand curve facing the seller is represented as a horizontal line; he can sell during a given time period any quantity of his product at the price set by the market forces of demand and supply, but at any higher price he could sell none at all.

2. The products sold by purely competitive sellers are described as being homogeneous; that is, the product of one firm is in no way differentiated from the product of other sellers in the market. A number of agricultural industries come close to this description of pure competition. The price of wheat, for example, is determined on a world market, and even a large-scale wheat farmer produces such a small fraction of the world's total wheat supply that he has no perceptible effect on the price of wheat. And he produces a homogeneous product; his wheat and that of other wheat producers will likely be placed together in a grain elevator, and the product of one farmer cannot be distinguished from that of another. Before the government undertook farm-price-support programs, the wheat market corresponded closely with the economist's model of pure competition.

Perfect competition has two additional requirements:

3. All producers, factors of production, and consumers in a perfectly competitive market have perfect knowledge of prices and other pertinent economic data. A worker, for example, would not accept a lower wage because of ignorance of the going wage rate, and consumers would never pay more than the current market price for a commodity because of ignorance of what the current price is.
4. All factors of production in a perfectly competitive market have perfect mobility. Workers can and will move promptly from low-wage to higher-wage jobs, and land will be quickly diverted from low-rent to high-rent uses.

In this book and in much of economic literature the distinction between perfect and pure competition is not observed. The terms are often used interchangeably and refer to markets where the number of sellers is large and all firms produce homogeneous products.

Monopolistic competition also assumes a large number of sellers, but this time each seller produces a product which in some way is differentiated from the products of other sellers. The products may actually be different in physical or chemical properties, or what is essentially the same product may be sold under a variety of trade names. By advertising and promotional activities of various sorts a seller may build up considerable consumer loyalty for his product, and he may be able to sell it at a price higher than the same or similar products sold under other trade names. That is to say that the demand curve for the monopolistically competitive seller, like that for all monopolistic sellers, is negatively inclined. The monopolistically competitive seller has a little monopoly of his particular trademarked commodity, but his product is so similar to that of other sellers that consumers can readily substitute one for the other, and competition among the several sellers may be quite intense.

Oligopoly is a market consisting of a few sellers. The products may be either homogeneous or differentiated, but most commodities sold by oligopolists to the final consumers are differentiated in some way.

Finally, pure monopoly means one seller. Like pure competition, cases of pure monopoly are rare in the real world. Before World War II the Aluminum Company of America was the only domestic producer of aluminum, and within geographical areas public utility companies frequently have no competitors in the production and sale of power and water, but like pure competition, pure monopoly is more important for purposes of economic analysis than it is in the real world.

Special terms have been invented to identify monopoly on the buying side of the market. Oligopsony is a market with a few buyers, and pure monopsony is a market with a single buyer. Oligopsonistic and monopsonistic markets are of some importance in markets where labor is bought and sold, and we will turn our attention to them in the later part of the book.

The Profit-Maximizing Assumption

Probably no statement is more familiar to elementary students in economics than this: to maximize profits a firm must produce to the point where marginal cost equals marginal revenue. The common sense of this statement is clear; if the additional cost of producing the Nth unit of output is less than the additional income derived from its production, the production of the Nth unit will add something to the firm's total profits. But is it "realistic" to assume that firms in fact think in marginal terms? And do firms uniformly and universally attempt to maximize profits? Firms are, of course, interested in profits, but is it not a distortion to assume that every entrepreneur is constantly straining every nerve to make the greatest possible amount of profit during every time period? Are there not other motives for the businessman, even in a private enterprise economy, in addition to profit maximization?

These are not idle questions, and economists have agonized over them from time to time.[9] If one is seeking an accurate description of reality, the profit-maximizing assumption will prove to be deficient. Some firms under some circumstances might prefer greater sales to greater profits even if the choice were clear-cut. Other firms might prefer smaller but adequate profits to maximum profits if the reduction in effort required were sufficiently attractive. A firm might deliberately choose less-than-maximum profits to avoid harassment by the Anti-Trust Division of the Department of Justice. And many successful businessmen may never have heard of marginal cost or marginal revenue.

The profit-maximizing assumption remains, however, a useful tool for economic analysis. For one thing, it gives price theory a precision which would not otherwise be possible. If we assume that some quantitative magnitude is to be maximized, the tools are available for determining under what conditions that end will be achieved. The analysis of labor union activity has been less precise because it is not clear what the unions are trying to maximize. Do they want to maximize the number of men employed? or the wage rate? or the total wage bill paid to the workers? None of these appears to describe accurately the behavior of labor unions, and labor economics is frequently more descriptive than analytical because of the lack of a suitable maximization hypothesis.

Even if it be argued that in the real world firms seldom attempt to

---

[9] For a discussion of these and related matters by an economist and a psychologist, see C. Addison Hickman and Manford H. Kuhn, *Individuals, Groups and Economic Behavior* (New York: Dryden Press, 1956).

maximize profits, the profit-maximizing assumption is still instructive. We can determine what the profit-maximizing output would be, and then make whatever adjustments are necessary to fit the analysis to the facts. We may assume that, *other things being equal,* the firm would prefer more to less profits. If all other things are not equal, we can attempt to take them into account and make the necessary adjustments after we have determined the equilibrium position on the basis of the profit-maximizing assumption. No analytical model will describe reality with complete accuracy, and price theory alone will solve few problems in the real world. But without some analytical framework the complexities of the real world will render an understanding of economic behavior difficult if not impossible. In the years ahead new assumptions and new techniques will undoubtedly add to our understanding of the world in which we live, but price theory as we have it today is one of the best of the tools we have for the understanding and manipulation of our economic environment to the end of increasing the production of goods to satisfy human wants.

POSTPRANDIUM

The social scientist, for the most part, deals with concepts which are familiar to the general public. The man on the street is not awed by the vocabulary of the social scientist because, presumably, he understands the meanings of such terms as government, taxes, family, labor, and income. And the general public feels free to debate and vote on issues in the area of the social sciences without guidance or advice from those who have made the study of these matters their life work. A person may, however, be quite illiterate in sociology or political science or economics without realizing it. If, on the other hand, one knows virtually nothing about chemistry or physics or biology, he is quite aware of his ignorance. It would be a rarity to find a man who is ignorant of physics but who holds dogmatic opinions about issues being debated by the physicists. And, indeed, it would probably do little harm to the general welfare if strong convictions about physics and chemistry were held by people with little or no information in those areas. But, unfortunately, it is precisely in the areas where the welfare of the public is affected that people so frequently hold strong convictions that are based on a minimum of information and analysis, and public policy reflects these opinions. Perhaps democratic institutions have found it possible to survive because frequently people reach the right conclusions for the wrong reasons.

The business or professional man is not only likely to hold exaggerated ideas of his own understanding of issues in the social sciences, but in addition, he may view the work of social scientists with suspicion, on the grounds that these men are too abstract and theoretical. "It may be true in theory, but it doesn't work out that way in practice," says the man of affairs.

Probably no statement more irritates the scientist. The practical man wants "fewer theories and more facts." But what, after all, is a "fact"?

A painting by Thornton Utz served as the cover for a popular magazine some months ago. The picture shows in the foreground a table loaded with good things to eat—hors d'oeuvres, ham, turkey, cheeses, chafing dishes, fruit, and fancy breads. Obviously, everything is in readiness for a party. The stack of plates indicates that some twenty guests have been invited. The host and hostess are standing in front of a big picture window waiting for the guests to arrive. Judging from the cigarette butts in the ash tray on the window ledge, it has already been a long wait. And the reason is easy to see. There has been a big snow storm, and it is still snowing. It begins to look as if there will be no party after all.

Now, what are the "facts" of this picture?

To the editor of the magazine on whose cover the painting appeared the picture undoubtedly appealed as an amusing and attractive cover that would help sell the magazine.

To an illustrator the painting might appear as an interesting study in color and form and perspective.

To an engraver it might demonstrate the technological progress that has made multi-color printing feasible and practicable.

An architect might note with horror that four large ceiling beams in the living room appear to be supported by the picture window.

To a psychologist the picture might represent a study in frustration.

A physician might note that several cases of indigestion have been prevented by a storm.

A meteorologist would likely find the storm itself the matter of chief interest.

To an economist the painting might indicate the high standard of living which is enjoyed by contemporary Americans.

And a communist might consider the picture an evidence of the decadence of capitalism—an extravagant waste of food while many are hungry.

What, indeed, are the "facts" of the picture?

We may say with reasonable accuracy that a theory is nothing more than the way we perceive facts; and it follows from this that we cannot perceive facts without a theory of some sort. The practical man with no regard for theory but with an insatiable appetite for facts is unconsciously putting to work some kind of intuitive theory. It is part of the work of the social scientist to make the theories which he uses explicit.

Some theories are better than others. One who bases his conclusions on a theory of which he is not even aware is not likely to hit upon the best possible explanation. The test of a theory is its usefulness in making predictions, and the ability to predict is important because it makes possible some degree of control over phenomena. This does not mean, for example, that the economist should be able to forecast business conditions for the next year or to determine what the price of wheat will be six months from today. But it does mean that the economist can say that if the price of wheat goes up and other things remain the same—among the "other things" would be consumer income and taste and the prices of other commodities—the amount of wheat demanded will decline. Or, if government reduces its rate of expenditure and other things remain the same, national money income will decline.

A theory is not an exact picture of reality. It is more like a road map than a photograph—it does not show every tree and twist in the road, but it *abstracts* from reality those elements which appear most likely to be significant. Since in any theory something is left out—the real world is much too complex for a theory to include all "other things"—there is always the hazard that the theorist will leave out of account some of the most important elements of the problem. Theories of this sort will likely prove to have little practical value, and they will in time be replaced by fuller explanations. Theories that are of the implicit or intuitive sort are usually unsatisfactory because they are almost certain to leave out of account some of the most significant features of the problem.

The social scientist is confronted by a task which in important respects is more difficult than that of the natural scientist. In the first place, social scientists are concerned with the behavior of human beings, and people do not react to a given stimulus as consistently as do chemical compounds or the phenomena of the physical world. A politician's winning smile or his charming wife may cause many voters to change party affiliations, and this may affect the country's policy with respect to the appropriation of funds for foreign aid or public education. Expectations for the future may be important. If people become convinced that a bank is in perilous condition, a run on the bank may cause it to close its doors whether it is actually in trouble or not.

Secondly, the social scientist may find it more difficult than the natural scientist to be objective; he may be affected personally if his recommendations are incorporated as part of public policy. If, for example, he recommends an increase in taxes for any of several reasons, he is urging a policy which may be detrimental to his own personal interests.

Certain modes of scientific inquiry which have proved fruitful to scientists in other areas are not available to the social scientist. The use of the experimental method, for example, is quite limited in most of the social sciences. A public utility commission might persuade a company which distributes electric power in several communities to experiment with electric rates in order to determine whether a reduction of rates would increase the consumption of power sufficiently to warrant a general policy of rate reduction. But the results likely would not be conclusive, largely because the "other things" that an experiment needs to keep constant might not in fact remain constant. A rate reduction might result in little increase in the use of power during the first year, but after ten years, when consumers had had time to replace worn-out gas appliances with electric appliances, the increased consumption of electricity might be considerable. And one could not be sure that the amount of increased consumption of electric power in one community would indicate the amount of increase in another if there were a comparable reduction of rates there; differences in rates of population growth in the two communities would be one disturbing factor, and there would undoubtedly be others.

Perhaps the chief difficulty confronting the social scientist as compared with the physical scientist is that the social scientist is concerned not only with what is but also with what should be. When the astronomer establishes that a planet follows an elliptical path around the sun, his job is done. He does not have the additional task of recommending that the path be changed to a circle or a triangle. The social scientist is subject to error, first, in determining the consequences of given actions, and, second, in determining the desirability of the consequences. The study of "what is" is sometimes referred to as "positive" or "factual" science; the study of "what ought to be," as "normative" or "regulative" science. The problems of positive science are formidable; in the field of normative science the social scientist may have little special competence.

Students of scientific method have suggested a variety of approaches to the task of increasing our understanding of the world in which we live. The prescriptions of Francis Bacon, René Descartes, Morris Cohen, and John Dewey, for example, differ in numerous important respects. In spite of the debates on scientific method, in which the partisans of one approach are likely to condemn all other approaches, it appears now to be pretty generally understood that there is not one scientific method but, in fact, many. A given researcher is likely to find one method best suited to his purposes, but the problems of the scientist, and particularly those of the social scientist, are so complex and varied that any method which promises new insights would appear to have some usefulness. Alfred Marshall very wisely observed many years ago that "a man is nearly sure to be right when affirming the usefulness of his own procedure, and wrong when denying that of others."[10]

There are those who insist that the so-called "social sciences" are not sciences at all and prefer the term "social studies." Whether a subject is a science turns on one's definition of science. Are biochemistry and meteorology sciences? Some would insist that they are not. But it should be understood that to designate a field of study as a science is a matter of description and not a matter of commendation or encomium. The distinction is often made between science and art. But when we talk about the art of self-defense and the science of the boxer, do we not mean essentially the same thing? In any event it is important that the economist and the sociologist use the tools and techniques which are most effective for his purposes whether or not they be construed as scientific.

[10] Marshall, *Principles of Economics*, p. 771.

One method which has in recent years assumed increasing importance among social scientists is the construction of simplified "skeletal" systems called models. Much of economic data is quantitative, and economists have made effective use of two kinds of models, mathematical and econometric. A mathematical model is a set of relations among a number of economic variables. An ordinary demand curve, which shows the relationship between the price of a commodity and the demand for it, is a simple mathematical model that has proved extremely useful in the analysis of prices. Mathematical models are tested chiefly on the grounds of consistency and reasonableness and provide only partial information about the real world. Econometric models differ in that they make more systematic use of actual statistical data in an effort to make them correspond more accurately with reality. But it should be clear that no model fully reflects the real world. The purpose of the model, indeed, is to abstract from reality only those elements which are significant, thereby reducing the number of variables to manageable proportions. If the irreducible number of significant variables remains large, mathematical techniques are the only ones by which the problem can be solved, and for some purposes the use of elaborate electronic computers provides the only feasible method of solution.

Model building, which constitutes much of the content of this text, is subject to important limitations. There is the possibility of attempting to use a model where it does not fit. And, since some mathematical techniques are easier to use than others, there is a temptation to use the simpler methods when the situation actually calls for more elaborate techniques. Economists frequently represent data as straight lines when it is clear that the relationship is nonlinear in character. Nonlinear relationships may, indeed, prove to be so complex that the model becomes almost as difficult to manipulate as the raw data. There has also been the charge that model builders become so fascinated with the mathematical manipulations that they lose sight of the essentially economic nature of the problem with which they started. This is less a criticism of model building than of model builders, but it represents a hazard which must be guarded against.

The chief limitation imposed on the model builder is that his technique is appropriate only for those variables which can be expressed quantitatively. In some areas we can measure with great precision—length, weight, and temperature, for example, are subject to accurate measurement. In other areas our measurements are less precise—measurements of intelligence, for example. And in still other areas we are not yet able to make measurements at all; we cannot say, for example, that John loves Mary 98 love units or that Jim gets 56 units of satisfaction from eating a piece of apple pie. And many factors which we have not yet learned to measure are important in the social sciences.

It should, finally, be observed that techniques of measurement are arbitrary, and they are invented. It has been only a relatively short time in the history of man that we have been able to measure temperature. Perhaps some day we will be able to measure those things which at the moment remain unmeasurable, and, if that happens, the scope of model building will expand. But the more important consideration is that already many things are measurable, and we have not to date done all that might be done with the quantitative data at our disposal.

SELECTED REFERENCES

Allen, Clark Lee, James M. Buchanan, and Marshall R. Colberg. *Prices, Income, and Public Policy*. Rev. ed. New York: McGraw-Hill Book Co., 1959. Chap. 1.

Boulding, Kenneth E. *Economic Analysis*. 3rd ed. New York: Harper & Row, Publishers, 1955. Chap. 1.

Ellis, H. S. "The Economic Way of Thinking," *American Economic Review*, 50 (March 1950), 1–12.

Fellner, William. *Emergence and Content of Modern Economic Analysis*. New York: McGraw-Hill Book Co., 1960. Chaps. 1 and 2.

Hickman, C. Addison. "Managerial Motivation and the Theory of the Firm," *Proceedings of the American Economic Association* (May 1955), pp. 544–554.

Lange, Oscar. "The Scope and Method of Economics," *Review of Economic Studies,* 13 (1945–46), 12–32.

Marshall, Alfred. *Principles of Economics*. 8th ed. London: Macmillan & Co., 1920. Books I and II.

Robbins, Lionel. *An Essay on the Nature and Significance of Economic Science,* 2nd ed. London: Macmillan & Co., 1935.

Schumpeter, Joseph. "The Nature and Necessity of a Price System," in *Economic Reconstruction*. New York: Columbia University Press, 1934. Reprinted in Clemence, R. V., *Readings in Economic Analysis*. Cambridge, Mass.: Addison-Wesley Press, 1950. II, 1–7.

Stackelberg, Heinrich von. *The Theory of the Market Economy*. New York: Oxford University Press, 1952. Chap. 1.

Stigler, George J. *The Theory of Price*. Rev. ed. New York: The Macmillan Co., 1952. Chaps. 1 and 2.

Zeuthen, F. *Economic Theory and Method,* Cambridge: Harvard University Press, 1955. Part I.

2

The Elements of
Purely Competitive Market
Price Determination

In a purely competitive market the basic price-determining forces are demand and supply. In product markets of all kinds demand plays an important role but, as we will see in subsequent chapters, the concept of supply becomes vague when monopoly elements appear. At the moment, we are taking a quick look at free-market price determination; this chapter is intended to refresh the student's memory concerning matters which he encountered in elementary economics and to serve as an introduction to the more detailed study of demand and supply in following chapters.

The Nature of Demand

As the term demand is used in ordinary speech and as it is sometimes defined in popular dictionaries, it means the amount of a good which people will buy at a given price. To the economist, however, demand means something different, and to avoid confusion it is important to distinguish the scientific from the popular use of the term. To the economist, demand implies the desire for a good plus the ability to pay for it plus the willingness to pay for it. If any of these conditions is lacking, potential demand may be said to exist. Numerous institutions have been formed in our society to convert potential into effective demand. Among them are advertising and salesmanship, which may act to create or increase the desire for a commodity, and credit and installment-purchase plans, which may increase the consumer's ability or willingness to pay.

The economist observes that the amount of a commodity or service demanded during a given interval of time depends upon the price charged for the good. To borrow the language of mathematics, the amount demanded is a function of the price. Stated in symbols,

$$D = q = f(P),$$

where D and q are the quantity of the good demanded, and P is the price of the good. By demand the economist means the entire functional relationship; the whole range of price-quantity combinations rather than the amount demanded at a particular price is, as the economist uses the term, the demand for a commodity. This view of demand is an abstraction and the definition is arbitrary. But a distinction must be made between the amount demanded at a given price and the whole schedule of quantities demanded at all relevant prices. If we use the same term to describe demand as the quantity demanded at a given price and as the schedule of quantities demanded at various prices, confusion is inevitable. Careless use of terminology might lead one to argue, for example, that the price of a commodity could not fall permanently because, if the price decreased, demand for the good would increase, and the increase in demand would cause the price to rise again. The difficulty here arises, of course, because in the first instance we have used demand to mean the amount demanded at a given price, and in the second to mean the schedule of amounts demanded at all prices. If the price of a commodity falls, the *quantity demanded* will increase, but the change in price will not in itself affect *demand* in the schedule sense; changes in price are not, accordingly, automatically self-canceling. When we mean the amount demanded at a particular price, we must use the somewhat cumbersome expression *quantity demanded* or *amount demanded* and reserve the term *demand* for the whole schedule of price-quantity relationships.

When we say that the amount demanded is a function of price, we state simply that for every price there is a corresponding quantity demanded. This statement does not in itself indicate the nature of the price-quantity relationship. Will the quantity demanded vary directly or inversely with the change in price? The expression $D = f(P)$ does not tell us. But common sense indicates that in general a decline in price is accompanied by an increase and not a decrease in the amount demanded. This comes about because a consumer's ability and willingness to pay will be enhanced by a reduction in the price of the commodity. This common-sense view will be confirmed analytically in subsequent chapters, but it seems clear on its face that the functional relationship between price and quantity demanded is an inverse and not a direct one: if the price falls, the amount of the commodity demanded will—other things remaining the same—increase; if the price rises, the quantity demanded will decrease. This principle has sometimes been called the Fundamental Law of Demand.

Suppose that the demand for a particular commodity for a given period of time is given by the equation

$$D = q = 10 - p,$$

where D and q are the amount demanded, and p is the price of the commodity. This equation may have been arrived at as result of statistical

TABLE 2–1

Price	Quantity Demanded
$10	0
9	1
8	2
7	3
6	4
5	5
4	6
3	7
2	8
1	9
0	10

observation of empirical data, or it may be taken to be a simple mathematical model which represents no actual real-world situation but rather a typical demand situation. Instead of a general functional relationship between the amount demanded and the price, we now have a specific demand by particular consumers for a given commodity during a given period of time. By substituting appropriately for p in the equation we can determine the amount that would be demanded at any price. As stated before, the higher the price, the smaller will be the quantity demanded. At a price of 10, none of this commodity will be demanded at all. If the commodity were a free good—that is, if the price were zero—consumers would want 10 units per time period. If $p = \$5.96$, the quantity demanded is 4.04 units per time period. But note that 4.04 is the quantity demanded and not the demand; demand is $D = q = 10 - p$.

It is often convenient to put the price-quantity relationships in tabular form; such a table is called a demand *schedule*. Using the function $D = q = 10 - p$, and substituting appropriate values for p, we get the demand schedule represented in Table 2–1. The entire table or schedule represents the demand for the commodity; each number in the right-hand column is the quantity demanded at the price indicated in the left-hand column. If we move from one price-quantity combination to another, we assume a change in the quantity demanded, but the demand does not change since the demand is the entire schedule, and that has remained constant.

We have represented demand as an algebraic function and as a table or schedule. A third way to represent demand is geometrically, as a demand *curve*. If we plot the demand function $D = q = 10 - p$, measuring price on the *y-axis* and the quantity demanded on the *x*-axis, we get a linear function with a negative slope, having an intercept at 10 on the price axis and an intercept of 10 on the quantity axis.

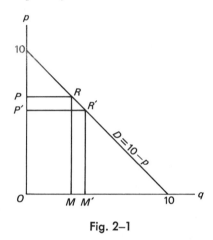

Fig. 2–1

A demand curve may be formally described as the locus of points representing alternative maximum quantities which a consumer or a group of consumers would be willing to buy per time period at all relevant prices. Demand curves may or may not be linear. They may be convex or concave to the origin, or they may be discontinuous, looking something like descending stairsteps. But they will normally have a negative slope; this reflects the inverse relationship between price and quantity demanded. If the price falls, the amount demanded will increase; if the price rises, the amount demanded will decrease. This may be stated symbolically as follows:

$$m = \frac{\Delta p}{\Delta q},$$

where m is the slope of the demand curve, Δp is the negative change in price, and Δq is the positive change in the quantity demanded. Since Δp and Δq have opposite algebraic signs, the slope of the demand curve is negative.

The distinction between demand and the quantity demanded may be made once again with reference to Figure 2–1. If the price of the commodity falls from OP to OP', the quantity demanded will increase from OM to OM'. This represents a movement from point R on the demand curve D to point R' on the same curve. Since the demand curve has not changed, demand has not changed; the effect of the change in price has been to change the amount demanded, but not demand. Under appropriate circumstances the demand curve itself might shift, and if it did, this would be a change in demand. If a change occurs in consumer money income or if there is a change in consumer tastes or if prices of complementary or rival goods change, the demand for the commodity in question might change. This would be represented by a new demand curve, to the right of the original curve if demand increased and to the left if it decreased.

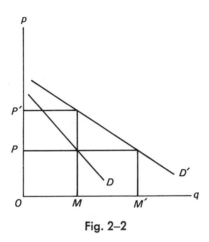

Fig. 2–2

An increase in demand is illustrated in Figure 2–2. The original demand is curve D. The new curve, D', is drawn to the right of D. At any price, such as OP, the quantity demanded on the new curve is greater than the quantity demanded at that price on the original curve. Or, alternatively, the same quantity demanded at price OP on the original curve will be demanded at a higher price on the new demand curve. The shift from D to D' is what the economist means by an increase in demand. A shift from D' to D would, of course, represent a decrease in demand. The proper way to read a demand curve may be indicated with reference to Figure 2–2. One says that *if* the price is OP' and the demand is D', the quantity demanded is OM; *if* the price falls to OP and the demand remains at D', the quantity demanded is OM'. Or *if* the demand is D and the price is OP, the quantity demanded is OM.

The Nature of Supply

The term supply also means something to the economist which is different from the meaning attached to the word in popular speech. Supply does not mean the stock or store of a good in existence at a given time, since at very low prices suppliers may choose not to offer the good for sale. They have what is sometimes called a "reservation price"; they will hold onto their goods rather than offer them for sale if they consider the price too low. Supply is the schedule of maximum quantities which will be offered by sellers at all relevant prices. This too may be stated in mathematical terminology:

$$S = q = f(P),$$

where S and q are the quantity supplied and P is price. This expression does not indicate the nature of the price-quantity relationship; it simply says that for any price there is a corresponding quantity which will be supplied. But this time common sense tells us that the relationship is direct and not inverse. At very low prices little or none of the good may be offered for sale. As the price rises, the quantity supplied would be expected to increase. This view will also be substantiated analytically in a subsequent chapter.

Instead of a general function which indicates that there is a quantity supplied corresponding to each price, we may represent a particular supply with an equation such as

$$S = q = 2p - 5.$$

If supply is given to us in this form, we may determine the quantity supplied at any price by substituting appropriately for p in the equation. At a price of $8.98, for example, the quantity supplied would be 12.96 units per time period.

A table showing the quantities supplied at various prices can be derived from the given supply equation; Table 2–2 is called a supply schedule.

TABLE 2–2

Price	Quantity Supplied
$10	15
9	13
8	11
7	9
6	7
5	5
4	3
3	1
2.50	0

At prices below $2.50 none of this commodity would be offered for sale; we assume that the idea of negative quantities offered for sale is meaningless.

The supply schedule can also be represented geometrically as a supply curve. It will be noted that the supply curve in this instance is linear and has a positive slope. Supply curves may or may not be linear, but since the relationship between price and quantity supplied is a direct one, the slope of a supply curve is normally positive; that is, since Δp and Δq have the same algebraic sign, $m = \Delta p / \Delta q$ is positive.

With reference to Figure 2–3, if the price should rise from $5 to $7.50, the quantity supplied would increase from 5 units to 10 units per time period. We would in effect move from point R to point R' on the supply curve. This would represent a change in price and a change in the quantity supplied, but since the supply continues to be represented by the same curve, this would indicate no change in supply. If the supply had changed, this would be shown by a new curve: to the right of S if the supply had increased, and to the left of S if the supply had decreased.

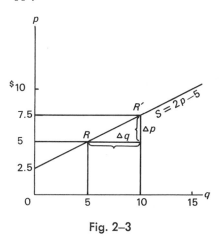

Fig. 2–3

Equilibrium Price

If we know the nature of both the demand function and the supply function, we can determine equilibrium price. We may suppose that the demand functions of all the individual buyers of a commodity in a given market are added up, and the demand for the commodity in the market is given by

$$D = q = 10 - p;$$

and in a similar fashion the supply functions of all of the sellers in the market have been added, and the supply of the commodity is given by

$$S = q = 2p - 5.$$

If the price is relatively high, the quantity demanded will be small and the quantity supplied will be large. If at a given price the quantity supplied is greater than the quantity demanded, sellers will tend to reduce their asking price; otherwise some of them would be unable to sell at all. Similarly, at relatively low prices, the quantity demanded will be large and the quantity supplied will be small. If the quantity demanded at a given price is greater than the quantity supplied at that price, buyers will tend to bid up the price; otherwise some buyers will be unable to buy any at all. But if there is a price at which the quantity demanded is just equal to the quantity supplied, that price is said to be the equilibrium price since once that price has been established, there will be no tendency for the price to rise or fall as long as supply and demand remain unchanged. Equilibrium price is the price toward which market price in a free market tends to gravitate. In the real world, even in a free-market situation, market price might seldom be at the equilibrium level since in many markets demand or supply or both are subject to frequent shifts, and before equilibrium price has been reached, a change in supply or demand may cause the equilibrium price itself to change. But in a free market, price is either at or moving toward the equilibrium point.

The equilibrium price is determined by locating the price at which the quantity demanded is just equal to the quantity supplied. In terms of our algebraic model, we want to determine where the supply function and the demand function have the same values for p and q. We may accomplish this by setting the two functions equal to each other and solving for p:

$$S = D$$
$$2p - 5 = 10 - p$$
$$3p = 15$$
$$p = 5.$$

Therefore

$$q_d = 10 - 5 = 5$$

and

$$q_s = 10 - 5 = 5$$

where q_d is the quantity demanded and q_s is the quantity supplied.

Suppose now that with no change in supply, demand for some reason shifts, and the new demand function is given by

$$D' = q = 13 - p.$$

The new demand represents an increase in demand since at any price more units will be demanded now than previously. We may determine the new equilibrium price as before by setting the supply function equal to the new demand function and solving for p:

$$S = D'$$
$$2p - 5 = 13 - p$$
$$3p = 18$$
$$p = 6.$$

Therefore

$$q_d = 13 - 6 = 7$$

and

$$q_s = 12 - 5 = 7.$$

It is frequently convenient to show the determination of market price geometrically with the use of demand and supply curves. In Figure 2–4, D represents the original demand function $D = q = 10 - p$, and S represents the supply function $S = q = 2p - 5$. The equilibrium price is seen to be 5, and the equilibrium quantity exchanged is 5. D' is the new demand $D' = q = 13 - p$, and after the increase in demand the new equilibrium price is 6 and the new equilibrium quantity exchanged is 7.

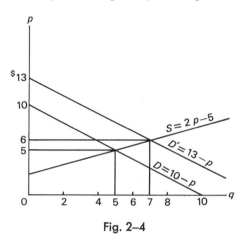

Fig. 2–4

If the demand curve has a negative slope and the supply curve has a positive slope, the equilibrium price represents a stable equilibrium; that is, if the equilibrium is disturbed, the price tends to return to the equilibrium level. An egg lying on its side is in neutral equilibrium. But an egg balanced on one end is in a position of unstable equilibrium; if it tumbles over, it will not return to the original equilibrium position. If both demand and supply curves had negative slopes and if the negative slope of the demand curve were greater than that of the supply curve, the intersection of the curves would represent a point of unstable equilibrium. As we have seen, supply curves normally have a positive slope, but in certain exceptional cases it is possible that the supply curve might be negatively inclined. Such a case will be discussed in a subsequent chapter.

Figure 2–5 represents an unstable equilibrium situation. Price OP is the equilibrium price since at this price the quantity demanded is equal to the quantity supplied. But if for some reason the price should fall, say to OP', the quantity supplied would be greater than the quantity demanded at this price, and instead of forcing the price back up to OP the excess of quantity supplied over the quantity demanded would force the price further downward without limit. A necessary condition, accordingly, for the forces of demand and supply to be effective as determinants of market price is for the demand and supply curves to have slopes appropriate for the establishment of a stable equilibrium.[1]

It may be noted that more units will be exchanged at the equilibrium price than would be exchanged at any other price, either higher or lower. In

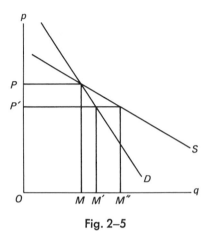

Fig. 2–5

Figure 2-6, it will be seen that at the equilibrium price of *OP* the number of units bought and sold is *OM*. If the price were higher than *OP*, for example *OP'*, the quantity demanded at this price would be less than *OM*, and, of course, no more units can be sold at a given price than are demanded at that

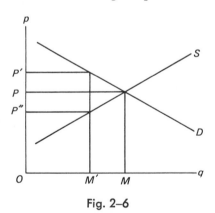

Fig. 2–6

price. If the price were lower than the equilibrium price, say *OP''*, the quantity supplied would be less than *OM*, and no more units can be sold at a given price than sellers will supply at that price. If price is not at the equilibrium level, accordingly, the maximum amount of the good is not being exchanged.

[1] For a brief discussion of stable and multiple equilibria, see Sidney Weintraub, *Price Theory* (New York: Pitman Pub. Corp., 1956), pp. 120–124.

The Ceteris-Paribus Assumption

When we say that $D = f(P)$, we assume that other things remain the same, or as it is frequently expressed, the amount of X demanded depends on the price of X, *ceteris paribus* (other things being equal). This is a convenient device for recognizing that the amount of X demanded depends, in fact, on a number of things, but we at the moment are concerned with the price-quantity relationship, and as far as possible we will ignore other influences on the amount demanded and will concentrate on the effect of changes in price. When several variables affect the demand for a commodity, it is necessary to hold all of them constant except the one whose influence we are directly concerned with. Suppose that we are interested in the demand for gasoline. If per capita income were $2,000, there would be one demand for gasoline, but with a per capita income of $3,000 there would be a different demand, that is, a new demand curve, for gasoline. Or if a 50 percent sales tax were levied on automobiles, there would undoubtedly be a decrease in the demand for gasoline; that is, a smaller quantity would be demanded at each price than before the tax.

The influence of factors other than the price of X on the demand for X is sometimes formally recognized by writing the demand function in the following form:

$$D_x = f(p_x,\ p_c,\ p_s,\ Y,\ T),$$

where D_x is the amount of X demanded; p_x is the price of commodity X; p_c represents prices of complementary goods, that is, goods whose prices tend to move in the opposite direction from the price of X; p_s is the prices of substitutes, that is, goods whose prices tend to move in the same direction as the price of X; Y is consumer income; and T is consumer tastes. The *ceteris-paribus* assumption holds all of these things constant except p_x and tries to discover what changes in the amounts demanded are attributable to changes in the price of X.

This is an analytical device and is not intended to be a description of reality. We may, curiously enough, hold one variable constant in order to see what changes in that variable will subsequently occur. If we draw a demand curve for margarine, for example, we assume among other things that the price of butter is held constant. But if the supply of margarine increases, say, because of the removal of a tax on margarine, the price of margarine will fall. The reduction of the price of margarine will tend to reduce the demand for butter—the demand-for-butter curve will shift to the left—and the price of butter, which was one of the things we held constant, will fall. The new lower price of butter will now cause the demand for margarine to shift to the left, lowering the price of margarine. And so on until the shifts become so small that their effects are imperceptible and a condition of equilibrium has been reached.

It may be noted that if the price of X falls, it is logically impossible for *everything* else to remain the same. If the price of X falls and all other prices remain the same, *relative* prices will have changed. Furthermore, if the price of X falls and all other prices and the consumer's money income remain the same, his *real* income will have increased. Or, if we keep his real income constant, we will have to assume a change in his money income. In either event *all* things have not remained the same. If the prices of all other commodities remain the same, the amounts spent on them remain unchanged, and the consumer's income and the amount he saves remain unchanged, the consumer would not be able to spend more on commodity X even if its price fell: where would the additional purchasing power come from? If we insisted on a rigid assumption that *everything* remains constant, we would have to confine our analysis to those commodities only on which the total expenditure remains constant as the price changes. As we will see in the next chapter, an interesting special case exists when consumer expenditure is unaffected by price changes, but this is hardly a typical case, and we do not wish to have to confine our analysis to this relatively rare phenomenon.

An insistence on all other things remaining unchanged would also involve us in logical difficulties when we view the effects of price changes on the whole economy. Consider a situation where all resources are fully employed and all industries are in equilibrium. We say that if the price of X falls, everything else remaining constant, the amount of X demanded will increase. But if the quantities of all other goods demanded remain the same, where will the resources—the men, materials, and machines—needed to produce the additional units of X come from? Unless less of something else is produced or total productivity is somehow increased, it will not be possible to produce more of X. The *ceteris-paribus* assumption must imply, accordingly, not that nothing else changes, but that there is no other *independent* source of change.

We conclude this section by repeating that the *ceteris-paribus* assumption is a convenient and necessary analytical tool for isolating the effects of one among many variables. Just as the chemist must be careful to see that changes in temperature or air pressure or other extraneous variables do not affect the results of his experiment, the economist uses the *ceteris-paribus* assumption as he undertakes what is a sort of intellectual experiment. But in a world where everything depends upon everything else, the purpose of the *ceteris-paribus* assumption must be understood to be methodological and not substantive in nature.[2]

---

[2] For a discussion of the problem of *ceteris paribus,* see Milton Friedman, *Price Theory* (Chicago: Aldine Publishing Company, 1962), pp. 23–30.

POSTPRANDIUM

In dealing with demand and supply analysis it is frequently convenient to work with models which can be expressed algebraically as well as geometrically. Since straight lines are easier to work with than nonlinear curves, we will normally express demand and supply as linear functions unless there is some special reason to do otherwise. If one knows the general form of linear functions, he can tell from inspection whether a given algebraic function represents a positively or a negatively inclined curve and where the intercepts on the x-axis and the y-axis will come. This is particularly useful to those who are preparing mathematical models showing price formation under conditions of pure competition, and in this postprandium we will investigate the matter of general linear equations of demand and supply.

The basic equation for a straight line is

$$y = mx + b,$$

where $m = \Delta y / \Delta x =$ slope, and $b =$ the y-intercept. Consider the function

$$y = -\tfrac{1}{2}x + 10. \tag{1}$$

The slope of this curve is $-\tfrac{1}{2}$ and its y-intercept is 10. The curve is plotted in Figure 2–7.

Equation (1) may be written in the form

$$\tfrac{1}{2}x + y - 10 = 0, \tag{2}$$

and this may be put in the general form

$$Ax + By - C = 0, \tag{3}$$

where A, B, and C are constants. Equation (3) is the general equation for a linear demand curve with a negative slope; A and B are positive and C is negative.

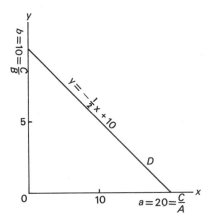

Fig. 2–7

We can determine the x-intercept in Equations (2) and (3) by setting y equal to zero and solving for x. This gives us

$$a = \frac{C}{A} = \frac{10}{\frac{1}{2}} = 20,$$

where a is the x-intercept of the curve. By setting x equal to zero and solving for y we can determine the y-intercept:

$$b = \frac{C}{B} = \frac{10}{1} = 10.$$

The slope of the curve can be determined as follows:

$$m = -\frac{b}{a} = -\frac{C}{B} \div \frac{C}{A} = -\frac{C}{B} \cdot \frac{A}{C} = -\frac{A}{B} = -\frac{\frac{1}{2}}{1} = -\frac{1}{2}.$$

These formulas for a, b, and m will hold for any negatively inclined linear demand curve when the demand function is given in the general form of Equation (3).

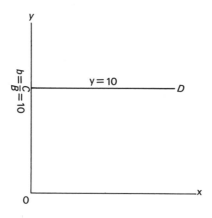

Fig. 2–8

Consider now a demand curve with a zero slope, as represented in Figure 2–8. If

$$m = -\frac{A}{B} = 0,$$

then A must equal zero, and the general equation for a demand curve with zero slope becomes

$$By - C = 0. \qquad (4)$$

In terms of Figure 2–8,

$$y - 10 = 0;$$

$$a = \frac{C}{A} = \frac{10}{0} = \infty;$$

$$b = \frac{C}{B} = \frac{10}{1} = 10;$$

$$m = -\frac{A}{B} = -\frac{0}{1} = 0.$$

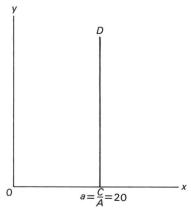

Fig. 2–9

Finally, we may consider a demand curve with infinite slope. If

$$m = -\frac{A}{B} = \infty,$$

then B must equal zero, and the general equation for a demand curve with infinite slope becomes

$$Ax - C = 0. \tag{5}$$

In terms of Figure 2–9,

$$\tfrac{1}{2}x - 10 = 0;$$

$$a = \frac{C}{A} = \frac{10}{\frac{1}{2}} = 20;$$

$$b = \frac{C}{B} = \frac{10}{0} = \infty;$$

$$m = -\frac{A}{B} = -\frac{\frac{1}{2}}{0} = -\infty.$$

To summarize: the general equation for a demand curve is given by

$$Ax + By - C = 0.$$

The C term is always negative. If the demand curve is negatively inclined, A and B will be positive. If the demand curve has a zero slope, A will be zero, and B will be positive. If the demand has an infinite slope, A will be positive, and B will be zero.

General Supply Equations

In similar fashion we can determine the general equations for the supply function. In addition to the cases when the slope of the supply function is equal to zero and when the slope is equal to infinity, where the equations for

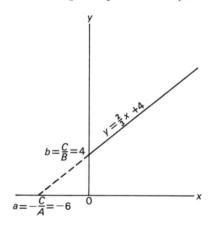

Fig. 2–10

the supply functions would have the same algebraic expression as demand curves of the same slopes, there are three cases of supply which are of interest to the economist: (a) when the y-intercept of the supply curve is above the origin, (b) when the y-intercept is below the origin, and (c) when the y-intercept is at the origin.

Since we are dealing with linear functions, the basic equation for a linear supply curve is

$$y = mx + b.$$

Consider the function plotted in Figure 2–10:

$$y = \tfrac{2}{3}x + 4.$$

This could be written as

$$-\tfrac{2}{3}x + y - 4 = 0.$$

Or, multiplying through by -1, this becomes

$$\tfrac{2}{3}x - y + 4 = 0.$$

The general equation for a linear supply curve with a positive y-intercept is

$$Ax - By + C = 0. \qquad (6)$$

We may generalize by saying that if the supply curve is linear and positively inclined with a positive y-intercept, A and B are of opposite algebraic signs and A and C have the same sign.

It may be noted further that

$$a = -\frac{C}{A} = -\frac{4}{\frac{2}{3}} = -6;$$

$$b = \frac{C}{B} = \frac{4}{1} = 4;$$

$$m = \frac{A}{B} = \frac{\frac{2}{3}}{1} = \frac{2}{3}.$$

In this case, since b is positive, C is positive.

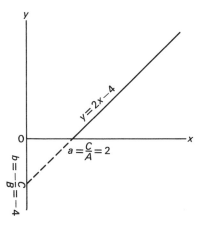

Fig. 2–11

Consider next a supply curve with a negative intercept on the y-axis. In Figure 2–11 we have drawn the function

$$y = 2x - 4.$$

This could be written

$$-2x + y + 4 = 0,$$

and by multiplying both sides by -1 we get

$$2x - y - 4 = 0.$$

In general terms this becomes

$$Ax - By - C = 0. \tag{7}$$

We may generalize by saying that if the supply curve is linear and positively inclined with a negative y-intercept, A and B are of opposite signs and B and C have the same sign.

In this case

$$a = \frac{C}{A} = \tfrac{4}{2} = 2;$$

$$b = -\frac{C}{B} = -\tfrac{4}{1} = -4;$$

$$m = \frac{A}{B} = \tfrac{2}{1} = 2.$$

Since b is negative, C is negative.

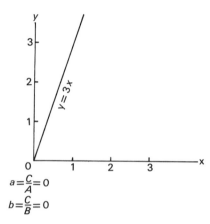

$$a = \frac{C}{A} = 0$$

$$b = \frac{C}{B} = 0$$

Fig. 2–12

Finally, consider a linear supply curve which passes through the origin. Figure 2–12 represents the function

$$y = 3x,$$

which can be written as

$$-3x + y = 0.$$

Multiplying through by -1 we get

$$3x - y = 0.$$

The general equation for supply curves of this type is

$$Ax - By = 0. \tag{8}$$

And

$$a = \frac{C}{A} = \tfrac{0}{3} = 0;$$

$$b = \frac{C}{B} = \tfrac{0}{1} = 0;$$

$$m = \frac{A}{B} = \tfrac{3}{1} = 3.$$

To summarize the general equations for supply functions: A will be positive and B will be negative; if b is positive, C will be positive; if b is negative, C will be negative; and if b is zero, C will be zero.

Shortages and Surpluses

We may conclude this postprandium with a word about the meaning of the terms "shortage" and "surplus." Under conditions of pure competition the quantity demanded will be just equal to the quantity supplied at the equilibrium price. All buyers who want to buy at that price and all sellers who wish to sell at that price will be able to do so. There is under these circumstances no problem of surplus or shortage; the equilibrium price is the one which just "clears the market." If due to unusually favorable weather conditions the quantity of an agricultural commodity which is brought to market is greater than usual, the price of the commodity will tend to fall, and all that is offered will be sold. Since the quantity demanded just equals the quantity supplied, there is in no real sense a surplus of the commodity. Or, if due to unfavorable conditions the harvest is abnormally small, the price will rise; all who are willing to pay the price will be able to buy the good, and it would not be accurate to say that there was a shortage of the good. In a communist economy, on the other hand, the available goods will be rationed among consumers according to some prearranged plan, and if the harvest is poor, consumers might with some point speak of the shortage of the commodity; if it should ever happen that the communist state should produce more of a commodity than consumers would choose to have, the overproduction might well be considered a surplus. But in a free-market economy price serves the function of eliminating the problems of shortages and surpluses.

Shortages and surpluses appear in a private-enterprise economy only when some outside constraint prevents prices from seeking their equilibrium

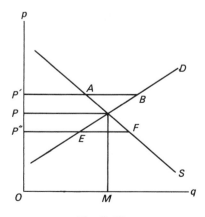

Fig. 2–13

levels. In Figure 2–13, equilibrium price is *OP* and equilibrium quantity exchanged is *OM*. There is no shortage or surplus at this price. But suppose that the government undertakes a price-support program and makes *OP'* the legal price. At this price buyers will be willing to buy only *P'A* units ·of the commodity, whereas sellers will offer *P'B* units for sale. The difference between what buyers will buy and what sellers will want to sell at this price is the surplus, which in the figure is equal to *AB* units of the commodity. In order to maintain the legal price the government will have to buy the units which consumers are unwilling to buy at that price, and the government will have either to store the surplus, destroy it, or sell it abroad. Whatever disposal the government makes of the surplus will involve costs and likely will have domestic or foreign political repercussions. When a price-support program is undertaken, these hazards are assumed in order to effect a redistribution of income among economic groups within the country. Whether the social gains outweigh the social costs of such a program is a much-debated issue.

Sometimes the government intervenes in an effort to protect the consumer from inflationary forces by setting a legal price below the equilibrium level. In time of war the government often sets maximum prices such as *OP''* in Figure 2–13. At this price consumers would like to buy *P''F* units of the commodity, whereas sellers would be willing to sell only *P''E* units at this price. The difference, *EF*, may properly be described as a shortage. Since there is less of the good than consumers want to buy at the legal price, it frequently becomes necessary for the government to ration commodities among consumers. The effective demand of the consumer now requires not only that he be able and willing to pay the money price; he must, in addition, be able and willing to provide the required ration coupons. When shortages are acute, it is difficult for the government to maintain the legal price. Many buyers and sellers will be willing to trade in the unlawful "black market" at prices above the legal maximum. In the United States during World War II black markets flourished in spite of patriotic appeals that price controls were necessary to prevent inflation and make victory possible. In Nazi Germany trading in black markets was a capital offense, but Hitler with all of the powers of a totalitarian state at his command was unable to stop black-market trading. The market forces of demand and supply are powerful and not easily diverted.

SELECTED REFERENCES

Alchian, Armen, and William R. Allen. *University Economics.* Belmont, Calif.: Wadsworth Publishing Co., Inc., 1964. Chap. 7.

Allen, Clark Lee. *Elementary Mathematics of Price Theory.* Belmont, Calif.: Wadsworth Publishing Co., Inc., 1962. Chaps. 3 and 4.

———, James M. Buchanan, and Marshall R. Colberg. *Prices, Income, and Public Policy.* 2nd ed. New York: McGraw-Hill Book Co., 1959. Chap. 4.

Boulding, Kenneth E. *Economic Analysis.* 3rd ed. New York: Harper & Row, Publishers, 1955. Chaps. 5 and 6.

Knight, Frank H. *Risk, Uncertainty and Profit.* Boston: Houghton Mifflin Co., 1921. Chap. 1.

Marshall, Alfred. *Principles of Economics.* 8th ed. London: Macmillan & Co., 1920. Book V. Chaps. 1–3.

PROBLEMS

PROBLEM I

In Figure 2–14, D and S represent the demand and supply for a given commodity. D′ represents the new demand if a tax is levied on the buyers; S′ represents the new supply if a tax is levied on the sellers.

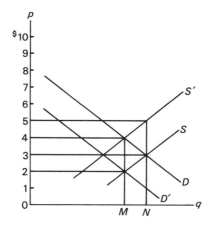

Fig. 2–14

1. When demand and supply are represented by D and S:
    (a) Equilibrium price is .   .   .   .   .   . _____
    (b) Equilibrium quantity is   .   .   .   .   . _____

2. Assume now that a tax of $2 per unit is levied on sellers:
    (a) Quantity exchanged now is   .   .   .   . _____
    (b) Price to the consumer is   .   .   .   . _____
    (c) Price to the seller after taxes is .   .   .   . _____

3. Now assume that the tax is levied on the buyer instead of the seller:
    (a) Quantity exchanged is now   .   .   .   . _____
    (b) Price to the buyer including tax is .   .   . _____
    (c) Price to the seller is   .   .   .   .   . _____

PROBLEM II

Draw curves on the charts below to demonstrate the effect on (a) price and (b) quantity exchanged in each of the following cases:

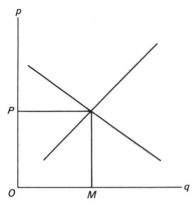

Fig. 2–15

1. An increase in demand and an equal increase in supply.

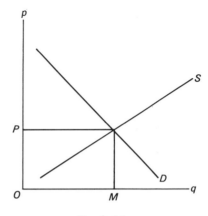

Fig. 2–16

2. An increase in demand and an equal decrease in supply.

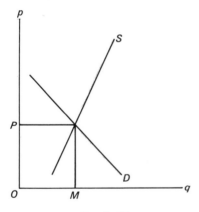

Fig. 2–17

3. A large increase in demand and a small decrease in supply.

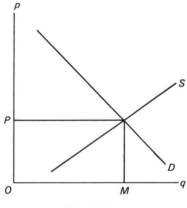

Fig. 2–18

4. A small increase in demand and a large increase in supply.

PROBLEM III

1. The price of gasoline was much lower in 1938 than in 1930. D and S in Figure 2–19 represent the demand and supply of gasoline in 1930. Draw in the chart the changes in demand and/or supply which represents the most reasonable explanation of this price change.

2. The price of cement was the same in 1930 as in 1900. D and S in Figure 2–20 represent the demand and supply of cement in 1900. Draw in the chart the changes in demand and/or supply which represent the most reasonable explanation of this constant price.

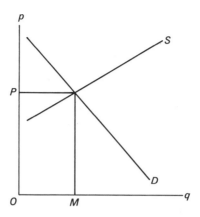

Fig. 2–19

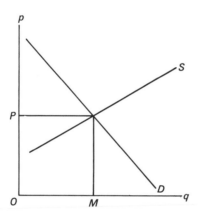

Fig. 2–20

PROBLEM IV

Given: $D = 6 - p/2;\ S = p.$

(a) What is the equilibrium price? . . . ._____
(b) What is the equilibrium quantity? . . ._____
(c) What is the x-intercept of the D curve? . ._____
(d) What is the y-intercept of the D curve? . ._____
(e) What is the slope of the D curve? . . . ._____
(f) What is the x-intercept of the S curve? . ._____
(g) What is the y-intercept of the S curve? . ._____
(h) What is the slope of the S curve? . . . ._____

Assume now that demand shifts to $D' = 9 - p/2$; S remains unchanged.

(i) What is the new equilibrium price? . . ._____

(j) What is the new equilibrium quantity? . ._____

(k) What is the x-intercept of the D' curve? . ._____

(l) What is the y-intercept of the D' curve? . ._____

(m) What is the slope of the D' curve? . . . ._____

(n) Does the shift from D to D' represent an increase in demand? . . . . ._____

3

The Price Elasticity
of Demand

The negative slope of a demand curve indicates that as the price of a commodity falls, the quantity demanded increases. But the prices of two commodities may fall equally and yet the change in the quantity demanded may be much greater for one than for the other. Then we may say that the demand for one commodity is more responsive to a change in price than the demand for the other, or that the price elasticity of demand is greater for one commodity than for the other.

The difference in the responsiveness of two demands to a given change in price, i.e., the difference in the elasticity of demand between two given prices, is illustrated in Figure 3–1. D_a represents the demand for commodity A, and D_b, the demand for commodity B. At price OP, the amount of each commodity demanded is OM. If the price of each commodity falls to OP', the amount demanded at the lower price is greater for both commodities than the amount demanded at the higher price, but the increase in the amount of B demanded is greater than the increase in the amount of A demanded. We may say, accordingly, that between prices OP and OP', the elasticity of D_b is greater than the elasticity of D_a.

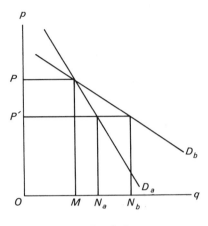

Fig. 3–1

Elasticity of Demand and Total Expenditure

It is possible, given the demand function, to measure the elasticity of demand with great precision. For many purposes, however, it is sufficient to determine whether the elasticity of demand between two prices is relatively great or relatively small. This can be done by observing the relation between a change in price and the corresponding change in total expenditure (or from the point of view of the seller, total revenue). In Table 3–1 we have drawn up a demand schedule with a Total-Expenditure column added. Total expenditure at any price is the product of price times quantity: $TE = pq$.

TABLE 3–1

Price	Quantity Demanded	Total Expenditure
$10	0	$ 0
9	1	9
8	2	16
7	3	21
6	4	24
5	5	25
4	6	24
3	7	21
2	8	16
1	9	9
0	10	0

It will be noted that, although the price each time falls by one unit and the corresponding quantity demanded increases by one unit, the product of price times quantity (pq) does not remain constant but rather increases, reaches a maximum, and then decreases. The reason for this is that, for example, while a drop in price from $9 to $8 represents about an 11 percent change in price, the corresponding increase in quantity demanded from 1 to 2 is a 100 percent increase in quantity. In this range the demand is highly responsive to a change in price, i.e., the price elasticity of demand is high. On the other hand, consider the effect of a drop in price from $2 to $1. This is a reduction of price of 50 percent, but the corresponding increase in quantity demanded from 8 units to 9 is only 12½ percent. If it takes a 50-percent decrease in price to effect a 12½-percent increase in the quantity demanded, the demand in this range is relatively unresponsive to a price change, or is inelastic. The point is illustrated in Figure 3–2.

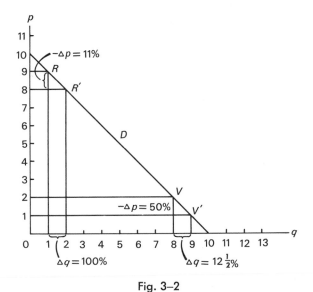

Fig. 3–2

The relationship between a change in price and a change in total expenditure may be generalized as follows: in a range where total expenditure and price move in opposite directions, the demand is said to be elastic; where total expenditure and price move in the same direction, it is said to be inelastic. Where total expenditure remains constant as price changes, the percentage reduction in price per unit is just offset by the percentage increase in number of units demanded, and the demand is neither elastic nor inelastic but has unitary elasticity, or an elasticity of one. An inelastic demand has a coefficient of elasticity of less than one and an elastic demand has a coefficient of elasticity greater than one.

The relation between elasticity of demand and total expenditure is indicated in Figure 3–3, in which the demand and total-expenditure schedules of Table 3–1 have been plotted. It will be noted that when the total expenditure is at a maximum, i.e., where for an infinitesimally small change in quantity the total expenditure remains constant (i.e., it has stopped increasing but has not yet begun to decrease), the elasticity of demand is one. This comes at precisely the midpoint of the linear demand curve. In the upper half of the demand curve, where a drop in price is associated with an increase in total expenditure, the elasticity of demand is greater than one; and in the lower half of the demand curve, where a drop in price is associated with a decrease in total expenditure, the elasticity of demand is less than one.

For many purposes this measure of elasticity of demand is sufficient. If a businessman contemplates reducing the price of his product, he assumes that at the lower price he can sell more units than at the higher price. But will his

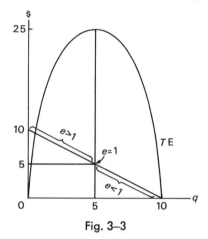

Fig. 3–3

total revenue increase as the price is reduced? It will if the elasticity of demand for his product between these prices is greater than one. If a railroad is in financial difficulty and proposes an increase in rates in order to increase its total revenue, it will be disappointed if the elasticity of demand for its services is greater than one. If a country devalues its currency in order to increase the value of its exports in terms of foreign currencies, the effort will fail if the foreign demand for its exports proves to be inelastic. If a football team has been drawing less-than-capacity crowds, a reduction in the admission charge will increase total revenue only if the elasticity of demand for watching football games is greater than one.

Point Elasticity of Demand

There are times, however, when it is desirable to know more about the elasticity of demand than a comparison of the movements of price and total expenditure will tell us. We may know, for example, that a 1-percent drop in price will cause more than a 1-percent increase in the quantity demanded, i.e., we may know that the elasticity of demand is greater than 1; but we may want to know *how much* greater. Our next task, accordingly, is to find a method for determining a precise coefficient of elasticity.

Elasticity of demand may be defined in mathematical symbols as

$$E_d = \frac{\frac{\Delta x}{x}}{\frac{\Delta y}{y}},$$

where E_d is elasticity of demand, Δx is the change in the quantity demanded, x is the original amount demanded, Δy is the change in price, and y is the original price. If a 1-percent change in price should be accompanied by a 1-percent increase in the amount demanded, the elasticity of demand would be

$$E_d = \frac{\frac{\Delta x}{x}}{\frac{\Delta y}{y}} = \frac{\frac{1}{100}}{\frac{1}{100}} = 1.$$

Similarly, if a 1-percent fall in price caused a 2-percent increase in the quantity demanded, the elasticity of demand would be 2. And if a 1-percent decrease in price resulted in a $\frac{1}{2}$-percent increase in the amount demanded, the demand would have a coefficient of elasticity of $\frac{1}{2}$.

A worrisome complication must be introduced at this point. If we assume that a drop in price is accompanied by an increase in quantity demanded, Δy in our formula will be negative and Δx will be positive, and the coefficient of elasticity will, accordingly, have a negative algebraic sign. When a drop of 1 percent in price is accompanied by an increase of 1 percent in quantity demanded, the elasticity of demand is actually -1 rather than $+1$. The coefficient of elasticity of a curve takes the same algebraic sign as the slope of the curve. This would be simple enough except that economists consider an elasticity of demand of -2 to be greater than an elasticity of -1, and, of course, -2 is not, in fact, greater than -1. Some writers have attempted to avoid this problem by defining elasticity of demand as

$$E_d = -\frac{\frac{\Delta x}{x}}{\frac{\Delta y}{y}},$$

thus making the coefficient of elasticity of demand positive. But if this convention is followed, we must use one formula for the elasticity of a negatively inclined curve, such as a demand curve, and a different formula for the elasticity of a positively inclined curve, such as a supply curve. We shall here follow the convention of representing the elasticity of demand as a negative number, but we consider a coefficient of elasticity of, for example, -3 to be greater than a coefficient of elasticity of -2. That is, for most purposes the algebraic sign can be ignored; it simply reflects the slope of the curve. But when a formula includes elasticity of demand in one of its terms, the value of the formula will be affected by the algebraic sign assigned to the coefficient of elasticity.

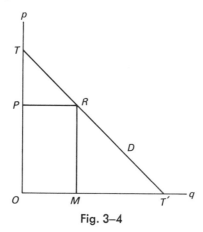

Fig. 3–4

The formula for the elasticity of demand is a ratio of two ratios, and in this form it is cumbersome. Fortunately, however, it can be stated as a simple ratio. We may begin by putting the basic formula in these terms:

$$E_d = \frac{\dfrac{\Delta x}{x}}{\dfrac{-\Delta y}{y}} = \frac{\Delta x}{x} \cdot \frac{y}{-\Delta y} = \frac{y}{x} \cdot \frac{\Delta x}{-\Delta y}.$$

In terms of Figure 3–4 this becomes

$$E_d = \frac{y}{x} \cdot \frac{\Delta x}{-\Delta y} = \frac{OP}{OM} \cdot \frac{PR}{-PT}$$

since $\Delta x / -\Delta y$ is the reciprocal of the slope of TT', and one measure of the slope of the curve is $-PT/PR$. But since $PR = OM$, we may write

$$E_d = \frac{OP}{OM} \cdot \frac{PR}{-PT} = \frac{OP}{OM} \cdot \frac{OM}{-PT} = -\frac{OP}{PT}. \tag{1}$$

Or to find a second expression for the elasticity of demand, we may write

$$E_d = \frac{y}{x} \cdot \frac{\Delta x}{-\Delta y} = \frac{OP}{OM} \cdot \frac{MT'}{-MR} = \frac{MR}{OM} \cdot \frac{MT'}{-MR} = -\frac{MT'}{OM}. \tag{2}$$

Or we may note that OT and $T'T$ may be viewed as transverse lines cut by the parallel lines PR and OT', and, since parallel lines cut transverse lines proportionately, that

$$E_d = -\frac{MT'}{OM} = -\frac{RT'}{RT}.\tag{3}$$

This gives us three formulas for the measurement of elasticity and all are equivalent to the complex formula:

$$E_d = \frac{\frac{\Delta x}{x}}{\frac{-\Delta y}{y}} = -\frac{OP}{PT} = -\frac{MT'}{OM} = -\frac{RT'}{RT},$$

where price $= OP$, quantity demanded $= OM$, the x-intercept of the demand curve is T', and the y-intercept of the demand curve is T.

If we assume that the change in price is infinitesimally small, the $-\Delta x/\Delta y$ term in our basic formula becomes $-dx/dy$, and the formula for the elasticity of demand at a point on the demand curve, which is known as point elasticity, becomes

$$E_d = \frac{y}{x} \cdot \frac{dx}{-dy} = \frac{OP}{-PT} = \frac{MT'}{-OM} = \frac{RT'}{-RT}.$$

If the demand curve is nonlinear, we can determine the elasticity of demand at any point by drawing a tangent to the curve at the given point, and, since at the point of tangency the linear and the nonlinear curves are identical for an infinitesimal distance, the elasticity of both curves at that point will be the same. In Figure 3–5, for example, the elasticity of the nonlinear curve D and the tangent TT' at point R is given by

$$E_d = -\frac{OP}{PT} = -\frac{MT'}{OM} = -\frac{RT'}{RT}.$$

The geometry of point elasticity of demand may also be illustrated with reference to Figure 3–5. If we know the intercepts of the linear curve TT', we may choose any value for OP and determine the values of TT', OM,

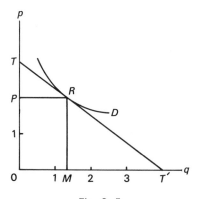

Fig. 3–5

MT', RT, RT', the slope of the demand curve, and the elasticity of demand at the given price.

Let

$$OT = 3$$

and

$$OT' = 4.$$

Then

$$TT' = \sqrt{3^2 + 4^2} = \sqrt{25} = 5.$$

Let

$$OP = 2;$$

and

$$m = -\frac{OT}{OT'} = -\tfrac{3}{4}.$$

Since

$$TP = OT - OP = 3 - 2 = 1,$$
$$m = -\frac{TP}{PR} = -\frac{1}{PR} = -\tfrac{3}{4}.$$

If

$$-\frac{1}{PR} = -\tfrac{3}{4},$$
$$3PR = 4$$
$$PR = \tfrac{4}{3} = OM,$$

and

$$MT' = OT' - OM = 4 - \tfrac{4}{3} = \tfrac{8}{3}.$$

Then at point R,

$$E_d = -\frac{OP}{PT} = -\tfrac{2}{1} = -2,$$

or

$$E_d = -\frac{MT'}{OM} = -\frac{\tfrac{8}{3}}{\tfrac{4}{3}} = -2.$$

but

$$E_d = -\frac{RT'}{RT} = -\frac{T'T - RT}{RT} = -\frac{5 - RT}{RT} = -\tfrac{2}{1}.$$

If

$$-\frac{5 - RT}{RT} = -\tfrac{2}{1},$$
$$2RT = 5 - RT,$$
$$3RT = 5,$$
$$RT = \tfrac{5}{3},$$

and

$$RT' = 5 - \tfrac{5}{3} = \tfrac{10}{3} \, .$$

Then

$$E_d = -\frac{RT'}{RT} = -\frac{\tfrac{10}{3}}{\tfrac{5}{3}} = -2.$$

It will be noted that if a demand curve is negatively inclined and linear, the coefficient of elasticity of demand will be different at every price. In Figure 3–6 at point R the elasticity of demand is given by OP/TP;[1] OP is less than TP, and the elasticity of demand at this price is, accordingly, less than one. At point R', OP' and TP' are equal, and the elasticity of demand is

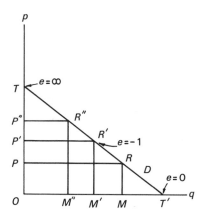

Fig. 3–6

unity. At point R'', elasticity of demand is given by OP''/TP''; since OP'' is greater than TP'', elasticity is greater than one. It will be noted furthermore that as one moves down the demand curve from point R, OP approaches zero, and the elasticity of demand correspondingly approaches zero. If we start at point R'' on the demand curve and move upward along the curve, we note that TP'' approaches zero, and the elasticity of demand accordingly approaches infinity. We may generalize by saying that on any linear negatively inclined demand curve drawn from its intercept on the y-axis to its intercept on the x-axis, the coefficient of elasticity varies from zero to infinity. It is not accurate to describe such a curve as either elastic or inelastic; it is proper to speak of the elasticity of the curve at a given point or between two given points, but it is inappropriate to speak of the elasticity of the curve as a whole.

If a demand curve is perfectly elastic throughout, or if it has an elasticity

[1] To avoid the use of the minus sign we may consider TP negative whereas PT would be positive.

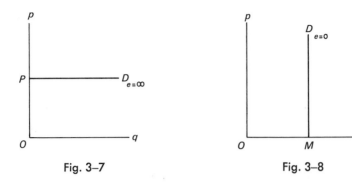

Fig. 3–7   Fig. 3–8

of zero at all points, it is not inappropriate to speak of the elasticity of the curve since the elasticity is uniform at all points or between any two points. The case of the perfectly elastic demand curve is an important one for price theory, and such a demand is represented in Figure 3–7. A demand curve of zero elasticity is represented in Figure 3–8.

If a demand curve has a uniform elasticity of anything between zero and infinity throughout its length, it will not be a linear curve. The general equation for such a curve is

$$q = \frac{K}{p^n} = Kp^{-n},$$

where p is price, q is quantity demanded, and K and n are constants. The elasticity of such a demand function is equal to $-n$ at all points. A case of special interest in price theory is the demand curve which has an elasticity of -1 at all points. Such a curve is known as a rectangular hyperbola. Suppose it is known that, regardless of price, total expenditure is always constant at 12. That is,

$$TE = pq = 12.$$

Then

$$q = \frac{12}{p}.$$

We know that if total expenditure remains constant as price changes, the elasticity of demand is equal to -1. The function $q = 12/p$ is drawn in Figure 3–9.

It will be noted that if we draw a tangent to the demand curve in Figure 3–9 at price = 6, the elasticity of demand, which is given by $-OP/PT$, is $-6/6 = -1$. The tangent to the curve at $p = 6$ has a y-intercept at 12. In general, if the demand curve is a rectangular hyperbola, the tangent to the curve at price = p will have a y-intercept at $2p$. The tangent to the curve at $p = 3$ has a y-intercept at 6. When price is 6, the quantity demanded is 2, and the total expenditure is 12. If the price is 3, the quantity demanded is 4,

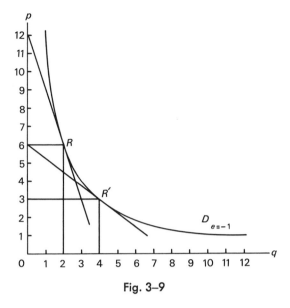

Fig. 3–9

and the total expenditure remains at 12. The area of any rectangle inscribed under this demand curve is equal to 12; the area of the rectangles represents total expenditure, i.e., price times quantity demanded, which the equation for the curve, $pq = K$, tells us must remain constant.

Elasticity and Slope

The ideas of slope and elasticity are quite different but are frequently confused. We have noted that the algebraic sign for the coefficient of elasticity and the slope of a curve is the same, and we have seen in Figures 3–7 and 3–8 that a horizontal demand curve has an elasticity of infinity at all points and a vertical demand curve has zero elasticity at all points. It is easy to make the mistake of assuming that the flatter the demand curve—that is, the closer it approaches the horizontal—the more elastic it will be, and the steeper the demand curve—that is, the closer it approaches the vertical—the less elastic it will be. This misconception must be dispelled once and for all.

In the first place, it will be noted in Figures 3–7 and 3–8 that when m, the slope of the curve, is zero, e, the elasticity of the curve, is infinity, and vice versa. Instead of being the same, slope and elasticity in these instances are opposites! The reason for this is indicated in the definitions of the concepts themselves. Slope is defined as

$$m = \frac{\Delta y}{\Delta x},$$

whereas elasticity is defined as

$$e = \frac{y}{x} \cdot \frac{\Delta x}{\Delta y} .$$

Elasticity is a more complex concept than slope, and it contains in its formula the *reciprocal* of the slope.

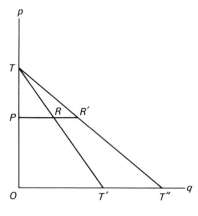

Fig. 3–10

It will also be recalled that whereas the slope of a straight line is constant throughout, the elasticity of a linear negatively inclined demand curve is different at each point, ranging from zero to infinity. It is appropriate to speak of the slope of a linear demand curve, but the elasticity of such a curve must be measured at a particular point on the curve.

Since the elasticity of a demand curve at price OP is given by the formula

$$E_d = -\frac{OP}{PT} ,$$

it follows that all negatively inclined linear demand curves with a common y-intercept have the same elasticity at any given price regardless of the slopes of the curves. In Figure 3–10 the elasticity of the demand curve TT' at point R is equal to $-OP/PT$; the elasticity of the curve TT'' at point R' is also $-OP/PT$. The curves have different slopes, but the elasticity at any given price will be the same.

Similarly, since the elasticity of a demand curve at quantity OM is given by

$$E_d = -\frac{MT'}{OM} ,$$

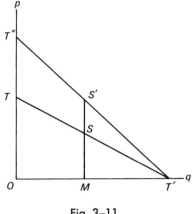

Fig. 3–11

all negatively inclined linear demand curves with a common *x*-intercept will have the same elasticity at any given *quantity* regardless of the slopes of the curves. In Figure 3–11 the elasticity of the demand curve *TT'* at point S is equal to the elasticity of curve *T''T'* at point S'; both are given by

$$E_d = -\frac{MT'}{OM}.$$

The curves have different slopes, but the elasticity at any given *quantity* is the same.

In Figure 3–12 we have drawn two demand curves with different slopes and different intercepts on both axes. Demand *TT'* has a relatively steep slope, and *T''T'''* has a lesser slope. But at any given price, the elasticity of the curve with the greater slope is greater than the elasticity of the other curve; that is, *OP/TP* > *OP/T''P*. It clearly is not true that the greater the

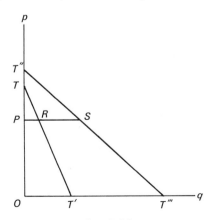

Fig. 3–12

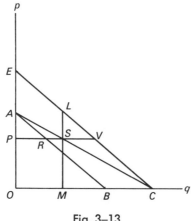

Fig. 3–13

slope of a demand curve, the less will be its elasticity. Slope and elasticity are quite different concepts, and they must not be confused.

Finally, we may distinguish between slope and elasticity by reference to Figure 3–13. AB and EC are parallel demand curves, i.e., they have the same slope. A third demand curve, AC, is drawn by connecting the y-intercept of AB and the x-intercept of EC, and its slope is less than that of the other curves. But at price OP curves AB and AC, which have different slopes, have the same coefficient of elasticity, which is given by OP/AP in each instance. But the elasticities of the parallel demand curves at that price are different: $OP/AP > OP/EP$. Again, the elasticity of the nonparallel curves AC and EC is the same at quantity OM, equal in each instance to CM/OM; but the curves with the same slope have different elasticities at quantity OM: $CM/OM > BM/OM$.

A convenient method of comparing elasticities of two demand curves at given points is indicated in Figure 3–14. AB and EC are two linear demand

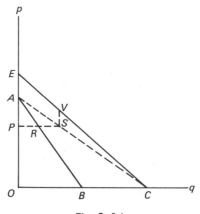

Fig. 3–14

curves. The problem is to locate the point on curve EC where the elasticity of demand is equal to the elasticity of curve AB at point R. We may draw a line from the y-intercept of AB to the x-intercept of EC. Since AB and AC have a common intercept on the y-axis, they will have the same elasticity at any given price; that is, the elasticity of AB at R is equal to the elasticity of AC at S. But AC and EC have a common intercept on the x-axis and, accordingly, have the same elasticity at any given quantity. The elasticity of AC at point S is, therefore, equal to the elasticity of EC at V, and the elasticity at V on curve EC, accordingly, is equal to the elasticity of curve AB at point R, which is given by OP/AP.

POSTPRANDIUM

It is possible to become involved with the mechanics of the measurement of the elasticity of demand to the point where one may lose sight of the significance of what is being measured. It is not too much to say that at one time in recent history the fate of an empire turned on the proper assessment of elasticity of demand, and we pause to take a brief look at the circumstances of that fateful decision.

Following World War II the nations of Western Europe found themselves economically exhausted. In England, for example, many factories had been bombed out of existence; plants that remained had been unable to maintain their capital equipment; foreign currencies had been largely liquidated; and in general the economic future looked dark. England and other European countries depended upon the United States for new capital equipment and even for a considerable quantity of goods for immediate consumption. All nations needed dollars to pay for American goods; this was the period of the "dollar shortage." In England the slogan was "Export or die," which really meant "Export so we can get foreign currencies to pay for imports or we die." But the price of the pound sterling had been pegged during the war at about $4.02, and at this rate British goods were so expensive in terms of dollars that the British found it difficult to export. The decision was finally made to devalue the pound from $4.02 to $2.80 in order to make English goods less expensive in dollar terms. The effect of the devaluation of the pound is illustrated in Table 3–2.

The first column shows the price of an MG sports car in pounds sterling.

TABLE 3–2

$£P_{MG}$	$\$P_£$	$\$P_{MG}$	Q_d	TR
£500	$4	$2,000	1,000	$2,000,000
£500	$3	$1,500	1,200 ⎫	⎧ $1,800,000
			1,333 ⎬	⎨ 2,000,000
			1,500 ⎭	⎩ 2,250,000

The second column shows the rate of exchange, i.e., the price of the pound in dollars. (The actual devaluation was somewhat greater than that indicated in the table, so our illustration understates the actual situation.) The third column indicates the price of an MG in dollars, i.e., the price of an MG in pounds multiplied by the dollar price of the pound, and the fourth column indicates the quantity demanded per time period in the United States at that price. The last column indicates the total revenue received by the British from the sale of MG's to Americans.

The objective of the English, as we have seen, was to increase the number of dollars available to them to spend on machine tools, raw materials, and food imports. If the pound is devalued to $3, the price of an MG in the American market becomes $1,500. Suppose that at that price Americans will buy 1,200 units per time period. The total revenue from the sale of MG's to Americans will then be only $1,800,000 as compared with $2,000,000 before devaluation. Since the total revenue and price moved in the same direction, the elasticity of demand in the American market between prices $2,000 and $1,500 is less than one. From the British point of view, this result would be disastrous; they would have exported more MG's, which were in very short supply in the British market, and would have received for them actually fewer dollars than before.

Suppose, however, that the elasticity of the American demand for MG's is equal to one. A reduction in the dollar price from $2,000 to $1,500 would be accompanied by an increase in the quantity demanded by American buyers from 1,000 to 1,333, and total revenue would remain constant at $2,000,000. If in general the American demand for English goods had an elasticity of one, the policy of devaluation of the pound would again prove to be a failure; the British would have to export more of their own goods, which were insufficient for their own requirements, and receive no more dollars than before devaluation.

Only if the American demand for British goods had an elasticity of more than one would the devaluation policy prove successful. If the reduction in the price of MG's from $2,000 to $1,500 resulted in increased sales in the American market from 1,000 per time period to 1,500, the total revenue of the English would increase from $2,000,000 to $2,250,000. Even in this instance it may be noted that the percentage increase in required exports is much greater than the percentage increase in the number of dollars made available to the British. And since no one knew in advance what the elasticity of the American demand for English goods would prove to be, the 1949 devaluation of the pound represented a desperate gamble for England.[2]

---

[2] For a discussion of the reasons for the 1949 devaluation of the pound and the attitudes of contemporary economists toward the proposed change, see Raymond F. Mikesell, *Foreign Exchange in the Postwar World* (New York: The Twentieth Cent. Fund, 1954), Chap. 7.

The Concept of Infinity

In this and subsequent chapters we are concerned from time to time with the idea of a variable which approaches infinity, and a word about the notion of infinity is in order. As it is popularly used, "infinite" means immense or to an exceedingly great degree, but literally it means without limit. A billion is no closer to infinity than is a dozen. Since our minds are finite and we are accustomed to thinking in finite terms, we can scarcely fathom the idea of limitlessness. Even the Bible starts with the phrase, "In the beginning . . ." But what about the day or the year or the eons before the beginning? Time, it would seem, has neither beginning nor end.

A question to which youngsters sometimes address themselves is, "What is the biggest number in the world?" For a preschool boy, that number is probably one hundred. A little later he learns about one thousand. And eventually he may decide that a quadrillion is the world's largest number. (Incidentally, just to increase the confusion, in American and French notation a quadrillion is one followed by 15 zeros, whereas in England a quadrillion is one followed by 24 zeros.) The term *googol* has been invented to name a very large number; a googol is equal to 10^{100}, which is one followed by 100 zeros, and a *googolplex* is one followed by a googol of zeros: a googolplex $= 10^{10^{100}}$. It has been estimated that the number of grains of sand on the beach at Coney Island is about 10^{20} or one followed by 20 zeros, and the total number of words spoken since the beginning of man, including all baby talk, love songs, and Congressional debates, is about 10^{16}—both considerably less than a googol.[3] But all of these numbers are finite; they are less than infinity. There is, of course, no "largest" number; take the biggest number you can think of and add one more zero, and the number becomes ten times larger. The number of integers is infinite.

The number of fractions between each pair of integers is also infinite. If we restricted ourselves to fractions in the decimal system and used only *ones,* the number of fractions between, say, 1 and 2 would be infinite. We could start in this way:

$$1.1$$
$$1.11$$
$$1.111$$
$$1.1111$$
$$1.11111$$

and so on until we had a googolplex of ones following the decimal point. We could then replace the first one after the decimal point with a two, and continue indefinitely, and so on.

[3] Edward Kasner and James Newman, *Mathematics and the Imagination* (New York: Simon & Schuster, Inc., 1952), pp. 18–37.

Now, if there is an infinity of integers and an infinity of fractions between each pair of integers, are there more integers or more fractions? Common sense might suggest that there are more fractions than integers, but if there is an infinity of each, there must be as many of one as of the other. One series cannot be more infinite than another. Infinity times infinity equals infinity. Infinity to the infinite power is infinity. Infinity is more than a big number; more even than a googolplex to the googolplex power to the googolplex power. . . .

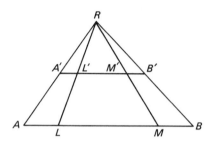

Fig. 3–15

Consider another aspect of infinity. How many points are there on a given straight line? Now a point has position but no dimensions—no width, no length, and no thickness. The concept of a point, like the concept of perfect competition, is a mental construct with no exact counterpart in the real world. If a point has no length or breadth, there is no limit to the number of points on a given line; the number of points is infinite.

. Consider the lines AB and $A'B'$ in Figure 3–15. AB is clearly longer than $A'B'$, but it has no more points on it than $A'B'$; the number of points on both is equal to infinity. This can be demonstrated by taking any point on AB, such as L and drawing a line from L to R. The line LR crosses $A'B'$ at point L'; L' is the point on $A'B'$ corresponding to point L on AB. Similarly, M' on $A'B'$ corresponds to point M on AB. For every point on AB there is a corresponding point on $A'B'$, and the number of points on the shorter line is, therefore, equal to the number of points on the longer line. And this would be true if AB were googol inches long and $A'B'$ were one inch long. Infinity is a concept quite different from the notion of very large or very small. And it is the concept on which much of mathematics, the most exact of the sciences, is built.

SELECTED REFERENCES

Allen, Clark Lee. *Elementary Mathematics of Price Theory*. Belmont, Calif.: Wadsworth Publishing Co., Inc., 1962. Chap. 16.

Bain, Joe S. *Pricing, Distribution, and Employment.* New York: Henry Holt, Rinehart & Winston, Inc., 1953. Chap. 2.

Marshall, Alfred. *Principles of Economics.* 8th ed. London: Macmillan & Co., 1920. Book III. Chaps. 3 and 4, and Mathematical Appendix, Note III.

Norris, Ruby Turner. *The Theory of Consumer's Demand.* Rev. ed. New Haven, Conn.: Yale University Press, 1952. Chap. 9.

Schultz, Henry. *The Theory and Measurement of Demand.* Chicago: University of Chicago Press, 1938.

Stigler, George J. *The Theory of Price.* Rev. ed. New York: The Macmillan Co., 1952. Chap. 4.

PROBLEMS

PROBLEM I

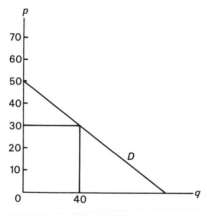

Fig. 3–16

1. What is the equation for the demand curve in the above figure? . . . . ._____

2. What is the x-intercept of D? . . . . . ._____

3. What is the elasticity of demand when $p = 30$? ._____

4. What is the elasticity of demand when $p = 20$? ._____

5. What is the elasticity of demand when $q = 70$? ._____

6. What is the elasticity of demand when $q = 10$? ._____

7. At what quantity is the elasticity of demand equal to $-\frac{1}{4}$? . . . . ._____

8. At what price is the elasticity of demand equal to $-\frac{1}{4}$? . . . . ._____

9. At what quantity is the elasticity of demand equal to -4? . . . . ._____

10. At what price is the elasticity of demand equal
to −4? . . . . _____

PROBLEM II

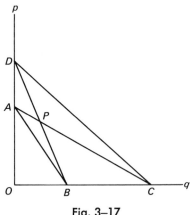

Fig. 3–17

1. Designate as *R*, *R′*, and *R″* the points on *AB*, *DB*, and *DC* respectively where the elasticity of demand is the same as at point *P* on *AC*.

2. Designate as *V*, *V′*, and *V″* the points on *DC*, *AC*, and *AB* respectively where the elasticity of demand is the same as at point *P* on *DB*.

PROBLEM III

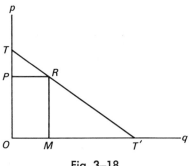

Fig. 3–18

Recalling that the elasticity of demand is always negative and that the elasticity of *TT′* at *R* is equal to $-OP/PT$, prove that the elasticity of *TT′* at *R* is also equal to $1 - OT/PT$.

PROBLEM IV

The equation for a linear demand curve is $Q = a(b - P)$, where *Q* is quantity demanded, *P* is price, and *a* and *b* are constants.

1. Show that *b* is the *y*-intercept of the demand curve and that *ab* is the *x*-intercept.

2. From the general formula $e = -OP/PT$, show that for the given curve $e = P/(P - b)$.

3. Show that the straight-line demand curve will have unitary elasticity where $P = b/2$.

4. Show that if we wish to describe the point on this demand curve that has any particular coefficient of elasticity, e, we may substitute the given elasticity in the formula $P = eb/(e - 1)$.

5. If we prefer these formulas in terms of Q rather than P, show that we may find the elasticity corresponding to any particular quantity by using the expression $e = 1 - (ab/Q)$.

6. If we want to find the quantity corresponding to any given elasticity, show that we may use the following formula: $Q = ab/(1 - e)$.

7. Show that the linear demand curve will have an elasticity of -1 when $Q = ab/2$.

8. If the linear demand curve has an intercept on the y-axis at 12, at what price will the elasticity of demand be -2?

9. If the linear demand curve has an intercept on the x-axis at 15, what will be the elasticity of demand when the quantity demanded is 5?

10. If the straight-line demand curve has an intercept on the x-axis at 18, at what quantity demanded will the elasticity of demand be -2?

PROBLEM V

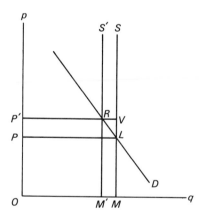

Fig. 3–19

In Figure 3–19, D and S are the demand and supply curves for a farm product. It is felt by the government that market price is too low. Three plans are proposed for increasing farmers' income, and each plan is analyzed below.

Plan A—Crop-Restriction Program

Assume that as a result of a program of crop restriction supply shifts from S to S' and price rises from OP to OP'.

1. Total farmers' income was originally . . . . ._____

2. After the crop-restriction program, farm income is ._____

3. If the elasticity of demand is less than one, the effect of the crop-restriction program will be to cause farm income to (rise, fall, remain the same) . . ._____

Plan B—Government-Purchase Program

Assume that D and S are demand and supply, but the government agrees to support price at OP' through commodity purchases.

1. Total farmers' income after the government-purchase program will be . . . . . . ._____

2. Total cost to the government of the purchase-program is . . . . ._____

3. Compared with Plan A above, this program would provide (greater, smaller, the same) income to farmers. . . . . ._____

Plan C—Producer-Subsidy Program

Assume that D and S are demand and supply but that the government pays a subsidy to farmers equal to PP' per unit of output.

1. Total farm income including subsidy is . . . ._____

2. Total cost to the government of the subsidy program is . . . . ._____

3. If the elasticity of demand is less than one, will Plan B or Plan C cost the government more? . ._____

PROBLEM VI

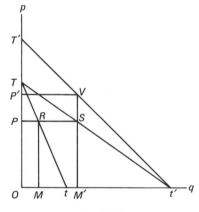

Fig. 3–20

Given: $OP = 6$, $OM = 2$, $Ot = 5$, $OM' = 6$, $OT' = 15$. Find:

1. Elasticity of demand at R . . . .─────────

2. $OT =$ . . . .─────────

3. Elasticity of demand at S . . . .─────────

4. $Ot' =$ . . . .─────────

5. Elasticity of demand at V . . . .─────────

6. $OP' =$ . . . .─────────

PROBLEM VII

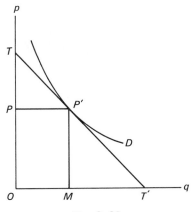

Fig. 3–21

Demonstrate geometrically that the elasticity of demand at price OP is given by $e = (OT'/OT) \cdot (OP/OM)$.

4

Arc Elasticity
of Demand and Supply

We have seen that the price elasticity of demand may be determined either at a given point or between two points on the demand curve. The elasticity at a point is called *point* elasticity, and the elasticity between two points is called *arc* elasticity of demand. In developing measures of point elasticity we considered the effect of a lower price on the amount demanded when the new price was only infinitesimally smaller than the original price. The two points on the demand curve representing the old and the new price-quantity combinations were so close together that they were in effect one point, and the elasticity of demand between these points was in effect the elasticity at a point. We found that we could measure point elasticity with great precision by using either the formula $e = OP/TP$ or $e = T'M/OM$. Because of the unambiguous nature of point elasticity, economists find it a very useful analytical tool. But in many applications we must concern ourselves with the elasticity of demand between two points on the curve which are separated by a finite distance, and for this purpose we need a measure of arc elasticity.

If a businessman contemplates lowering the price of his product, he is interested in how many more units he can sell at the lower price. He may never have heard of elasticity of demand, but he is, nonetheless, interested in it. And the businessman's interest is not likely to be in point elasticity; he wants to know what the change in his total revenue will be if he lowers or raises his price by a finite amount. If we attempt to measure the arc elasticity of demand from one point near the y-intercept of a linear demand curve to a second point near the x-intercept of the curve, we might get a coefficient of elasticity of about -1; but since in the neighborhood of the first point the elasticity would approach infinity, and in the neighborhood of the second point it would approach zero, a coefficient of -1 would be meaningless.

At best, the arc elasticity of demand is a kind of average of elasticities between the points on the curve, and no single coefficient always gives the most satisfactory measure of arc elasticity. There are, in fact, several formulas for arc elasticity; each is a perfectly rational measure, but when applied to a given problem, they give somewhat different results. For some purposes one formula serves best, and for some, another does. But in spite of this ambiguity, it is sometimes necessary to resort to the concept of arc elasticity.

Arc Elasticity Formulas

The first elasticity formula we used was an arc elasticity formula. It can be written

$$e = \frac{\frac{\Delta q}{q}}{\frac{\Delta p}{p}} = \frac{p}{q} \cdot \frac{\Delta q}{\Delta p} \, . \tag{1}$$

This formula related the change in price to the original price and the change in quantity to the original quantity. But it would be just as reasonable to relate the change in price to the new price and the change in quantity to the original quantity, and this would give us a second formula:

$$e = \frac{\frac{\Delta q}{q}}{\frac{\Delta p}{p + \Delta p}} = \frac{p + \Delta p}{q} \cdot \frac{\Delta q}{\Delta p} \, . \tag{2}$$

Or we could relate the change in price to the original price and the change in quantity to the new quantity:

$$e = \frac{\frac{\Delta q}{q + \Delta q}}{\frac{\Delta p}{p}} = \frac{p}{q + \Delta q} \cdot \frac{\Delta q}{\Delta p} \, . \tag{3}$$

Or we could relate the change in price to the new price and the change in quantity to the new quantity:

$$e = \frac{\frac{\Delta q}{q + \Delta q}}{\frac{\Delta p}{p + \Delta p}} = \frac{p + \Delta p}{q + \Delta q} \cdot \frac{\Delta q}{\Delta p}. \tag{4}$$

Or, what is most commonly done, we could relate the change in price to an average of the two prices and the change in quantity to an average of the two quantities:

$$e = \frac{\frac{(q_1 - q_2)/(q_1 + q_2)}{2}}{\frac{(p_1 - p_2)/(p_1 + p_2)}{2}} = \frac{q_1 - q_2}{q_1 + q_2} \cdot \frac{p_1 + p_2}{p_1 - p_2}$$

$$= \frac{\Delta q}{q_1 + q_2} \cdot \frac{p_1 + p_2}{\Delta p} = \frac{p_1 + p_2}{q_1 + q_2} \cdot \frac{\Delta q}{\Delta p}. \tag{5}$$

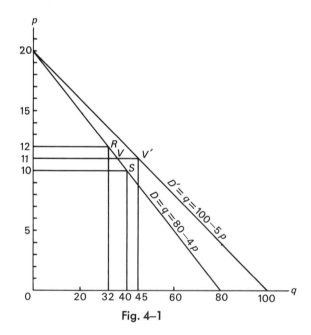

Fig. 4–1

Consider the demand function

$$D = q = 80 - 4p,$$

where q = quantity demanded and p = price. Suppose we want to determine the elasticity of demand between $p = 12$ and $p = 10$. By applying each of the arc elasticity formulas we get the following results:

$$(1) \quad e = \tfrac{12}{32} \cdot \frac{8}{-2} = -\tfrac{3}{2} \cdot$$

$$(2) \quad e = \frac{12 - 2}{32} \cdot \frac{8}{-2} = -\tfrac{5}{4} \cdot$$

$$(3) \quad e = \frac{12}{32 + 8} \cdot \frac{8}{-2} = -\tfrac{6}{5} \cdot$$

$$(4) \quad e = \frac{12 - 2}{32 + 8} \cdot \frac{8}{-2} = -1.$$

$$(5) \quad e = \frac{12 + 10}{32 + 40} \cdot \frac{8}{-2} = -\tfrac{11}{9} \cdot$$

It will be noted that all of the formulas except (4) give a coefficient of elasticity of more than one, but the differences among the several formulas are considerable. The discrepancies among the formulas diminish as the arc over which elasticity is measured becomes smaller and smaller. It will also be noted that if two demand curves have a common y-intercept, the arc elasticity between any two prices will be the same on both curves regardless of which formula is used. In Figure 4–1 the demand function $D = q = 80 - 4p$ is plotted along with the function $D' = q = 100 - 5p$, and, as the student can confirm for himself, arc elasticity between any two prices is the same on both curves regardless of which formula is employed.

Finally, it may be noted that formula (5) gives us the point elasticity of the curve at the price midway between the two given prices. The arc elasticity of both curves D and D' between prices 12 and 10 by formula (5) is $-11/9$. The point elasticity of both curves at price 11 is given by $OP/TP = -11/9$.

Arc Elasticity and Total Expenditure

We have seen that when demand is elastic, price and total expenditure move in opposite directions; when demand is inelastic, price and total expenditure move in the same direction; and when demand has an elasticity of one, total expenditure remains constant as price changes. The precise nature of the relationship between arc elasticity and total expenditure can be demonstrated with the use of Figure 4–2.

The total expenditure at price p is pq and is represented by the sum of the areas A_1 and A_2. When price is $p - \Delta p$, total expenditure is $(p - \Delta p)(q + \Delta q)$ and is the sum of the areas A_1 and A_3. The change in total expenditure as price changes from p to $(p - \Delta p)$ may be represented as

$$\Delta E = (A_1 + A_2) - (A_1 + A_3)$$
$$= A_2 - A_3.$$

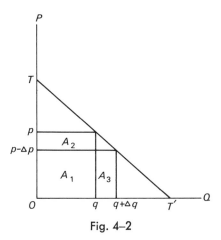

Fig. 4–2

Since the area A_2 is equal to $q\Delta p$ and the area A_3 is equal to $\Delta q(p - \Delta p)$, we may write

$$\Delta E = q\Delta p - \Delta q(p - \Delta p).$$

If the elasticity of demand between these prices is equal to -1, we know that there will be no change in total expenditure as price changes. Accordingly, if $e = -1$,

$$\Delta q(p - \Delta p) = q\Delta p.$$

Dividing both sides of this equation by $-q\Delta p$, we get

$$\frac{\Delta q(p - \Delta p)}{-q\Delta p} = -1.$$

Since Δp is negative, we may write

$$\frac{\Delta q(p + \Delta p)}{q\Delta p} = -1 = e,$$

or

$$e = \frac{p + \Delta p}{q} \cdot \frac{\Delta q}{\Delta p},$$

which is the same as our formula (2) for arc elasticity. It will be noted that this measure of arc elasticity gives us the lower price divided by the smaller quantity multiplied by $\Delta q/\Delta p$.

The formula

$$e = \frac{p + \Delta p}{q} \cdot \frac{\Delta q}{\Delta p}$$

may be written as

$$e = \frac{(p + \Delta p)\Delta q}{q \Delta p} \ .$$

The numerator of this fraction represents the area A_3 in Figure 4–2, and the denominator, the area A_2. It follows, accordingly, that:

if $(p + \Delta p)\Delta q > q \Delta p$, $e > 1$;
if $(p + \Delta p)\Delta q = q \Delta p$, $e = 1$;
if $(p + \Delta p)\Delta q < q \Delta p$, $e < 1$.

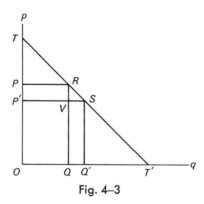

Fig. 4–3

We may use this formula to devise an additional measure of arc elasticity, this time relating directly the change in expenditure and elasticity of demand. In Figure 4–3 the total expenditure at price OP is $OPRQ$ and the total expenditure at price OP' is $OP'SQ'$. The change in total expenditure as price changes from OP to OP' may be written as

$$\Delta E = OP'SQ' - OPRQ$$
$$= QVSQ' - P'PRV$$
$$= \Delta q(p - \Delta p) - q \Delta p.$$

Dividing both sides by $-q\Delta p$, we get

$$\frac{\Delta E}{-q\Delta p} = \frac{\Delta q(p - \Delta p) - q\Delta p}{-q\Delta p} \ .$$

Since Δp is negative, we may write

$$\frac{\Delta E}{q\Delta p} = \frac{\Delta q(p + \Delta p) + q\Delta p}{q\Delta p}$$

$$= \frac{\Delta q(p + \Delta p)}{q\Delta p} + \frac{q\Delta p}{q\Delta p}$$

$$= \left(\frac{p + \Delta p}{q} \cdot \frac{\Delta q}{\Delta p} \right) + 1;$$

and by formula (2) for arc elasticity we get

$$\frac{\Delta E}{q \Delta p} = e + 1$$

$$e = \frac{\Delta E}{q \Delta p} - 1. \tag{6}$$

We may check this formula by reference to Figure 4–1. The arc elasticity of demand D between prices 12 and 10 by formula (2) is

$$e = \frac{p + \Delta p}{q} \cdot \frac{\Delta q}{\Delta p} = \frac{12 - 2}{32} \cdot \frac{8}{-2} = -\tfrac{5}{4} .$$

The arc elasticity of demand D between the same two prices by formula (6) is

$$e = \frac{\Delta E}{q \Delta p} - 1 = \frac{400 - 384}{32(-2)} - 1 = \frac{36}{-64} - 1 = -\tfrac{1}{4} - 1 = -\tfrac{5}{4} .$$

The arc elasticity of demand D between prices 11 and 9 by formula (6) is

$$e = \frac{\Delta E}{q \Delta p} - 1 = \frac{396 - 396}{36(-2)} - 1 = -1.$$

Between prices 6 and 5 arc elasticity of D is

$$e = \frac{\Delta E}{q \Delta p} - 1 = \frac{300 - 336}{-56} - 1 = \tfrac{9}{14} - 1 = -\tfrac{5}{14} .$$

Cross Elasticity of Demand

We have noted that the demand for commodity X is a function not only of the price of X but also of the prices of complementary goods and substitute goods and of consumer income and consumer tastes. This may be expressed in the form

$$D_x = (p_x, \ p_c, \ p_s, \ Y, \ T).$$

The arc-elasticity concept provides a convenient method for determining whether two commodities are complements or substitutes, and provides a measure of the degree of their complementarity or substitutability. If the demand for a commodity is the function of the prices of two or more commodities, we are concerned with what is called the partial elasticity of demand; the partial elasticity of demand for one commodity with respect to the price of another commodity is known as cross elasticity.

Suppose that it is known that when the price of beef is 50, the quantity of pork demanded is 100; when the price of beef rises to 60, the quantity of pork demanded increases to 120:

Beef	Pork
$P = 50$	$Q = 100$
$P' = 60$	$Q' = 120$

The cross elasticity of demand for pork with reference to the price of beef may be determined by using an arc-elasticity formula relating the change in the price of beef to the change in the quantity of pork demanded. By formula (5),

$$E_{p,b} = \frac{P_b + P_b'}{Q_p + Q_p'} \cdot \frac{\Delta Q_p}{\Delta P_b} = \frac{50 + 60}{100 + 120} \cdot \tfrac{20}{10} = +1.$$

Suppose now that when the price of bread is 25, the quantity of margarine demanded is 100; when the price of bread is 30, the quantity of margarine demanded is 90:

Bread	Margarine
$P = 25$	$Q = 100$
$P' = 30$	$Q' = 90$

By applying the cross-elasticity formula we get

$$E_{m,b} = \frac{P_b + P_b'}{Q_m + Q_m'} \cdot \frac{\Delta Q_m}{\Delta P_b} = \frac{25 + 30}{100 + 90} \cdot \frac{-10}{5} = -\tfrac{11}{19} \cdot$$

It will be noted that the coefficient of cross elasticity of demand for pork in terms of the price of beef is positive, whereas the coefficient of cross elasticity of demand for margarine in terms of the price of bread is negative. In this instance the algebraic sign of the coefficient of elasticity is significant. If an increase in the price of one commodity causes a decrease in the amount demanded of the other, the goods must be in a complementary relationship. An increase in the price of bread reduces the amount of bread demanded and, accordingly, the amount of margarine demanded; bread and margarine must be used together as complements, and the algebraic sign of cross elasticity will be the same as the algebraic sign of the elasticity of demand for either with respect to its own price. On the other hand, an increase in the price of beef causes a reduction in the amount of beef demanded and an increase in the amount of pork demanded. Pork and beef must, accordingly, be substitutes for each other; the change in the price of one will be in the same direction as the change in the quantity of the other, and the algebraic sign of the coefficient of cross elasticity will be positive. The absolute value of the coefficient of cross elasticity is a measure of the degree of complementarity or substitutability of the commodities: of complementarity if the sign is negative and of substitutability if the sign is positive.

Income Elasticity of Demand

Before now, when we have spoken of the elasticity of demand, we meant the responsiveness of the demand to a change in price. This has been referred to as the price elasticity of demand. But we have noted that the demand for a good is a function of consumer income as well as of the price of the good and of complementary and substitutable goods. The responsiveness of demand to a change in consumer income, prices of all goods assumed to remain constant, is called *income* elasticity of demand. We shall encounter this concept in subsequent chapters, but it is introduced here since, if we are considering the effect of a finite change in income on the amount of a given commodity demanded, we must use some sort of arc elasticity formula to determine the coefficient of income elasticity of demand.

Suppose that when a consumer's income is $100 per time period, he buys 5 quarts of milk, but if his income increases to $110, his purchases of milk increase to 6 quarts:

Income	Milk
$Y = 100$	$Q = 5$
$Y' = 110$	$Q' = 6$

The precise value we get for the coefficient of income elasticity of demand will depend on which formula for arc elasticity we employ. Suppose that we adapt formula (1) to this purpose:

$$E_y = \frac{Y}{Q} \cdot \frac{\Delta Q}{\Delta Y} = \frac{100}{5} \cdot \frac{1}{10} = \frac{100}{50} = 2.$$

If, however, we base our income elasticity formula on formula (5), we get

$$E_y = \frac{Y + Y'}{Q + Q'} \cdot \frac{\Delta Q}{\Delta Y} = \frac{100 + 110}{5 + 6} \cdot \frac{1}{10} = \frac{210}{110} = \frac{21}{11},$$

which is, of course, slightly less than 2.

It will be noted that the coefficient of income elasticity in this instance has a positive algebraic sign. This reflects the fact that as the income increases, the quantity of milk demanded also increases, and for most commodities this is the usual case. There are instances, however, when an increase in income is accompanied by a decrease in the amount demanded of certain goods. If a very poor family receives an increase in income, they may buy less margarine and more butter, less dried beans and more fresh vegetables, less bread and molasses and more cake, fewer potatoes and more fruit.

Goods for which the demand decreases as income increases are called inferior goods; the coefficient of income elasticity for inferior goods is negative. As in the case of cross elasticity, accordingly, the algebraic sign of the coefficient of income elasticity is significant. For inferior goods the coefficient of income elasticity is negative; for normal goods; it is positive; and the greater the absolute value of the coefficient of elasticity, the greater the responsiveness of the demand to a change in income.

Elasticity of Supply

The elasticity concept has several applications in addition to its use as a measure of the responsiveness of demand to a change in price or income.[1] We may, for example, be interested in the response of a supply function to a change in price, that is, in the elasticity of supply. If a relatively small percentage change in price results in a relatively large percentage change in the quantity supplied, the supply is said to be elastic; if a relatively large change in price results in only a small change in quantity supplied, the supply is said to be inelastic; and if, say, a 1-percent change in price results in a 1-percent change in quantity supplied, the supply is said to have an elasticity of one. This is, of course, analogous to the concept of demand elasticity, but since the change in price and quantity moves in the same direction, the coefficient of elasticity of supply has a positive rather than a negative algebraic sign. A perfectly inelastic supply, like a perfectly inelastic demand, is represented by a vertical line, and a perfectly elastic supply, like a perfectly elastic demand, is represented by a horizontal line.

The basic formula for the elasticity of supply is identical with the formula for the elasticity of demand:

$$E_s = \frac{y}{x} \frac{\Delta x}{\Delta y},$$

where E_s is the elasticity of supply, y = price and x = quantity supplied.

Since $\Delta x / \Delta y$ is the reciprocal of the slope, and one measure of the slope of the supply curve in Figure 4–4 is TP/PR, we may write PR/TP for $\Delta x/\Delta y$ in the general formula, and the elasticity of supply in terms of Figure 4–4 is

$$E_s = \frac{y}{x} \frac{\Delta x}{\Delta y} = \frac{OP}{OM} \frac{PR}{TP} = \frac{OP}{OM} \frac{OM}{TP} = \frac{OP}{TP},$$

and this is the same as one of the measures of elasticity of demand derived in the preceding chapter.

[1] For additional applications of the elasticity concept see Clark Lee Allen, *Elementary Mathematics of Price Theory* (Belmont, Calif.: Wadsworth Publishing Co., Inc., 1962), Chap. 17.

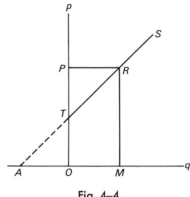

Fig. 4–4

It is also possible to get a measure of elasticity of supply in terms of values on the *x*-axis. A second measure of the slope of the supply curve in Figure 4–4 is MR/AM, and we can substitute AM/MR for $\Delta x/\Delta y$ in the general formula:

$$E_s = \frac{y}{x}\frac{\Delta x}{\Delta y} = \frac{MR}{OM}\frac{AM}{MR} = \frac{AM}{OM},$$

where A is the intercept of the supply curve on the *x*-axis.

Since OP in Figure 4–4 is greater than TP and AM is greater than OM, the elasticity of supply at price OP or at quantity OM is greater than one:

$$\frac{OP}{TP} = \frac{AM}{OM} > 1.$$

In general, if a linear supply curve has a positive intercept on the *y*-axis (or, what is the same thing, a negative intercept on the *x*-axis), the elasticity of supply at any point on the curve is greater than one. But note that the elasticity of supply will be different at each point on the supply curve; for every value of OP there will be a different value for OP/TP. As the price falls and approaches OT, TP approaches zero and the elasticity of supply approaches infinity. We may generalize by saying that at every point on the supply curve in Figure 4–4 the elasticity of supply is greater than one; the higher the price the closer the elasticity of supply approaches one, with elasticity approaching infinity as we move along the supply curve toward the *y*-axis.

If the supply curve has a negative intercept on the *y*-axis (or a positive intercept on the *x*-axis), the elasticity of supply at any point on the curve will be less than one. In terms of Figure 4–5, elasticity of supply is again measured by OP/TP or AM/OM, and since OP is less than TP and AM is less than OM, elasticity of supply will always be less than one. If we start at point R on the curve and move toward the *x*-axis, AM becomes smaller,

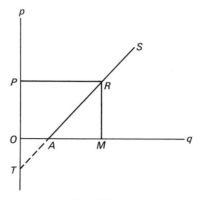

Fig. 4–5

approaching zero, and as price approaches zero, the elasticity of supply approaches zero. At higher and higher prices the elasticity of supply becomes greater. OP will always be less than TP by an amount equal to TO, but at very high values for OP this difference becomes relatively smaller, and the elasticity of supply approaches one as a limit as price rises indefinitely.

The third possibility is that a linear supply curve might pass through the origin, as represented in Figure 4–6. In this instance, the y-intercept, T, and the x-intercept, A, both come at O. It follows, accordingly, that OP/TP is the same as OP/OP, and AM/OM is the same as OM/OM, and the elasticity of supply at any point on the curve is equal to one.

The three cases are represented in Figure 4–7. It will be noted that although the three supply curves have equal slopes, the elasticity of each at any price or at any quantity is different from the other two, pointing up again that slope and elasticity are quite different concepts. Whereas a demand curve with an elasticity equal to one at any point took the form of a rectangular hyperbola, a supply curve with an elasticity of one at all points

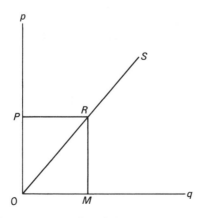

Fig. 4–6

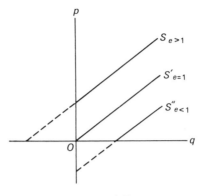

Fig. 4–7

takes the form of a linear curve through the origin. And whereas a linear demand curve drawn from the y-axis to the x-axis represents a range of elasticities from infinity to zero, a supply curve with the same range of elasticities would of necessity be nonlinear and take the general form of the supply curve in Figure 4–8.

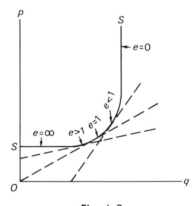

Fig. 4–8

The arc elasticity formula can be used to measure the elasticity of supply. Suppose that the supply function is given by

$$S = q = p + 2,$$

and we wish to determine the elasticity between points R and R' in Figure 4–9. By formula (5):

$$E_s = \frac{p_1 + p_2}{q_1 + q_2} \cdot \frac{\Delta q}{\Delta p} = \frac{2 + 4}{4 + 6} \cdot \frac{2}{2} = \frac{6}{10} \cdot \frac{1}{1} = \frac{3}{5}.$$

Again, this measure of arc elasticity is equivalent to point elasticity at the point midway between R and R'. Point elasticity at point R'' is given by:

$$E_s = \frac{OP}{TP} = \tfrac{3}{5} = \frac{AM}{OM} = \tfrac{3}{5}.$$

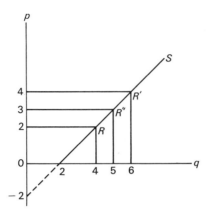

Fig. 4-9

POSTPRANDIUM

There is some degree of substitutability between virtually all commodities which the consumer buys. Many commodities, of course, have zero substitutability in use; examples of independent goods of this sort are parsnips and parachutes, cheese and gasoline, and velvet and portland cement. But even if commodities A and B are goods of this type and the price of A falls and the demand for A is highly elastic, the increased expenditure on A may result in a reduction of the quantity of B purchased due to budgetary constraints. In a sense all commodities are competitors for the consumer's dollar. During a strike idle workers may spend more money on gasoline and correspondingly less on bread. The demand for commodity A, as we have seen, is a function not only of the price of A, but also of the prices of complements and substitutes. The closer the degree of substitutability, as indicated by the coefficient of cross elasticity, the greater will be the impact of a change of price of the substitute on the price of the commodity in question, but the prices of all commodities are to some degree interdependent.

Examples of goods in highly complementary or joint demand come readily to mind. Right and left gloves, gasoline and oil, pens and ink, pipes and tobacco, and coffee and cream are illustrations frequently cited. Examples of substitute or competitive demand are also familiar: beef and lamb, nylon and silk, electricity and gas for home heating, trains and planes, brand *A* cornflakes and brand *B* cornflakes. Again, the coefficient of cross elasticity between these goods may be great or small, but the phenonema of joint and competitive demand are commonplace.

Joint and competitive relationships are also encountered on the supply side of the market. Two commodities are said to be in complementary or joint supply if an increase in the supply of one results in an increase in the supply of the other. Examples are mutton and wool, lumber and sawdust, and grain and straw. If the production of sheep increases in response to an increased demand for mutton, the production of wool will perforce also increase. If there has been no change in the demand for wool, the price of wool may be expected to fall. If this condition persists, it may be possible in the long run to breed a new variety of sheep which will produce more mutton and less wool, but in the short run when the ratio between mutton and wool is fixed, an increase in the price of one is likely to be accompanied by a decrease in the price of the other.

If, on the other hand, an increase in the supply of one commodity requires a decrease in the supply of another, the goods are said to be in substitutive or competitive supply. This comes about when the same facilities are used to produce two or more commodities and the common facility is used at full capacity. If a farmer puts more of his acreage in corn due to high corn prices, he will have less land on which to raise soybeans. If a furniture factory turns out more tables, it may have to produce fewer chairs. If an automobile assembly line turns out more convertibles, it may have to produce fewer sedans. Prices of competitive goods are likely to move in the same direction. If the price of corn rises, farmers will produce more corn and less soybeans; if the demand for soybeans has not changed, the price of soybeans will also rise.

Two factors affect the relationships between demands and supplies of commodities. The first is elasticity of demand and supply. If the supply of wool is highly elastic and the demand for wool increases, the increased price of wool will result in a considerable increase in the production of sheep and, accordingly, of mutton. If the demand for mutton is highly inelastic, the increased supply of mutton will cause a considerable drop in the price of mutton.

The second factor is the degree of rigidity of the proportions of commodities in the production and consumption processes. If a consumer insists upon cream in his coffee, anything which affects the amount of coffee that he drinks will in the same degree affect the amount of cream he uses. If the ratio between sawn lumber and sawdust produced is fixed, anything which affects the amount of lumber produced will also affect the amount of sawdust produced. Sawdust may be a valuable by-product of the lumber industry, but if the output of lumber increases at the same time that the demand for sawdust decreases, sawdust may come to be of negative value to the lumber firm.

SELECTED REFERENCES

Allen, Clark Lee. *Elementary Mathematics of Price Theory.* Belmont, Calif.: Wadsworth Publishing Co., Inc., 1962. Chap. 17.

Bain, Joe S. *Pricing, Distribution, and Employment.* New York: Holt, Rinehart & Winston, Inc., 1953. Chap. 3.

Dean, Joel. *Managerial Economics.* Englewood Cliffs, N.J.: Prentice-Hall, Inc., 1951. Chap. iv.

Norris, Ruby Turner. *The Theory of Consumer's Demand.* Rev. ed. New Haven, Conn.: Yale University Press, 1952. Chap. 9.

Schultz, H. *The Theory and Measurement of Demand.* Chicago: University of Chicago Press, 1938.

Stigler, George J. *The Theory of Price.* Rev. ed. New York: The Macmillan Co., 1952. Chap. iv.

Tintner, Gerhard. *Mathematics and Statistics for Economists.* New York: Holt, Rinehart & Winston, Inc., 1954. Pp. 41–42, 119–120.

PROBLEMS

PROBLEM I

Given: $D = x = 4 - y;\ S = x = 2y - 2.$

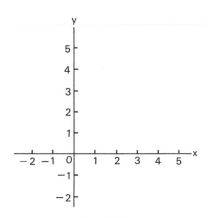

Fig. 4–10

1. Plot the demand, supply, and total-revenue curves on the chart above.

2. Equilibrium price = ..._____

3. Equilibrium quantity = ..._____

4. Total revenue at the equilibrium quantity = . ._____

5. E_d at equilibrium price = ..._____

6. E_s at equilibrium quantity = ..._____

Now assume that supply shifts to $S' = x = 2y + 2$; demand remains unchanged.

7. Plot the new supply curve.

8. The new equilibrium price = ..._____

9. The new equilibrium quantity = ..._____

10. E_d at the new equilibrium quantity = ..._____

11. E_s at the new equilibrium price = ..._____

12. The shift from S to S' represents (an increase, a decrease) in supply.

PROBLEM II

Given: $D = Q = 6 - P$; $S = Q = P + 2$.

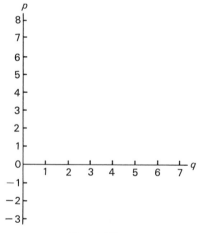

Fig. 4–11

1. Plot the demand and supply curves on the chart above.

2. What is equilibrium price? . . . . . ._____

3. What is equilibrium quantity? . . . . ._____

4. What is elasticity of demand at $P = 5$? . . ._____

5. What is elasticity of demand at $P = 3$? . . ._____

6. What is elasticity of demand at $P = 2$? . ._____

7. What is elasticity of demand at $Q = 2$? . . ._____.

8. What is elasticity of demand at $Q = 3$? . . ._____

9. What is elasticity of demand at $Q = 5$? . . ._____

10. What is elasticity of supply at $P = 3$? . . . ._____

11. What is elasticity of supply at $P = 2$? . . . ._____

12. What is elasticity of supply at $P = 4$? . . . ._____

13. What is elasticity of supply at $Q = 4$? . . . ._____

14. What is elasticity of supply at $Q = 2$? . . . ._____

15. What is elasticity of supply at $Q = 3$? . . . ._____

PROBLEM III

1. Suppose that a market consists of two cities. The demand for a given commodity in each city is given by $p = 120 - q$, where p is price and q is quantity demanded. The total market will, of course, take twice as much at any given price as either city alone will take at that price. What is the demand function for the total market? . . . . ._____

2. If the market consists of four cities instead of two, each with the demand function given above, what is the total market demand function? . . . . ._____

3. Determine the arc elasticity of demand between prices of $80 and $70 for each city and for the market as a whole.

For each city, arc elasticity = ..._____
For the whole market, arc elasticity = ..._____

PROBLEM IV

Suppose that we know two points on a linear demand curve: P_1 is the point where $x = 3$ and $y = 6$; P_2 is the point where $x = 4$ and $y = 4$.

1. What is the slope of the demand curve? . . . ._____

2. What is the y-intercept of the demand curve? ._____

3. What is the x-intercept of the demand curve? ._____

4. Using formula (5) for arc elasticity, determine the arc elasticity of demand between points P_1 and P_2. ._____

5. At what price is the point elasticity of demand equal to the arc elasticity of demand between P_1 and P_2? ._____

6. At what quantity is the point elasticity of demand equal to the arc elasticity of demand between points P_1 and P_2? . . . . ._____

PROBLEM V

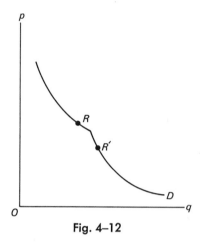

Fig. 4–12

Arc elasticity of demand between points R and R' on the curve above is equal to OP/TP. Locate P and T on the figure.

PROBLEM VI

Given the demand function $2x + y = 12$, where $y =$ price and $x =$ quantity demanded.

1. What is point elasticity of demand at $y = 8$? . .————————————

2. Using the arc elasticity formula

$$e = \frac{y_1 + y_2}{x_1 + x_2} \cdot \frac{\Delta x}{\Delta y},$$

determine arc elasticity of demand between $y = 7$ and $y = 9$ . . . .————————————

PROBLEM VII

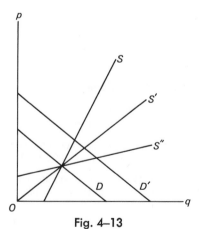

Fig. 4–13

In Figure 4–13, D and D' are parallel demand curves, and S, S', and S'' are supply curves. Indicate the elasticity of demand and the elasticity of supply (equal to, less than, or greater than one) at *market price* if:

1. Demand $= D$ and supply $= S$: $E_d = $ _____ $E_s = $ _____

2. Demand $= D$ and supply $= S'$: $E_d = $ _____ $E_s = $ _____

3. Demand $= D$ and supply $= S''$: $E_d = $ _____ $E_s = $ _____

4. Demand $= D'$ and supply $= S$: $E_d = $ _____ $E_s = $ _____

5. Demand $= D'$ and supply $= S'$: $E_d = $ _____ $E_s = $ _____

6. Demand $= D'$ and supply $= S''$: $E_d = $ _____ $E_s = $ _____

PROBLEM VIII

When A's income was $300, he bought 20 quarts of milk per month. When his income increased to $350, he took 24 quarts per month. Assuming no change in the price of milk, what was A's income elasticity of demand? .   .   .   .   . _____

PROBLEM IX

When the price of X was $5, 100 units of Y were sold. When the price of X fell to $4, 120 units of Y were sold with no change in the price of Y.

1. What is the cross elasticity of demand for Y in terms of the price of X?   .   .   .   . _____

2. Are X and Y substitutes? .   .   .   . _____

5

Marginal Utility
and Consumer Demand

To this point we have assumed as a matter of common sense that demand curves normally have negative slopes; that is, as the price of a commodity decreases, the amount of it which consumers will buy increases. This follows from the fact that demand implies the ability to pay for the good plus the willingness to pay for it. As the price falls, both ability and willingness to pay increase. At a lower price the cost of the good to the consumer declines, not only in money terms, but—what is actually more important—in terms of foregone alternatives. Other things remaining the same, a lower price for commodity A means an increase in consumer purchasing power or in consumer real income. As real income increases the consumer is likely to buy more of commodity A and of other commodities as well. This is referred to as the *income effect* of a price change. Further, if the price of commodity A falls and other prices remain the same, commodity A is now relatively cheaper, and there may be some tendency to substitute the cheaper commodity for other relatively more expensive goods. This is the *substitution* effect of a price change.

As reasonable as all this may seem, it is possible to demonstrate the characteristic negative slope of the demand curve somewhat more precisely, and this will be the task of this and the following chapter. In this chapter we will demonstrate the negative inclination of the demand curve with the use of marginal-utility analysis; in the next chapter we will use a newer technique, indifference curves.

Diminishing Marginal Utility

By *utility* the economist means the ability or the power of a good to satisfy a want. Utility or satisfaction is, of course, a very real thing. If one eats a piece of apple pie and enjoys it, it may be said to provide a degree of satisfaction to the consumer; it possesses *utility*. But to date no one has devised a measure of the degree of utility provided by a given commodity. One may say, "The apple pie is excellent," or "I enjoyed the pie very much," or "I never ate a better piece of pie than this." But if one's hostess asked, "How much did you enjoy the pie?" one could scarcely reply, "About six," and convey any meaningful intelligence. Perhaps some day psychologists or physiologists will devise a method for measuring degrees of utility, but to date we must content ourselves by speaking of utility in terms of great or small and more or less.

Although it is not possible to measure utility by any absolute standard, it has long been noted that if one consumes unit after unit of a given commodity, the additional utility (*marginal* utility) derived from the consumption of each succeeding unit after a certain point becomes smaller and smaller. This is the familiar principle of diminishing marginal utility. We can be sure that this principle is valid because if the marginal utility of commodity A divided by the price of A were greater than the marginal utility of all other commodities divided by their prices, and if the marginal utility of all commodities were constant as the consumption of them increased, the consumer would spend his entire income on commodity A and nothing on other commodities. But clearly consumers do not in fact behave in this way.

Although there is no known way to measure marginal utility, it will be analytically useful to pretend that we can measure it. Suppose that utility is measurable and that the units of utility are called *utils.* We can now tell our hostess that her excellent apple pie provided us with 12 utils of satisfaction, and we may add that no pie in our previous experience had ever before exceeded 10 utils. With this tool in our possession, let us observe the behavior of twelve-year-old Johnny as he eats his breakfast. Johnny is having his favorite food, pancakes. After he has eaten the first one, he reports that it was excellent—it provided him with 9 utils of satisfaction. The second one tasted even better; it hit 10 on the utility scale. And the third went to 11. But number 4 provided only 9 utils of satisfaction, the fifth 6 utils, the sixth only 3 utils, and the seventh provided zero utils of utility. Johnny's mother says, "There is enough batter for one more. How about it?" And Johnny replies, "No thanks. That one would make me sick—probably minus 5 utils." A graph of Johnny's marginal-utility schedule is given in Figure 5–1.

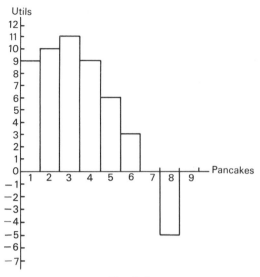

Fig. 5–1

It will be noted that marginal utility increased to the third pancake, but after the third pancake—that is, after the point of diminishing marginal utility—the additional utility resulting from the consumption of each additional pancake diminished. Marginal utility may or may not increase for a time, but it will eventually in any event decrease, and it is the negatively inclined portion of the marginal utility curve which is significant. It will also be noted that the *total* utility at any point is the sum of the marginal utilities to that point. The marginal utility of the fifth pancake was 6 utils; the total utility of eating five pancakes was $9 + 10 + 11 + 9 + 6 = 45$ utils. In general, the area under a marginal-utility curve from the y-axis to any point on the x-axis is the total utility at that point.

Marginal utility may also be represented algebraically. Suppose that the marginal-utility function for commodity A is given by

$$MU_a = y = 150 - 2a,$$

where a is the quantity of commodity A. The graph of this function is given in Figure 5–2. When 25 units of A are consumed, the marginal utility of A is 100 utils; when 50 units are consumed, marginal utility is 50 utils. Total utility is equal to the area under the marginal-utility curve. When the amount of A consumed is 25, the area under the marginal utility is a trapezoid with a base of 25, one side of 150, and the other side of 100. Total utility at that point is given by

$$TU = \frac{150 + 100}{2} \times 25 = 3,125 \text{ utils.}$$

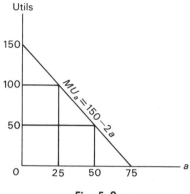

Fig. 5–2

Average utility, i.e., utils per unit of commodity A, would be

$$AU = \frac{TU}{25} = 3125 \div 25 = 125 \text{ utils.}$$

If we wish to know the marginal utility per dollar spent on commodity A, we would write

$$\frac{MU_a}{P_a} = \frac{150 - 2a}{P_a}.$$

In Figure 5–3 we have plotted MU_a/P_a for three prices: $P_a = 1$; $P_a = 2$; and $P_a = 3$.

Comparing MU_a and MU_a/P_a as represented in Figures 5–2 and 5–3, it will be noted that the y-intercept of MU_a/P_a is equal to the y-intercept of MU_a divided by P_a; the x-intercept of MU_a/P_a is the same as the x-intercept of MU_a. The logic of this is clear. If the marginal utility of commodity A is equal to 148 when one unit of A is consumed and if the price of A is \$1, the marginal utility of a dollar spent on A is 148. If, however, the

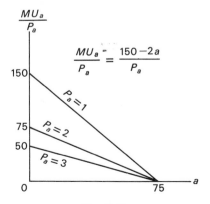

Fig. 5–3

price of A is \$2, and the consumer buys one unit of A, the marginal utility of a dollar spent on A is 148 ÷ 2 or 74 utils per dollar. And if the price of A is \$3, the marginal utility of a dollar spent on A is one-third of 148. On the other hand, the marginal utility of A is zero when 75 units of A are consumed. The marginal utility per dollar spent on A will also be zero when 75 units of A are consumed regardless of the price of A.

Marginal Utility Curves and Demand Curves

If the consumer has a given amount of money to spend on commodities A, B, C, . . . , N, and wants to maximize his total satisfaction, he must allocate his expenditures so that the marginal utils per dollar spent on one commodity are equal to the marginal utils per dollar spent on each of the other commodities. If this turns out not to be the case—if, for example, he gets more utils per dollar from the last dollar spent on commodity A than he does from the last dollar spent on commodity B—he can increase his total utility by buying less of B and more of A until $MU_a/P_a = MU_b/P_b$. In general, consumer equilibrium can be described as meeting the following conditions:

$$\frac{MU_a}{P_a} = \frac{MU_b}{P_b} = \frac{MU_c}{P_c} = \cdot \cdot \cdot = \frac{MU_m}{P_m},$$

where MU_m is the marginal utility of money and P_m is the price of money. But since the price of a dollar is 1, the denominator of the last fraction may be omitted.

If we assume that in the short run the marginal utility of money is constant, and if we wish to concentrate on commodity A, we may write

$$\frac{MU_a}{P_a} = MU_m.$$

Suppose that as before the marginal utility of commodity A is given by

$$MU_a = y = 150 - 2a,$$

and suppose that the marginal utility of money is constant at 3; that is

$$MU_m = K = 3.$$

We may write

$$\frac{MU_a}{P_a} = MU_m$$
$$\frac{150 - 2a}{P_a} = 3$$
$$3P_a = 150 - 2a$$
$$P_a = y = 50 - \frac{2a}{3}.$$

This function expresses the relation between the amount of commodity A demanded, a, and the price of A, y; and it is, accordingly, the demand function for commodity A which has been derived from the marginal utility function. We may write the demand function explicitly in terms of a as follows:

$$y = 50 - \frac{2a}{3}$$

$$\frac{2a}{3} = 50 - y$$

$$D_a = a = 75 - \frac{3y}{2}.$$

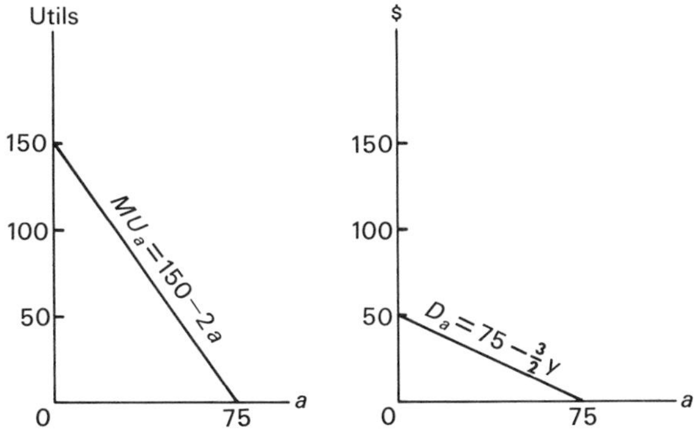

Fig. 5–4

The MU_a curve and the D_a curve are plotted in Figure 5–4. It will be noted that the y-intercept of D_a is equal to the y-intercept of MU_a divided by MU_m. The x-intercept of the D_a curve is the same as the x-intercept of the MU_a curve. We may generalize by saying that if the marginal-utility function for a given commodity is linear, we may derive the corresponding demand curve for that commodity by using as the y-intercept of the demand curve the y-intercept of the marginal-utility curve divided by the marginal utility of money and making the x-intercept for the demand curve equal to the x-intercept of the marginal-utility curve.

Marginal Utility of Expenditure

In determining the optimum allocation of expenditure on two commodities it is convenient to think of the marginal utility of expenditure on the commodities rather than the marginal utilities of the commodities themselves. Consumer equilibrium does not require that the marginal utility of commodity A equal the marginal utility of commodity B, but it does require that the marginal utility of dollars spent on commodity A must equal the marginal utility of dollars spent on commodity B. That is to say, the utility of the last can of beans purchased is not expected to be equal to the utility of the last television set purchased, but the utility from the last dollar spent on beans *is* expected to be equal to the utility from the last dollar spent on a television set, and both should be equal to the marginal utility of money. When one says that he cannot afford a new television set, what he presumably means is that the marginal utility of dollars spent on a television set is less than the marginal utility of his money itself.

If we are to think in terms of the marginal utility of dollars spent on commodities, it becomes necessary to convert the marginal utility function for commodity A into a marginal-utility function for dollars spent on commodity A. Let $x =$ the number of dollars spent on commodity A and, as before, let us suppose that

$$\frac{MU_a}{P_a} = \frac{150 - 2a}{P_a}.$$

The number of dollars spent on commodity A will be the price per unit times the number of units purchased; that is,

$$x = aP_a$$

and

$$a = \frac{x}{P_a}.$$

We may then write

$$\frac{MU_a}{P_a} = \frac{150 - \dfrac{2x}{P_a}}{P_a} = \frac{150}{P_a} - \frac{2x}{P_a^2} = MU_x.$$

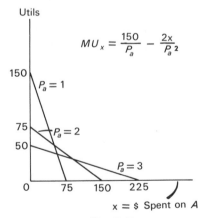

Fig. 5–5

In Figure 5–5 the MU_x function has been plotted for values of P_a equal to \$1, \$2, and \$3. It will be noted that the y-intercept of MU_x is equal to the y-intercept of MU_a divided by P_a; the x-intercept of MU_x is equal to the x-intercept of MU_a multiplied by P_a. This is logical since the higher the price of commodity A, the smaller will be the marginal utility of the first dollar spent on A; and the higher the price of commodity A the more dollars that will have to be spent before the marginal utility of dollars spent on A becomes zero; in this case, 75 units of A have to be bought before that happens.

Consumer Equilibrium

The conversion of the marginal-utility function for commodity A into a marginal-utility function for dollars spent on commodity A is a convenient device for simplifying the determination of the optimum position for a consumer who wants to maximize his satisfaction resulting from an allocation of income among two or more commodities. The principle is, of course, that the marginal utility of expenditure on commodity A must equal the marginal utility of expenditure of commodity B. This point is demonstrated in Figure 5–6.

Suppose that a consumer has a total budget of $N'M'$ dollars to be spent on commodities A and B. Let MU_x represent the marginal utility of expenditure on commodity A and MU_z the marginal utility of expenditure on commodity B. In Figure 5–6 the unit on the x-axis is dollars spent; the right-hand section is read in the usual way from left to right, but on the left-hand side the scale on the x-axis runs from the origin to the left. Suppose initially the consumer divided his $N'M'$ dollars in such a way as to spend ON' on commodity A and OM' on commodity B. With this allocation of expenditure the marginal utility of expenditure on commodity A is $N'R'$, which is less

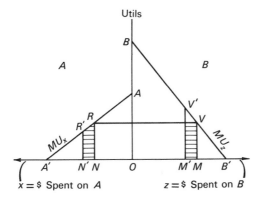

Fig. 5–6

than the marginal utility of expenditure on commodity B, which is $M'V'$. The total utility of expenditure on A is the area under the marginal-utility curve, that is, $N'R'AO$; the total utility of expenditure on B is $OBV'M'$. Since MU_x is less than MU_z, the consumer must, if he is to maximize total satisfaction, spend less on commodity A and more on commodity B; this will cause MU_x to increase and MU_z to decrease. MU_x equals MU_z when ON is spent on commodity A and OM is spent on B. The reduction of expenditure on A, which is $N'N$, is equal to the increase in expenditure on B, which is $M'M$. With ON dollars spent on commodity A, the MU_x is equal to NR, which in turn is equal to MV, which is MU_z. No additional gains to the consumer can accrue from further modifications in the expenditure pattern.

It can easily be seen that the consumer's total satisfaction is greater with the new allocation of funds. When the consumer spends ON dollars on commodity A, his total utility is equal to $NRAO$, which is less than the total utility of spending ON' (or $N'R'AO$) on A. The loss of satisfaction from the reduced expenditure on A is equal to the trapezoid $N'R'RN$. But the total utility derived from the expenditure on commodity B is now greater than it was before. Whereas the total utility of expenditure on B was originally $OBV'M'$, it is now $OBVM$, which is an increase equal to $M'V'VM$. The short side of the trapezoid representing gain is equal to the long side of the trapezoid representing loss, and the net effect of the reallocation of expenditure on these commodities has been to increase the consumer's total utility: $NRAO + OBVM$ is greater than $N'R'AO + OBV'M'$.

It is sometimes more convenient to solve income allocation problems algebraically than it is to solve them geometrically. Suppose that we have given the marginal utility of expenditure functions for two commodities and the total amount to be spent on these commodities, and we are to determine how much should be spent on each.

Let

$$x = \text{the dollars to be spent on commodity } A$$

and

$$z = \text{the dollars to be spent on commodity } B,$$

and let

$$x + z = 50; \text{ that is, } x = 50 - z.$$

Let

$$MU_x = y = 40 - x$$

and

$$MU_z = y = 80 - 2z.$$

The consumer will maximize his total satisfaction when $MU_x = MU_z$:

$$40 - x = 80 - 2z.$$

Substituting $(50 - z)$ for x:

$$40 - (50 - z) = 80 - 2z$$
$$40 - 50 + z = 80 - 2z$$
$$3z = 90$$
$$z = 30$$

and

$$x = 50 - 30 = 20.$$

At $x = 20$, $MU_x = 40 - x = 40 - 20 = 20$; and at $z = 30$, $MU_z = 80 - 2z = 80 - 60 = 20$. The marginal dollar spent on both commodities provides 20 utils of utility, and, accordingly, the best allocation of the $50 to be spent on these commodities is $20 on commodity A and $30 on B.

A geometric solution of this problem is given in Figure 5–7.

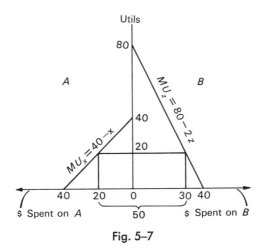

Fig. 5–7

Measurement of Marginal Utility

As we have noted, there is actually no way to measure utility, and this inability reduces the usefulness of the marginal utility analysis. But since we know the general shape of marginal-utility functions even though we have no way of determining their precise form, this analysis does provide us with certain insights into economic behavior. It is possible, moreover, to set upper and lower limits to the change in a consumer's marginal utility which results from the change in the price of a commodity, and this may add to the usefulness of this type of analysis.

In Figure 5–8 we have represented a consumer's demand curve. If the price is OP, the consumer will buy OM units and spend a total of $OPSM$ on

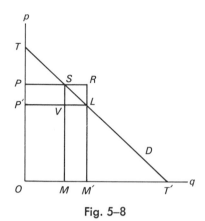

Fig. 5–8

this commodity. If the price falls to OP', the consumer will buy OM' units and spend $OP'LM'$. The fall in the price of the commodity has increased the consumer's consumption of it by an amount equal to MM'. The gain to the consumer represented by the additional MM' units purchased may be evaluated either at the original price or at the new price. If we use the new price, the additional units have a value of $MVLM'$, which is equal to $\Delta q(p - \Delta p)$. This may be taken as the lower limit of the increase in utility to the consumer. If the price were OP', the consumer could pay a tax equal to $MVLM'$ and still have as much of the commodity as he had at price OP with no tax.

Suppose now that the price remains at OP but the consumer buys OM' units, the amount that he would normally buy at the lower price. The total expenditure on OM' units at price OP would be $OPRM'$. This is an increase of $MSRM'$ over what the consumer spent when he bought OM units at price OP. The reduction in price from OP to OP' has been equivalent to a subsidy of $MSRM'$ at the old price. This subsidy is equal to $p\Delta q$, and this may be taken to be the upper limit of the increase in utility. So while we have no absolute measure of a consumer's utility, we may say that the increase in utility resulting from a decrease in price lies between $q\Delta p$ and $\Delta q(p - \Delta p)$, and if Δp is small, we come close to a measure of utility.

POSTPRANDIUM

This is a convenient place to develop the precise relationship between total utility and marginal utility. Among the most important tools of the price theorist are the relations between total, marginal, and average quantities, and we will utilize these concepts not only with reference to utility but also with reference to revenue, cost, and other economic magnitudes. If total is expressed as a simple algebraic function, it is often easy to derive the corresponding marginal function, and if we did not take the time to learn the method, we would be needlessly handicapping ourselves.

Suppose we have given the total utility function

$$U = 10x - x^2,$$

where U = total utility and x = the amount of commodity X consumed. Now suppose that the amount of commodity X consumed increases from x to $(x + \Delta x)$. This will cause total utility to increase to some amount which we may represent as $(U + \Delta U)$. We may rewrite our total utility function by replacing x with $(x + \Delta x)$:

$$
\begin{aligned}
U + \Delta U &= 10(x + \Delta x) - (x + \Delta x)^2 \\
&= 10x + 10\Delta x - (x^2 + 2x\Delta x + \Delta x^2) \\
&= 10x + 10\Delta x - x^2 - 2x\Delta x - \Delta x^2.
\end{aligned}
$$

By substracting U from the left-hand side of the equation and its equivalent, $10x - x^2$, from the right-hand side we get

$$\Delta U = 10\Delta x - 2x\Delta x - \Delta x^2.$$

To determine the additional utility per additional unit of commodity X we divide by Δx:

$$\frac{\Delta U}{\Delta x} = \frac{10\Delta x - 2x\Delta x - \Delta x_2}{\Delta x} = 10 - 2x - \Delta x.$$

If we assume that Δx becomes infinitesimally small, we write dU/dx instead of $\Delta U/\Delta x$:

$$\lim_{\Delta x \to 0} \frac{\Delta U}{\Delta x} = \frac{dU}{dx} = 10 - 2x.$$

The expression dU/dx is read, "the derivative of U with respect to x," and it is the rate of change of the total function which, in terms of the economics of the problem, is the marginal utility function. If, then, total utility is given by the function

$$U = 10x - x^2,$$

marginal utility will be given by the function

$$M = \frac{dU}{dx} = 10 - 2x.$$

The general rule may be stated as follows: the derivative with respect to x of the nth power of x is equal to n times x to the $(n - 1)$ power. If the total function is given by

$$T = ax^n,$$

where a and n are constants, then

$$M = nax^{n-1},$$

where M is marginal. For example, if

$$T = 3x^4,$$

then

$$M = 12x^3.$$

Or if

$$T = x - 5,$$

then

$$M = 1,$$

since $x^{1-1} = x^0$, and anything to the zero power is equal to one; the derivative of 5 with respect to x is zero since the derivative of a function is the rate of change of the function, and the rate of change of a constant is, of course, zero.

By way of summary we may say that the derivative of a function is the rate of change of the function; viewed geometrically, the derivative of a function gives us the slope of the function at any x-value; in terms of economics, the derivative of a total function is the marginal function.

To return to our original example, if

$$U = 10x - x^2,$$

then

$$M = 10 - 2x.$$

Since average utility would be the total utility of consuming x units divided by x, we may add

$$A = \frac{U}{x} = 10 - x.$$

Recalling that the equation for a straight line is $y = mx + b$, where m is the slope of the curve and b is the y-intercept, it will be noted that the absolute value of the slope of the marginal curve is twice that of the average curve.

In Figure 5–9 the total-, marginal-, and average-utility curves have been plotted. It will be noted that at $x = 3$, marginal utility is 4. At $x = 3$, the slope of the tangent to the total-utility curve is also 4: $m = \Delta y / \Delta x = 12/3 = 4$. Geometrically, the marginal value for any point on the x-axis is the slope of the total curve at that point. For x-values from zero to 5, marginal utility is positive and the slope of the total-utility curve is positive. At $x = 5$, the slope of the total curve is zero, and marginal utility at that point is zero. From $x = 5$ to $x = 10$, marginal utility is negative and the slope of the total-utility curve is negative. *Marginal utility is the slope or the rate of change of the total-utility curve.*

We may note, finally, that the figure gives us three measures of total utility. We may read total utility directly from the total-utility curve and note that when $x = 3$, total utility $= 21$. Or, when $x = 3$, average utility $= 7$; total utility, accordingly, is $7 \times 3 = 21$. Or, total utility is the area under the

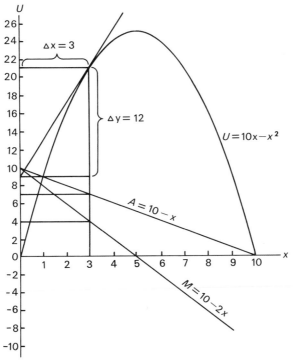

Fig. 5–9

marginal-utility curve; when $x = 3$, that area is a trapezoid with a base of 3, one side of 10, and one side of 4: $U = 3x(10 + 4)/2 = 21$.

Elasticity of Demand Once More

To illustrate the myriad uses of the derivative in price theory we may use it to derive an algebraic measure of the elasticity of demand. Suppose that the demand function is given as

$$D = x = 6 - \tfrac{1}{2}y.$$

This function is plotted in Figure 5–10.

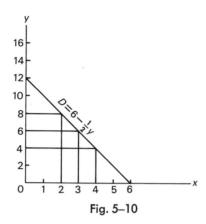

Fig. 5–10

The elasticity formula may be put in the following form:

$$E_d = \frac{y}{x} \cdot \frac{dx}{dy}.$$

The derivative of the demand function is

$$\frac{dx}{dy} = -\tfrac{1}{2}.$$

Substituting $-\tfrac{1}{2}$ for dx/dy and $(6 - \tfrac{1}{2}y)$ for x in the elasticity formula:

$$E_d = \frac{y}{x} \cdot \frac{dx}{dy} = \frac{y}{6 - \frac{1}{2}y} \cdot \frac{-\frac{1}{2}}{1} = \frac{-\frac{1}{2}y}{6 - \frac{1}{2}y}.$$

With this formula we can determine the elasticity at any price by substituting appropriately for y.

$$\text{If } y = 8, \; E_d = \frac{-4}{6 - 4} = -2 = \frac{OP}{TP}.$$

$$\text{If } y = 6, \; E_d = \frac{-3}{6 - 3} = -1 = \frac{OP}{TP}.$$

$$\text{If } y = 4, \; E_d = \frac{-2}{6 - 2} = -\tfrac{1}{2} = \frac{OP}{TP}.$$

The demand function may be given in terms of y as

$$y = 12 - 2x.$$

To determine the elasticity of demand we will now need the derivative of y in terms of x instead of the derivative of x in terms of y. But $dx/dy = 1/(dy/dx)$, and the basic elasticity formula may be written

$$E_d = \frac{y}{x} \cdot \frac{1}{\dfrac{dy}{dx}}.$$

Since the derivative of the function $y = 12 - 2x$ is -2, we may substitute this for dy/dx, and we may substitute $(12 - 2x)$ for y in the elasticity formula:

$$E_d = \frac{y}{x} \cdot \frac{1}{\dfrac{dy}{dx}} = \frac{12 - 2x}{x} \cdot \frac{1}{-2} = \frac{12 - 2x}{-2x} .$$

The elasticity of demand at any quantity may now be determined by substituting appropriately for x.

$$\text{If } x = 2, \; E_d = \frac{12 - 4}{-4} = -2 = \frac{MT'}{OM} .$$

$$\text{If } x = 3, \; E_d = \frac{12 - 6}{-6} = -1 = \frac{MT'}{OM} .$$

$$\text{If } x = 4, \; E_d = \frac{12 - 8}{-8} = -\tfrac{1}{2} = \frac{MT'}{OM} .$$

This method may also be used to determine the elasticity of a nonlinear demand curve. Suppose that we consider a situation where total expenditure is constant as price changes, and the elasticity of demand is, accordingly, equal to one at all points on the curve:

$$xy = 12$$
$$y = \frac{12}{x} = 12x^{-1}.$$

$$E_d = \frac{y}{x} \cdot \frac{1}{\dfrac{dy}{dx}} = \frac{12x^{-1}}{x} \cdot \frac{1}{-12x^{-2}} = \frac{12x^{-1}}{-12x^{-1}} = -1.$$

Consumer's Surplus

We turn our attention now to a matter pertinent to the subject matter of this chapter. Alfred Marshall, in his classic *Principles of Economics*, noted that the price which a person pays for a thing can never exceed the maximum amount which he would be willing to pay rather than go without it, but he may very well have to pay less than the maximum amount he would be willing to pay. In Marshall's words, "The excess of the price which he would be willing to pay rather than go without the thing, over that which he actually does pay, is the economic measure of this surplus satisfaction. It may be called *consumer's surplus*."[1] Marshall's concept of consumer's surplus is illustrated in Figure 5–11.

In Figure 5–11 we are again using the demand function

$$y = 50 - \tfrac{2}{3}a.$$

[1] Alfred Marshall, *Principles of Economics*, 8th ed. (London: Macmillan & Co., 1920), p. 124.

Suppose that the price of commodity A is \$14; the quantity demanded at that price would then be 54 units per time period. The demand curve tells us that the consumer would be just willing to pay \$14 for the 54th unit of commodity A, but would have been willing to pay somewhat more, if necessary, for each of the units up to that point. For each of the first 53 units purchased, accordingly, the consumer enjoys a "surplus satisfaction." The total consumer's surplus is represented in Figure 5–11 by the right triangle bounded by the upper part of the demand curve, the y-axis, and the horizontal line

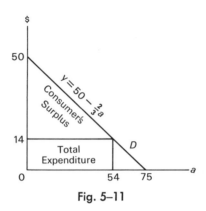

Fig. 5–11

$y = 14$. This gives a measure of consumer's surplus in dollars, and in terms of Figure 5–11 is equal to

$$CS = \frac{54 \cdot \$36}{2} = \$972.$$

Using the techniques developed in this chapter, consumer's surplus may also be measured directly in terms of utility. In Figure 5–12 the marginal-utility curve corresponding to the demand curve of Figure 5–11 is drawn, again on the assumption that the marginal utility of money is constant at 3. The equation for the marginal-utility curve is

$$y = 150 - 2a.$$

We have seen that if the price of commodity A is \$14, the consumer will take 54 units of A per time period. If the consumer buys 54 units of A, the marginal utility of A, as indicated in Figure 5–12, is 42 utils. This is consistent with the fact that by assumption the marginal utility of money is constant at 3 utils per dollar, and the marginal utility of 14 dollars must be 14×3 utils $= 42$ utils. The *total* utility to the consumer of 54 units of A is the area under the marginal-utility curve, which is represented in the figure by a trapezoid with a base of 54, one side of 150, and the other side of 42:

$$TU_a = \frac{150 + 42}{2} \times 54 = 5{,}184 \text{ utils.}$$

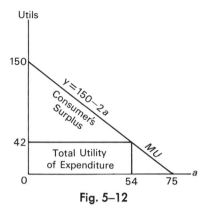

Fig. 5–12

The total utility of the money spent on 54 units of commodity A is represented by the rectangle with a height of 42 and a length of 54:

$$TU_m = 42 \times 54 = 2,268 \text{ utils.}$$

Consumer's surplus measured in utils is equal to

$$CS = TU_a - TU_m$$
$$= 5,184 - 2,268 = 2,916 \text{ utils.}$$

This is, of course, equal to the right triangle with a height of 108 and a base of 54:

$$CS = \frac{54 \times 108 \text{ utils}}{2} = 2,916 \text{ utils.}$$

Since marginal utility of money is assumed constant at 3, the consumer's surplus measured in utils is three times the consumer's surplus measured in dollars:

$$CS = 972 \times 3 \text{ utils} = 2,916 \text{ utils.}$$

SELECTED REFERENCES

Alchian, Armen A. "The Meaning of Utility Measurement," *American Economic Review*, 43 (March 1953), 26–50.

Allen, Clark Lee. *Elementary Mathematics of Price Theory*. Belmont, Calif.: Wadsworth Publishing Co., Inc., 1962. Chaps. 6, 7, and 11.

Marshall, Alfred. *Principles of Economics*. 8th ed. London: Macmillan & Co., 1920. Book III. Chaps. 5 and 6.

Stigler, George J. "The Development of Utility Theory," *Journal of Political Economy*, 58 (August 1950), 307–324.

Strotz, Robert H. "Cardinal Utility," *American Economic Review*, 43 (May 1953), 384–397.

PROBLEMS

PROBLEM I

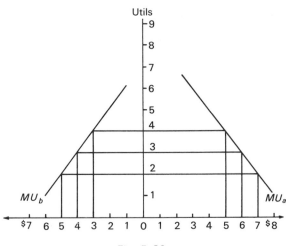

Fig. 5–13

In the figure above, MU_a represents the marginal utility of dollars spent on commodity A, and MU_b represents the marginal utility of dollars spent on B for a given consumer.

1. If the consumer has a total of $12 to spend on commodities A and B, in order to maximize his total satisfaction he should spend $_____ on commodity A and $_____ on commodity B.

2. If the consumer has a total of $10 to spend on commodities A and B, in order to maximize his satisfaction he should spend $_____ on commodity A and $_____ on commodity B.

3. If the consumer has a total of $8 to spend on commodities A and B, in order to maximize his satisfaction he should spend $_____ on commodity A and $_____ on commodity B.

4. If the consumer has a total of $1 to spend on commodities A and B, in order to maximize his satisfaction he should spend $_____ on commodity A and $_____ on commodity B.

PROBLEM II

Mr. R is a rich man, and Mr. P is a poor man. Both have the same marginal-utility-of-money schedule, represented in the figure by MU_m. Mr. R's income is OR, and Mr. P's income is OP.

1. What is the MU_m for Mr. R? .   .   .   .   .   ._____

2. What is the TU_m for Mr. R? .   .   .   .   .   ._____

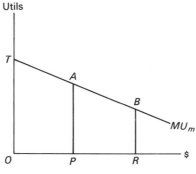

Fig. 5–14

3. What is the MU_m for Mr. P? .   .   .   .   .   ._____

4. What is the TU_m for Mr. P? .   .   .   .   .   ._____

5. Indicate on the figure the reallocation of the total incomes of Mr. R and Mr. P which would provide the maximum TU_m for the two men combined.

6. The reallocation of income would cause a loss in TU_m to Mr._____

7. The reallocation of income would cause a gain in TU_m to Mr._____

8. Mark the area of loss of TU_m with L.

9. Mark the area of gain of TU_m with G.

10. The net effect of the reallocation of income between Mr. R and Mr. P would be a (gain, loss) in TU_m.

PROBLEM III

Given:

$$MU_a = y = 50 - x$$
$$MU_b = y = 50 - 2u$$
$$x + u = 60,$$

where x = amount spent on commodity A, u = amount spent on commodity B, and y = marginal utility measured in utils.

1. Plot the marginal utility curves for commodities A and B on Figure 5–15 on page 108, and indicate the amount the consumer should spend on each commodity in order to maximize his satisfaction.

2. What is the marginal utility of expenditure on each commodity after the consumer's expenditure has been properly allocated? .   .   .   .   .   .   ._____

3. What would be the marginal utility of expenditure if the total amount to be spent on these two commodities were 30?   .   .   .   .   ._____

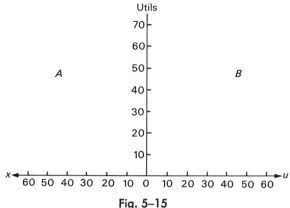

Fig. 5–15

4. What would be the marginal utility of expenditure if the total amount to be spent on these two commodities were 75? . . . . ._____

PROBLEM IV

Let $MU_a = 12 - 2x$ and $MU_m = 3$, where MU_a is the marginal utility of commodity A and MU_m is the marginal utility of money for a given consumer.

1. Draw the MU_a curve on the axes below.
2. Draw the demand curve for commodity A and label it D_a.
3. What is the equation for the demand curve? $y =$ _____
4. Label the y-axis in the figure.

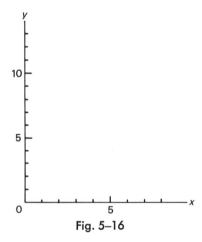

Fig. 5–16

PROBLEM V

Given the demand function $D = x = 10 - y$, where $x =$ the quantity demanded and $y =$ price.

1. Using the elasticity formula

$$e = \frac{y}{x} \times \frac{dx}{dy},$$

   determine algebraically E_d at $x = 6$ . . . . ._____

2. State the demand function explicitly in terms of
   $y.$ . . . $y =$ . . . . ._____

3. Using the elasticity formula

$$e = \frac{y}{x} \times \frac{1}{\dfrac{dy}{dx}},$$

   determine algebraically E_d at $y = 4$ . . . . ._____

PROBLEM VI

Given:

$$MU_a = 100 - 2a$$
$$MU_m = K = 5$$
$$P_a = 8.$$

1. What is the demand function for commodity A? $y =$ _____

2. Plot MU_a and D_a on the axes below:

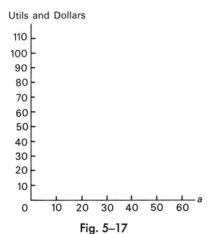

Utils and Dollars

Fig. 5–17

3. What is the function for the marginal utility of expenditure on commodity A when $P_a = 8$? $MU_x =$ _____

4. Plot MU_x when $P_a = 8$ on the axes of Figure 5–18 on page 110.

5. What is the elasticity of demand for commodity
   A at $P_a = 8$? . . . . ._____

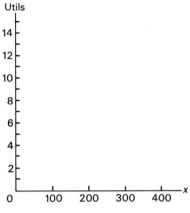

Fig. 5–18

6. What is consumer's surplus in terms of dollars at $P_a = 8$? . . . . ._____

7. What is consumer's surplus in terms of utils at $P_a = 8$? . . . . ._____

8. Shade the areas in Figures 5–17 and 5–18 representing consumer's surplus measured in dollars.

9. Shade the area in Figure 5–17 representing consumer's surplus measured in utils.

10. MU_x equals MU_m when the consumer buys _____ units of A at $P_a = 8$, and his total expenditure on A is $_____.

6

Theory of Demand: Indifference Curves

In the preceding chapter we discovered that if a consumer's marginal-utility function for a commodity is given and if we know the marginal utility of money and assume that it is constant in the short run, the demand function for the commodity is not difficult to derive from the marginal-utility function. Since there is no absolute measure of utility, the marginal-utility approach to the theory of consumer demand is subject to significant limitations but, in spite of this handicap, makes possible the setting up of models and the development of principles for consumer equilibrium. For many years this was the only approach to demand theory available to students of economics. A more recent tool, known as indifference curves, avoids the necessity of making specific measurements of utility. This device can be employed to derive demand curves and can serve as a useful tool as well in numerous other economic applications, some of which will be demonstrated in this chapter.

The advantage of indifference curves over the marginal-utility approach to the theory of consumer demand lies in the fact that indifference curves involve only *ordinal* rather than *cardinal* measures of utility. When we say that when Johnny eats the fourth pancake its marginal utility is nine utils of satisfaction, we are making a cardinal measure of utility, and such measures of utility are not, in fact, available to us. But for purposes of indifference-curve analysis it is only necessary that the consumer be able to determine that one combination of commodities is more or less desirable than another combination; it is not necessary to make the further assumption that the consumer can determine *how much* more or less. The consumer must be able to arrange various combinations of commodities in order of their increasing or decreasing attractiveness. The housewife must make such ordinal measures of utility each time she visits the supermarket or dress shop. Since the indiffer-

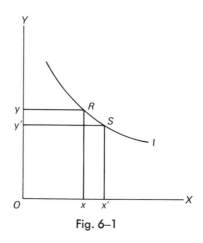

Fig. 6–1

ence-curve technique makes one less assumption than the marginal-utility analysis—i.e., it does not make the assumption that the consumer can determine *how much* better one combination of commodities is than another combination—the indifference-curve analysis is scientifically simpler than the marginal-utility analysis and is accordingly to be preferred.

Suppose that a consumer has y units of commodity Y and x units of commodity X. It may be presumed that the consumer would be willing to give up a certain amount of commodity Y, which may be designated as Δy, if in exchange he received an appropriate additional amount of commodity X, which may be designated as Δx. If Δx is properly chosen, the consumer's total satisfaction would be the same whether he had y units of commodity Y plus x units of commodity X or $(y - \Delta y)$ units of commodity Y plus $(x + \Delta x)$ units of commodity X. Or if the consumer had still less of Y, say, $(Y - \Delta y -\Delta y')$ of Y, but had appropriately more of X, say, $(x + \Delta x + \Delta x')$ of X, his condition of well-being would not be affected. The consumer would be indifferent as to which of the three combinations of Y and X he had since all would provide the same amount of total satisfaction or total utility. An indifference curve is the locus of all points representing combinations of Y and X which would provide the consumer with the same total satisfaction.

In Figure 6–1 a consumer's indifference curve has been drawn with the amount of commodity X measured on the x-axis and the amount of commodity Y measured on the y-axis. Each point on the indifference curve represents a combination of X and Y which will provide the consumer with equal degrees of satisfaction or utility. Combination R represents Oy of Y plus Ox of X. If the consumer gives up yy' of Y but acquires an additional xx' of X, he moves from point R on the indifference curve to point S. The loss in total utility resulting from giving up yy' units of Y is just compensated for by the gain in total utility from getting the additional xx' units of X. The particular form assumed by the consumer's indifference curve will depend on the consumer's tastes, and through time as the consumer's tastes change there will be a shift in the position of the consumer's indifference curve, so an indifference curve reflects a given consumer's taste pattern at any given moment.

Properties of Indifference Curves

Certain significant properties of indifference curves can be described. Among them are the following:

1. Indifference curves slope downward from left to right. In terms of the utility vocabulary, if the marginal utility of a commodity is always assumed to be positive—that is, if more of a commodity is preferred rather than less of it —one must have more of commodity X to compensate for less of commodity Y; i.e., if ΔY is negative, ΔX must be positive: $\Delta Y/\Delta X < 0$. Indifference curves that were positively inclined would indicate that more of both X and Y would leave the consumer's state of well-being unaffected, and this would violate the assumption that both commodities were utility-yielding goods.

2. Indifference curves are normally convex to the origin. If a consumer is on a point on an indifference curve which represents a large amount of commodity Y and a small amount of commodity X, we may assume that he will be willing to give up a certain amount of Y in order to get an additional unit of X. The number of units of Y which the consumer will give up in order to get an additional unit of X is called the *marginal rate of substitution* of X for Y and is written $MRS_{xy} = \Delta Y/\Delta X$. According to this statement, the marginal rate of substitution of X for Y is equal to the slope of the indifference curve at any given point on the indifference curve.

$$MRS_{xy} = \frac{\Delta Y}{\Delta X} = m.$$

If we start with a point on the indifference curve representing a large amount of Y and a small amount of X, we may assume that, in order to maintain his level of satisfaction, the consumer will be willing at first to give up a considerable amount of Y to get an additional unit of X, and as we move down the curve from left to right and the amount of Y decreases as the amount of X increases, he will give up smaller and smaller amounts of Y to acquire an additional unit of X. This is known as the principle of diminishing marginal rate of substitution of X for Y. The absolute slope (i.e., without reference to algebraic sign) of the indifference curve diminishes as the quantity of X increases, and the indifference curve is convex to the origin. This is illustrated in Figure 6–2.

   3. An indifference curve to the right of and above another indifference

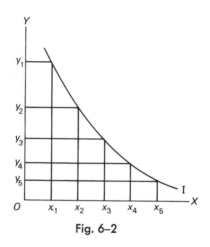

Fig. 6–2

curve is a "higher" indifference curve. It is assumed that any point in the "indifference field" between the y-axis and the x-axis lies on some indifference curve. There must be, accordingly, an infinity of indifference curves which make up the consumer's "family of indifference curves." Two of the infinite number of such curves are represented in Figure 6–3. Indifference curve II is a "higher" indifference curve than I; that is, any point on curve II represents a combination of commodities X and Y which will provide more satisfaction

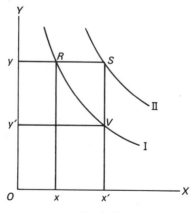

Fig. 6–3

to the consumer than any point on curve I. Combination S on curve II in Figure 6–3 is better than combination R on curve I since S represents the same quantity of commodity Y plus a greater quantity of commodity X. Combination S on curve II is better than combination V on curve I since it represents the same amount of commodity X plus more of commodity Y. Since any point on curve II provides the same satisfaction as point S and any point on curve I provides the same satisfaction as points R or V, any point on curve II represents a combination of commodities X and Y which is preferable to any combination represented by a point on curve I.

4. Since any point on a given indifference curve provides the consumer with the same satisfaction as any other point on the same curve, indifference

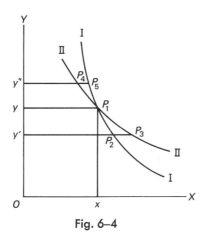

Fig. 6–4

curves cannot intersect. Consider the two indifference curves in Figure 6–4 which are drawn so as to intersect at point P_1. At the point of intersection the consumer would have Ox of X and Oy of Y whether he were on curve I or curve II. But at point P_3 on curve II the consumer would be better off than at point P_2 on curve I since he would have the same amount of Y but a greater amount of X. Below the point of intersection, accordingly, II is higher than I. At point P_5 on curve I, however, the consumer would be better off than at point P_4 on curve II since he would have the same amount of Y and more of X. Above the point of intersection curve I is a higher curve than curve II. But since any point on curve I provides the same utility as any other point on that curve, and any point on curve II provides the same utility as any other point on that curve, curve I can't be both higher and lower than curve II; intersecting indifference curves would involve us in logical inconsistency.

The Price Line

Suppose that a consumer has budgeted a certain amount of money to be spent on commodities X and Y; let that amount be designated R. Suppose the price of X is given and is designated P_x; the price of Y is given and is designated as P_y. Let the number of units of X purchased be x and the number of units of Y purchased be y. The total expenditure on commodity X will then be xP_x and the total expenditure on Y will be yP_y, and we may write

$$xP_x + yP_y = R.$$

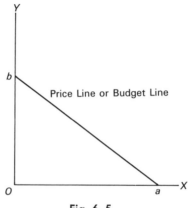

Fig. 6–5

If the total budget R were spent on commodity X, the number of units of X which could be purchased would be $R \div P_x$; in terms of Figure 6–5, $R/P_x = Oa$; that is, Oa is the amount of X which could be purchased if the total budgeted amount were spent on X and none was spent on Y. Similarly, if the entire amount were spent on Y and none on X, the amount of Y which could be purchased would be $R/P_y = Ob$. With the same total expenditure, therefore, the consumer could buy either Oa of X or Ob of Y.

It can be demonstrated that all of the combinations of both X and Y which could be purchased with the total expenditure R lie on the linear curve ba. We begin with the equation

$$xP_x + yP_y = R.$$

Dividing each term by R, we get

$$\frac{xP_x}{R} + \frac{yP_y}{R} = 1.$$

Dividing the numerator and denominator of the first term by P_x and the numerator and denominator of the second term by P_y, we get

$$\frac{x}{\dfrac{R}{P_x}} + \frac{y}{\dfrac{R}{P_y}} = 1.$$

But as we have seen, $R/P_x = Oa$ and $R/P_y = Ob$, so we may write

$$\frac{x}{Oa} + \frac{y}{Ob} = 1,$$

and this is the equation for a straight line with an x-intercept at a and a y-intercept at b and is usually written in the form

$$\frac{x}{a} + \frac{y}{b} = 1.$$

That is to say that all of the combinations of X and Y which can be purchased with a total expenditure of R at the given prices for X and Y will lie on the linear curve ba. For this reason ba is sometimes called the *budget line* or the *opportunity* line or the line of *attainable combinations*.

The line ba is also called the *price line* because the slope of ba represents the price of X in terms of the price of Y; that is, the slope of $ba = P_x/P_y$.

Referring again to Figure 6–5, we note that the slope of $ba = m = Ob/Oa$. But $Ob = R/P_y$ and $Oa = R/P_x$, so we may write

$$m = \frac{Ob}{Oa} = \frac{R}{P_y} \div \frac{R}{P_x} = \frac{R}{P_y} \cdot \frac{P_x}{R} = \frac{P_x}{P_y}.$$

Note that it is the *slope* of the price line which represents the price of X in terms of Y; any other price line drawn parallel to ba would represent the same price of X in terms of Y as does ba. If the price of X should increase relative to the price of Y, a would move to the left, and the slope of ba would increase. If the price of X should fall, a would move to the right, and the slope of ba would decrease (without reference to algebraic signs).

Consumer Equilibrium

We can now indicate the optimum allocation of a given expenditure on two commodities when the consumer's indifference map is given and when we know the total amount to be spent on the commodities and their prices. In Figure 6–6 we have represented four of the indifference curves from the consumer's family of indifference curves together with the budget line. We know that the consumer could, with the prices of X and Y given, buy either Ob of Y or Oa of X or any combination of both X and Y which lies on the budget line ba. Among these possible combinations are those designated L, S, T, W, and V. Since L and V both lie on indifference curve I, these combinations of X and Y would be equally attractive to the consumer. It is also true that combinations S and W would be equally attractive to the consumer since they both lie on indifference curve II. But since S and W are on a higher indifference curve than L and V, either S or W would be preferred to either L or V. But point T also lies on the line of attainable combinations, and it is on a still higher indifference curve, so the combination of X and Y represented by T indicates the best attainable combination. The consumer would, of course, like to move to a still higher indifference curve such as IV, but with the budget constraint given and the prices of X and Y given, combination T, which represents Ox of X plus Oy of Y is the best the consumer can do. The general rule is that a consumer will have maximized his satisfaction when he has moved to the combination represented by the point of tangency between the budget line and an indifference curve.

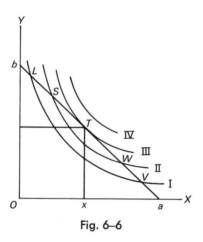

Fig. 6–6

It will be noted in Figure 6–6 that at the optimum point T the slope of indifference curve III is equal to the slope of the budget line ba. Since the slope of the indifference curve is the marginal rate of substitution of X for Y and the slope of the budget line is the price of X in terms of Y, we may say that the consumer has maximized his satisfaction when $MRS_{xy} = P_x/P_y$.

Limiting Cases

We have noted that indifference curves are normally convex to the origin, and are therefore nonlinear. But let us see what the implications of linear indifference curves would be. Suppose that a consumer's indifference map is made up of linear curves such as I, II, and III in Figure 6–7. Since the curves are linear, the slopes of the curves are constant, and if the slopes are constant the marginal rates of substitution are constant. If the figure is drawn so that $OB = OC$, for the indifference curve III the $MRS_{xy} = 1$. That is, the consumer would at all times be willing to give up one of Y in order to get one more of X, and X and Y are, accordingly, perfect substitutes for each other. If a consumer has no preference for one brand of cornflakes over another, he

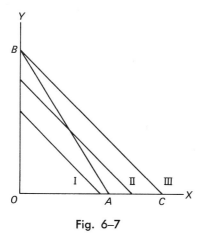

Fig. 6–7

would be perfectly willing to give up a box of Y-brand cornflakes in order to get an additional box of X-brand cornflakes.

If the price of X is equal to the price of Y, i.e., if $P_x/P_y = 1$, the slope of the budget line will be -1; and in Figure 6–7 the budget line BC is identical with indifference curve III. The consumer will, accordingly, be indifferent as to which of the infinite combinations of X and Y represented by points on the budget line he will buy. If, however, the prices of X and Y are not the same, the consumer will buy the cheaper brand only. If the price line is represented by BA, for example, X is more expensive than Y, and the consumer will buy OB of Y and none of X. Perfect substitutes may be regarded as a limiting case; normally the degree of substitutability between two commodities is less than infinite. Or it might be argued that if two goods are perfect substitutes for each other, they are not actually different commodities at all even though they be differentiated by brand names or in some other way.

Another case in which the consumer would choose all of one commodity and none of the other is represented by indifference curves concave to the origin. We have argued that indifference curves are convex to the origin, and further evidence for that contention is obtained by noting what would happen if indifference curves were concave. In Figure 6–8 indifference curve I is tangent to the budget line BA at point R. This is not, however, a point of consumer equilibrium but rather a point of *minimum* satisfaction. Any other point on the budget line would put the consumer on a higher indifference curve—for example, points S and T are on indifference curve II. The highest indifference curve which the consumer could reach would be curve III at point B, where the consumer buys OB of Y and none of X. If a utility-maximizing consumer buys some of both X and Y, we may conclude, accordingly, that the indifference curves are neither linear and down-sloping nor concave to the origin.

The second limiting case is that of perfect complements. If two commod-

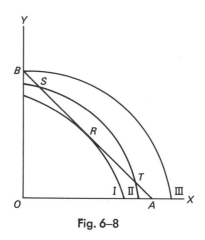

Fig. 6–8

ities must be used in fixed proportions, the indifference map would assume the form indicated in Figure 6–9. In this instance we have assumed that commodities X and Y must be used in the proportion $OC/OD = 1$. An example of perfect complements might be right shoes and left shoes. One

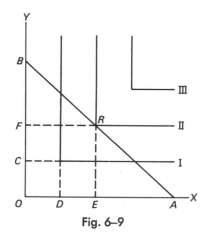

Fig. 6–9

right shoe plus one left shoe would provide the same satisfaction as one right shoe and two left shoes or two right shoes and one left shoe. A special sale announced by the local bootery which would give the customer an extra right shoe at no additional cost would not be likely to stimulate sales perceptibly. Two right shoes and two left shoes would put the consumer on a higher indifference curve, but three right shoes and two left shoes would not be better than two of each. In the case of perfect complements, it will be noted that the point of maximum satisfaction will always come at a corner of an indifference curve. If the budget line is BA in Figure 6–9, consumer equilibrium will be at point R, which represents OE of X and OF of Y.

Changes in Income and Prices

For many purposes in indifference-curve analysis it is convenient to plot on the *y*-axis income in dollars rather than a second commodity Y. In this way we can measure the quantity of commodity X purchased *versus* "all other goods." In Figure 6–10 we measure commodity X on the *x*-axis and income on the *y*-axis. We begin by assuming that the consumer's income is OB. If he spends all of his income on commodity X, he could buy OA units of X. The price line is BA, and the slope of the price line, OB/OA, is the price of X in terms of the price of Y. But since we are measuring income on the *y*-axis in dollars, and since the price of a dollar is $1, the slope of the price line gives us the price of X in dollars.

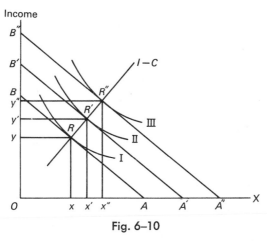

Fig. 6–10

If the consumer's income is OB and the price of X is OB/OA, the consumer will move to combination R on indifference curve I. Combination R represents Ox of X and Oy of Y. But if the consumer has Oy of income left after he has bought Ox of X, he must have spent $OB - Oy = yB$ dollars on Ox units of X. This is confirmed when we note that just as an expenditure of OB dollars on X would buy OA units of X, so would an expenditure of yB dollars on X buy $yR = Ox$ units of X.

Suppose now that the consumer's income increases from OB to OB′ and the price of X remains unchanged. If the entire income were spent on X, the consumer could buy OA′ units of X, and, since the price of X has not changed, the slope of the new price line will be the same as the slope of the original price line; that is, B′A′ is parallel to BA. The consumer will move from point R on indifference curve I to point R′ on indifference curve II; the effect of the increase in income has been to permit the consumer to move to a higher indifference curve. Similarly, if the income increases further to OB″, the consumer will be able to move to point R″ on indifference curve III. A

line drawn through the points of tangency between price lines and indifference curves is called the *income-consumption* curve,[1] and it indicates the
amounts of X which the consumer will buy at all income levels.

The effect of a change in the price of X on the amount of X purchased
while consumer income remains constant is illustrated in Figure 6–11. Suppose that consumer income is OB and that if the entire income were spent on
X the amount of X which could be purchased would be OA. The slope of the
price line, OB/OA, is the price of X. With this price of X and this income,

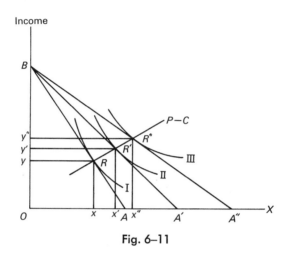

Fig. 6–11

the consumer would move to point R on indifference curve I, which would
represent a purchase of Ox units of X and a total expenditure on X of yB. If
now the price of X falls and the income remains constant, the total income
would buy more of X than before, and the slope of the price line (without
regard to algebraic sign) would diminish. Suppose the new price line is BA';
the consumer would move from point R on indifference curve I to point R'
on indifference curve II. The consumer would buy Ox' of X and spend
y'B on X. As drawn in Figure 6–11, as the price of X falls the total expenditure
on X declines. A further drop in the price of X as represented by price line
BA'' would cause the consumer to move to a still higher indifference curve.
The line drawn through the points of tangency between price lines and
indifference curves is called the *price-consumption* line. Although the price-
consumption line shows the relation between the price of X and the amount
of X demanded, it is not a conventional demand curve because we are
measuring income on the y-axis whereas a demand curve is drawn with price
measured on the y-axis.

[1] A curve showing the various quantities of a given commodity a consumer would
take at various income levels, other things remaining the same, is frequently called an
Engel curve, after Christian Lorenz Ernest Engel, a nineteenth-century German statisti-
cian who pioneered in consumer budget studies.

Deriving Demand Curves from Indifference Curves

Although the price-consumption line is not a demand curve, deriving a demand schedule from indifference curves is not difficult, and the demand curve may be plotted from the demand schedule. In Figure 6–12 we have represented a consumer's indifference map with indifference curves I to VII and price lines BA_1 to BA_7. The consumer's income is OB, which we may take to be $120. When the price of commodity X is represented by the price line BA_1, the price of X is the slope of $BA_1 = OB/OA_1 = \$120/2 = \$60$. When the price of X is $60, the consumer will buy one unit of X, as is indicated by the point of tangency between indifference curve I and price line BA_1. In similar manner we can determine the quantities demanded at each of the prices indicated by the other price lines, and we may draw up the following demand schedule:

P	Q_d
$60	1
40	2
30	3
20	4
15	5
12	6
10	7

The demand schedule is plotted in Figure 6–13.

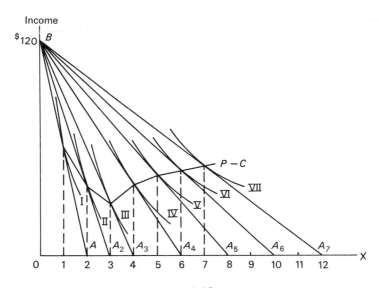

Fig. 6–12

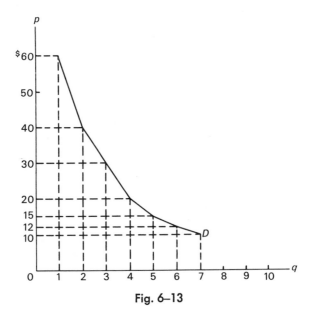

Fig. 6–13

Income and Substitution Effects

We have seen earlier that when the price of commodity X falls, the amount of X demanded increases for two reasons. First, if the price of X falls and other prices remain the same, X is now relatively cheaper than other commodities, and there will be a tendency to substitute the cheaper for the dearer goods; this is the substitution effect of a price change. Second, if the price of X falls and the consumer's money income remains the same, the consumer's real income will increase, and this will cause him to buy more goods, including more of commodity X; this is the income effect of a price change. Through the use of the indifference-curve technique, it is possible to isolate the income effect from the substitution effect of a change in price, and we will demonstrate two methods of doing that here.

In Figure 6–14 we begin with the consumer in equilibrium at point R on indifference curve I. The consumer's income is OB and he is consuming OM units of commodity X. Suppose now that the consumer's income increases to OB′ with no change in the price of X; he will move to indifference curve II at point S. In this new equilibrium the consumer will consume ON units of commodity X. It is clear that the effect of the increase in income from OB to OB′ has been to increase the consumption of X by MN units.

But the increase in the consumer's well-being represented by his movement from indifference curve I to indifference curve II might have been accomplished by an appropriate decrease in the price of X rather than an increase in the consumer's money income. Suppose that the consumer is able to move from indifference curve I to indifference curve II by virtue of a decrease in the price of X, represented by a shift of the price line from BA to BA″, money income remaining constant at OB. The consumer is as well off now as he was in the first case when money income increased and there was no change in the price of X, but he is buying more of X at point V on indifference curve II than he would have bought at point S on the same indifference curve: the effect of the change in money income was to increase the consumption of X by MN units, whereas the effect of the decrease in the price of X (which had the same real-income effect as the change in money income) was to increase the consumption of X by MM′ units. In the case of

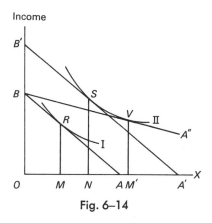

Fig. 6–14

an increase in money income, the increased consumption of X was due entirely to the change in income; in the case of a price decrease, there was not only an increase in real income, but there was also a substitution effect. We may say, accordingly, that of the total MM′ increase in the consumption of X resulting from a decrease in the price of X, MN was due to the real-income effect of the price change, and NM′ was due to the substitution effect of the price change. The consumer's movement (from point R on indifference curve I to point V on indifference curve II) which resulted from a decrease in the price of X may be visualized as a movement (from point R on indifference curve I to point S on indifference curve II) resulting from income effect and a movement (from point S to point V on indifference curve II) resulting from the substitution effect of the price change.

The income and substitution effects of price change can be seen in another way in Figure 6–15. Initially, the consumer is assumed to be in equilibrium at point R on indifference curve I. His income is OB; he buys OM units of X; and his total expenditure on X is R′B. Now the price of X falls (see price line BA'), the consumer moves to point S on indifference curve III, and his consumption of X increases by an amount equal to MM'. If the consumer had chosen to continue to buy OM units of X at the new lower price, his total expenditure on the OM units would have been reduced from $R'B$ to $L'B$, an increase in purchasing power of $R'L'$, which is equal to $q\Delta p$, when q is quantity purchased and Δp is change in price. Suppose that the increase in purchasing power resulting from the decrease in the price of X is taken from the consumer as income tax. The income tax will accordingly

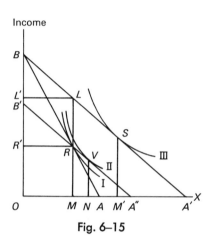

Fig. 6–15

be equal to $RL = R'L' = B'B$. The consumer's income after tax will be OB' and the budget line will now be $B'A''$ which is parallel to BA'. The new budget line will pass through point R on indifference curve I since. $RL = B'B$. That is, the consumer could, after the price of X has fallen and the tax been levied, be at the same point on indifference curve I that he occupied in the original equilibrium situation. But since the price line passes through R and is not tangent to indifference curve I at R, R no longer represents a point of equilibrium. The consumer will, in fact, buy more than OM units of commodity X and will find the new equilibrium at point V on indifference curve II.

This analysis indicates that if the entire increase in purchasing power which results from a decrease in the price of X is taken away as income tax, the price reduction will nevertheless put the consumer on a higher indifference curve. The explanation is that, although the income tax has cancelled the income effect of the price change, the substitution effect remains. In Figure 6–15 the total effect of the decrease in price represented by a shift from price line BA to BA' is MM' additional units of X consumed. Of this increase in the consumption of X, NM' is due to the income effect of the price change (which was eliminated by the income tax), and MN was the substitution effect, which remains in spite of the tax.

Effect of a Consumer Subsidy

An impression of the benefits and costs of a consumer subsidy may be obtained from Figure 6–16. Suppose that the original price of commodity X is represented by price line BA. Then it is lowered through the government's paying a part of it. Low-cost housing may be taken as an example: the price paid to the landlord is OB/OA, but the tenant pays only OB/OA', the difference being paid by the government.

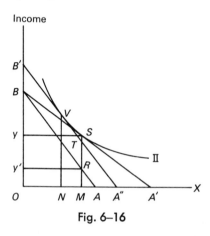

Fig. 6–16

We begin by determining the cost of the subsidy to the government. When the price of X is indicated by price line BA', the consumer will buy OM units of X. The total expenditure on X at this price is yB. But the seller of X receives a price indicated by the price-line BA, and his total receipts for OM units are equal to y'B. The total cost to the government is the difference between what the seller receives and what the consumer pays, or yy' = RS.

As an alternative to the subsidy on commodity X, the government could make a cash payment to the consumer which would place him on the same indifference curve. In Figure 6–16 this would require a payment of BB', which would increase the consumer's income from OB to OB'. The new price line B'A'' is parallel to BA, and the consumer would be in equilibrium at point V on indifference curve II. But the amount required to move the consumer to the higher indifference curve is smaller in the form of a cash payment to the consumer than in the form of a subsidy on commodity X; that is, BB' = RT < RS. An improvement in the overall well-being of the consumer can be accomplished more economically by a cash payment to him than by a subsidy on commodity X. However, the consumption of X is greater when a subsidy is paid on it than when a cash payment is made to the consumer: OM > ON. If we are afraid that the consumer would spend the cash payment at the local tavern and we want to increase his consumption of X, we should subsidize X. If commodity X represents surplus food which the government has acquired as result of its farm-price-support program, and if the objective is not only to help the poor but also to dispose of surplus food, the subsidy device is preferable to cash payment.

Negative Income and Price Effects

We have assumed that in general if the price of a commodity decreases or the consumer's income increases, the amount of a commodity demanded will increase. There are, however, certain exceptions to this rule.

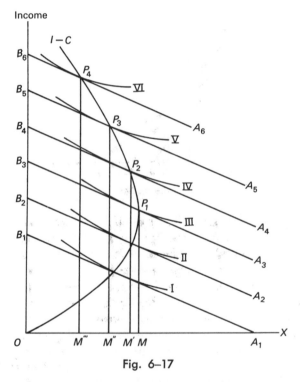

Fig. 6–17

First, where *inferior goods* are involved, the amount of commodity X consumed will decrease as income increases. This is an instance of so-called negative income effect. It is illustrated in Figure 6–17. A poor family may spend a considerable part of its food budget on navy beans because they are inexpensive and nourishing. The family feels that it can "afford" little except beans. If we begin at point P_1 on indifference curve III with income at OB_3, we note that the family buys OM units of beans per time period. If the income rises above OB_3, however, the purchase of beans decreases, and the family presumably buys more meat and fresh vegetables. Above point P_1 the income-consumption curve has a negative slope. Below P_1 the income-consumption curve has a positive slope, and the relation between income and consumption is positive.

Figure 6–18 represents a negative price effect, or what is commonly called the Giffen effect.[2] If we start with price line BA_1 and the consumer in equilibrium at point P_1 on indifference curve IV, and then assume that the price of X increases, as is indicated by a shift to price line BA_2, we note that the consumption of X increases from OM to OM'. An increase in price will

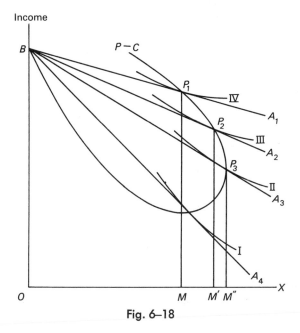

Fig. 6–18

be associated with an increase in the amount of X demanded until we get to point P_3 on indifference curve II; thereafter the amount of X demanded will decrease as the price of X increases. This case is also sometimes encountered in real life. Suppose that OB is a low income and that commodity X is bread. When the price of bread is represented by price line BA_1, the family buys a great deal of bread because it is inexpensive and wholesome. Suppose now that the price of bread increases, and, although it is more expensive than it was before, it is still the cheapest food the family can buy. They may, accordingly, buy even less of other foods and more of bread. If the price of

[2] After a Sir R. Giffen who, according to Alfred Marshall, noted cases where a rise in the price of bread "makes so large a drain on the resources of the poorer labouring families and raises so much the marginal utility of money to them, that they are forced to curtail their consumption of meat and the more expensive farinaceous foods: and, bread being still the cheapest food which they can get and will take, they consume more, and not less of it. But such cases are rare; when they are met with, each must be treated on its own merits." Alfred Marshall, *Principles of Economics*, 8th ed. (London: Macmillan & Co., 1920), p. 132.

bread continues to rise, however, there will come a point when the family's purchases of bread will decline—past point P_3 in Figure 6–18. On the assumption that if the price of X becomes sufficiently high, purchases of X will fall to zero, the price-consumption curve will start at B.

Indifference Curves and Elasticity of Demand

It is possible to determine both income elasticity of demand and price elasticity of demand from the consumer's indifference map. We begin with income elasticity of demand because its geometry is somewhat simpler.

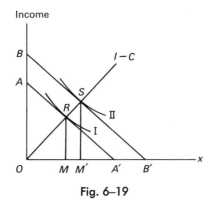

Fig. 6–19

To measure income elasticity of demand we may use the basic elasticity formula

$$e_y = \frac{\Delta x}{x} \div \frac{\Delta y}{y}.$$

In terms of Figure 6–19 this becomes

$$e_y = \frac{\Delta x}{x} \div \frac{\Delta y}{y} = \frac{MM'}{OM} \div \frac{AB}{OA} = \frac{MM'}{OM} \cdot \frac{OA}{AB}.$$

But $MM'/OM = RS/OR$, and $OA/AB = OR/RS$, and we may write

$$e_y = \frac{RS}{OR} \cdot \frac{OR}{RS} = 1.$$

We may generalize by saying that if the income-consumption line is linear and passes through the origin, the income elasticity of demand is equal to one.

Suppose now that the income-consumption curve has a *y*-intercept above

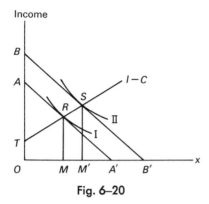

Fig. 6–20

the origin, as in Figure 6–20. The income elasticity of demand between incomes OA and OB may be measured as follows:

$$e_y = \frac{\Delta x}{x} \div \frac{\Delta y}{y} = \frac{MM'}{OM} \div \frac{AB}{OA} = \frac{MM'}{OM} \cdot \frac{OA}{AB} = \frac{RS}{TR} \cdot \frac{OA}{AB}$$

$$= \frac{AB}{TA} \cdot \frac{OA}{AB} = \frac{OA}{TA} > 1.$$

We may generalize by saying that the income elasticity of demand can be measured by OA/TA, where A is the y-intercept of the original budget line and T is the y-intercept of the linear income-consumption line. If T is at the origin, the income elasticity of demand is equal to one; if T comes above the origin, the income elasticity of demand is greater than one; and if T comes below the origin, the income elasticity of demand is less than one.

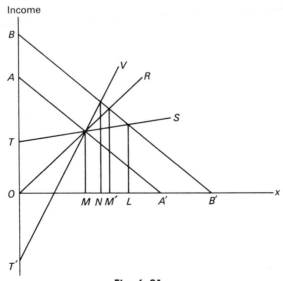

Fig. 6–21

The common sense of this argument is indicated in Figure 6–21. *AA'* and *BB'* are budget lines, and it is assumed that the income increases from *OA* to *OB*. At the original income, *OM* units of commodity *X* are consumed. If the income increases to *OB* and the income-consumption curve is *OR*, the consumption of *X* increases by *MM'* units and the income elasticity of demand is equal to one. If, however, the income-consumption line is *TS*, the increase in the consumption of *X* resulting from the same change in income is *ML*, which is greater than *MM'*. If the income-consumption line has a positive intercept on the *y*-axis, the income elasticity of demand must, accordingly, be greater than one. On the other hand, if *T'V* is the income-con-

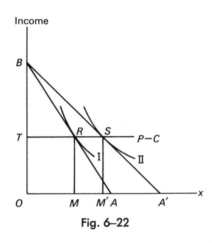

Fig. 6–22

sumption line, the increase in income from *OA* to *OB* results in an increase in the consumption of *X* of only *MN* units, which is less than *MM'*, and the income elasticity of demand must be less than one. In the first case $e_y = OA/OA = 1$; in the second case $e_y = OA/TA > 1$; in the last case $e_y = OA/T'A < 1$.

Now we turn to price elasticity of demand. With the use of Figure 6–22 we can devise a method for determining whether the price elasticity of demand is equal to, less than, or greater than one. It is clear from the figure that the elasticity of demand between the prices represented by the price lines *BA* and *BA'* is equal to one since, as the price changes, the total expenditure remains constant at *TB*. If the price-consumption line had a positive slope instead of being horizontal, the increase in the consumption of commodity *X* resulting from the indicated decrease in the price of *X* would have been less than *MM'*, and the elasticity of demand would, therefore, have been less than one. And if the price consumption curve had had a negative slope, the indicated decrease in the price of *X* would have caused a greater increase in the consumption of *X* than *MM'*, and the elasticity of demand between these prices would, accordingly, have been greater than one. What we are seeking, therefore, is an algebraic confirmation of what common sense tells us.

For this purpose we use the arc elasticity formula:

$$e = \frac{q_1 - q_2}{q_1 + q_2} \cdot \frac{p_1 + p_2}{p_1 - p_2}.$$

In terms of Figure 6–22, $q_1 = OM$; $q_2 = OM'$; $p_1 = OB/OA$; and $p_2 = OB/OA'$. We may write

$$e = \frac{OM - OM'}{OM + OM'} \cdot \frac{OB/OA + OB/OA'}{OB/OA - OB/OA'}.$$

Putting the numerator and the denominator of the second term over the common denominator $OA \cdot OA'$, we get:

$$e = \frac{-MM}{OM + OM'} \cdot \frac{\dfrac{OB \cdot OA' + OB \cdot OA}{OA \cdot OA'}}{\dfrac{OB \cdot OA' - OB \cdot OA}{OA \cdot OA'}}.$$

Multiplying the numerator and denominator of the second term by $OA \cdot OA'$:

$$e = \frac{-MM}{OM + OM'} \cdot \frac{OB \cdot OA' + OB \cdot OA}{OB \cdot OA' - OB \cdot OA}.$$

Dividing the numerator and the denominator of the second term by OB:

$$e = \frac{-MM}{OM + OM'} \cdot \frac{OA' + OA}{OA' - OA} = \frac{-MM}{OM + OM'} \cdot \frac{OA' + OA}{AA'}.$$

But $MM' = RS$; $OM = TR$; $OM' = TS$; and, since parallel lines cut transverse lines proportionately, $(OA' + OA)/AA' = (TS + TR)/RS$. We may write, accordingly:

$$e = \frac{-RS}{TR + TS} \cdot \frac{TS + TR}{RS} = -1.$$

To summarize: if the price-consumption line is horizontal, the price elasticity of demand is equal to one; if the price-consumption line has a positive slope, the price elasticity of demand is less than one; and if the price-consumption line has a negative slope, the price elasticity of demand is greater than one (ignoring the algebraic sign of the coefficient of elasticity).

POSTPRANDIUM

One of the best-known problems to which the indifference-curve technique has been applied relates to the question of the comparative effect of an excise tax and an income tax on a single consumer. Suppose that an excise or sales tax is levied on cigarettes, and that each week Mr. A pays a constant amount as cigarette tax. The payment of the tax reduces the consumer's well-being and puts him on a lower indifference curve than he would be on in the absence of the tax; the effect of the excise tax is to raise the price of cigarettes to Mr. A.

Now suppose that the excise tax is removed and an income tax added. The income tax takes from Mr. A in the form of a withholding tax the same amount each week that he was previously paying as an excise tax. The effect of the income tax is also to puṭ Mr. A on a lower indifference curve than he would be on in the absence of the tax. Now the question is, Does the *kind* of tax he has to pay make any difference to Mr. A, as a consumer? The common sense of the matter would seem to suggest that it shouldn't. But the indifference-curve analysis indicates that it does: Mr. A will be somewhat better off if he pays the amount as income tax rather than as excise tax.

This unexpected conclusion can be verified with the use of Figure 6–23.

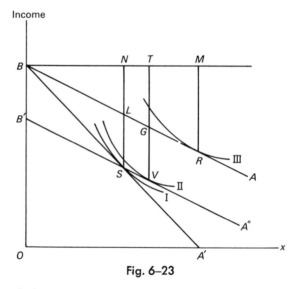

Fig. 6–23

We begin with the consumer in equilibrium at point R on indifference curve III. The consumer's income is equal to OB. The price of commodity X is indicated by the slope of the price line, BA; at this price the consumer buys BM units of commodity X and pays a total of RM dollars for this amount. Now the price of commodity X is increased by virtue of the imposition of an excise tax on the commodity, and the new price is indicated by the slope of the new price line, BA'. At the new price the consumer is in equilibrium at point S on indifference curve I. At the new price the consumer takes BN units of commodity X and pays a total of SN dollars for it. Now, at the original price, before the excise tax, the consumer could have bought BN units of commodity X at a total outlay of only LN dollars. The difference between SN and LN or SL dollars must, accordingly, be the total amount which the consumer pays to the government as excise tax on the BN units purchased.

Suppose now that there is no excise tax and the price goes back to the original price represented by the slope of BA. But the government levies an income tax which takes from the consumer an amount equal to the SL dollars which he paid as excise tax on commodity X. The income tax in effect reduces the consumer's income; $B'B$, which is equal to SL, represents the amount of the income tax. The consumer's income after tax is OB'. The price line is now $B'A''$, which has the same slope as BA, and $B'A''$ passes through point S on indifference curve I since SL equals $B'B$. This means that the consumer could now, if he chose, move to point S on indifference curve I and be as well off as he was under the excise-tax arrangement. But since indifference curve I is not tangent to price line $B'A''$ at S, point S does not represent the consumer's equilibrium position. The new equilibrium will be reached at point V on indifference curve II, a higher indifference curve than the consumer could reach with the excise tax even though the total amount paid as tax is the same in either instance. Since indifference curves by their nature cannot intersect, and indifference curve II is tangent to $B'A''$, II is necessarily higher than I.

Now how can we rationalize this conclusion? If the consumer pays a like amount under both tax arrangements, why is he left better off in one case than in the other? The answer seems to be that although in both instances the consumer is subjected to the same adverse income effect, in the case of the excise tax there is in addition an adverse substitution effect imposed upon the consumer which is absent in the case of the income tax. With the income tax, the consumer is free to spend what he has left after taxes without further restraint, but with the excise tax, both the consumer's real income is reduced and relative prices are disturbed. Extensive revisions in the consumer's expenditure pattern may as a result become necessary.

This analysis applies to the individual consumer and not to the economy as a whole. The nation's resources are the same whatever system of taxation is employed, and the aggregate well-being of the community could be the same under either tax arrangement. But it does make a difference to the individual consumer whether money is taken from him by taxes on commodities or taxes on income. And it may surprise the student to learn that subtle differences of this sort are revealed by a technique which is based on the set of general logical propositions which comprise the characteristics of indifference curves.

Profit Maximization Again

In Chapter 1 we noted that the usual assumption made in the study of price theory is that firms attempt to maximize their profits. We observed that although this is not an accurate description of actual business behavior, it probably represents the best single assumption that can be made for purposes of economic analysis. The indifference curve technique provides us with a method of considering alternative assumptions with reference to the businessman's attitude toward profits, and it may provide some basis for estimating the frequency of deviations from the profit-maximizing behavior we have assumed.

In Figure 6–24 a three-part chart is drawn with income measured on the *y*-axis and output on the *x*-axis. A profit curve, π, is drawn in each section, indicating that at very small and very large outputs the firm operates at a loss. The maximum point on each π curve indicates the output where marginal revenue equals marginal cost. Indifference curves between income and output are drawn in each section. For firm *A* the indifference curves have positive slopes, indicating an increasing marginal rate of substitution. Firm *A* will be willing to produce a greater output only if it expects the increased

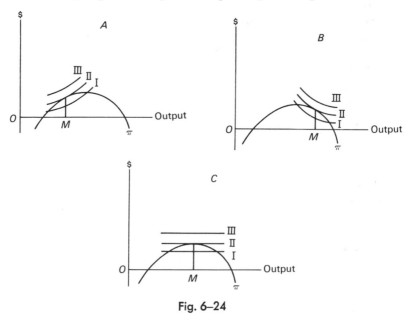

Fig. 6–24

output to result in sufficiently greater profits to justify the increased effort required to produce and sell the greater output. If a smaller output with smaller profits left the entrepreneur with more time for fishing, he would like this as well as a greater output with larger profits but with less leisure time. The point of tangency between the π curve and an indifference curve will determine the optimum output, and for this firm that will come to the left of the maximum-profit output.

Firm *B* is more interested in sales than in maximum profits. The indifference curves for this firm reflect a decreasing marginal rate of substitution. Somewhat smaller profits with greater sales is as attractive to this firm as greater profits with fewer sales. The firm would, if necessary, sacrifice profits to attain the prestige of being a large-scale producer, and its optimum output will be to the right of the $MR = MC$ output.

Firm *C* is the profit-maximizing firm of standard theory. It has no interest in a large output for its own sake; it is concerned only with making the greatest possible profit. The indifference curves for this firm are horizontal lines, and the optimum output is where profits are greatest, which is, of course, where $MR = MC$.

There can be little doubt that firms of all three types are common in the real world. Which case represents the most common attitude of businessmen cannot be determined by armchair speculation, though each of us can likely think of instances of each sort. If one is interested in a description of reality, he must turn to empirical research for his answers, and even these may prove to be less than conclusive.[3]

SELECTED REFERENCES

Allen, Clark Lee. *Elementary Mathematics of Price Theory.* Belmont, Calif.: Wadsworth Publishing Co., Inc., 1962. Chap. 19.

Friedman, Milton. "The 'Welfare' Effects of an Income Tax and an Excise Tax," *Journal of Political Economy,* 60 (February 1952), 25–33. Reprinted in Milton Friedman, *Essays in Positive Economics.* Chicago: University of Chicago Press, 1953.

Hicks, John R. *Value and Capital.* 2nd ed. Oxford: Clarendon Press, 1946. Chaps. 1 and 2.

Norris, Ruby Turner. *The Theory of Consumer's Demand.* 2nd ed. New Haven, Conn.: Yale University Press, 1952.

Ryan, W. J. L. *Price Theory.* London: Macmillan and Company, 1958. Chap. i.

Stonier, Alfred W., and Douglas C. Hague. *A Textbook of Economic Theory.* 3rd ed. New York: John Wiley & Sons, Inc., 1964. Chap. 3.

Vickrey, William S. *Microstatics.* New York: Harcourt, Brace and World, Inc., 1964. Chap. 2.

PROBLEMS

PROBLEM I

1. The change in the price of X is indicated by a shift from price-line *AB* to price-line *AB'*. This represents (a decrease, an increase) in the price of X.

2. Before the change in the price of X:
   (a) Total consumption of X = ..._____
   (b) Amount of income retained = ..._____
   (c) Total expenditure on X = ..._____

3. After the change in the price of X:
   (a) Total consumption of X = ..._____
   (b) Amount of income retained = ..._____
   (c) Total expenditure on X = ..._____

---

[3] For the argument that firms attempt to maximize sales revenue rather than profits, see William J. Baumol, *Business Behavior, Value and Growth* (New York: The Macmillan Co., Publishers, 1959), Chaps. 6 and 7.

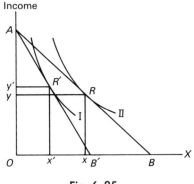

Fig. 6–25

4. On the figure draw the price-consumption line and label it P-C.

5. The elasticity of demand between the prices indicated is (equal to one, less than one, greater than one).

PROBLEM II

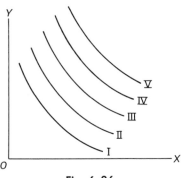

Fig. 6–26

Curves I to V in Figure 6–26 are consumer-indifference curves. Construct on the figure an income-consumption curve on the assumption that the prices of X and Y are equal. Label the income-consumption curve I-C.

PROBLEM III

In Figure 6–27 two indifference curves from a consumer's indifference map are indicated. Income is measured on the y-axis, and the quantity of commodity X on the x-axis.

1. If the price line is AB, the price of X is .   .   .   ._____

2. If the price line is AC, the price of X is .   .   .   ._____

3. The marginal rate of substitution at point R on curve
   I is .   .   .   .   ._____

4. The marginal rate of substitution at point S on curve
   II is .   .   .   .   ._____

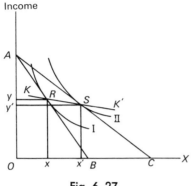

Fig. 6–27

5. *KK'* is the (income-consumption, price-consumption, expansion) curve.

6. Between the prices indicated by *AB* and *AC* the elasticity of demand is (equal to, less than, greater than) one.

7. If the demand curve had been a rectangular hyperbola, *KK'* in the figure would have been a _____ line.

8. Suppose that the price of X remains at the level indicated by *AB* but income increases to *OD* so that the consumer is as well off as if income had remained at *OA* and the price of X had fallen to *AC*. Locate *D* on the figure, draw the appropriate price-line, and label it *DE*.

PROBLEM IV

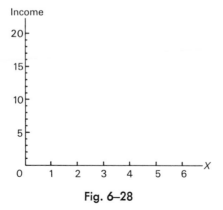

Fig. 6–28

A given consumer's income is assumed to be $12, and his demand schedule for commodity X is given in the table below:

P	Q_d
$6	1
4	2
3	3
2	4

1. On the axes in Figure 6–28 draw the price lines and the indifference curves which reflect this demand schedule.

2. Sketch in the price-consumption curve, and label it P-C.

3. Between prices $6 and $3 the elasticity of demand is (equal to, less than, greater than) one.

4. Between prices $3 and $2 the elasticity of demand is (equal to, less than, greater than) one.

5. Between prices $4 and $2 the elasticity of demand is (equal to, less than, greater than) one.

PROBLEM V

Given: $D = 6/p$, where D is the quantity demanded and p is price:

1. Complete the demand schedule in the table below:

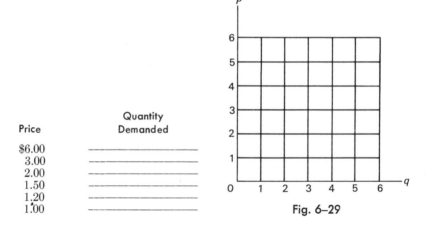

Price	Quantity Demanded
$6.00	_____
3.00	_____
2.00	_____
1.50	_____
1.20	_____
1.00	_____

Fig. 6–29

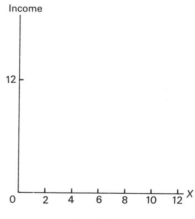

Fig. 6–30

2. Plot the demand curve in Figure 6–29.

3. What would be the *y*-intercept of a line drawn tangent to the demand curve

   at $p = 3$? .   .   .   ._____

   at $p = 1.2$? .   .   .   ._____

4. Assume that the consumer has an income of 12. Draw in Figure 6–30 the price lines and the price-consumption curve which reflect the above demand curve.

PROBLEM VI

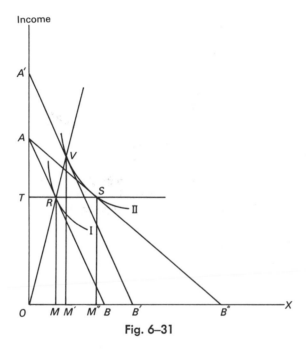

Fig. 6–31

1. When the consumer is at point R, the price of X is _____, and consumer income is _____.

2. When the consumer is at point V, the price of X is _____, and consumer income is _____.

3. When the consumer is at point S, the price of X is _____, and consumer income is _____.

4. If the consumer moves from point R to point V, the income elasticity of demand between income _____ and income _____ _____ is _____.

5. If the consumer moves from point R to point S, the price elasticity of demand between price _____ and price _____ is _____.

6. As result of the indicated change in the price of X the consumption of X increases by _____; of this _____ units are due to the income effect and _____ units are due to the substitution effect.

PROBLEM VII

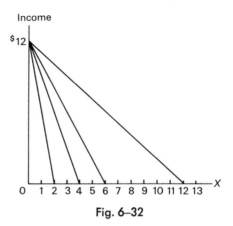

Income

$12

0 1 2 3 4 5 6 7 8 9 10 11 12 13   X

Fig. 6–32

The demand for commodity X has a price elasticity of − 1 throughout. It is known that when price = $3, the quantity demanded = 2. In the figure above sketch in the appropriate indifference map and the price-consumption curve.

PROBLEM VIII

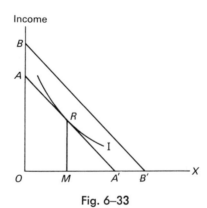

Income

B

A

R

I

O   M   A' B'   X

Fig. 6–33

The consumer is in equilibrium at R on indifference curve I when income is OA and the price line is AA'. Suppose that income increases to OB and there is no change in the price of X. Draw the Income-Consumption line and the appropriate indifference curve on the assumption that the income elasticity of demand is equal to one.

PROBLEM IX

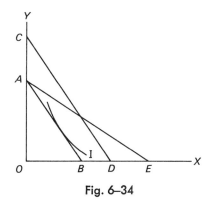

Fig. 6–34

Draw indifference curve II to indicate that when the price of X changes from OA/OB to OA/OE, the price elasticity of demand is −1, and when the income changes from OA to OC, the income elasticity of demand is + 1.

PROBLEM X

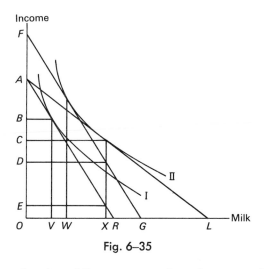

Fig. 6–35

1. Assume that the indifference curves above show some of the combinations of milk and other goods which provide equal satisfaction to an individual on relief during a depression. The amount which the individual receives in relief payments, his income, is OA. The disposition which he can make of this income at prevailing prices is shown by the price-line AR.

    (a) How much milk will the individual purchase? ._____

    (b) How much will he pay for it? . . . . ._____

2. In the 1930s people on relief were often permitted to buy agricultural products at a price less than market price. The government paid the

producers the difference between the market price and the price paid by
those on relief. Assume that such a policy is adopted and the price line for
those on relief now becomes AL instead of AR, but the price received by
milk producers remains unchanged.

(a) How much milk will the individual purchase? ._____

(b) How much will he pay for it? .   .   .   ._____

(c) How much will the government pay? .   .   ._____

3. Assume that the two-price system is abandoned by the government. In
order that the person on relief may be as well off as he was under the two-
price system, an additional money payment is made to him.

(a) How much will this additional payment be? ._____

(b) How much will the government save through
the use of this policy instead of the two-price
system? .   .   .   .   ._____

(c) Milk producers would (prefer the two-price policy, prefer the income-
subsidy policy, be indifferent).

7

Average, Total, and
Marginal Revenue

We noted in Chapter 2 that the quantity of a commodity demanded is a function of the price of the commodity, and this relationship can be expressed as

$$D = x = f(y),$$

where x is the quantity demanded and y is the price. The demand function may be represented geometrically as in Figure 7–1, and the demand curve is read as follows: if the price is OP, the amount demanded will be OM. If, however, the curve TT' is viewed as the demand curve for the product of a given firm, we might start with the quantity and see at what price that amount of the commodity could be sold: if the quantity offered for sale is OM, that amount could be sold at a price of OP per unit. The price OP is the revenue per unit of output, and from the point of view of the firm this is properly called the average revenue. The curve TT' may, accordingly, with equal propriety be considered either the demand curve or the average-revenue curve. The average-revenue function may be expressed as the function of the quantity sold and written as

$$AR = y = f(x).$$

If we assume that the demand function is given by

$$D = x = 10 - y,$$

the corresponding average-revenue function is

$$AR = y = 10 - x.$$

Both functions when plotted give us curve TT' in Figure 7–1.

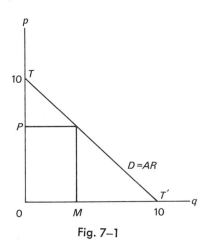

Fig. 7–1

If the average revenue function is

$$AR = y = 10 - x,$$

the total revenue function is revenue per unit multiplied by the number of units sold and may be written as

$$TR = xy = x(10 - x) = 10x - x^2.$$

The marginal function, as we saw in Chapter 5, is the derivative of the total function:

$$MR = \frac{dTR}{dx} = 10 - 2x.$$

The average-, total-, and marginal-revenue curves are plotted in Figure 7–2, and, since these are among the most important relationships in price theory, this chapter and two subsequent chapters will be devoted to average, total, and marginal curves.

It will be noted that Figure 7–2 gives us three distinct measures of total revenue. When, for example, the quantity is OM, we may read the total revenue directly from the total-revenue curve: $TR = MS$. Or, since total revenue is equal to average revenue multiplied by the number of units sold,

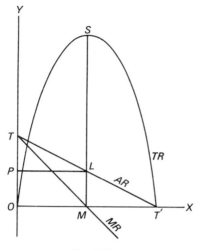

Fig. 7–2

$$TR = OP \cdot OM = OPLM.$$

Or, since total revenue is equal to the area under the marginal-revenue curve, $TR = OTM$. One measure of total revenue is a line, one measure is a rectangle, and one measure is a triangle, and all are equal to total revenue. Now it is clear that a line cannot equal an area, and the mathematical purist may object that total revenue cannot be properly measured as the length of a line and also as the area of a rectangle and of a triangle. But note that we are measuring price per unit of output on the y-axis, and price per unit times the number of units gives us total revenue in dollars. We are not multiplying dollars times dollars to get square dollars; the area of the rectangle represents the total number of dollars spent by the buyer and received by the seller, just as the line MS represents total revenue in dollars.

This argument is confirmed if we substitute numerical values for the letters in the figure. Point M represents the quantity where marginal revenue is zero. We may write

$$MR = 10 - 2x = 0$$
$$-2x = -10$$
$$x = 5.$$

When $x = 5$, total revenue is 25:

$$TR = 10x - x^2$$
$$= 50 - 25 = 25.$$

MS in Figure 7–2 is, accordingly, equal to 25. When the quantity sold is 5, the average revenue is 5:

$$AR = 10 - x$$
$$= 10 - 5 = 5.$$

Total revenue viewed as the area $OPLM$ is, therefore, equal to $5 \times 5 = 25$. The y-intercept of the marginal-revenue curve is 10:

$$MR = 10 - 2x;$$

when $x = 0$,

$$MR = 10 - 0 = 10.$$

Total revenue viewed as the triangle OTM, which represents the area under the marginal revenue curve, is equal to

$$TR = \frac{10 \times 5}{2} = 25.$$

The line MS, the rectangle $OPLM$, and the triangle OTM all tell us that when OM units of commodity X are sold, the total revenue is 25.

We may note in passing the relationship between the elasticity of demand and the average-, total-, and marginal-revenue curves. When OM units of X are sold at a price of OP, the elasticity of demand at point L on the average-revenue curve is given by

$$E_d = \frac{OP}{TP} = \frac{5}{-5} = -1.$$

That is to say that at the midpoint of the average-revenue curve its elasticity is equal to -1. It may also be noted that when the elasticity of demand is -1, marginal revenue is equal to zero and total revenue is at a maximum. For quantities less than 5, the elasticity of demand would be greater than -1 (in absolute terms), marginal revenue would be greater than zero, and total revenue would be less than the maximum. For values of x greater than 5, the elasticity of demand would be less than -1; marginal revenue would be negative; and total revenue would be beyond the maximum point.

One further observation may be made at this point. Marginal revenue is the rate of change of the total revenue as quantity changes. Geometrically this means that the marginal revenue at any x-value is the slope of the total-revenue curve at that x-value. It will be noted that when the slope of the total-revenue curve is positive, marginal revenue is positive; when the slope of the total-revenue curve is zero, marginal revenue is zero; when the slope of the total-revenue curve is negative, marginal revenue is negative.

Average Revenue and Marginal Revenue

We are now ready to look at average-marginal-total relationships in somewhat greater detail. First we turn our attention to the relationship between average revenue and marginal revenue.

When the average-revenue function is

$$AR = 10 - x,$$

we have seen that the corresponding marginal-revenue function is

$$MR = 10 - 2x.$$

Remembering that the equation for a straight line is

$$y = mx + b,$$

where m is the slope of the curve and b is its y-intercept, we note that both the average- and marginal-revenue curves have a y-intercept at 10, but the slope of the average-revenue curve is equal to -1 whereas the slope of the marginal-revenue curve is -2. This may be stated generally as follows: if the average-revenue curve is linear, the marginal-revenue curve will be linear and have the same y-intercept as the average curve, but the slope (without reference to algebraic sign) of the marginal-revenue curve will be twice the slope of the average-revenue curve.

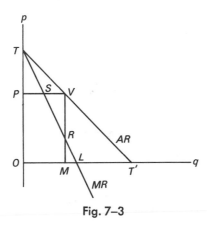

Fig. 7–3

The relationship between average-revenue curves and marginal-revenue curves can be demonstrated with the use of Figure 7–3. If OM units are sold, the average revenue will be OP and total revenue will be equal to TR $= OPVM$. But since total revenue is also equal to the area under the marginal-revenue curve, we may write $TR = OTRM$. It follows, accordingly, that $OPVM = OTRM$. But $OPVM = OPSRM + SVR$ and $OTRM = OPSRM$ $+ PTS$, so we may write

$$OPSRM + SVR = OPSRM + PTS.$$

Subtracting the area common to both sides, we get $SVR = PTS$ in area. But angles TPS and SVR are right angles and are therefore equal; angles PST and RSV are opposite angles and are equal; so the third angles PTS and SRV must be equal. SVR and PTS are equal in all respects, or $SVR \cong PTS$. Since SVR and PTS are congruent triangles, the base of one must equal the base of the other, or $PS = SV$. We may generalize as follows: if the average-revenue curve is linear and we wish to draw the corresponding marginal-revenue curve, start at the y-intercept of the average curve and bisect any horizontal line drawn from the y-axis to the average curve. It will be noted in Figure 7–3 that $PS = SV$ and $OL = LT'$. When average revenue equals $OP = MV$, marginal revenue is MR; when the quantity sold is OL, marginal revenue is zero; and when the quantity is greater than OL, marginal revenue is negative.

If the average-revenue curve is nonlinear, the marginal-revenue curve will usually be nonlinear, and the construction of a marginal-revenue curve corresponding to a given nonlinear average-revenue curve becomes a bit tedious since the points on the marginal-revenue curve must be located one at

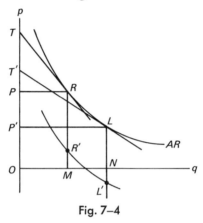

Fig. 7–4

a time. Referring again to Figure 7–3, we may note that since triangles TPS and SVR are congruent, side PT of the first one must be equal to the corresponding side VR of the second. An alternate method of drawing the marginal-revenue curve corresponding to the average-revenue curve TT' follows: Mark off a distance VR on the line MV so that VR equals PT. The marginal-revenue curve starts at point T and passes through point R. When average revenue is MV, marginal revenue is MR.

The alternate method of drawing a marginal-revenue curve may be employed when the average-revenue curve is nonlinear; its advantage consists in the fact that for each point on the marginal-revenue curve one less line has to be drawn. In Figure 7–4 choose a point R on the average-revenue curve where price is OP and the quantity demanded is OM. Draw a tangent to the average-revenue curve at R; call the y-intercept of the tangent T. Now measure the distance PT and mark off on line MR the distance RR' so that RR' equals PT. Point R' will lie on the marginal-revenue curve: when average revenue is MR, marginal revenue will be MR'. Now repeat the process to determine the point on the marginal-revenue curve corresponding to point L on the average-revenue curve. Mark off on the line NL a distance equal to $P'T'$. This will take us below the x-axis; when average revenue is NL, marginal revenue will be negative NL'. After a sufficient number of points on the marginal curve have been determined in this fashion, a smooth curve can be drawn through them, and this will be the marginal-revenue curve corresponding to the average-revenue curve *AR*. Since the geometric determination of a nonlinear marginal-revenue curve is tedious, economists usually either draw the average- and marginal-revenue curves as straight lines or they assume an algebraic expression for total revenue and derive from that the corresponding average- and marginal-revenue functions.

Price, Quantity, Slope, and Marginal Revenue

A useful formula can be developed with the use of Figure 7–5 showing the relationship between average revenue or price, quantity demanded at that price, the slope of the average-revenue curve, and the marginal revenue at that quantity.

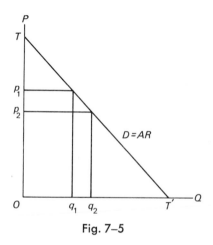

Fig. 7–5

The change in total revenue as price falls from p_1 to p_2 is given by

$$\Delta TR = p_2 q_2 - p_1 q_1.$$

But

$$p_2 q_2 = p_2 q_1 + p_2 (q_2 - q_1) = p_2 q_1 + p_2 \Delta q$$

and

$$p_1 q_1 = p_2 q_1 + q_1 (p_1 - p_2) = p_2 q_1 - q_1 \Delta p.$$

We may write

$$\Delta TR = (p_2 q_1 + p_2 \Delta q) - (p_2 q_1 - q_1 \Delta p)$$
$$= p_2 q_1 + p_2 \Delta q - p_2 q_1 + q_1 \Delta p$$
$$= p_2 \Delta q + q_1 \Delta p.$$

Since marginal revenue is the change in total revenue divided by the change in quantity sold, we may write

$$MR = \frac{\Delta TR}{\Delta q} = \frac{p_2 \Delta q}{\Delta q} + \frac{q_1 \Delta p}{\Delta q} = p_2 + \left(\frac{\Delta p}{\Delta q}\right) q_1.$$

As Δq approaches zero,

$$MR = \frac{dTR}{dp} = p + \left(\frac{dp}{dq}\right) q.$$

Since dp/dq is the slope of the average-revenue curve,

$$MR = p + mq$$

or

$$MR = y + mx,$$

where y = price, x = quantity demanded, and m = slope of the average-revenue curve. This result may be obtained directly by using the rule for the derivative of a product:

$$TR = pq$$
$$MR = \frac{d(pq)}{dq} = p + \frac{dp}{dq} q.$$

Consider the average-revenue function

$$AR = y = 10 - x.$$

If plotted, this average-revenue curve would have a y-intercept at 10 and an x-intercept at 10, and the slope of the curve would be -1. Our formula tells us that

$$MR = y + mx.$$

By substituting $(10 - x)$ for y and -1 for m we get

$$MR = (10 - x) + (-1)x = 10 - 2x.$$

This is the same result we get if we take the derivative of the total-revenue function:

$$AR = 10 - x$$
$$TR = 10x - x^2$$
$$MR = 10 - 2x.$$

It will be noted from the formula

$$MR = y + mx$$

that if the slope of the average-revenue curve is negative, marginal revenue at any output will be less than average revenue; that is, marginal revenue is equal to price minus something. If the slope of the average-revenue curve is zero, average revenue and marginal revenue will be equal; that is, marginal revenue is equal to price minus zero.

Continuous and Discrete Marginal Revenue

We have seen that if we have the total-revenue function given and if output can be varied continuously—that is, Δx can assume any value including the infinitesimally small—the marginal-revenue function may be derived by taking the derivative of the total-revenue function. If, for example,

$$TR = 10x - x^2,$$

then

$$MR = \frac{dTR}{dx} = 10 - 2x.$$

Sometimes, however, output can be increased only by discrete units, which we may designate Δx, or we may have the total revenue given for each of a limited number of values of x, as in a total-revenue schedule. In this event, since we do not know the total-revenue function, we must determine marginal revenue without the help of the calculus. We may get a measure of marginal revenue if we take total revenue when output is x and subtract from that total revenue at output $(x - \Delta x)$, and divide this difference by Δx:

$$MR = \frac{\Delta TR}{\Delta x} = \frac{TR_x - TR_{x-\Delta x}}{\Delta x}.$$

The first of the measures of marginal revenue we may designate as continuous marginal revenue:

$$MR_c = \frac{dTR}{dx},$$

and the second as discrete marginal revenue:

$$MR_d = \frac{\Delta TR}{\Delta x}.$$

These two measures of marginal revenue will give slightly different values, but the closer Δx approaches zero, the less will be the discrepancy.

In Table 7–1 the price and quantity-demanded columns are derived from the function

$$AR = y = 10 - x.$$

TABLE 7–1

P	Q_d	TR	MR_c	MR_d
$10	0	$ 0	$10	—
9	1	9	8	$9
8	2	16	6	7
7	3	21	4	5
6	4	24	2	3
5	5	25	0	1
4	6	24	−2	−1
3	7	21	−4	−3
2	8	16	−6	−5
1	9	9	−8	−7
0	10	0	−10	−9

The total-revenue column is derived from

$$TR = xy = 10x - x^2.$$

The continuous marginal-revenue column is derived from

$$MR_c = \frac{dTR}{dx} = 10 - 2x.$$

The discrete marginal-revenue column is derived from

$$MR_d = \frac{\Delta TR}{\Delta x} = \frac{TR_x - TR_{x-\Delta x}}{\Delta x}.$$

It will be noted that the MR_c and MR_d columns in Table 7–1 are not identical; the MR_d is in this instance always one more than the MR_c for any x value. To explain this discrepancy, let

$$TR = ax - bx^2,$$

where a and b are positive constants. It follows that continuous marginal revenue is given by

$$MR_c = a - 2bx.$$

Discrete marginal revenue is

$$MR_d = \frac{\Delta TR}{\Delta x} = \frac{TR_x - TR_{x-\Delta x}}{\Delta x}.$$

We may let

$$TR_x = ax - bx^2$$

and

$$TR_{x-\Delta x} = a(x - \Delta x) - b(x - \Delta x)^2.$$

Discrete marginal revenue then becomes

$$MR_d = \frac{(ax - bx^2) - [a(x - \Delta x) - b(x - \Delta x)^2]}{\Delta x}$$

$$= \frac{ax - bx^2 - [ax - a\Delta x - b(x^2 - 2x\Delta x + \Delta x^2)]}{\Delta x}$$

$$= \frac{ax - bx^2 - [ax - a\Delta x - bx^2 + 2bx\Delta x - b\Delta x^2]}{\Delta x}$$

$$= \frac{ax - bx^2 - ax + a\Delta x + bx^2 - 2bx\Delta x + b\Delta x^2}{\Delta x}$$

$$= a - 2bx + b\Delta x.$$

It will get noted that MR_d is greater than MR_c by an amount equal to $b\Delta x$. If

$$TR = ax - bx^2 = 10x - x^2,$$

then

$$a = 10$$

and

$$b = 1.$$

Discrete marginal revenue is then equal to

$$MR_d = a - 2bx + b\Delta x = 10 - 2x + \Delta x;$$

if $\Delta x = 1$,

$$MR_d = 10 - 2x + 1.$$

At, for example, $x = 3$,

$$MR_d = 10 - 6 + 1 = 5,$$

which is the value of MR_d when the quantity demanded equals 3 in Table 7–1. As Δx approaches zero, $b\Delta x$ also approaches zero, and the values of MR_d and MR_c become identical. But as long as Δx is greater than zero, MR_d will be greater than MR_c by an amount equal to $b\Delta x$, which for the functions used in Table 7–1 equals $1 \times 1 = 1$, since $b = 1$ and $\Delta x = 1$.

We can make the discrepancy between the continuous and discrete measures of marginal revenue appear to disappear by placing the discrete marginal-revenue values between the lines as in Table 7–2. It might be argued that, for instance, when total revenue increases from $16 to $21, the marginal revenue is $5; but, one might say, this is not marginal revenue when total revenue is $21; this is marginal revenue *between* total revenues of $16 and $21. We may, accordingly, put the marginal revenue values between the lines of the table. If we plot the marginal values, not at the given x-values, but midway between them, we get the same curve for continuous and discrete marginal revenue, and this device is sometimes resorted to in order to avoid the necessity of distinguishing between the two. The fact is, however, that we

TABLE 7–2

P	Q$_d$	TR	MR$_c$	MR$_d$
$10	0	$ 0	$10	
				$9
9	1	9	8	
				7
8	2	16	6	
				5
7	3	21	4	
				3
6	4	24	2	
				1
5	5	25	0	
				−1
4	6	24	−2	
				−3
3	7	21	−4	
				−5
2	8	16	−6	
				−7
1	9	9	−8	
				−9
0	10	0	−10	

do have two measures of marginal revenue. If we know the total-revenue function, it is usually more convenient to use the continuous measure of marginal revenue. If we must determine marginal revenue from a table which gives us total revenue at only certain specified x-values, we have no choice but to use the discrete measure of marginal revenue. And if we can take Δx sufficiently small, the difference between continuous and discrete marginal revenue will not be great in any event.

Total Revenue and Average Revenue

We know that average revenue is total revenue divided by the quantity sold. If the total-revenue function is

$$TR = ax - bx^2,$$

where a and b are positive constants and x is the quantity sold, then

$$AR = \frac{ax - bx^2}{x} = a - bx.$$

But suppose we have given a total-revenue curve and we do not know the equation for the curve. There is a simple geometric method for determining the general form of the average-revenue curve, and this method is explained with the use of Figure 7–6.

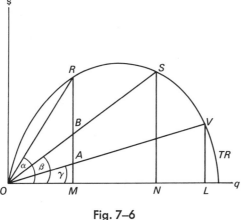

Fig. 7–6

Figure 7–6 tells us that when OM units are sold, the total revenue is MR. It follows that when OM units are sold, average revenue is equal to $MR \div OM$, that is, total revenue divided by the quantity sold. If we draw a vector RO from point R on the curve to the origin, we form the right triangle OMR. From the point of view of the angle at the origin, $\angle ROM$, which we have designated α, MR is what in trigonometry is called the *opposite* side and OM is called the *adjacent* side. Average revenue at quantity OM, which is measured by MR/OM, is, accordingly, equal to the opposite side, MR, divided by the adjacent side, OM. In trigonometry the opposite side divided by the adjacent side is given the name *tangent* of the angle, and this is abbreviated *tan*. We may then say that when OM units of commodity X are sold, average revenue is equal to tan α:

$$AR = \frac{MR}{OM} = \tan \alpha.$$

To say that $AR = \tan \alpha$ is to say no more than $AR = MR/OM$. But there is a significant advantage in expressing average as the tangent of an angle. This follows from the fact that the smaller the angle, the smaller is the tangent of the angle. Note in Figure 7–6 that tan β is equal to MB/OM. Angle β is smaller than angle α, and MB/OM is less than MR/OM. Angle γ is smaller than angle β, and tan γ, which is equal to MA/OM, is less than MB/OM. To repeat: *the smaller the angle, the smaller the tangent of the angle*. It will be noted that when the total-revenue curve assumes the form of TR in Figure 7–6, average revenue decreases as the quantity sold increases. At $q = OM$, $AR = \tan \alpha$; at $q = ON$, $AR = \tan \beta$; at $q = OL$, $AR = \tan \gamma$. Total revenue increases for a time as quantity increases, reaches a maximum, and then decreases; but average revenue decreases continuously as quantity increases. This relationship between total and average is readily apparent when we understand that average revenue is measured by the tangent of the angle formed by a line from the given point on the total curve to the origin and the x-axis, but without this technique this relationship would not be so obvious.

Total Revenue and Marginal Revenue

The tangent of an angle may also be used to derive the marginal revenue from the total-revenue curve at any x-value. The basic concept here is that marginal revenue represents the rate of change of total revenue as the quantity sold changes, which is interpreted geometrically as meaning the slope of the total curve.

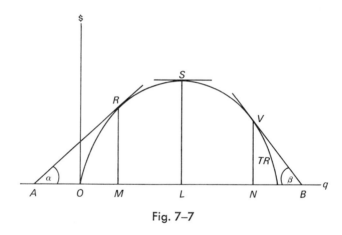

Fig. 7–7

In Figure 7–7 when the quantity sold is OM, total revenue is MR. Marginal revenue at quantity OM is the slope of the total revenue curve at point R. To measure marginal revenue at that point, draw a tangent to the total-revenue curve at R and extend it to the x-axis (or any other convenient horizontal line). Marginal revenue at output OM is equal to the slope of the TR curve at point R, which is equal to the slope of the tangent AR, which, in turn is equal to MR/AM, and this is equal to $\tan \alpha$. By similar argument, the marginal revenue for quantity ON is equal to $-NV/NB = -\tan \beta$. The rule may be stated as follows: to determine marginal revenue corresponding to total revenue at any point on the total-revenue curve, draw a tangent at that point on the total curve, extend the tangent to the x-axis, and the tangent of the angle formed by the tangent to the total curve and the x-axis is marginal revenue. It will be noted in Figure 7–7 that as quantity increases from zero, marginal revenue decreases; for quantities less than OL, marginal revenue is positive; at OL marginal revenue is equal to zero; and for quantities greater than OL, marginal revenue is negative.

Summary

The important relationships between average, marginal, and total revenue and the elasticity of demand may be summarized with reference to Figure 7–8. This time let

$$AR = p = 6 - q$$
$$TR = pq = 6q - q^2$$
$$MR = \frac{d(pq)}{dq} = 6 - 2q.$$

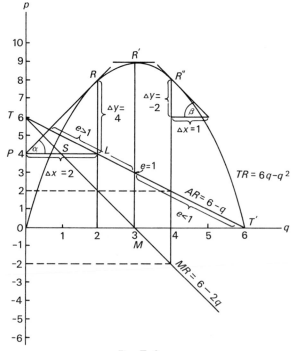

Fig. 7–8

1. If the average revenue curve is linear and negatively inclined, the marginal revenue curve has the same y-intercept as the average-revenue curve and bisects any horizontal line from the y-axis to the average curve; e.g., $PS = SL$ and $OM = MT'$.
2. If average revenue is decreasing as the quantity sold increases, marginal revenue is less than average revenue at any quantity.
3. When marginal revenue is positive, total revenue is increasing as q increases; e.g., at $q = 2$, $MR = +2$ and total revenue at point R has a positive slope.
4. When marginal revenue is zero, total revenue is at a maximum; at $q = 3$, $MR = 0$, and TR has a slope of zero at point R'.

5. When marginal revenue is negative, total revenue is decreasing as q increases; e.g., at $q = 4$, $MR = -2$, and the slope of the total-revenue curve at point R'' is negative.

6. Viewed geometrically, marginal revenue *is* the slope of the total revenue curve; e.g., when $q = 2$, $MR = 2$ and the slope of the total-revenue curve at point R is $4/2 = \tan \alpha = 2$; when $q = 4$ $MR = -2$ and the slope of the total-revenue curve at point R'' is $-2/1 = \tan \beta = -2$.

7. When total revenue is at a maximum, marginal revenue is zero.

8. When total revenue is at a maximum, the elasticity of demand is equal to one (without regard to algebraic sign).

9. When total revenue is increasing as q increases, the elasticity of the average-revenue curve is greater than one.

10. When total revenue is decreasing with an increase in q, elasticity of average revenue is less than one.

11. When marginal revenue is positive, elasticity of average revenue is greater than one.

12. When marginal revenue is equal to zero, elasticity of demand is one.

13. When marginal revenue is less than zero, elasticity of average revenue is less than one.

14. When $q = 1$, average revenue equals total revenue.

POSTPRANDIUM

A useful formula can be developed showing the relationship between average revenue, marginal revenue, and elasticity of average revenue. We know that in terms of Figure 7–9 elasticity of average revenue at price OP is given by

$$e = \frac{OP}{-PT}.$$

Since $ML = OP$ and $RL = PT$, we may write

$$e = \frac{ML}{-RL}.$$

But ML is average revenue, which we may symbolize by a, and since MR is marginal revenue, which we may call m, it follows that RL is $(ML - MR)$ or $(a - m)$. We may then write

$$e = \frac{ML}{-RL} = \frac{ML}{-(ML - MR)} = \frac{a}{-(a - m)} = \frac{a}{m - a}.$$

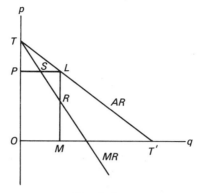

Fig. 7–9

This formula may be made explicit in terms of m as follows:

$$e = \frac{a}{m - a}$$
$$em - ea = a$$
$$em = a + ea$$
$$m = \frac{a}{e} + a.$$

Or, to put the formula in terms of a:

$$e = \frac{a}{m - a}$$
$$em - ea = a$$
$$-ea - a = -em$$
$$a(e + 1) = em$$
$$a = m\left(\frac{e}{e + 1}\right).$$

These formulas may be checked with reference to Figure 7–8. The figure tells us, for example, that when $AR = 4$, $MR = 2$. According to our formula,

$$e = \frac{a}{m - a}$$
$$= \frac{4}{2 - 4} = -2 = \frac{OP}{-PT} = \frac{4}{-2}.$$

The figure also indicates that when $AR = 2$, $e = OP/-PT = 2/-4 = -\frac{1}{2}$.

$$m = \frac{a}{e} + a$$
$$= \frac{2}{-\frac{1}{2}} + 2 = -4 + 2 = -2,$$

which is the value of MR when $AR = 2$.

Finally the figure shows that when $MR = -4$, $e = -\frac{1}{5}$, and $AR = 1$.

$$a = m\left(\frac{e}{e+1}\right)$$

$$= -4\left(\frac{-\frac{1}{5}}{-\frac{1}{5}+1}\right) = -4\left(\frac{-\frac{1}{5}}{\frac{4}{5}}\right) = -4(-\frac{1}{4}) = 1.$$

Retail Mark-ups and Elasticity of Demand

Elasticity of demand is an economist's term and may not be a part of the working vocabulary of the local businessman. However, the concept of elasticity, if not the term itself, is important to the businessman, and prices charged by retailers often reflect estimates of the elasticity of the demands for products. Often trade associations suggest to their members appropriate mark-ups to be applied to retailers' costs, and it is presumed that the retail prices arrived at in this way will, from the seller's point of view, be optimal. Suppose, for example, that a retail furniture dealer uses a mark-up of 100 percent: what costs him $100 he sells for $200. This, we may suppose, is the price which the seller believes will maximize his profit. But this mark-up, as we shall see, makes an implicit assumption that the elasticity of demand for the seller's product is -2. If in fact the elasticity of demand is something other than -2, a mark-up of 100 percent is inappropriate to establish the profit-maximizing price.

For this analysis we use the formula

$$e = \frac{a}{m - a},$$

where e is elasticity of demand, a is average revenue or price, and m is marginal revenue. But since we are seeking the elasticity of demand at the profit-maximizing price and at that price marginal cost equals marginal revenue, m in this instance is also marginal cost. Suppose that the cost of a table to the retailer is $100, and on the basis of his 100 percent mark-up, he prices it at $200. We may substitute $200 for a and $100 for m and solve for e:

$$e = \frac{200}{100 - 200} = \frac{200}{-100} = -2.$$

Suppose now that a grocer uses a mark-up of 12 percent. The assumed elasticity of demand for his product is then:

$$e = \frac{112}{100 - 112} = \frac{112}{-12} = -9\frac{1}{3}.$$

On the face of it, this is a curious result. In general, the elasticity of demand reflects the availability of good substitutes; the more readily available the substitutes, the greater the elasticity of demand. Although there are few good substitutes for furniture, substitutes for groceries are nonexistent; and yet our formula indicates that the elasticity of demand for groceries is greater than the elasticity of demand for furniture. The answer to this paradox is that we are considering the demand of an individual seller and not the demand for furniture or groceries in general. There are no good substitutes for food, but the groceries of firm A are a very good substitute for those offered by firm B. If firm B's beans cost 2 cents more than firm A's, and a particular grocer carries the brand of firm B, many housewives will go to another store where the price is lower. In most communities the number of grocery stores is relatively large, and the closer the situation approaches the conditions of pure competition, the higher will be the elasticity of demand for the products they carry. If the elasticity of demand equals infinity, as it would under pure competition, selling price would equal marginal revenue:

$$m = \frac{a}{e} + a$$

$$m = \frac{a}{\infty} + a = a.$$

SELECTED REFERENCES

Allen, Clark Lee. *Elementary Mathematics of Price Theory.* Belmont, Calif.: Wadsworth Publishing Co., Inc., 1962. Chaps. 12, 14, and 15.

Levenson, Albert M., and Babette S. Solon. *Outline of Price Theory.* New York: Holt, Rinehart & Winston, Inc., 1964. Chap. 3.

Robinson, Joan. *The Economics of Imperfect Competition.* London: Macmillan & Co., 1942. Chap. 2.

Stigler, George J. *The Theory of Price.* Rev. ed. New York: The Macmillan Co., 1952. Chap. 3.

PROBLEMS

PROBLEM I

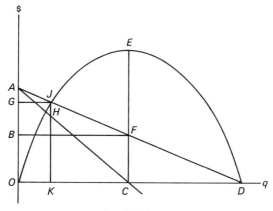

Fig. 7–10

In Figure 7–10 *AD* is a demand curve, *AC* is the marginal-revenue curve, and the parabola *OED* is the total-revenue curve.

1. If the price is *OB*, the quantity demanded is . . . _____

2. If the quantity demanded is *OC*, average revenue is _____
    or _____

3. When price is *OB*, total revenue is represented by
    the line . . . . ._____
                    or by the rectangle . . ._____
                    or by the triangle . . . ._____

4. When the quantity demanded is *OC*, elasticity of
    demand is . . . . ._____

5. When the price is *OB*, elasticity of demand is . ._____

6. If the price is *OG*, total revenue is represented by
    line . . . . ._____
                    or by rectangle . . . ._____
                    or by trapezoid . . . ._____

7. When quantity demanded is *OK*, average reve-
    nue is . . . . ._____

8. When price is *OG*, elasticity of demand is equal to _____

9. What is the numerical value of *OK*? . . . ._____

PROBLEM II

1. If total revenue increases as *q* increases, marginal revenue is (positive, negative, zero).

2. If total revenue decreases as *q* increases, marginal revenue is (positive, negative, zero).

3. If total revenue is at a maximum, marginal revenue is (positive, negative, zero).

4. If average revenue decreases as *q* increases, marginal revenue is (less than, greater than, equal to) average revenue.

5. If total revenue increases as *q* increases, elasticity of average revenue is (equal to, greater than, less than) one.

6. If total revenue decreases as *q* increases, elasticity of average revenue is (equal to, less than, greater than) one.

7. If total revenue is at a maximum, elasticity of average revenue is (equal to, greater than, less than) one.

8. If elasticity of average revenue is greater than one, marginal revenue is (positive, negative, zero).

9. If elasticity of average revenue is less than one, marginal revenue is (positive, negative, zero).

10. If elasticity of average revenue is equal to one, marginal revenue is (positive, negative, zero).

PROBLEM III

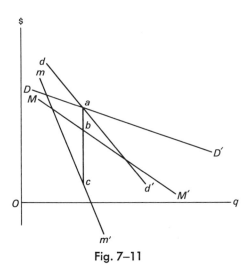

Fig. 7–11

Figure 7–11 shows four demand curves: DD', dd', Dad', and daD'; for each demand curve there is a corresponding marginal-revenue curve.

1. The marginal-revenue curve corresponding to DD' is . . . . _____

2. The marginal-revenue curve corresponding to dd' is . . . . _____

3. The marginal-revenue curve corresponding to Dad' is . . . . _____

4. The marginal-revenue curve corresponding to daD' is . . . . _____

5. The segment Da at any price is (more, less) elastic than da at the same price.

6. The segment aD' at any price is (more, less) elastic than ad' at the same price.

7. The segment Da at any quantity is (more, less) elastic than da at the same quantity.

8. The segment aD' at any quantity is (more, less) elastic than ad' at the same quantity.

PROBLEM IV

Given: $e = -OP/PT$.

1. Prove that $e = a/(m - a)$, where e = elasticity of demand, m = marginal revenue, and a = average revenue.

2. If $p = \$2$ and marginal revenue = $\$1.40$, what is e?_____

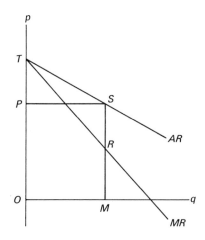

Fig. 7–12

3. What is e when $a = m$? . . . . ._____

4. What is e when $m = 0$? . . . . ._____

5. What is m when $e = 0$? . . . . ._____

PROBLEM V

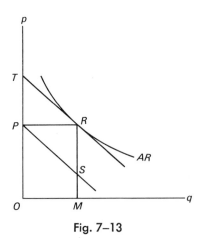

Fig. 7–13

Given: $a =$ average revenue; $m =$ marginal revenue; $e =$ elasticity of demand; and $m = a + a/e$. PS is parallel to TR. Without adding any lines or letters to the figure, prove that MS is marginal revenue at output OM.

PROBLEM VI

Assume that a linear demand curve has an elasticity of $-\frac{1}{4}$ at a price of 18.

1. The quantity demanded will become zero at price _____

2. Elasticity of demand will be -1 at price . . .———————

3. Marginal revenue at price $18 is . . . . .———————

4. If total revenue is at a maximum at $x = 1,800$, the equation for the demand curve is . . . . .———————

5. The equation for the total-revenue curve is . . .———————

6. The equation for the marginal-revenue curve is . .———————

7. Plot the average-revenue and marginal-revenue curves below:

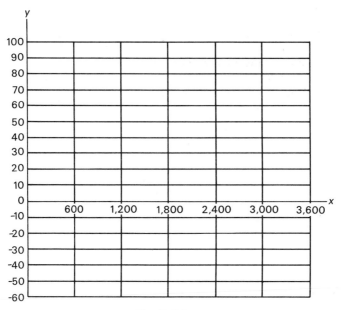

Fig. 7–14

PROBLEM VII

The equation for a demand curve is

$$\frac{x}{4} + \frac{y}{12} = 1.$$

1. The x-intercept of the demand curve is . . .———————

2. The y-intercept is . . . .———————

3. The slope of the curve is . . . .———————

4. Write the equation for the demand curve in the form $AR = y = mx + b$, where m is slope and b is the y-intercept. . . . .———————

5. The equation for the total-revenue curve is . . .———————

6. The equation for the marginal-revenue curve is . .———————

PROBLEM VIII

1. Suppose that it is known that the equation for a particular demand curve is $D = x = 5(10 - y)$, where $x =$ quantity demanded and $y =$ price.
   (a) What is the intercept of the demand curve on the y-axis? . . . . ._____
   (b) What is the intercept of the demand curve on the x-axis? . . . . ._____
   (c) What is the equation for average revenue? . ._____
   (d) What is the equation for total revenue? . ._____
   (e) What is the equation for marginal revenue? ._____

2. Now suppose that the equation for the demand curve is given by the general formula $D = x = a(b - y)$, where a and b are constants.
   (a) What is the intercept of the demand curve on the y-axis? . . . . ._____
   (b) What is the intercept of the demand curve on the x-axis? . . . . ._____
   (c) What is the equation for average revenue? . ._____
   (d) What is the equation for total revenue? . ._____
   (e) What is the equation for marginal revenue? ._____

PROBLEM IX

Given the demand function $AR = y = 10 - 2x$. Show that when $MR = 0$, $e = -1$, where MR is marginal revenue and e is elasticity of demand.

PROBLEM X

Given the demand function $AR = p = a - bx$, where a and b are positive constants.

1. What is the equation for total revenue? . . . ._____
2. What is the equation for marginal revenue? . ._____
3. What is the x-intercept of the demand curve? . ._____
4. What is the y-intercept of the demand curve? . ._____
5. What is the y-intercept of the marginal-revenue curve? . . . . ._____
6. What is the x-intercept of the marginal-revenue curve? . . . . ._____
7. What is the slope of the demand curve? . . . ._____
8. What is the slope of the marginal-revenue curve? ._____
9. Make a general statement about relative slopes and intercepts of linear demand curves and their corresponding marginal-revenue curves.

PROBLEM XI

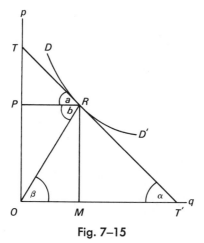

Fig. 7–15

Demonstrate that the elasticity of the demand curves DD' and TT' at point R is given by

$$e = -\frac{\tan b}{\tan a} = -\frac{\tan \beta}{\tan a}.$$

8

Average, Total, and Marginal Cost

The cost of a thing is what must be given up in order to acquire it. What is given up may be money, goods, leisure, income, security, or prestige. The cost of a year at college consists not only of the payments for tuition and fees, room and board, books, and clothes; more important in the aggregate than all of these is the income which the student might have made if he were not in college. The cost of a suit of clothes, instead of being thought of as $50, might accurately be viewed as the shoes, shirts, hat, movie tickets, and milkshakes which might have been bought with the $50 if it had not been spent on a suit. If a man invests money in his own business, a part of the cost of being in business for himself is the income which he could have enjoyed from investing his funds in the securities of another business. A part of the cost of owning one's own home is the loss of income that one could have had if the money had been invested in government bonds. This view of cost is known as *alternative* or *opportunity* cost, and is the meaning of cost in the most basic sense. Factors of production, such as labor and raw materials, must be paid for because they have alternative uses. To acquire factors for a particular use they must be bid away from other uses. If one uses walnut paneling in his den, he must bid the paneling from those who make cabinets for television sets. The bidding process in a private enterprise economy establishes prices, and costs are usually measured in money terms. But underlying money costs are opportunity costs.

Costs are of prime importance to economists and businessmen because in a private enterprise economy profits are the motivating force for productive activity. And profit is the difference between total revenue and total cost, or

$$\pi = TR - TC,$$

where π is profit, TR is total revenue, and TC is total cost. This seemingly obvious statement contains one complication. A part of the cost of doing business may consist of the return on one's own funds invested in one's business which could earn an income if invested elsewhere. Another part of the firm's cost may consist of the *imputed* cost to the owner of his working in his own business; if he were not working for himself, he could get an income by hiring out his services to someone else. There is a minimum "profit" which the firm must expect to earn to induce it to remain in business; this "normal" profit, as it is usually called, is the cost of keeping the firm in business, and it must be included as a part of total cost. Although profit is the difference between total revenue and total cost, it follows that total cost must include normal profit. When we say that a firm's total cost equals its total revenue, i.e., that the firm is "breaking even," we mean that the firm is making "normal" profit but is not making anything in excess of normal profit.

Business costs may be variously classified, and the classification which is best depends upon the uses to which it is to be put. The accountant's analysis of costs differs in certain respects from that of the economist, and presumably each classification serves the purposes of its users. From the point of view of the economist, all costs are divided into two parts, fixed and variable, or

$$TC = FC + VC.$$

Fixed costs are those which remain constant as output changes. Examples of fixed costs are: rent paid for land and buildings, which is a given amount per month or per year and is not affected by the output of the firm; the corporation president's salary, which is stipulated as a given amount per year; and certain kinds of insurance costs that are independent of the firm's rate of output. Fixed cost may also be viewed as the firm's total cost at zero output. If the plant should be closed by a strike, or if the owner should padlock his firm and go fishing, certain costs would nonetheless continue; these are the fixed costs.

Variable costs are those which do change as output changes. Most labor costs are variable costs—the greater the output, the more labor must be hired. Raw materials represent variable costs; it takes more leather to make 1,000 pairs of shoes than to make 500 pairs. Electric power costs are for the most part variable; the firm would have a certain minimum cost for electricity even at output zero, but beyond that, power costs increase as output increases.

Total and Average Costs

Because total cost is made up of two components, the relationship between average cost and total cost is somewhat more complex than average-total relationships as applied to other economic magnitudes such as utility and revenue. Average total cost is the summation of average fixed cost and average variable cost:

$$atc = afc + avc.$$

We begin with an analysis of the relationship between total fixed cost and average fixed cost.

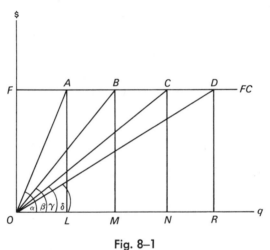

Fig. 8–1

The distinguishing characteristic of total fixed costs is that they remain constant as output changes; that is,

$$FC = K,$$

where K is a constant. Average fixed cost is, accordingly, total fixed cost divided by output:

$$afc = \frac{K}{x}.$$

This means that average fixed cost becomes smaller as output increases, approaching but never reaching zero as output becomes very great. In Figure 8–1, total fixed cost is equal to OF at any output, and the total fixed cost curve is the horizontal line FC. At output OL the average fixed cost is the total fixed cost, LA, divided by the output OL, which is the tangent of angle *a.* At the greater output *OM*, average fixed cost is the tangent of angle β. But since angle β is smaller than angle α, average fixed cost is less at output *OM* than at output *OL*. As output continues to increase, the angle formed by a line from the *FC* curve to the origin and the *x*-axis becomes smaller, and the average fixed cost becomes smaller as output increases.

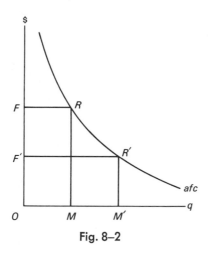

Fig. 8–2

A typical average fixed-cost curve is represented in Figure 8–2. This curve is of the general form

$$y = \frac{K}{x},$$

where K is a constant. Such a curve is described by mathematicians as a rectangular hyperbola. As x increases, y approaches but never reaches the x-axis. At $x = 1$, $y = K$; i.e., average fixed cost equals total fixed cost when output equals one. For values of x less than one, y increases and approaches but never reaches the y-axis. That is, the average fixed-cost curve is asymptotic to both axes. In Figure 8–2, when output is *OM*, average fixed cost is *OF*. If we multiply the fixed cost per unit of output by the output, we get total fixed cost. At output *OM*, accordingly, total fixed cost is *OF* × *OM* which is equal to the rectangle *OFRM*. If we now consider output *OM'*, which is twice as great as *OM*, average fixed cost will be *OF'*, which is one-half of *OF*, and the rectangle *OF'R'M'*, which represents total fixed cost at the larger output, is equal to rectangle *OFRM*. Any rectangle which can be inscribed under the average fixed-cost curve will have the same area as *OFRM*, which reflects the fact that total fixed cost is a constant. This may be written

$$xy = K,$$

where *x* is output, *y* is average fixed cost, and *K* is a constant equal to total fixed cost.

It is apparent that if fixed costs comprise a large part of total costs, average total cost will decline over a wide range as output increases. Decreasing costs are usually thought of as being characteristic of public utilities such as power and transportation companies, since such a large part of their total costs are fixed; their cost per unit of output decreases over a wide range as their output increases. Suppose that a die to stamp out the right front fender of a Chevrolet costs $1,000,000. If the die is used to produce only one car, the die cost per car is, of course, $1,000,000. But if the die can be used in the production of 1,000,000 Chevrolets, the die cost per car is only $1. And if the die could be used in the production of 10,000,000 cars, the die cost per car

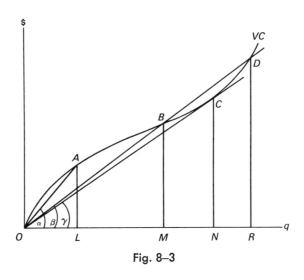

Fig. 8–3

would be only 10¢! It is clear that businesses characterized by high fixed costs need to operate on a large scale in order to bring down unit costs. This also explains why automobile manufacturers frequently use the same basic body shells for their luxury cars and their less expensive cars.

Next we turn to the relationship between total variable cost and average variable cost. It is generally assumed that the total variable-cost curve for most firms assumes the general form of curve *VC* in Figure 8–3. It will be noted that at output *OL* average variable cost is equal to tan *α*; at output *OM* average variable cost is equal to tan *β*; and at *ON* average variable cost is equal to tan *γ*. But since these angles become smaller as output becomes greater, average variable cost decreases from output *OL* to output *ON*. At *ON* average variable cost is at a minimum; if the angle were any smaller than *γ*, the line from the origin would miss the *VC* curve entirely. The minimum average variable cost is, accordingly, tan γ. As output increases from *ON* to *OR*, average variable cost increases; average variable cost at *OR* is equal to average-variable cost at *OM*, both being equal to tan β.

The average variable-cost curve corresponding to the total variable cost curve of Figure 8–3 is drawn in Figure 8–4. Average variable cost decreases as output increases until an output of *ON* is reached. At *ON* average variable cost is at a minimum. Beyond *ON* average variable cost increases as output increases. At outputs *OM* and *OR* average variable costs are equal. In general we may argue that if the average variable-cost curve assumes the U-shape of the *avc* curve of Figure 8–4, the total variable-cost curve must have the general form of the *VC* curve of Figure 8–3.

The relationship between the total cost curve and the average total-cost curve is essentially the same as between total variable cost and average

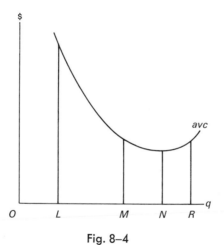

Fig. 8–4

variable cost. In Figure 8–5 both total cost and total variable-cost curves are drawn. It will be noted that the total cost curve is identical to the total variable-cost curve except that it has been raised vertically by the amount of the total fixed cost. At any output the total cost is equal to the total variable cost plus the total fixed cost. At output *ON*, for example, $TC = NV + VR$, and $VR = OF$. It will also be noted that the average variable cost reaches a minimum at output *OM*, where average variable cost is equal to tan α. Average total cost is at a minimum at output *ON*, and at this point is equal to tan β. The minimum average total cost always comes at a greater output than the minimum average variable cost.

The relationship between average and total costs can, of course, be demonstrated algebraically. Suppose that we have given the total cost function

$$TC = x^3 - 4x^2 + 8x + 4.$$

Since 4 is the only term which does not change as x (output) changes, the total fixed cost must be 4. This is confirmed by letting $x = 0$; at output zero

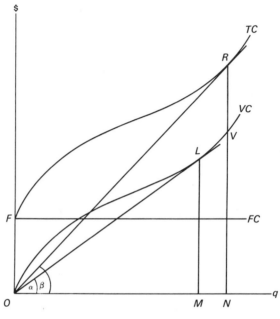

Fig. 8–5

the total cost is 4; as we have seen, the total cost at output zero is the total fixed cost. We may, accordingly, write

$$FC = 4.$$

Total cost minus total fixed cost is total variable cost. The terms in the total-cost function which contain the variable x will comprise total variable cost:

$$VC = x^3 - 4x^2 + 8x.$$

Average total cost is total cost divided by x:

$$atc = \frac{TC}{x} = x^2 - 4x + 8 + \frac{4}{x}.$$

Similarly,

$$afc = \frac{FC}{x} = \frac{4}{x},$$

and

$$avc = \frac{VC}{x} = x^2 - 4x + 8.$$

Average and total costs are computed in Table 8–1, and average costs are plotted in Figure 8–6 and total costs in Figure 8–7.

TABLE 8–1

Output	FC	VC	TC	afc	avc	atc
0	4	0	4	—	—	—
1	4	5	9	4	5	9
2	4	8	12	2	4	6
3	4	15	19	$1\frac{1}{3}$	5	$6\frac{1}{3}$
4	4	32	36	1	8	9
5	4	65	69	$\frac{4}{5}$	13	$13\frac{4}{5}$

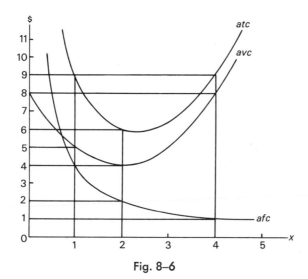

Fig. 8–6

It will be noted in Figure 8–6 that the *afc* curve decreases as *x* increases. When $x = 1$, $afc = 4$, and FC is 4; when $x = 2$, $afc = 2$, and $FC = 4$; when $x = 4$, $afc = 1$, and $FC = 4$. Both *avc* and *atc* are U-shaped curves; they decrease, reach a minimum, and then increase as *x* increases. The vertical distance between the *avc* and *atc* curves at any output is equal to the average fixed cost at that output. When, for example, $x = 1$, $atc = 9$ and $avc = 5$, a difference of 4, and *afc* at $x = 1$ is 4. When $x = 4$, $atc = 9$ and $avc = 8$, a difference of 1, and *afc* at $x = 4$ is 1. The average fixed cost at any output could be determined even if the *afc* curve had not been plotted, and for this reason the *afc* curve is often omitted from average-cost charts.

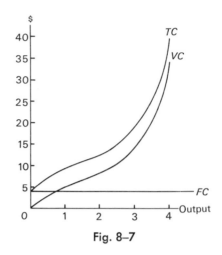

Fig. 8–7

Total and Marginal Costs

Marginal cost is the rate of change of the total cost as output changes. Viewed geometrically, marginal cost at any output is the slope of the total-cost curve at that output. Marginal cost is frequently described as the additional cost of producing an additional unit of output. As in the case of marginal revenue, it is necessary to distinguish between discrete and continuous measures of marginal cost. If we know the total-cost function and if x is continuously variable, the marginal-cost function is the derivative of the total-cost function:

$$mc_c = \frac{dTC}{dx}.$$

If, however, we do not have the total-cost function, or if output can be varied only by discrete increments, we must use discrete marginal cost, which is the change in total cost divided by the change in output:

$$mc_d = \frac{\Delta TC}{\Delta x}.$$

If $\Delta x = 1$, discrete marginal cost is the additional cost of producing an additional unit of output.

Since the only component of total cost which changes as output changes is variable cost, marginal cost is also the rate of change of variable cost as output changes. Viewed analytically, the only difference between the total-cost function and the variable-cost function is a constant term, and since the derivative of the constant term is zero, the derivative of the total-cost function and the derivative of the total variable-cost function are equal, and we may write

$$mc_c = \frac{dVC}{dx},$$

and

$$mc_d = \frac{\Delta VC}{\Delta x}.$$

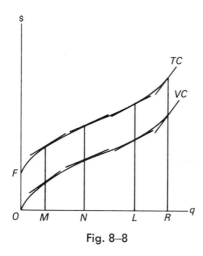

Fig. 8–8

In Figure 8–8 typical total-cost and total variable-cost curves have been plotted. Several points with reference to the relationship between marginal cost and total cost may be noted:

1. The slopes of the total-cost curve and the total variable-cost curve are positive at all outputs. Since the slope of the total-cost curve at any output *is* the marginal cost at that output, marginal cost must everywhere be greater than zero. This means simply that it always costs more to produce a greater output than a smaller output.

2. At any output the slope of the TC curve is equal to the slope of the VC curve at that output; that is, the tangent to the TC curve at any x-value is parallel to the tangent of the VC curve at that x-value. If total fixed cost should increase, the TC curve would slide vertically up the y-axis, but the slope of the TC curve at any output would be unchanged. A change in fixed cost, accordingly, will not affect marginal cost. An increase in rent, for example, will not affect the *additional* cost of producing an additional unit of output since the higher rent will have to be paid whether or not the additional unit of output is produced.

3. In Figure 8–8, as output increases from OM to ON, the slope of the total curve decreases. But as output increases from ON to OL and from OL to OR, the slope of the total curves increases. This

means that for small outputs total cost is increasing at a decreasing rate; it will be noted that at outputs OM and ON the tangents to the total curves lie above the curves. For greater outputs, total costs are increasing at an increasing rate; the tangents to the total curves at outputs OL and OR lie below the total curves. This means that marginal cost for small outputs, although positive, is decreasing; for larger outputs marginal costs are increasing, making the marginal-cost curve also U-shaped.

Average and Marginal Costs

As we have seen, if

$$TC = x^3 - 4x^2 + 8x + 4,$$

then

$$afc = \frac{FC}{x} = \frac{4}{x}$$

and

$$avc = \frac{VC}{x} = x^2 - 4x + 8$$

and

$$atc = \frac{TC}{x} = x^2 - 4x + 8 + \frac{4}{x}.$$

Since marginal cost is the derivative of the total-cost function, which is equal to the derivative of the variable-cost function, we may write

$$mc = \frac{dTC}{dx} = \frac{dVC}{dx} = 3x^2 - 8x + 8.$$

The average-cost columns of Table 8–1 have been reproduced in Table 8–2 with continuous marginal-cost and discrete marginal-cost columns added. The average and marginal curves have been plotted in Figure 8–9.

Several observations about the relationship between average- and marginal-cost curves may be made from Figure 8–9 and Table 8–2:

1. As previously noted, the vertical distance between the *avc* curve and the *atc* curve at any given output is equal to the average fixed cost at that output.
2. Although it is meaningless to talk about the average cost of producing zero units, it will be noted that in a purely mathematical sense the average variable-cost curve and the marginal-cost curve have the same intercept on the y-axis.
3. As long as average variable cost is decreasing as output increases,

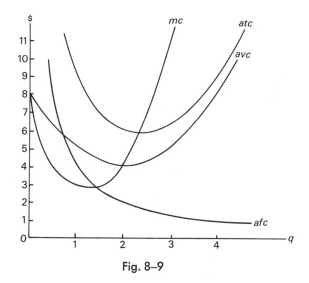

Fig. 8–9

marginal cost is less than average variable cost. (Note that this is not the same thing as saying that as long as average variable cost is decreasing, marginal cost is decreasing; the fact is, as reference to Figure 8–9 will indicate, that for some range of output marginal cost will be increasing as average variable cost is decreasing.)

4. When average variable cost is at a minimum, marginal cost equals average variable cost.

5. When average variable cost increases as output increases, marginal cost is greater than average variable cost.

6. When average total cost is decreasing as output increases, marginal cost is less than average total cost.

7. When average total cost is at a minimum, marginal cost equals average total cost.

8. When average total cost increases with an increase in output, marginal cost is greater than average total cost.

9. As previously noted, a change in total fixed cost will not affect the marginal-cost curve; if there is a change in total fixed cost, the average total-cost curve will slide along the marginal-cost curve in such a way as to make the marginal-cost curve cut the new average total-cost curve at the lowest point on the average total-cost curve.

TABLE 8–2

Output	afc	avc	atc	mc_e	mc_d
0	—	—	—	8	—
1	4	5	9	3	5
2	2	4	6	4	3
3	$1\frac{1}{3}$	5	$6\frac{1}{3}$	11	7
4	1	8	9	24	17
5	$\frac{4}{5}$	13	$13\frac{4}{5}$	43	33

POSTPRANDIUM

Empirical studies of firms' costs made in recent years have led a number of economists to believe that cost curves do not always assume the forms typically assigned to them in price theory, but, on the contrary, are linear. A brief consideration of this matter will illustrate both the usefulness and limitations of price theory.

One cannot, of course, determine the cost functions of a particular firm without analyzing actual empirical data. Even when the cost accountant's data are available, the determination of actual cost functions is difficult because many of the accountant's figures are estimates made on the basis of standard rules and assumptions, and, as we have seen, since the objectives of the cost accountant differ in significant respects from the objectives of the

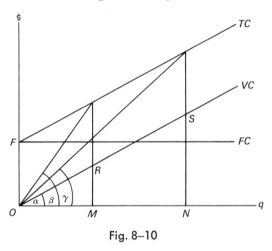

Fig. 8–10

price theorist, his figures do not provide the economist with the data which he needs or in the form in which he needs it. The construction by an economist of cost curves from accounting data is, accordingly, perilous, and errors in the transformation of data may result and lead to invalid conclusions.

Suppose that our study of the cost data of a particular firm causes us to believe that the total variable-cost function is linear. Since the total fixed-cost function is linear, the total-cost function will also be linear. The three total curves will assume the form of Figure 8–10.

Let us see what this implies with respect to the shape of the average- and marginal-cost curves. In terms of Figure 8–10, average variable cost is equal to tan a for any output. This means that the average variable-cost curve is linear and horizontal. The marginal cost is the slope of the total variable-cost curve, and this too is equal to tan a; this means that at all outputs $mc = avc = K$. The average total-cost curve will, however, be nonlinear. At output OM, *atc*

= tan β, and at output ON, atc = tan γ. As output increases, average total cost decreases. Since the *atc* curve and the *avc* curve are separated at any output by the amount of the average fixed cost at that output, and since *afc* decreases as output increases, the *atc* curve will approach the horizontal *avc* as

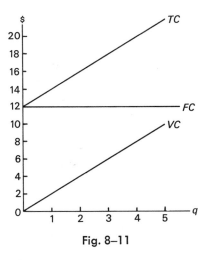

Fig. 8–11

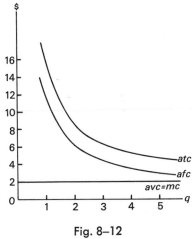

Fig. 8–12

a limit. This means that the *atc* will never reach a minimum but will always decrease with an increase in output.

Suppose that the total-cost function is given by

$$TC = 2x + 12.$$

It follows that

$$FC = 12$$
$$VC = 2x$$
$$atc = 2 + \frac{12}{x}$$
$$afc = \frac{12}{x}$$
$$avc = 2$$
$$mc = 2.$$

The total curves are represented in Figure 8–11 and the average and marginal curves in Figure 8–12.

If this firm is assumed to sell in a market which is less than purely competitive, its average-revenue curve will be negatively inclined, and so will its marginal-revenue curve. As we will see in the next chapter, the firm will maximize profits if it produces to the point where marginal cost equals marginal revenue. If the cost curves assume the forms represented in Figure 8–12, there is no problem with the conventional analysis. The firm will, of course, be operating in a range where average total costs are decreasing, but this is also normally true if we make the usual assumption that the atc curve assumes U shape. If, however, the firm sells in a purely competitive market, its average-revenue and marginal-revenue curves will be horizontal. If both marginal-cost and marginal-revenue curves are horizontal, they will never intersect. If the horizontal marginal-revenue curve lies above the horizontal marginal-cost curve, one would suppose that the firm would increase its output to infinity. Since as a matter of fact purely competitive firms do not increase their outputs infinitely, we must conclude either that such firms do not have linear total variable-cost functions or that they do not attempt to maximize profits. Even if we reject the profit-maximizing assumption, it would appear that purely competitive firms would tend to become so large that the number of them which the market could support would be limited, and if the number of firms became small, the market would no longer be purely competitive, and the firms' marginal-revenue curves would no longer be horizontal! The conclusion seems inevitable, accordingly, that if the total-variable-cost function is linear, the firm must be operating in a less than purely competitive market. And this we can determine without consulting any empirical data.

A second conclusion sometimes drawn from empirical studies of firms' costs may be rejected out-of-hand. Studies of costs have led some writers to believe that, at least over a wide range of outputs, the average total-cost function is linear and constant. Let us see why, on strictly theoretical grounds, such a case is most unlikely.

If the average total-cost curve is a horizontal line, the total-cost curve, on the basis of principles we have developed, must also be linear and pass through the origin. If the total-cost curve is linear, the total variable-cost curve must be linear and parallel to the total-cost curve, the vertical distance between the total-cost curve and the total variable-cost curve at any output being equal to the total-fixed cost. This means that at output zero, total variable cost must be negative, the negative variable cost just cancelling the positive fixed cost, making the total cost equal to zero. The nature of total and average costs implied by constant average total costs is indicated in Figures 8–13 and 8–14.

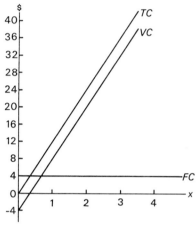

Fig. 8–13

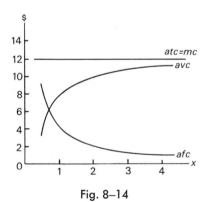

Fig. 8–14

In Figure 8–13 the total variable-cost function is given by

$$VC = 12x - 4$$

and

$$FC = 4$$

so that

$$TC = 12x - 4 + 4 = 12x.$$

It follows, accordingly, that

$$atc = 12$$
$$mc = 12$$
$$afc = \frac{4}{x}$$
$$avc = 12 - \frac{4}{x}.$$

Now, it would seem to be clear that at output zero, total variable cost—payments, for example, for labor and materials—cannot in fact be less than zero. It follows, therefore, that the average-total-cost curve cannot be a horizontal line throughout its entire length. But might it not be possible for the average-total-cost curve to be horizontal over a wide range, say between outputs 2 and 4 in Figure 8–14? Even this would seem to be highly unlikely and certainly not a representative case. Our average-variable-cost function tells us that at any output average variable cost is equal to the constant average total cost minus the average fixed cost at that output. As a matter of definition average fixed cost must constantly decrease as output increases; but what would cause average variable cost to increase as output increases just enough to offset the decrease in average fixed cost? If through some unlikely coincidence this should happen, the slightest change in either total fixed cost or total variable cost would upset the delicate balance, and average total cost would no longer be constant. If empirical data seem to suggest that the average-total-cost curve is a horizontal line, it seems reasonable to conclude either that the data are inaccurate or that they have been improperly interpreted.

SELECTED REFERENCES

Allen, Clark Lee. *Elementary Mathematics of Price Theory*. Belmont, Calif.: Wadsworth Publishing Co., Inc., 1962. Chap. 7.

Bain, Joe S. *Price Theory*. New York: Holt, Rinehart & Winston, Inc., 1952. Pp. 83–110.

Bober, M. M. *Intermediate Price and Income Theory*. Rev. ed. New York: W. W. Norton & Company, Inc., 1955. Pp. 146–167.

Hall, R. L., and C. J. Hitch. "Price Theory and Business Behavior," *Oxford Economic Papers*, 2 (May 1939), 12–33.

Leftwich, Richard H. *The Price System and Resource Allocation*. 3rd ed. New York: Holt, Rinehart & Winston, Inc., 1966. Pp. 126–141, 152–155.

Levenson, Albert M. and Babette S. Solon. *Outline of Price Theory*. New York: Holt, Rinehart & Winston, Inc., 1964. Pp. 139–144.

Machlup, Fritz. "Marginal Analysis and Empirical Research," *American Economic Review*, 36 (September 1946), 519–554.

Staehle, Hans. "The Measurement of Statistical Cost Functions: An Appraisal of Some Recent Contributions," *American Economic Review*, 32 (1942),

321–333. Reprinted in George J. Stigler and Kenneth E. Boulding, eds., *Readings in Price Theory.* Homewood, Ill.: Richard D. Irwin, Inc., 1952. Pp. 264–279.

PROBLEMS

PROBLEM I

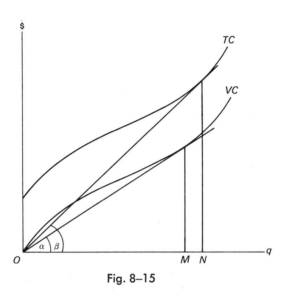

Fig. 8–15

1. When average variable cost is a minimum, output = ..._____

2. When average variable cost is a minimum, average variable cost = tan . . . . ._____

3. When average total cost is a minimum, output = _____

4. When average total cost is a minimum, average total cost = tan . . . . ._____

5. When average variable cost is a minimum, marginal cost is (equal to, greater than) average variable cost.

6. For outputs less than *OM,* marginal cost is (equal to, less than, greater than) average variable cost.

7. For outputs greater than *OM,* marginal cost is (equal to, less than, greater than) average variable cost.

8. When average total cost is a minimum, marginal cost is (equal to, less than, greater than) average total cost.

9. For outputs less than *ON,* marginal cost is (equal to, less than, greater than) average total cost.

10. For outputs greater than ON, marginal cost is (equal to, less than, greater than) average total cost.

11. At output OM, average variable cost is (equal to, less than, greater than) average total cost.

12. At output OM, marginal cost is (equal to, less than, greater than) average variable cost, which is (equal to, less than, greater than) average total cost.

13. If at output OM, marginal cost is (equal to, less than, greater than) average total cost, OM must represent a (larger, smaller) output than ON; i.e., minimum average variable cost must come at a (smaller, larger) output than minimum average total cost.

PROBLEM II

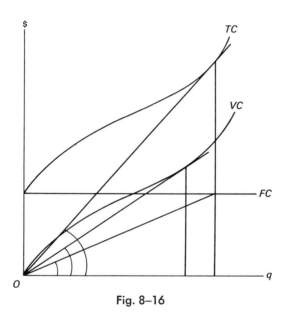

Fig. 8–16

Locate the following points on the above figure:

1. VC when AVC is a minimum is AB.

2. AVC when AVC is a minimum is tan a.

3. TC when ATC is a minimum is CD.

4. ATC when ATC is a minimum is tan b.

5. FC when ATC is a minimum is OE.

6. AFC when ATC is a minimum is tan c.

7. Output when AVC is a minimum is .   .   .   ._____

8. Output when ATC is a minimum is .   .   .   ._____

9. Output when $MC = AVC$ is . . . . . . _____

10. Output when $MC = ATC$ is . . . . . . _____

PROBLEM III

Complete the following table:

Output	TC	FC	VC	MC	ATC	AFC	AVC
0	$ 20						
1	30						
2	45						
3	70						
4	125						
5	225						

Fig. 8–17

PROBLEM IV

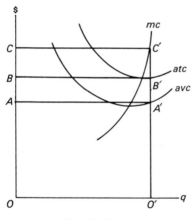

Fig. 8–18

At output OO':

1. $avc =$ . . . . ._____ or _____

2. $VC =$ . . . $= ATC$ . . . . . ._____

3. $atc =$ . . . . ._____ or _____

4. $TC =$ . . . . ._____

5. $afc =$ . . . . ._____ or _____

6. $FC =$ . . . . ._____

7. $mc =$ . . . . ._____ or _____

PROBLEM V

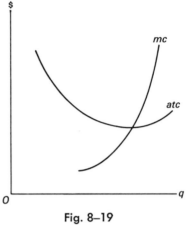

Fig. 8–19

The above figure represents the basic cost data for a given firm. Assume a significant increase in fixed costs. Make the appropriate changes in the figure.

PROBLEM VI

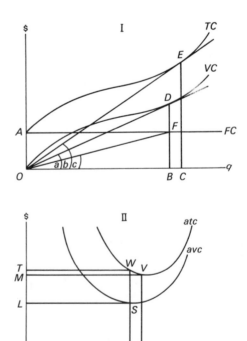

Fig. 8–20

Although the scales on both *x*- and *y*-axes are different, Chart I and Chart II are assumed to represent the same cost data. The problem consists of locating the point, line, or area on Chart II which corresponds to the indicated part of Chart I.

1. *OB* _____

2. *BD* _____

3. *OC* _____

4. *CE* _____

5. tan *a* _____

6. tan *b* _____

7. tan *c* _____

8. *OA* _____

PROBLEM VII

1. If $TC = ax^2$ where *a* is a constant, what are:

   (a) *MC* . . . . _____
   (b) *ATC* . . . . _____
   (c) *FC* . . . . _____
   (d) *AFC* . . . . _____
   (e) *VC* . . . . _____
   (f) *AVC* . . . . _____

2. For what value of *x* will
   (a) $MC = TC$? . . . . _____
   (b) $ATC = TC$? . . . . _____

PROBLEM VIII

Fill in the following table from the data given below:

Output	TC	MC	ATC	AFC	VC	AVC
0						
1						
2						
3						
4						
5						
6						
7						
8						

Fig. 8–21

1. *AFC* for 5 units of output is 1,008.

2. *AVC* for 4 units of output is 850.

3. *TC* is increased by 900 when the 5th unit of output is produced.

4. The *ATC* of 6 units of output is 1,740.

5. *TC* for 7 units of output is 11,840.

6. *TVC* is increased by 2,000 when the 8th unit of output is produced.

7. *AFC* plus *AVC* for 2 units of output is 3,470.

8. *ATC* is decreased 890 when output is increased from 2 to 3 units.

9. It costs 1,000 more to produce 1 unit of output than to remain shut down.

9

Prices and Output
under
Pure Competition

The principal distinguishing characteristic of a purely competitive market is the inability of one firm to affect the prices of the factors which it buys or of the products which it sells. This comes about because by definition a purely competitive market is one which includes a large number of buyers and sellers, so many that no one of them can exert any perceptible influence on prices. Rather, prices are determined by the impersonal demand-and-supply forces of the market. After market price has been established by demand and supply each individual firm is free to make such output adjustments as are appropriate, but the firm must accept the price which has been determined for it and for all other firms in the market. Price competition is completely foreign to the purely competitive market. No firm can sell any output at a price even slightly higher than market price, and since each firm can sell all of its output at market price, there is no inducement for it to cut prices. In a purely competitive market, also, the product of one firm is indistinguishable from that of all other firms in the market.

In earlier chapters we have considered the nature of the demand function. We have derived demand curves from marginal-utility curves and from indifference curves, and we have discussed the concept of elasticity of demand. Before we can explore pricing in a purely competitive market, we must consider the supply function. But before doing that we must give attention to the question of a firm's most profitable output.

Competitive Firm's Most Profitable Output

One of the most important propositions in price theory is that, as has already been mentioned, if a firm is to maximize profits, it must produce to the point where marginal cost equals marginal revenue. This maxim holds in all cases, whether the firm sells in a competitive or a monopolistic market. Since for the purely competitive firm marginal revenue is equal to price at all outputs, the rule in this special case may be put in this form: produce to the point where marginal cost equals price. The validity of this proposition may

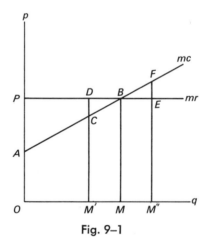

Fig. 9–1

be established as a matter of common sense. If the production of an additional unit of output will add more to the firm's revenue than to its costs, the production of that unit will add something to the firm's total profits. If, however, the additional cost of producing one more unit is greater than the resulting additional revenue, the firm's profits will be reduced if the production of that unit is undertaken. In order to maximize profits, the firm should expand output as long as marginal cost is less than or equal to marginal revenue.

This point can be demonstrated with reference to Figure 9–1. The marginal-revenue curve is represented as a horizontal line so that marginal revenue at all outputs is equal to price, OP. That this is characteristic of purely competitive firms may be demonstrated as follows:

We begin by noting that

$$TR = pq,$$

where p is price and q is quantity sold. A change in price and quantity would result in a change in total revenue:

$$\Delta TR = (p + \Delta p)(q + \Delta q) - pq$$
$$= q\Delta p + p\Delta q + \Delta p\Delta q = (p + \Delta p)\Delta q + q\Delta p.$$

It follows that marginal revenue is given by

$$MR = \frac{\Delta TR}{\Delta q} = p + \Delta p + q\frac{\Delta p}{\Delta q}.$$

For a firm selling in a purely competitive market, price is constant for all outputs, and a change in output is accompanied by a Δp of zero. But if $\Delta p = 0$,

$$MR = p + 0 + q\frac{0}{\Delta q} = p.$$

In Figure 9–1 the marginal-revenue curve is a horizontal line, and as a matter of convenience, the marginal-cost curve is also represented as a linear function. Marginal cost and marginal revenue are equal at output OM, and this is the profit-maximizing output. At this output the firm's total revenue is equal to the area under the marginal-revenue curve, which is the rectangle $OPBM$. The area under the firm's marginal-cost curve is total variable cost; this is the trapezoid $OABM$. The difference between total revenue and total variable cost is the triangle APB. Total profit will be the difference between the area of APB and the firm's total fixed cost, which cannot be determined from Figure 9–1. If total fixed cost is greater than APB, the firm will operate at a loss, but the loss will be smaller at output OM than at any other output, either greater or smaller. If total fixed cost is less than APB, profit will be positive and greater at output OM than at any other output.

Let us assume for convenience that total fixed cost is zero. The area APB in Figure 9–1 can then be called profit. At any smaller output than OM, profit will be less than APB. At output OM', for example, total revenue would be $OPDM'$, total cost would be $OACM'$, and total profit would be $APDC$, which is less than APB by an amount equal to CDB. Since at output OM' marginal cost is $M'C$ and marginal revenue is $M'D$, and $M'C$ is less than $M'D$, it is clear that OM' is less than the profit-maximizing output. On the other hand, consider an output greater than OM, such as OM''. Total revenue at this output is $OPEM''$, total cost is $OAFM''$, and total profit is APB minus BFE, which is clearly less than APB. At output OM'', marginal cost, $M''F$, is greater than marginal revenue, $M''E$, and this is a signal to the firm that it must contract output if it is to maximize profits.

This point can also be made with the use of total-revenue and total-cost curves. We know that total profit is the difference between total revenue and total cost:

$$\pi = TR - TC.$$

We also know that total revenue is equal to price times quantity:

$$TR = y = pq,$$

where p is the constant price and q is the quantity of output. Recalling that the equation for a straight line is

$$y = mx + b,$$

it follows that in the total-revenue function p is equal to m, the slope of the total-revenue curve, and b is equal to 0; that is, for a purely competitive firm, the total-revenue curve is linear and passes through the origin with a slope equal to price.

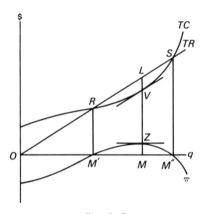

Fig. 9–2

In Figure 9–2 such a total-revenue curve together with a typical total-cost curve has been drawn. It will be noted that at outputs OM' and OM'' total cost and total revenue are equal; these are the break-even points. Between OM' and OM'' total revenue is greater than total cost, and at any output the profit is equal to the vertical distance between the cost and revenue curves. A tangent to the total-cost curve parallel to the total-revenue curve has been drawn in the figure; the tangent touches the total-cost curve at point V. It is clear by inspection that the distance VL is greater than any other vertical distance between the total-cost and total-revenue curves between outputs OM' and OM''. That is to say that profits are maximized at output OM, where total revenue is ML, total cost is MV, and profit is VL. But at output OM, the slope of the total-cost curve is equal to the slope of the total-revenue curve. Since, as we have seen in earlier chapters, the slope of the total-cost curve is marginal cost and the slope of the total-revenue curve is marginal revenue, the most profitable output is determined at the point where marginal cost equals marginal revenue. We may say that total profit will be maximized when

$$\frac{dTC}{dq} = \frac{dTR}{dq}.$$

In Figure 9–2 the profit function has also been sketched in. It will be noted that for outputs less than OM' and outputs greater than OM'' profit is negative. At output OM profit is at a maximum and equal to MZ, which, in turn, is equal to VL. When profits are at a maximum, the slope of the profit function is equal to zero. That is to say that profits are maximized when

$$\frac{d\pi}{dq} = 0.$$

One modification of the marginal-cost-equals-marginal-revenue rule must be made. It is possible that marginal revenue and marginal cost may be equal at more than one output. In Figure 9–3 marginal revenue and marginal cost are equal at outputs OM' and OM, and $d\pi/dq = 0$ at both outputs. At output OM', however, profits are at a minimum value rather than a maximum. In order for $d\pi/dq = 0$ to establish a maximum-profit output, the slope of the MR curve must be less than the slope of the MC curve. That is, for maximum profits

$$\frac{dMR}{dq} < \frac{dMC}{dq}.$$

At output OM', the slope of the marginal-revenue curve is zero and the slope of the marginal-cost curve is less than zero. Since the slope of the MR curve is greater than the slope of the MC curve, OM' represents an output of minimum and not maximum profits. At output OM, however, the slope of the MR curve is zero and the slope of the MC curve is greater than zero, and OM is an output of maximum profits. In general, if the intersection of MC and MR curves is to locate a maximum-profit output, the MC curve must cut the MR curve from below.

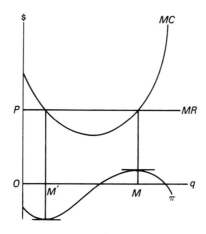

Fig. 9–3

Marginal Cost and the Firm's Supply Curve

We are now ready to derive the competitive firm's supply curve. In Figure 9–4 the average-total-cost, average-variable-cost, and the marginal-cost curves have been drawn. If the price is OP_1, the average-revenue and marginal-revenue curves will be represented by the same horizontal line drawn from P_1; marginal revenue will equal marginal cost at point B, and the most profitable output will be OM_1. We may reason, accordingly, that if the price is OP_1, the firm will supply OM_1 units of output, and the profit per unit will be equal to AB. If, however, the price falls to OP_2, total cost per unit of output will just equal total revenue per unit, and the firm will be at the break-even output. At price OP_3 the firm will supply OM_3 units of output, and the loss per unit of output will be equal to DE. But note that DE is the average fixed cost at output OM_3; this is true since the total unit cost at this output is M_3E and the variable unit cost is M_3D, and the difference, DE, must be the fixed unit cost. The total loss at output OM_3, accordingly, is equal to the firm's total fixed cost; at price OP_3 the firm just covers variable costs, and fixed costs represent a loss. At any price lower than OP_3 the firm would not even cover all variable costs, and its losses would exceed its total fixed cost. But if the firm shuts down and produces zero output, it can limit its total loss to an amount equal to total fixed cost. The firm, if it is to maximize profits (or, in this case, if it is to minimize losses) will not produce at all below price OP_3. Price OP_3 is, accordingly, the shutdown price, and output OM_3 is the shutdown output. At any price below OP_3, the firm will supply zero units; at price OP_3 it will supply OM_3 units; at price OP_2 it will supply OM_2 units; and at price OP_1 it will supply OM_1 units. We may generalize by saying that that part of a competitive firm's marginal-cost curve which lies above its average-variable-cost curve is its short-run supply curve.

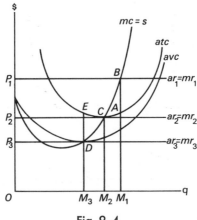

Fig. 9–4

Elasticity of Supply

The part of the competitive firm's marginal-cost curve which lies above its average-variable-cost curve is its *short-run* supply curve because we have assumed sufficient time for the firm to make appropriate modifications in its purchases of variable factors in response to a change in price but not sufficient time for it to change the amount of fixed factors which it employs. The period of time during which the firm can adjust its use of variable factors but cannot change its use of fixed factors is what the economist means by the short-run period. The firm's short-run supply curve normally has a positive slope because that part of its marginal-cost curve which lies above its average-variable-cost curve normally has a positive slope. As the price rises, the quantity supplied increases. But the responsiveness of supply to a change in price may vary from time to time and from commodity to commodity; that is, supply may exhibit varying degrees of price elasticity.

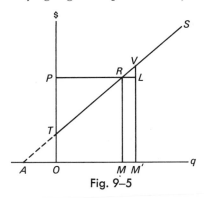

Fig. 9–5

As was pointed out in an earlier chapter, the basic formula for measuring the price elasticity of supply is the same as that used for measuring the elasticity of demand:

$$E_s = \frac{\dfrac{\Delta x}{x}}{\dfrac{\Delta y}{y}}.$$

In terms of Figure 9–5 we may write

$$E_s = \frac{\Delta x}{x} \div \frac{\Delta y}{y} = \frac{MM'}{OM} \div \frac{LV}{MR} = \frac{MM'}{OM} \cdot \frac{MR}{LV} = \frac{RL}{OM} \cdot \frac{MR}{LV} = \frac{RL}{LV} \cdot \frac{MR}{OM}$$

$$= \frac{AM}{MR} \cdot \frac{MR}{OM}$$

$$= \frac{AM}{OM} = \frac{AR}{TR} = \frac{OP}{TP} > 1.$$

The last of these measures of elasticity of supply,

$$E_s = \frac{OP}{TP},$$

where OP is price and T is the y-intercept of the supply curve, is the same as one of the measures of price elasticity of demand developed in an earlier chapter. If T lies above the origin, OP/TP will always be greater than one. If T lies below the origin, OP/TP will be less than one. If T is at the origin, OP/TP is equal to one.

In Figure 9–5, as OP falls, approaching OT, the value of OP/TP approaches infinity; as price increases, the value of OP/TP decreases. We may generalize by saying that if the supply curve has a positive y-intercept, the elasticity of supply will be greater than one at all prices, and the higher the price, the closer will the coefficient of elasticity of supply approach one. The various degrees of elasticity of supply are summarized in Figures 9–6 and 9–7.

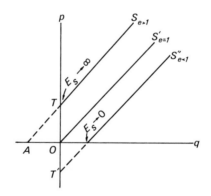

Fig. 9–6

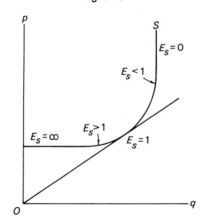

Fig. 9–7

Equilibrium Price

If for a given commodity the individual demand curves of all the consumers in a market are added together, the resulting curve is the market demand curve. And if the marginal-cost curves of all the firms producing the commodity in the purely competitive market are added together, the resulting curve is the market supply curve. In a purely competitive market, price is determined by the intersection of the market-demand and the market-supply curves. At any price higher than the one determined in this way, the amount supplied would exceed the amount demanded, and the competitive forces of the market would force the price down. At any price lower than the equilibrium price, the quantity demanded would be greater than the quantity supplied, and the competitive forces of the market would force the price up.

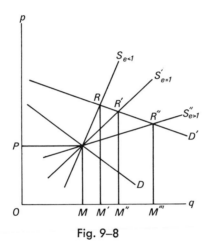

Fig. 9–8

If changes in demand and/or supply take place frequently in a given market, it is possible that before an equilibrium position has been reached, changes in demand and supply will determine a new equilibrium, and the equilibrium position may seldom if ever be attained. But, as was explained in an early chapter, in a purely competitive market, price and output are always at or moving toward equilibrium.

In Figure 9–8, if market demand is D and market supply is S, S', or S'', equilibrium price will be OP, and equilibrium output will be OM. OP is the price which each firm in the industry will have to accept, and OM is the summation of the outputs of all of the firms at price OP. Suppose now that demand increases from D to D'. The effect of the increase in demand will be to raise price and increase the quantity exchanged. But the degree to which price and quantity will be affected by the change in demand will depend upon the elasticity of supply. If supply is represented by S, whose elasticity at all points is less than one, price will rise to $M'R$ and the quantity exchanged will increase to OM'. If, however, supply is represented by S', whose elasticity is equal to one at all points, price will rise only to $M''R'$ and quantity will increase to OM''. If the elasticity of supply is greater than one, as illustrated by curve S'', the increase in price will be less and the increase in the quantity exchanged will be greater. We may generalize by saying that for a given increase in demand, the price will increase less and the quantity exchanged will increase more as the elasticity of supply is greater.

Long-Run Supply

Since time is required for firms to make output adjustments in response to changes in price, the elasticity of supply is likely to be greater as the time period under consideration is greater. Three time periods may be distinguished, and two significant cases—constant long-run supply and increasing long-run supply—may be described.

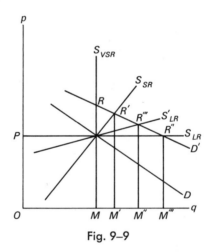

Fig. 9–9

With reference to Figure 9–9, suppose that initially price is OP and the firms in this purely competitive industry are producing a total of OM units of output per time period. Now assume that market demand increases from D to D'. In the very-short-run time period the firms are unable to make any adjustments in the quantity of variable factors which they employ, and they can, of course, make no adjustments in the quantity of fixed factors used. The full impact of the increase in demand will be reflected in a higher price. The very-short-run supply curve, S_{VSR} in Figure 9–9, will be perfectly inelastic, and price will rise from OP to MR.

The short-run time period is a period long enough to permit firms to make adjustments in their use of variable factors but not sufficiently long for them to change their use of fixed factors. The short-run supply curve for each firm in a purely competitive industry, as we have seen, is that portion of its marginal-cost curve which lies above its average-variable-cost curve. In Figure 9–9 curve S_{SR} is the sum of the individual firm's short-run supply curves. The short-run equilibrium price is $M'R'$, and short-run equilibrium output is OM'. The short-run supply curve at any price is more elastic than the very-short-run supply curve; short-run price is lower than the very-short-run price, and short-run output is greater than very-short-run output.

Finally, we come to a consideration of the long-run time period. The long run is a period of time sufficiently great to allow firms to modify their use of fixed as well as of variable factors. That is, firms in the long run can add new machines, or build additions to their plants or establish new ones. Also, new firms may enter the industry. Again in terms of Figure 9–9, if at price OP the firms in this industry are making normal profits, after the increase in demand and short-run adjustments are made, the firms should make better-than-normal profits with the short-run equilibrium price of $M'R'$. Attracted by the high rate of profits, old firms may, in the long run, be expected to expand facilities and new firms may be expected to enter the market. The entry of new firms will cause a shift in the market supply curve, and the form taken by the long-run supply curve will depend upon whether the industry is characterized by constant or increasing costs.

If the industry is a constant-cost industry, the long-run equilibrium price will be the same as the initial price; in Figure 9–9, $M'''R'' = OP$. The long-run supply curve, S_{LR}, implies that even though new firms enter the market, the resulting increased demand for labor and materials used by these firms will have no effect on their prices, and the firms' costs after the increased demand for the product will be the same as before. This would be possible only in the event that the industry's use of variable factors constituted but a small part of the total demand for them. If, however, the entry of new firms into this industry resulted in increased prices of the factors employed by the industry, the long-run supply curve would have a positive slope and would assume the form of S'_{LR} in Figure 9–9. In this event the new long-run equilibrium price would be higher than the initial price, OP.

Market and Firm Equilibrium

The nature of the responses of individual firms to changes in the market forces of demand and supply can be demonstrated with the use of Figure 9–10. The left side of the figure represents market demand and supply; the right side of the figure represents the cost and revenue curves for a typical firm in the market. We begin with demand and supply represented by the curves D and S; market price is OP and the amount exchanged is OM. The price OP is established for each firm; the firm's average-revenue and marginal-revenue curves are represented by the same horizontal line drawn from point P. Marginal revenue equals marginal cost at output Om. The scale on the y-axis is the same for both sections of the chart, but the scale on the x-axis of the two sections is different. If the market consists of 1,000 identical firms, OM equals 1,000 times Om.

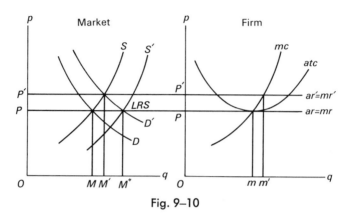

Fig. 9–10

OP is the equilibrium price. As long as demand and supply are properly represented by D and S there is no tendency for market price to rise above or fall below OP. It is also true that the firm is in short-run equilibrium since it has made the appropriate output adjustment to equalize marginal cost and marginal revenue. Finally, the industry is in long-run equilibrium since the average total cost of each firm is equal to average revenue; each firm is at the break-even point, and there is no inducement for new firms to enter this industry or for old firms to get out; all firms are making normal profits, and in the long run in a purely competitive market that is all they can expect to do. Since there is no tendency for the number of firms in the market to increase or decrease, the market is said to be in long-run equilibrium.

Suppose now that the equilibrium is upset by an increase in market demand to D'. The short-run effect of the increase in demand is for market price to rise to OP'. This means that for each individual firm the average-revenue and marginal-revenue curve rises to $ar' = mr'$. The appropriate short-run adjustment for each firm is to increase output to Om', and the output for the industry as a whole will, accordingly, increase to OM'. When each firm's output has been increased to Om', the firms will be again in short-run equilibrium. But at price OP', each firm's cost per unit of output will be less than its revenue per unit of output, and firms will be enjoying "supernormal" profits. Attracted by these profits, new firms will enter the industry, and, as they do, the market-supply curve will shift to the right, causing prices to fall. If this is a constant-cost industry—that is, if the addition of new firms to the market does not affect the prices of the factors which these firms buy—firms will continue to enter the market, and supply will continue to increase until the original price, OP, has been reestablished. At this price each firm will again produce *Om* units of output per time period, but the total output of the entire market will now be *OM″* since the number of firms has increased, each of them producing an output of *Om*. When the price of *OP* has been reestablished and each firm is producing at the rate of *Om* units per time period, each firm will again be in short-run equilibrium since *mr = mc*, and the market as a whole will be in long-run equilibrium since there is no longer any tendency for the number of firms in the industry to change; each firm is again just making normal profits.

Next, let us consider the somewhat more complex case of the adjustments of firms to a change in demand in an increasing-cost industry. This time we will assume that as new firms enter the market, the resulting increased demand for the factors which these firms employ will cause their prices to rise and the costs of the firms to increase. We are in essence

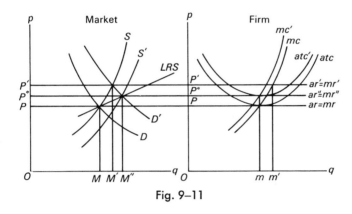

Fig. 9–11

assuming that the slopes of the supply curves for factors of production used by these firms are positive rather than horizontal.

In Figure 9–11 we again utilize a two-part diagram with the market conditions represented on the left side and the cost and revenue curves of the typical firm on the right side as before. We again begin with market price set by demand and supply at *OP*, with each firm producing *Om* units of output, and the market as a whole producing *OM* units. At price *OP* and output *Om*, each firm is in short-run equilibrium since *mr = mc*, and the industry is in long-run equilibrium since for each firm *ar = atc*. As before we assume that the equilibrium is disturbed by an increase in market demand from *D* to *D′*, causing market price to rise to *OP′*. At the higher price each firm in the short run will adjust its output to *Om′* and the total quantity exchanged for the industry as a whole will be *OM′*. But at output *Om′*, *ar′* is greater than *atc*, and each firm is making supernormal profits. Attracted by the profits in this industry, additional firms will enter the market, and the supply curve will shift to the right, causing price to decline. But this time as new firms enter the market, the prices of the things which the firms buy increase, and the firms' costs rise. Two things are now happening as new firms enter the market: price is falling and average-total costs are rising. At some price between OP and OP' each firm's average-revenue curve will become tangent to its average-total-cost curve, and supernormal profits will disappear. There will then be no further inducement for more new firms to enter the industry, and long-run equilibrium will be attained at some price above OP but below OP'. In Figure 9–11 the new long-run equilibrium price is OP'', each firm is again producing Om units of output per time period, and the total output of the whole market is OM''.

As drawn in Figure 9–11, each firm is producing an output of Om units under the new long-run equilibrium conditions, just as under the initial equilibrium conditions. Whether the new output will be the same, greater than, or less than the initial output depends on what form the change in costs takes. We may assume that all costs, fixed and variable, will increase by some specified amount, or that only fixed costs will increase (or fixed costs will increase more than variable costs will), or that only variable costs will increase (or variable costs will increase more than fixed costs will).

Suppose that the total-cost function is given by

$$TC = ax^3 - bx^2 + cx + f,$$

where a, b, c, and f are constants and x is output. It follows that average-total cost will be

$$ATC = \frac{TC}{x} = ax^2 - bx + c + fx^{-1}.$$

Under conditions of long-run equilibrium the average-revenue curve will be tangent to the average-total-cost curve, and since the average-revenue curve is a horizontal line, the point of tangency must come at the minimum value of the average-total-cost curve, or where $dATC/dx = 0$. Since the marginal-cost curve cuts the average-total-cost curve at its lowest point, under conditions of long-run equilibrium marginal cost will equal marginal revenue when $dATC/dx = 0$. We may write

$$\frac{dATC}{dx} = 2ax - b - fx^{-2}.$$

Setting this function equal to zero, we get

$$2ax - b - fx^{-2} = 0,$$

or

$$2ax - b - \frac{f}{x^2} = 0.$$

Multiplying through by x^2:

$$2ax^3 - bx^2 - f = 0,$$

or

$$2ax^3 - bx^2 = f. \qquad (1)$$

By substituting appropriately for a, b, and f, we could get the value of x, which corresponds with Om in Figure 9–11.

Now suppose that total cost increases to ϕTC, where ϕ is some number greater than one. If both variable and fixed costs have increased by this factor, we may write

$$\phi TC = \phi ax^3 - \phi bx^2 + \phi cx + \phi f$$
$$\phi ATC = \phi ax^2 - \phi bx + \phi c + \phi fx^{-1}$$
$$\frac{d\phi ATC}{dx} = 2\phi ax - \phi b - \frac{\phi f}{x^2} = 0$$
$$2\phi ax^3 - \phi bx^2 = \phi f$$
$$2ax^3 - bx^2 = f. \qquad (2)$$

Since equation (2) is identical with equation (1), it follows that if all costs increase by a given factor, the new long-run equilibrium output will be the same as the original equilibrium output, and this is the case illustrated by Figure 9–11.

Now suppose that as new firms enter the industry only fixed costs are increased. This means that the marginal-cost curve will not be affected by the increase in costs, and as the average-total-cost curve rises, it will slide along the old marginal-cost curve, and its lowest point will come at greater outputs as average costs increase. This means that in terms of Figure 9–11 the final equilibrium output of each firm would be greater than Om but less than Om'. Thus, if only fixed cost increases, the new total-cost function will be

$$TC' = ax^3 - bx^2 + cx + \phi f$$
$$ATC' = ax^2 - bx + c + \phi fx^{-1}$$
$$\frac{dATC'}{dx} = 2ax - b - \frac{\phi f}{x^2}.$$

Setting $dATC'/dx = 0$ to locate the lowest point on the ATC' curve:

$$2ax - b - \frac{\phi f}{x^2} = 0$$
$$2ax^3 - bx^2 = \phi f. \qquad (3)$$

Since ϕ is greater than one, the value of x in equation (3) must be greater than the value of x in equation (1), and if only fixed costs increase as new firms enter the market, the new long-run equilibrium output for each firm will be greater than it would be in the constant-cost case or in the case where both variable and fixed costs increased by a given factor.

Suppose finally that only variable costs increase as new firms enter the industry, fixed costs remaining unaffected. We may write

$$TC'' = \phi a x^3 - \phi b x^2 + \phi c x + f$$

$$ATC'' = \phi a x^2 - \phi b x + \phi c + f x^{-1}$$

$$\frac{dATC''}{dx} = 2\phi a x - \phi b - \frac{f}{x^2}.$$

$$2\phi a x - \phi b - \frac{f}{x^2} = 0$$

$$2\phi a x^3 - \phi b x^2 = f$$

$$\phi(2a x^3 - b x^2) = f. \tag{4}$$

Since ϕ is greater than one, the value of x in this equation must be less than the value of x in equation (1), and if only variable costs increase as new firms enter the industry, the new long-run equilibrium output for each firm will be less than the original equilibrium output.

Decreasing-Cost Industries

We have confined our analysis in the preceding paragraphs to two cases: constant-cost and increasing-cost industries. We have assumed that when new firms enter an industry, the resulting increased demand for factors of production either does or does not cause the prices of those factors to rise. Formally there is a third possibility, namely decreasing-cost industries. This appears to be an unlikely situation in the real world, but brief note may be made of what kind of market this case would imply.

Suppose that in terms of Figure 9–12 the initial equilibrium price is OP

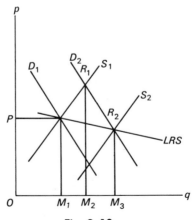

Fig. 9–12

and the industry is producing OM_1 units of output per time period. Now the demand for the product of this industry increases from D_1 to D_2. In the short run price rises to M_2R_1 and output increases to OM_2. Attracted by the supernormal profits resulting from the new high price, additional firms enter the industry, causing the supply curve to shift to the right. If this is a decreasing-cost industry, as supply increases both price of the product and costs of production will fall until a new long-run equilibrium is reached; in Figure 9–12 this will come when price is M_3R_2 and output is OM_3.

But what would cause costs to fall as the demand for factors increased? It is conceivable that in a young industry as new firms are formed transportation facilities might be improved; widened highways, improved air transport, new waterway facilities might to some extent lower production costs. It is also possible that improved marketing facilities might be developed as the industry matured, and this might contribute to lower costs of production. These changes would result in what are called external economies, since they come about outside the industry and are beyond the control of the firms within it. But a young industry is not likely to consist of so many firms that none has the power to affect the price of its product, and this means, of course, that young industries are not likely to be purely competitive. For older, established, purely competitive industries, external economies would not seem likely to be sufficiently great to cause average-total-cost curves to fall as more firms enter the industry, and the case of the decreasing-cost purely competitive industry would appear to be a rare one. The evidence seems to indicate that most industries fall into the increasing-cost or constant-cost category.

Long-Run Average Costs

The day-to-day decisions of the managers of purely competitive firms are short-run decisions relating to whether output should be expanded or contracted. From time to time, however, a long-run decision may have to be made as to whether a new plant should be established or an old plant abandoned. If it is decided to build a new plant, one of the critical decisions will relate to the size of the plant. In general it may be assumed that if the size of the plant is either too small or too large, the firm will suffer from diseconomies of size; and unit costs, even if the plant is operated at its lowest-cost output, will be excessive. But since in a purely competitive market any supernormal profits will attract new firms until the entry of new firms, by causing the market supply to increase, will cause such profits to disappear, firms with plants larger or smaller than the optimum size will be suffering losses when the optimum-size firms are earning normal profits. This means that firms in purely competitive industries have no practical choice as to the size of the plants which they build; they must build plants of the optimum size in order to subsist in the long run.

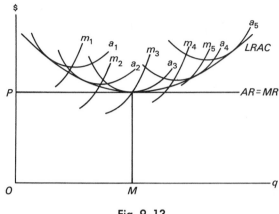

Fig. 9–13

If we assume that the size of plants is infinitely variable, we can draw short-run average-total-cost curves of plants of various sizes on the same chart. In Figure 9–13 five such plants are represented with their average-total-cost curves ranging from a_1 to a_5, each with its own short-run marginal-cost curve. These are to be taken as representative of the infinite number of sizes of plants which might be constructed. As plant size increases from a_1 to a_3, the minimum average total cost diminishes as the scale of the plant increases. This may be taken to reflect the economies of large-scale production. But as the size of the plants continues to increase, from a_3 to a_5, diseconomies of large-scale production outweigh the economies, and minimum average total costs increase as size of plant increases. If we draw an envelope curve just tangent to each of the short-run average-total-cost curves, the resulting curve is U-shaped and is called the long-run-average-cost curve or the planning curve. Since in the long run no costs are fixed but all are variable, we do not have to distinguish between long-run-average-total cost and long-run-average-variable cost. Clearly the optimum-size plant is a_3. The long-run equilibrium price would be OP. At this price the optimum-size plants would break even, but any other size, either larger or smaller, would operate at a loss at this price and eventually would have to be abandoned.

If price is OP and each plant is of a_3 size and produces at the rate of OM units of output per time period, this situation may be characterized as follows:

$$AR = MR = MC = ATC = LRAC.$$

The fact that $AR = MR$ indicates that the firm sells in a purely competitive market. If the firm sold in a monopolistic market, its demand curve would be negatively inclined, and at any output marginal revenue would be less than average revenue. The fact that $MR = MC$ indicates that the firm is maximizing profits; that is, the firm is in short-run equilibrium. The fact that $MC = ATC$ indicates that the firm is operating at the lowest point on the average-total-cost curve. The fact that $AR = ATC$ tells us that the firm is making only normal profits. And the fact that $MC = ATC = LRAC$ tells us that the optimum-size plant is operating at optimum output. All of this taken together means that in a purely competitive market when firms are in long-run equilibrium consumers can buy the product at the lowest price which current techniques make possible.

POSTPRANDIUM

If a purely competitive industry in long-run equilibrium is one which provides consumers with the maximum of goods at the lowest prices consistent with current technology, it is not surprising that it has significant normative value as a model. Even in situations where pure competition is clearly not feasible, such as in the public utilities, it might be helpful to policy officials to determine approximately what price and output would be if the industry *were* purely competitive, and a regulatory commission might set prices *as if* pure competition prevailed. But even the normative uses of pure competition are subject to important limitations.

It is not certain that most of us would enjoy living in a world of pure competition. Let us imagine what might happen if all industries were purely competitive. From our analysis in this chapter we would judge that they would provide consumers with maximum goods at the lowest possible prices; allocation of resources both between industries and within industries would be optimum; consumers would get goods at average cost of production; there would be no exploitation of workers by employers or of consumers by producers; flexibility of factor and product prices would presumably provide full employment of all resources; this would seem, in short, to be "the best of all possible worlds." But some things would also be missing. There would be no advertising, for example. This would mean that the resources currently used for advertising and promotional activities would be released, an even greater output of consumer goods thereby becoming possible. But a world without advertising would take getting use to. For good or ill, Madison Avenue's frenzied efforts—the poor taste, the extravagant claims, the misrepresentations—would be lost in a purely competitive economy. Free commercial television would disappear, newspapers and magazines would cost more—and can we visualize newspapers and magazines as homogeneous products? Brand names and trade marks would also be casualties of pure competition. Perhaps even the supermarket would disappear. There would be in each community many grocery shops where bread would be bread and beans would be beans. Perhaps we would see a return of the old pickle barrel and bulk sales of most staples. Almost certainly there would be reduced emphasis on the packaging of goods. One's choice of coffee might be limited to the 50¢-per-pound, the 75¢-per-pound, and the $1-per-pound varieties, and it would be the same story in the store across the street. If one wanted to buy a new car, one's choice might be limited to the small, the middle-size, and the big car. It begins to sound as if life under pure competition might in significant respects be as dull as life under pure communism! Opposite economic philosophies might prove to be surprisingly similar in their consequences.

But pure competition could not persist in many industries which enjoy significant economies of scale. The existence of large numbers of firms in industries such as steel, automobiles, and aluminum would require intolerable sacrifices of efficiency. Suppose, then, that some industries were purely competitive while others were to some degree monopolistic. Would this approximate the optimum use of resources?

The prime allocation problem is the allocation of resources among industries. If all industries were purely competitive, we might assume that resources would be allocated strictly in accordance with consumer preferences. But if only some industries are purely competitive, resource allocation must be less than optimum. The model of pure competition assumes demand, factor prices, and production techniques as given. The existence of monopolistic industries in the economy would affect the demand for goods produced by purely competitive firms, and this would upset the general equilibrium. Factor prices and income distribution would also be affected by the presence of monopoly. And whether all or only some industries were purely competitive, there is a question as to whether purely competitive firms would be as progressive as monopolistic firms. If an innovation promised reasonably certain cost reductions, the presumption is that it would be undertaken by the purely competitive seller since it would provide him in the short run with supernormal profits. But if the change promised only uncertain results, the purely competitive seller would probably feel that he could not afford the risk. Research expenditures would likely be smaller under pure competition than under monopoly. The net result might be that the purely competitive firm, selling at average cost but using obsolete production techniques, would have to charge prices as high as or higher than those charged by a monopolist using more advanced techniques.

But important as the purely competitive model is for its significant normative value, it in itself provides few answers to questions of economic policy. It is false to reason that if government pursued a hands-off policy, pure competition would follow, or that if it did it would bring us to the millennium. There is no guarantee that if government followed a hands-off policy pure competition would result, and, even if it did, many of us would be disappointed in the economic world in which we found ourselves.

Nevertheless, in assessing the economic efficiency of the economy we must turn to pure competition as the norm. In a private-enterprise economy resources are allocated through the price system. Price serves as a signalling device to firms, whether they are competitive or monopolistic. If price is higher than the average cost of production, firms will expand output and in the long run new firms will enter the market if entry is free. And under pure competition, entry is always free. Goods will be produced, accordingly, in response to the wants of the consumer.

Under conditions of pure competition price is independent of the amount the consumer purchases; there will be no price discrimination among consumers on the basis of how much they buy or who they are. The price is the same to all comers. In terms of the marginal-utility analysis, the consumer will allocate his expenditures on commodities X and Y in order to maximize his satisfaction, so that $MU_x/P_x = MU_y/P_y$, or, in terms of the indifference-curve analysis, he will allocate his expenditures on X and Y so that the $MRS_{xy} = P_x/P_y$. Since the prices of the products are the same for all consumers, the marginal rate of substitution between any two commodities will be the same for all consumers who buy them. This means that the most efficient distribution of goods among consumers has been achieved; with consumer incomes and tastes given, there would be no way to redistribute goods to increase aggregate consumer satisfaction.

Under long-run equilibrium conditions under pure competition, $P = MR = MC = ATC$. If we use the term marginal social cost to describe what society gives up in order to get an additional unit of a commodity, marginal social cost will, under conditions of pure competition, equal price; on the other hand, if a market is less than purely competitive, price will be greater than marginal cost, indicating that the firm's output is less than the economically most efficient output.

If the value of the product of a factor used by a given firm would be greater in some other use, it would be shifted to that use under conditions of pure competition, increasing the aggregate value of goods produced. In this way the value of the output of the economy would be maximized.

SELECTED REFERENCES

Bain, Joe S. *Price Theory.* New York: Holt, Rinehart & Winston, Inc., 1952. Chap. 4.

Boulding, Kenneth E. *Economic Analysis.* Vol. I, 4th ed. New York: Harper & Row, Publishers, 1966. Chap. 19.

Chamberlin, Edward Hastings. *The Theory of Monopolistic Competition.* 5th ed. Cambridge: Harvard University Press, 1946. Chap. 2.

Colberg, Marshall R., Dascomb R. Forbush; and Gilbert R. Whitaker, Jr. *Business Economics: Principles and Cases.* 3rd ed. Homewood, Ill.: Richard D. Irwin, Inc., 1964. Chap. 5.

Due, John F., and Robert W. Clower. *Intermediate Economic Analysis.* 4th ed. Homewood, Ill.: Richard D. Irwin, Inc., 1961. Chap. 9.

Leftwich, Richard H. *The Price System and Resource Allocation.* 3rd ed. New York: Holt, Rinehart & Winston, Inc., 1966. Chap. 9.

Liebhafsky, H. H. *The Nature of Price Theory.* Homewood, Ill.: The Dorsey Press, Inc., 1963. Chaps. 8 and 9.

Marshall, Alfred. *Principles of Economics.* 8th ed. London: Macmillan & Co., 1920. Book V, Chaps. 4 and 5.

Robinson, Joan. *Economics of Imperfect Competition.* London: Macmillan and Company, 1933. Chaps. 5 and 6.

Stigler, George J. *The Theory of Price.* Rev. ed. New York: The Macmillan Co., 1952. Chaps. 9 and 10.

Stonier, Alfred W., and Douglas C. Hague. *A Textbook of Economic Theory.* 3rd ed. New York: John Wiley & Sons, Inc., 1964. Chaps. 5 and 6.

Viner, Jacob. "Cost Curves and Supply Curves," *Zeitschrift für Nationalökonomie,* 3 (1931), 23–46; reprinted in George J. Stigler and Kenneth E. Boulding, eds., *Readings in Price Theory.* Homewood, Ill.: Richard D. Irwin, Inc., 1952. Pp. 198–232.

PROBLEMS

PROBLEM I

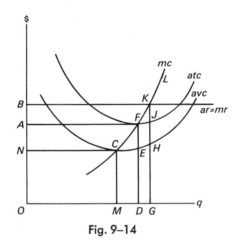

Fig. 9–14

Circle the correct answer in each instance:

    1. Most profitable output: *OA, OB, OM, OG.*

    2. Market price: *BK, AF, GK, MC.*

    3. Average revenue: *OB, BK, OG, DF.*

    4. Marginal revenue: *OA, AF, GK, DF.*

    5. Average total cost at most profitable output: *OB, OD, MC, GJ.*

    6. Average variable cost at most profitable output: *GH, GJ, MC, DF.*

    7. Profit per unit at most profitable output: *AB, JK, HJ, EF.*

    8. Average fixed cost at most profitable output: *EF, JH, AB, MC.*

9. Long-run equilibrium output: *OD, OM, OG, ON.*

10. Short-run supply curve: *OM, CL, AF, BK.*

PROBLEM II

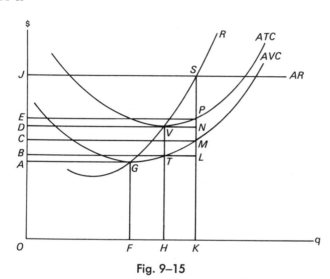

Fig. 9–15

In each blank put the number of the best answer for each question.

1. The firm whose costs and revenues are indicated in Figure 9–15 sells (a) competitively, (b) monopolistically.   .   .   .   .   ._____

2. The firm (a) is, (b) is not, in short-run equilibrium if it is producing at a rate of *OK* units per time period. .   .   .   .   ._____

3. The industry of which this firm is a part (a) is, (b) is not, in long-run equilibrium.   .   .   ._____

4. The firm's total revenue is (a) *OAGF,* (b) *OBLK,* (c) *OEPK,* (d) *OJSK.* .   .   .   .   ._____

5. Market price is (a) *FG,* (b) *KL,* (c) *OE,* (d) *OJ.* .   .   .   .   .   .   ._____

6. Total profit is (a) *PS,* (b) *EJSP,* (c) *DJSN,* (d) *OEPK.* .   .   .   .   .   .   ._____

7. Total variable cost is (a) *OBLK,* (b) *OCMK,* (c) *ODNK,* (d) *OEPK.*   .   .   .   ._____

8. Long-run equilibrium price is (a) *OA,* (b) *KN,* (c) *FG,* (d) *KS.*   .   .   .   .   .   ._____

9. The firm's short-run supply curve is (a) *JS,* (b) *GR,* (c) *EP,* (d) *DN.*   .   .   .   ._____

10. The firm's marginal-revenue curve is (a) *JS*,
    (b) *GR*, (c) *EP*, (d) *DN*. . . . . . . ._____

11. The shut-down price is (a) *OA*, (b) *OB*, (c)
    OC, (d) *OD*. . . . . ._____

12. The break-even price is (a) *OA*, (b) *OB*,
    (c) *OC*, (d) *OD*. . . . . ._____

13. The shut-down output is (a) *OF*, (b) *OH*,
    (c) *OK*, (d) *OD*. . . . . ._____

14. The break-even output is (a) *OF*, (b) *OH*,
    (c) *OK*, (d) *OD*. . . . . ._____

15. Long-run equilibrium output is (a) *OF*, (b) *OH*,
    (c) *OK*, (d) *OD*. . . . . ._____

16. *ATC* at profit-maximizing output is (a) *FG*,
    (b) *KM*, (c) *KP*, (d) *KS*. . . . . . ._____

17. *AVC* at profit-maximizing output is (a) *FG*,
    (b) *KM*, (c) *KP*, (d) *KS*. . . . . . ._____

18. Total fixed cost is (a) *BDNL*, (b) *BEPL*, (c)
    OAGF, (d) *BDVT*. . . . . ._____

19. *MC* at profit-maximizing output is (a) *OJ*, (b)
    FG, (c) *HV*, (d) *KP*. . . . . . . ._____

20. *AFC* at profit-maximizing output is (a) *TV*, (b)
    MP, (c) *BD*, (d) *BE*. . . . . . . ._____

PROBLEM III

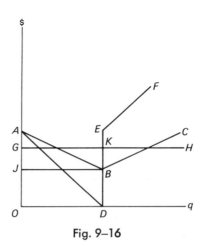

Fig. 9–16

In the above figure, cost and revenue data are represented as straight lines. *ABC* is
the average-total-cost curve, and *GH* is the average-revenue curve.

1. What is the marginal-revenue curve? . . . ._____

2. What is the marginal-cost curve? . . . . ._____

3. What is the most profitable output? . . . ._____

4. What is market price? . . . . . . ._____

5. What is the elasticity of demand? . . . . ._____

6. What is marginal revenue at the most profitable
   output? . . . . ._____

7. What is total revenue at the most profitable
   output? . . . . ._____

8. What is total cost at the most profitable output? ._____

9. What is total profit at the most profitable output? ._____

10. What is average total cost at the most profitable
    output? . . . . ._____

11. What is total variable cost at the most profitable
    output? . . . . ._____

12. What is average variable cost at the most profit-
    able output? . . . . ._____

13. What is total fixed cost at the most profitable
    output? . . . . ._____

14. What is average fixed cost at the most profitable
    output? . . . . ._____

15. Does this firm sell competitively? . . . . ._____

PROBLEM IV

Given: $TC = x^3 - 4x^2 + 8x + 4$

$TR = 4x.$

1. What is the equation for the firm's average-
   revenue curve? . . . . ._____

2. What is the equation for the firm's marginal-
   revenue curve? . . . . ._____

3. What is total revenue at $x = 4$? . . . . ._____

4. What is the equation for marginal cost? . . ._____

5. What is the equation for the average-total-cost
   curve? . . . . ._____

6. What is the firm's total fixed cost? . . . ._____

7. What is the firm's average fixed cost at $x = 5$? ._____

8. What is the firm's total variable cost at $x = 3$? ._____

9. What is the y-intercept of the firm's demand
   curve? . . . . ._____

10. What is the equation for the firm's total profit? ._____

11. What is the most profitable output? .   .   .   ._____

12. At what price can the most profitable output be
sold?   .   .   .   .   ._____

13. What is the elasticity of demand at the most
profitable price?   .   .   .   .   ._____

14. What is marginal revenue at the most profitable
output? .   .   .   .   ._____

15. What is total revenue at the most profitable
output? .   .   .   .   ._____

16. What is total variable cost at the most profitable
output? .   .   .   .   ._____

17. What is total cost at the most profitable output? ._____

18. What is total profit at the most profitable output? ._____

19. What is total profit at $x = 2\frac{1}{2}$? .   .   .   .   ._____

20. In what kind of market does this firm sell? .   ._____

PROBLEM V

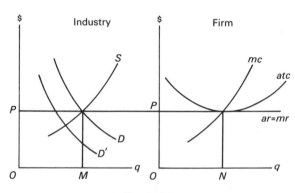

Fig. 9–17

In the above figure the market price is established at OP, the industry is producing
OM units of output per time period, and each firm is selling ON units. Assume
that market demand shifts from D to D'.

1. Indicate on the figure the new market price as OP', the new output of
the industry as OM', and the new output of each firm as ON'.

2. Each firm is now (making a profit, suffering a loss, breaking even), and
as a result there will be in the long run (an entry of new firms into the
industry, an exit of firms from the industry, no change in the number of
firms); this will result in a shift in the industry's short-run supply curve
to the (right, left).

3. Assume that this is a constant-cost industry. Draw the short-run supply curve which will reestablish long-run equilibrium, and label it S'.

4. The new long-run equilibrium price is . . . ._____

5. The output of each firm under the new equilibrium condition is . . . . ._____

6. The output of the industry under the new equilibrium is (equal to, less than, greater than) the original equilibrium output because the number of firms has (increased, decreased, remained the same).

7. Label the long-run supply curve *LRS*.

PROBLEM VI

Assume that a firm sells in a purely competitive market. Prepare on the axes below a two-part chart. (1) In the upper part draw a total-revenue curve and a total-cost curve. Indicate the output where profits will be maximized. Sketch in the total-profit curve. (2) In the lower part of the chart, using the same x-axis scale and any convenient scale on the y-axis, sketch in the corresponding average-revenue, marginal-revenue, average-total-cost, and marginal-cost curves. Check the critical points which make the upper and lower charts correspond. Shade the area in the lower chart representing total profit at the most profitable output.

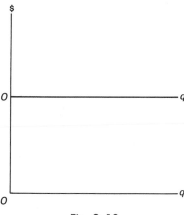

Fig. 9–18

10

Prices and Output
under Pure Monopoly

In the preceding chapter we considered pricing and output under conditions of pure competition. The analytical significance of pure competition stems in part from its contrast to the purely monopolistic market, which is the subject of this chapter. Pure monopoly—that is, literally one seller in the market—is as rare as pure competition in the real world, but it too has analytical significance. Intermediate cases such as oligopoly and monopolistic competition—which are what most real-world markets are actually like—are the subjects of the next two chapters.

A distinguishing characteristic of pure competition, as was pointed out in the preceding chapter, is that the demand curve of each firm is a horizontal line at the level of market price, which in turn is determined by market demand and supply. Since the demand or average-revenue curve is a horizontal line, marginal revenue is at all outputs equal to average revenue, and the elasticity of demand for the purely competitive firm is equal to infinity; that is, the short-run demand of each competitive firm is perfectly elastic. The purely competitive firm has no control over the price of its product, but it can sell any quantity which it can produce during a given time period at the price established by market demand and supply.

In contrast, in an industry consisting of one firm, the monopoly, industry demand and firm demand must be identical; since the market demand curve has a negative slope, the demand curve for the firm's product must also have a negative slope. In algebraic terms, a linear negatively inclined demand curve is

$$AR = y = b - mx,$$

where b is the y-intercept of the demand curve, and m is its slope. It follows that total revenue is given by

$$TR = xy = bx - mx^2,$$

and

$$MR = \frac{dTR}{dx} = b - 2mx.$$

It will be noted that if the average-revenue curve is linear and negatively inclined, the marginal-revenue curve will also be linear and negatively inclined, having the same y-intercept as the average-revenue curve and twice the slope of the average-revenue curve. At any output, accordingly, for the monopolist marginal revenue will be less than average revenue, or, what is the same thing, marginal revenue will be less than price at any output: $P > MR$.

If the monopolist's demand curve is linear and is drawn from the y-axis to the x-axis, the elasticity of demand will be different at every price, ranging from zero at the x-intercept to infinity at the y-intercept. In an earlier chapter we developed the following formula showing the relationship between average revenue, marginal revenue, and elasticity of average revenue:

$$e = \frac{a}{m - a},$$

where e is elasticity of demand expressed as a negative number, a is average revenue, and m is marginal revenue. It follows that when $m = 0$, $e = -1$. As we have seen, m is less than a at any output. If m is less than a but greater than 0, e must be greater than 1 (without reference to algebraic sign); if m is less than 0, e is less than 1. These relationships are demonstrated in Figure 10–1.

An important corollary may be drawn from these basic relationships. If we assume that marginal cost is always greater than zero, that is, if it always costs more to produce a somewhat greater output than a smaller output, the profit-maximizing monopolist will always operate in the range where the elasticity of demand is greater than one, since if marginal cost is greater than zero and marginal cost equals marginal revenue, marginal revenue must be greater than zero, and if marginal revenue is positive, the elasticity of demand is greater than one. In the unlikely case that marginal cost is equal to zero, the elasticity of demand would be equal to one, but if marginal cost is greater

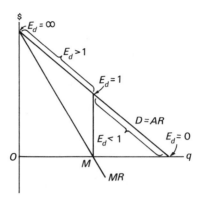

Fig. 10–1

than zero, elasticity of demand is greater than one. In terms of Figure 10–1 this means that the profit-maximizing firm would never deliberately produce an output in excess of OM units per time period.

Profit-Maximizing Output and Price

The monopolist knows that he can increase the quantity of his sales per time period by lowering his price, and he knows that he can raise his price without losing all of his sales. When the monopolist changes his output, the change will affect the price at which the output can be sold. This is not the case with a firm in a purely competitive industry. The monopolist has the choice of selling more units at a lower price or fewer units at a higher price. It will not be his object to get the highest possible price; we assume that he is seeking the price-output combination which will maximize profits.

The profit-maximizing output is determined in the same way for the monopolist as it is for the purely competitive seller: he should produce to the point where marginal cost equals marginal revenue. The common sense of the matter is also familiar: if the production of one more unit will add more to the firm's total revenue than it will add to its total costs, the production of that unit will add something to the firm's total profit; if, however, it adds more to costs than to revenue, it will reduce total profit.

The monopolist's profit-maximizing output is represented in Figure 10–2. The total-cost curve is the typical curve which reflects a U-shaped average-total-cost curve and is of the same general form as the total-cost curve of the competitive firm of the preceding chapter. But this time the total-revenue curve is nonlinear. In fact, as we have seen in a preceding chapter, if the average-revenue curve is linear and negatively inclined, the total-revenue curve will be parabolic. We know in advance that if the firm is attempting to maximize profits, it will never produce an output in excess of OR units per time period. Beyond OR, total revenue is decreasing and total cost is increas-

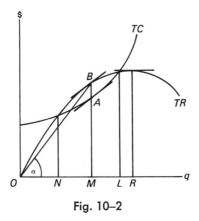

Fig. 10–2

ing as output increases. If the firm were producing more than OR units, it could increase profits simply by reducing the rate of output. Beyond output OR, marginal revenue is negative, and marginal cost could equal marginal revenue only if marginal cost were negative, that is, if total costs were decreasing as output increased. At output OR, the elasticity of demand is equal to -1; at outputs greater than OR the firm would be operating in the inelastic range of its demand curve, and, as we have just seen, the profit-maximizing firm operates only in the elastic segment of its demand curve.

Furthermore, the firm would incur losses if it produced less than ON units or more than OL units per time period. These are the break-even outputs, and anywhere between ON and OL, as Figure 10–2 is drawn, the firm will enjoy positive profits. Our task, accordingly, is to locate the output between ON and OL where the vertical distance between the TR and TC curves is greatest. Recalling that the slope of the total-revenue curve is marginal revenue and the slope of the total-cost curve is marginal cost, we may express the task geometrically as locating the output where the slope of the TR curve is equal to the slope of the TC curve; that is, we must determine at what output the tangents to the TC and TR curves are parallel. This output is OM in Figure 10–2. At this output total revenue is MB, total cost is MA, and total profit is AB. At output OM average revenue or price may be determined as follows:

$$AR = \frac{TR}{x} = \frac{MB}{OM} = \tan \alpha.$$

We may conclude that if a monopolist's cost and revenue curves are properly represented by Figure 10–2, the firm's most profitable output is OM units per time period, and the profit-maximizing price is $\tan \alpha$.

The marginal-cost-equals-marginal-revenue rule can be demonstrated more directly with the use of Figure 10–3, in which costs and revenue are represented by average and marginal curves rather than by total curves.

Again we can by inspection restrict the range of appropriate outputs. At output *OR* marginal revenue is equal to zero and the elasticity of demand is equal to −1, and output for the profit-maximizing monopolist will not exceed *OR* regardless of how the cost curves are drawn. For outputs less than *ON* and greater than *OL* average cost exceeds average revenue; between the break-even outputs, average revenue is greater than average cost. The firm will, if it is to maximize profits, produce somewhere between *ON* and *OL* units of output per time period. But at output *OM* marginal cost is equal to marginal revenue, and this is, accordingly, the most profitable output. At output *OM*, average-total cost is *MK = OC*, and total cost is *OCKM*. At output *OM* average revenue is *MJ = OP*, and total revenue is *OPJM*. Since

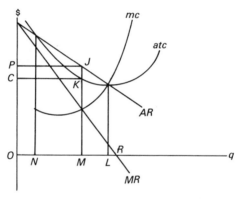

Fig. 10–3

total profit = *TR − TC*, profit in Figure 10–3 is *CPJK*; no other output, either greater or smaller than *OM*, will produce a profit this great. The profit-maximizing output is, accordingly, *OM*, and the profit-maximizing price is *OP*. If Figures 10–2 and 10–3 are based on the same data, *OM* in Figure 10–3 is equal to *OM* in Figure 10–2, and *CPJK* in Figure 10–3 is equal to *AB* in Figure 10–2.

One difference between the application of the *MC = MR* rule in the competitive and monopolistic cases needs to be made. We noted in the preceding chapter that marginal cost might be equal to marginal revenue at more than one output, and to determine an output of maximum and not minimum profits it was necessary to locate the output where the slope of the marginal-revenue curve was less than the slope of the marginal-cost curve; that is, a profit-maximizing output requires that

$$MC = MR$$

and

$$\frac{dMC}{dx} > \frac{dMR}{dx}.$$

Since the slope of the marginal-revenue curve for a purely competitive firm is everywhere equal to zero, at the profit-maximizing output the marginal-cost curve must have a positive slope. To locate a maximum- and not a minimum-profit output for a pure monopolist, it is still necessary that the slope of the marginal-revenue curve be less than the slope of the marginal-cost curve, but this condition could be met even if both curves had negative slopes. This means that the profit-maximizing output for the monopolist may come where the marginal-cost curve is approaching its minimum value, that is, where its slope is negative.

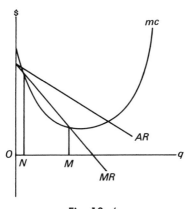

Fig. 10–4

In Figure 10–4 the marginal-revenue curve is drawn so that it intersects the marginal-cost curve at outputs *ON* and *OM*. At output *ON* the slope of the marginal-revenue curve is greater than the slope of the marginal-cost curve (a smaller negative value, which is a greater absolute value); this, therefore, is an output where profits are at a minimum rather than at a maximum. On the other hand, at output *OM*, the slope of the marginal-revenue curve is less than the slope of the marginal-cost curve, and this is, accordingly, a profit-maximizing output. But note that even at output *OM*, the marginal-cost curve has a negative slope. If this were a purely competitive firm, the profit-maximizing output could not come at a point where the marginal-cost curve was negatively inclined. In Figure 10–4 it is quite possible that even at output *OM* the firm is operating at a loss; since the average-total-cost curve has not been drawn, we have no way to compare average total cost with average revenue. But if the firm does encounter losses at output *OM*, its losses at this rate of output are smaller than they would be at any other output, larger or smaller. Output *OM* is the profit-maximizing or loss-minimizing output as the case may be. The necessary condition for *MC* = *MR* to establish the profit-maximizing output is simply this: at outputs somewhat less than the profit-maximizing output, *MC* < *MR*; for outputs somewhat greater than the profit-maximizing output, *MC* > *MR*.

Long-Run Costs

In the long run, the firm can build new plants or make additions to the old one. This means, as we have seen, that in the long run even the so-called fixed costs are variable. Suppose that a monopoly firm is contemplating building a new plant to replace the old one. For this firm, as for the purely competitive firm, the size of the plant to be built is a critical matter. But the nature of the crisis is somewhat different. The competitive firm must determine what the optimum size is—optimum in this connection meaning the scale of plant whose minimum average total cost is lowest—and then build a plant of the optimum size. This is essentially an engineering question, and the competitive firm has no real choice as to the size of plant. If its plant size is smaller or larger than optimum, it will not be able to survive under

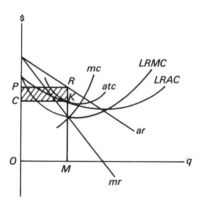

Fig. 10–5

conditions of long-run equilibrium, when the optimum-size plants are just breaking even. On the other hand, the monopoly firm has some discretion as to the scale of plant which it can build. There is a size which is optimum in the sense that with that size plant the firm's profits will be greatest, but the optimum-size plant may or may not be the one with the lowest minimum average-total costs. And even if the size of plant built proves to be larger or smaller than optimum for the output actually produced, the monopoly firm may be able to survive in the long run anyway, and quite possibly operate with a substantial profit.

In Figure 10–5 a long-run-average-cost curve is drawn, and, as in the preceding chapter, this is represented as U-shaped. The long-run average-cost curve, or the planning curve, in effect indicates the lowest cost at which any output, given the appropriate size plant, can be produced. For very small outputs, average costs will be relatively high. As output and scale of plant increase, average costs decrease .for a time, reach a minimum, and then increase. In Figure 10–5 we have also drawn in the long-run marginal-cost curve, which bears the same relation to the $LRAC$ curve that the mc curve bears to the atc curve; it indicates the additional cost of producing an additional unit of output as scale of plant is appropriately adjusted. The all-wise monopolist would take into account the $LRAC$ and $LRMC$ curves when he is planning a new plant; after the plant has been built, he is concerned only with the atc and mc curves; that is, his decisions then are short-run decisions.

Suppose that the monopolist decides that his plant will be called upon to produce an output of OM units per time period. The appropriate scale of plant to produce OM units at the lowest possible average total cost will be the one whose short-run marginal cost will equal the long-run marginal cost at that output. But if long-run and short-run marginal costs are equal at output OM, the short-run average-total-cost curve will be tangent to the long-run average-cost curve at that output. In Figure 10–5, $mc = LRMC$ at output OM, and atc is tangent to $LRAC$ at that output. The output of OM can be produced with the plant whose short-run cost curve is represented by atc at a cost of $MK = OC$ per unit, and this is the lowest cost at which this output can be produced with the techniques currently available. The firm's total cost will be $OCKM$; its total revenue will be $OPRM$; and its total profit will be $CPRK$. This is the output which maximizes profits for a plant of this size, and this scale of plant can produce this output at a lower average cost and hence with a greater profit than any other size plant.

If the firm whose cost and revenue curves are represented in Figure 10–5 produces OM units of output per time period at a price of OP, the situation may be summarized as follows:

$$AR > MR = MC < ATC = LRAC > LRMC.$$

The fact that $AR > MR$ indicates that the firm is selling in a less than perfectly competitive market. We do not know from this whether the firm is selling in a purely monopolistic, an oligopolistic, or a monopolistically competitive market, since in all these cases the firm's demand curve would be negatively inclined, but we do know that the firm is not a purely competitive seller. The fact that $MR = MC$ indicates that the firm is maximizing short-run profits. The fact that $MC < ATC$ indicates that the firm is operating to the left of the lowest point on its average-total-cost curve; that is, the firm is operating in the range of decreasing costs. The fact that $ATC = LRAC$ indicates that the scale of plant utilized by the firm is optimum for the output which it is producing even though it is smaller than the most efficient size plant in a strictly engineering sense, as is demonstrated by the fact that $LRAC > LRMC$. It is clear that a plant of "optimum" size in the engineering sense could produce the output OM only at a cost considerably in excess of MK.

If, after the plant of the size represented by atc in Figure 10–5 has been built, there is a shift in demand either to the right or to the left, the firm could continue to operate, and very likely at a profit, by making $mc = mr$. At the new output, however, atc would not equal $LRAC$, and this means that the firm would be producing the new output at a higher cost than a firm designed to produce the new output could produce it. If entry to the industry is difficult or impossible, the now greater or less than "optimum" size plant may be able to survive indefinitely, and very likely enjoy handsome if not maximum profits during the period.

When the "economically optimum" size plant is smaller than the "engineering optimum" size, the condition gives rise to what is frequently called "natural" monopoly. If in terms of Figure 10–5, the market will take only OM units of output per time period and that output can be produced at lowest cost by a relatively small plant, it is virtually impossible for competitive conditions to obtain. This is sometimes expressed by saying that decreasing costs and competition are incompatible. Suppose that there were even two firms in this market instead of one. Each firm could expect to sell approximately one-half of OM units per time period. The optimum-size plant to produce an output of one-half OM would, of course, be smaller than the plant whose short-run cost curve is atc. The aggregate demand for the product of the two firms would still be ar; the total output of the two firms would be OM; and the price to the consumer would be OP as before. The net effect of the entry of the second firm would be to reduce the profits of the producers without any benefit to consumers. The economy's resources would be utilized less efficiently, and this would contribute to a reduction in national income. In the long run each firm might be tempted to build larger plants to reduce costs, and, since cost per unit of output decreases as output increases, there might be an effort on the part of both firms to cut prices in order to increase sales until prices were actually below average costs. The final outcome would be either the failure of one firm, in which event monopoly would be restored, or the two firms would enter into an agreement as to prices and output, and in this event competition would also have disappeared. Decreasing costs tend to lead to "cutthroat" competition, which, in turn, leads to some form of monopoly. Since in fact some of the "natural" monopolies produce goods or services which are essential—electric power, water, and transportation are prime examples—in the United States these industries have been declared to be "affected with a public interest," and they are either owned by some agency of the state or are subjected to regulation of rates and service by a public authority. An exclusive franchise is usually given to one company to provide the service within an area, thus making the firm a "legal" as well as a "natural" monopoly, and then the firm is subjected to some measure of control by a regulatory commission. Some of the basic questions relating to the control of such privately owned public utilities will be considered later in this chapter.

It is possible that market demand might warrant the construction of a plant which would be of optimum size from the engineering point of view.

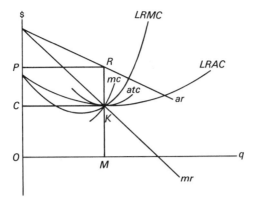

Fig. 10–6

Such a situation is represented in Figure 10–6. Here the plant is the size which provides the maximum engineering efficiency, and the firm is producing at its lowest-cost output. There is no way to produce OM units of output per time period at a lower cost than $MK = OC$. But note that instead of selling at a price equal to OC, as a purely competitive firm in long-run equilibrium would do, this firm sells at price $MR = OP$ and enjoys a supernormal profit equal to $CPRK$. Or it may be that the monopoly firm's plant is larger than the engineering optimum, as in Figure 10–7. In this case it will be noted that not only is the plant larger than the most efficient size, but in addition the firm is operating beyond its lowest-cost output.

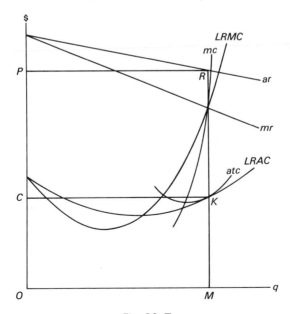

Fig. 10–7

Taxation of Monopolies

The monopolist is generally believed to enjoy excess profits—a belief which is often but not necessarily true—and it is sometimes proposed to regulate monopoly profits through taxation. The effect of the tax on the monopolist's price and output will depend upon whether it is a variable tax, such as a tax on each unit of the firm's output, or a lump-sum tax, such as a franchise tax levied on a firm for the right to do business in a given area. The specific tax adds to the variable costs of the firm in much the same way that an increase in the cost of inputs would add to them; the greater the firm's output, the more tax it has to pay. The lump-sum tax, on the other hand, is a fixed charge; so much per year is charged the firm, and this amount does not vary with output.

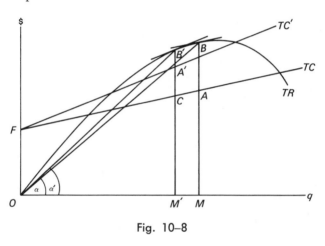

Fig. 10–8

In Figure 10–8 the cost and revenue curves for a monopoly firm have been drawn. The total-revenue curve has been drawn in the conventional manner, reflecting a linear negatively inclined demand curve. The total-cost curve, however, has been represented as a linear function in order to keep the chart as simple as possible. The total-revenue curve is TR and the total-cost curve before the imposition of a specific (variable) tax is TC. The slope of the total-revenue curve is equal to the slope of the total-cost curve at output OM. At this output total cost is MA; total revenue is MB; and total profit is AB. Now suppose that it is felt that this profit is excessive, and the government levies a tax on each unit of output. The new total-cost curve is TC'. It has the same y-intercept as the TC curve, indicating that total fixed cost has not changed, but the variable cost at any output has now increased by the amount of the total tax paid on that output. If the total-cost function was originally of the form

$$TC = y = mx + b,$$

where m is the slope of the curve and b is the amount of the fixed cost, the new total-cost function will be

$$TC' = y = (m + t)x + b,$$

where t is the amount of the tax levied on each unit of output. In Figure 10–8 the slope of the total-revenue curve is equal to the slope of the new total-cost curve at output OM'; total revenue is now $M'B'$; total cost is $M'A'$; total profit is reduced to $A'B'$; and the firm pays to the government an amount in taxes equal to CA'. This tax has succeeded in reducing the monopolist's profits, and by increasing the tax rate the profits could be eliminated entirely. But the tax has also reduced the firm's output from OM to OM', and, since the firm's demand curve has a negative slope, the reduced output will be sold at a higher price. This is confirmed in the figure. The original price was tan a, whereas the price after the tax is tan a', a higher price. The burden or incidence of the tax, accordingly, falls on both the monopolist and the consumer; the profits of the monopolist are reduced, but the price to the consumer is increased and the output of the firm is reduced.

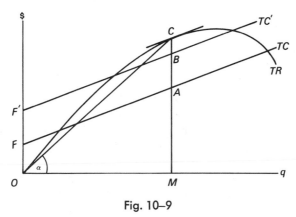

Fig. 10–9

The situation is quite different if the tax imposed on the monopolist is a lump-sum tax. In Figure 10–9 the total-cost curve is again represented as linear. When the total-revenue curve is TR and the total-cost curve is TC, the most profitable output is OM. This is where the slope of the TR curve is equal to the slope of the TC curve, which is to say where marginal revenue equals marginal cost. Now suppose that the firm's fixed costs are increased from OF to OF' by virtue of a franchise tax or some other form of lump-sum tax. The change in the fixed cost will not affect the marginal cost, and the slope of the new total-cost curve will be the same as the slope of the original total-cost curve; that is, TC' is parallel to TC. Since marginal cost has not been affected by the fixed tax, marginal cost and marginal revenue will be equal at the same output as before the tax. The most profitable output, accordingly, remains at OM. At this output total cost has increased by the amount of the tax $AB = FF'$. Profits have been reduced from AC to BC. Since output has not been affected by the tax, the price remains unchanged and equal to tan a. The full incidence of the lump-sum tax falls on the monopolist in the form of reduced profits; the consumer buys the same output at the same price as before the tax. The lump-sum tax might have the further advantage of encouraging the monopolist to seek more efficient methods of production and reduce his total costs in order to increase his profits. Or it might have the opposite effect. If the monopolist assumed that if he were able to increase his profits the government would raise the tax and eliminate his extra profits, there would be little incentive to investigate new cost-cutting techniques.

Regulation of Natural Monopolies

Political considerations have frequently outweighed economic analysis in the determination of public policy toward privately owned public utilities in the United States, and, because of practical as well as theoretical difficulties, commission regulation has often been less than satisfactory. The ends of public policy in this area have frequently been obscure, and the means for achieving the ends have often been inadequate. The basic consideration seems to be that monopoly is "natural" in the area of the public utilities; more than one firm serving a given geographic area would result in diseconomies of small scale and inefficient utilization of resources. An uncontrolled privately owned monopoly providing an essential service, however, would be in a position to exploit the consuming public, and, accordingly, regulatory commissions have been set up to maintain standards of service and prices which will be reasonable from the points of view of both the utility company and its customers. But what may seem reasonable from one point of view may be objectionable from the other. The courts have held that the utility company is entitled to a "fair return on a fair investment." Anything less would "deprive the company of property without due process of law," and would therefore be unconstitutional. In many decisions over the years the courts have tried to define "fair return" and "fair investment," but the terms remain essentially as vague as the economist's "normal profits." We shall call the price which would eliminate all monopoly profits but retain normal profits the "fair" price.

In Figure 10–10 we have represented the cost and revenue curves of a public utility company. If the company were permitted to maximize its profits, it would produce to the point where marginal cost equals marginal revenue; the most profitable output would be OM units per time period, and monopoly price would be MP_m. Since this price would provide monopoly profits for the utility company, we may assume that the regulatory commission would insist upon a price reduction. If the firm produced to the point where average total cost equals average revenue, cost per unit of output would equal revenue per unit, and all monopoly profit would be eliminated; since average total cost includes normal profit, the $atc = ar$ rule will establish the "fair" price. In Figure 10–10, fair price is $M'P_f$, and the corresponding output is OM'. We may assume that this is the price and output which an all-wise regulatory commission would establish.

But even the "fair" price does not provide the ideal allocation of resources. It will be noted in Figure 10–10 that the marginal cost of producing all units of output in excess of OM'' is greater than the prices consumers are willing to pay for them. It may be argued, accordingly, that the "ideal" price is $M''P_i$ and the ideal output is OM''. As long as consumers are willing to

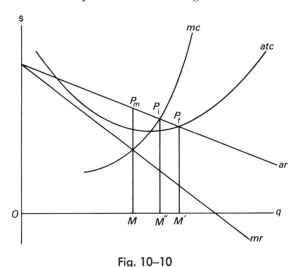

Fig. 10–10

pay more for a unit of output than its marginal cost of production, that unit should be produced. The ar curve tells us that consumers would rather have these units of this commodity at the indicated prices than anything else they might buy; otherwise they would not be willing to take the quantities at the various prices indicated on the demand curve. If resources are to be used in accordance with consumer preferences, a given commodity should be produced as long as marginal cost at any output is less than average revenue. As the curves are drawn in Figure 10–10, the "ideal" price would be lower than "monopoly" price but higher than the "fair" price, and the firm would enjoy some monopoly profit. If the demand curve had been drawn so that $ar = mc$ below the atc curve, however, the "ideal" price would be less than average total cost, and the firm would have to operate at a loss. An omniscient socialist state might be able to tax away any monopoly profits accruing from the application of the ideal-price principle and use the funds garnered in this way to subsidize those firms which suffered losses from the application of the rule. At this point one recalls with some nostalgia the world of pure competition. Without any regulatory commissions to enforce pricing rules, the purely competitive long-run-equilibrium condition is characterized by $mr = mc$, $ar = atc$, and $ar = mc$. No public utility commission and no socialist state can match that!

Price Discrimination

We have assumed to this point that the monopoly firm sells its product to all buyers at the same price. Under some circumstances, however, it may be possible for the monopolist to sell to different buyers at different prices. Electric power companies, for example, usually have one schedule of rates for commer-

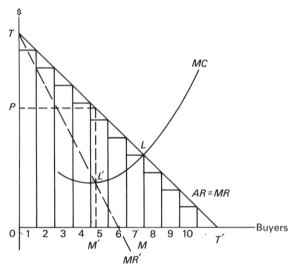

Fig. 10–11

cial buyers and a different and higher schedule for domestic users. Physicians sometimes make different charges for the same service, based on their estimates of their patients' ability to pay. Let us first consider the case of perfect discrimination. Suppose that a monopolist is able to list its buyers in decreasing order of the prices they are willing to pay for the firm's product. In terms of Figure 10–11, Buyer 1 is willing to pay the highest price, Buyer 2 the next highest, and so on until we reach Buyer 10, who is willing to pay the lowest price. Since the sale of an additional unit of the product does not affect the prices already being charged the other buyers, the price received for the additional unit of output adds that much to the firm's total revenue. Thus, in the case of the perfectly discriminating monopolist, the marginal-revenue curve and the average-revenue curve are identical. If the firm's marginal-cost curve is represented by *MC*, the profit-maximizing output will be *OM* and each buyer will be charged a different price. Since the firm's total revenue is represented by the area under the marginal-revenue curve, TR will be equal to $OTLM$. If the firm were a nondiscriminating monopolist with a single price to all buyers, profit-maximizing output would be OM' and monopoly price would be OP. The total revenue of the nondiscriminating monopolist would be the area under its marginal-revenue curve, which is $OTL'M'$. The increase in total revenue resulting from a policy of perfect price discrimination is given by

$$\Delta TR = TR_d - TR_n \\ = OTLM - OTL'M' = M'L'TLM,$$

where TR_d is the total revenue of the discriminating monopolist and TR_n is the total revenue of the nondiscriminating monopolist. The increased cost of the additional $M'M$ units produced by the discriminating monopolist is the area under the MC curve between OM' and OM:

$$\Delta TC = M'L'LM.$$

The increase in profits resulting from the policy of perfect price discrimination is given by

$$\Delta \pi = \Delta TR - \Delta TC \\ = M'L'TLM - M'L'LM = L'TL.$$

Cases of perfect price discrimination are rare if not nonexistent in the real world, but some degree of discrimination is not uncommon. One form of price discrimination employed by some monopolists is geographic price discrimination. Such firms sell at one price in one market area and at a higher or lower price in another. When geographic price discrimination is feasible, it adds to the profits of the seller. In order for a monopolist to be able to discriminate in this way, two conditions are necessary. First, those who buy at the lower price must not be able to resell to those who are charged the higher price by the monopolist; otherwise, the firm's customers would become its competitors. Secondly, the elasticity of demand for the product must be different in the two markets to make different prices profitable. In general, the monopolist will have to charge a lower price in the market where the elasticity of demand is greater. This point requires some elaboration.

Suppose that a monopolist sells in two markets, Market I and Market II. In Figure 10–12 AR_1 and MR_1 are the average-revenue and marginal-revenue curves for Market I, and AR_2 and MR_2 are the corresponding curves for Market II. The firm's marginal-cost curve is MC. The marginal-revenue curves for both markets have been added horizontally, giving us the total-marginal-revenue curve, MR_t. It will be noted that the average-revenue curves for both markets have a common y-intercept at T, and this means that the elasticity of demand at any price is the same in both markets; at price OP, for example, the elasticity of demand is given by OP/TP in both markets.

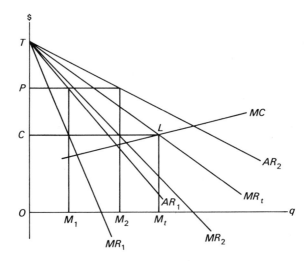

Fig. 10–12

The intersection of the MR_t and MC curves will indicate the profit-maximizing output for the two markets combined. At this output marginal cost is equal to M_tL or OC. Sales should be made in each market until the marginal revenue in that market is equal to OC. In Market I, sales will be equal to OM_1, and in Market II sales will be OM_2. Total sales in both markets will be

$$OM_1 + OM_2 = OM_t.$$

But OM_1 units can be sold at price OP in Market I, and OM_2 units can also be sold in Market II for price OP. When the elasticity of demand is the same in both markets, profit-maximizing price will be the same in both markets.

The reason for this may be seen more clearly if we call once again upon the formula

$$e = \frac{a}{m - a},$$

where e is elasticity of demand, a is average revenue, and m is marginal revenue. This formula may be restated explicitly in terms of a:

$$a = m\left(\frac{e}{1 + e}\right).$$

Now if e is the same in both markets and if m is also the same in both markets, it follows that a or profit-maximizing price must also be the same in both markets. But if e is different in the two markets and m is equal in both, there is opportunity for profitable price discrimination by the monopolist.

Suppose the elasticity of demand is -2 in Market I and -4 in Market II. For Market I:

$$a = m\left(\frac{-2}{1-2}\right) = 2m.$$

For Market II:

$$a = m\left(\frac{-4}{1-4}\right) = \frac{4}{3}\,m < 2m.$$

Profit-maximizing price will be lower in the market where the elasticity of demand is greater.

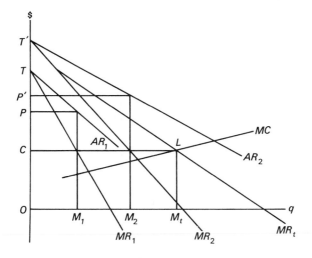

Fig. 10–13

This case is illustrated in Figure 10–13. Again we have average-revenue and marginal-revenue curves for two markets. But this time AR_1 is more elastic at any given price than is AR_2; at price OP, for example, the elasticity of AR_1 is OP/TP, whereas the elasticity of AR_2 at that price is $OP/T'P$, and $OP/TP > OP/T'P$. We should expect, accordingly, that the profit-maximizing price would be higher in Market II than in Market I. When MR_1 and MR_2 are added together horizontally we get total marginal revenue of MR_t. The intersection of MR_t and MC comes at total output OM_t, where marginal cost is equal to M_tL or OC. In Market I, marginal revenue equals OC at output OM_1, and in Market II marginal revenue equals OC at output OM_2; $OM_1 + OM_2 = OM_t$. But in Market I, OM_1 units of output can be sold for price OP; in Market II, OM_2 units of output can be sold at price OP', and OP' is a higher price than OP.

Competition and Monopoly Contrasted

We may conclude this chapter by noting a number of significant differences between the pure-monopoly and pure-competition models. About the only point they have in common is that in each case profits are maximized when $MR = MC$. But even here there is a difference. For the purely competitive firm, profits are at a maximum only if the marginal-cost curve is rising at the point where $MC = MR$; for the monopoly firm, marginal cost may be decreasing, constant, or increasing at the profit-maximizing output, provided that the MC curve cuts the MR curve from below.

1. The most obvious geometric difference between the competitive and monopolistic models is that the average-revenue curve of the perfectly competitive firm is represented by a horizontal line, whereas the average-revenue curve of a firm in a less than purely competitive market has a negative slope.

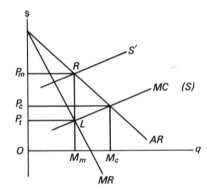

Fig. 10–14

2. The output where $P = MC$ may be called the competitive output, and the output where $P > MR = MC$ may be called the monopoly output. It is not to be inferred that if a monopoly could somehow be disintegrated into many purely competitive firms, the sum of the marginal-cost curves of the several firms would be the same as the marginal-cost curve of the monopoly firm. An industry in which a single firm supplies the entire market with a smaller than optimum-size plant operating at less than optimum output cannot be meaningfully compared with an industry which requires a very large number of optimum-size plants, each operating at optimum output. But if we mean by monopoly output the output where $P > MR = MC$ and competitive output the output where $P = MC$, we may argue that in general monopoly output is less than competitive output, and monopoly price is higher than competitive price. It is clear that the monopolist at least has the power to raise price by restricting output, whereas the competitive firm has no control over price.

In Figure 10–14 a monopolist's marginal-cost curve is represented by

MC, and the market demand is *AR.* The firm's marginal-revenue curve is *MR,* and the monopoly output is OM_m. Monopoly price, M_mR or OP_m, is greater than marginal revenue at output OM_m, which is M_mL. That is, $P > MR = MC$. Now suppose that *AR* is the market demand in a purely competitive industry, *MC* is the market supply curve, which is the summation of the marginal-cost curves of the firms within the industry. Competitive output, where $P = MC$, is OM_c, and competitive price is OP_c. Competitive price, as here defined, is lower than monopoly price, and competitive output is greater than monopoly output.

The effect of monopoly on price and output is much the same as the effect of a tax levied on each unit of output of the competitive seller. Suppose in Figure 10–14 that an excise tax equal to *LR* is levied on each unit of output of competitive firms. The effect of the tax would be to raise the market supply curve to *S′*; the price after the tax would be equal to OP_m, and OM_m units of output would be sold. This is, of course, the same as the original monopoly price and output, but the difference is that the amount of the tax, P_tP_mRL, would be paid to the government instead of going to the monopolist.

3. As we have seen, in a purely competitive industry all firms must be of optimum size since in long-run equilibrium even the optimum-size plants are just covering total costs including normal profits. There is no distinction between the most efficient size plant in an engineering sense and the optimum size in the economic sense. In a monopoly market, however, the optimum size plant to produce the most profitable output may be equal to, smaller than, or larger than the most efficient size plant in an engineering sense.

4. Under conditions of long-run equilibrium purely competitive firms are operating optimum size plants at optimum output. Under conditions of monopoly the firm may be using a less-than-optimum size plant at less-than-optimum output.

5. Purely competitive firms under conditions of long-run equilibrium will make no more than normal profits. Monopoly firms, on the other hand, may even in the long run earn supernormal profits.

6. Pure competition eliminates the necessity of making a number of ethical decisions and avoids the necessity of employing regulatory commissions to prevent firms from exploiting consumers. In long-run equilibrium under perfectly competitive conditions, equilibrium price is the fair price since $AR = ATC$, and equilibrium price is also the ideal price since $AR = MC$. Under conditions of monopoly, however, if there is no public regulation of prices, equilibrium price is likely to be higher than fair price or ideal price, and if a regulatory commission is set up to control prices, it must choose between the fair price and the ideal price since only in the special case where the demand curve cuts the average-total-cost curve at the minimum point on the *atc* curve are the two the same.

7. Our final observation in this section may come as something of a surprise: only in a purely competitive industry is market price determined by demand and supply. This is true by virtue of the fact that a less than purely competitive firm has no supply curve—there is no unique quantity which the firm will supply at a given price, and there is no unique price at which a given output will be sold. The amount produced by a firm possessing any degree of monopoly power—that is, a firm whose demand curve is negatively inclined—will be a function of both the firm's marginal revenue and its marginal costs. If the marginal-cost curve remains constant but the marginal-revenue curve shifts, monopoly output and monopoly price will change. Any output less than competitive output—that is, less than the output where $P = MC$—might be produced by a monopoly firm at a given price if appropriate shifts occur in the average- and marginal-revenue curves. Or, a given

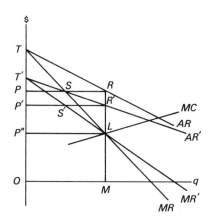

Fig. 10–15

output might be produced at any price higher than competitive price if appropriate changes occur in the average-revenue curve.

In Figure 10–15, *AR* and *MR* are a monopoly firm's revenue curves, and *MC* is the firm's marginal-cost curve. Monopoly output will be *OM* and monopoly price will be *OP*. But price *OP* and output *OM* are not a unique combination; output *OM* might be produced by this firm at any price above *OP″* even if there were no shift in the *MC* curve, provided that appropriate shifts took place in the firm's demand curve. Let us demonstrate the nature of the changes in the revenue curves which would make an arbitrary price, such as *OP′*, the monopoly price corresponding to output *OM*.

It will be recalled from the discussion of elasticity of demand in an earlier chapter that triangle *PTS* is congruent to triangle *SRL*; it follows that side *PT* must be equal to side *LR*. This means that the vertical distance from the marginal-revenue curve to the average-revenue curve at any price is equal to the distance on the *y*-axis from price to the intercept of the average-revenue curve. If we arbitrarily choose OP' as monopoly price, then the distance $P'T'$ must be equal to LR'. The average-revenue curve which will make OP' the profit-maximizing price, accordingly, will have a y-intercept at T' and pass through R'. The corresponding marginal-revenue curve will have a y-intercept at T' and pass through L. Monopoly output remains at OM, but monopoly price for this output is now OP'. As the y-intercept falls, approaching P'', monopoly price falls. If the y-intercept were at P'' and profit-maximizing output remained at OM, the average-revenue curve would be a horizontal line, indicating that the firm had no monopoly power. Competitive price is, therefore, OP'' when output is OM, and, if a monopolist produced this output, it would be at a higher than competitive price.

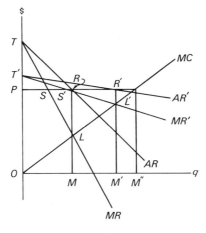

Fig. 10–16

We can also demonstrate that a monopoly firm may produce any output less than competitive output at a given price, depending upon what the nature of the demand curve happens to be. If in Figure 10–16 the monopolist's revenue curves are represented by AR and MR, monopoly output will be OM, and monopoly price will be OP. Suppose now that we want to show that this firm might produce the output OM' at price OP and indicate the appropriate changes in revenue curves to make this come about. If we measure a distance along the y-axis so that PT' equals $L'R'$, the appropriate average-revenue curve will have a y-intercept at T' and pass through R'. The corresponding marginal-revenue curve will have a y-intercept at T' and pass through L'. Profit-maximizing output is now OM' and profit-maximizing price remains at OP. It will be noted that competitive output is OM'', and this output would be produced at price OP only if the average-revenue curve were a horizontal line. We may conclude, therefore, that if monopoly price equals competitive price, monopoly output will be less than competitive output.

POSTPRANDIUM

Perfect price discrimination, which has been discussed in this chapter—like pure competition and pure monopoly, which were the subjects of the last two chapters—is rare or nonexistent in the real world. But less-than-perfect forms of price discrimination are commonplace now and other widespread types of price discrimination have been outlawed as contrary to the general welfare. Wherever price discrimination appears, the seller must enjoy some degree of monopoly power, since in a purely competitive market the seller has no control over the price of the product he sells but must sell at market price to all comers alike. A brief excursion into the nature of common forms of price discrimination is appropriate, accordingly, in a chapter on monopoly.[1]

Probably the most familiar form of price discrimination consists of quantity discounts; the buyer of a large quantity pays a smaller price per unit of product than does the buyer of a few units. In the supermarket one often sees prices quoted at "two for 25¢," the price of a single item presumably being 13¢. Or the large economy size may come at a lower cost per ounce than the regular size. In electric utilities it is commonplace to resort to "block rates," where the cost per kilowatt-hour declines as the consumption of power increases. A magazine may offer a two-year subscription for less than twice the cost of a single year's price. To the extent that quantity discounts reflect reduced costs to the seller it has generally been felt that price discrimination of this sort is not contrary to the public interest, but in 1936 Congress felt it necessary to incorporate into the Robinson-Patman Act restrictions on quantity discounts which did not reflect savings to the sellers.

Price discrimination is sometimes based on the wealth of the buyer. Physicians, lawyers, and horse breeders frequently charge different prices to different buyers based on their estimate of the buyer's ability to pay. A public speaker may charge more for an address to a conference of industrialists than to a teachers' convention. A television personality may demand more for an appearance on the Ed Sullivan show than on the Tonight show.

A buyer may be willing to pay discriminatory prices in order to avoid inconvenience and uncertainty. A reserved seat at a ball game or a theater may be little or no better than many of the general-admission seats, but, if one has a reserved seat, he knows in advance what he is getting for his money.

Time may affect the price of a good or service. Prices at a moving-picture theater are often less in the afternoon than at night; prices at resorts are higher on weekends and holidays and during the "season." This reflects changes in demand, but the price differentials are likely to be greater if services are sold monopolistically.

[1] This section is based largely on Clark Lee Allen, James M. Buchanan, and Marshall R. Colberg, *Prices, Income, and Public Policy,* rev. ed. (New York: McGraw-Hill Book Co., 1959), chap. 27.

Under some circumstances the prestige of the buyer may get for him a lower price. If a corporation president or a college dean is buying real estate, he may be able to buy at a discount because the seller hopes that junior executives and college professors will be more anxious to live in the subdivision if their superiors have homes there. This scheme on the part of the land developer may, of course, backfire, but that is beside the point.

Price discrimination may assume the form of multiproducts sold by the same seller. Often similar commodities are sold at prices which differ by more than the amount of the cost differential. The dealer's mark-up on the "extras" which a buyer may add to his new car is usually greater than the mark-up on the car itself. Sometimes the same commodity is sold under different trade names at a considerable difference in price so that the firm will have something to sell to those buyers who are not satisfied with the cheapest goods.

Spatial price discrimination has historically been common in this country but has been much reduced by federal legislation. The "Pittsburgh plus" system employed for years by the steel industry is probably the most familiar example. Under that system the freight charged a buyer of steel was figured from Pittsburgh to destination regardless of where the steel actually came from. A Chicago buyer, for example, who purchased his steel from nearby Gary, Indiana, paid freight as if the steel had come from Pittsburgh. For many years freight on automobiles was figured from Detroit even though the car had been assembled at some nearby point. The portland-cement industry used a multiple "basing-point" system until the United States Supreme Court upheld a Federal Trade Commission cease-and-desist order, and since that time cement and steel prices have been quoted on an f.o.b. mill basis.

Blanket freight rates are still employed in some instances. California oranges in carload lots, for example, are shipped for the same cost to any point between Denver and the North Atlantic coast. This practice discriminates against buyers in Kansas City and Chicago, for example, in favor of buyers in Philadelphia and New York City.

Discrimination may be based on the uses to which a commodity is to be put. A monopoly seller of salt may, for example, sell a "table brand" at one price, a "commercial brand" at a lower price, and a "livestock brand" at a still lower price. Milk of the same quality may be sold as Class I for fluid use, Class II for cream separation, and Class III for cheese making, and the price differential between classes may be considerable. It is reported that a plastic known as methyl methacrylate, which was produced by two domestic firms, was sold for industrial purposes at 85¢ per pound and for dental uses at $45 per pound.[2]

Before the days of federal regulation of railroad rates, competition among carriers often became ruinous or "cutthroat"; that is, since the firms

[2] Vernon A. Mund, *Government and Business* (New York: Harper & Row, Publishers, 1950), p. 127.

were characterized by great fixed costs, the more business they had the lower the cost per unit, and there was a great struggle to get more and more business, with the result that rates were reduced, often below the average-variable cost of the service. The consequence was that either the railroads finally got together and made collusive agreements as to rates, or one or more lines was forced out of business, leaving the surviving line with monopolistic power. It is reported that during these early days in the history of the railroads cattle were hauled from Chicago to the Atlantic seaboard for $5 per car, and sometimes for $1 per car, when the normal charge was $110 per car. At these rates the railroads couldn't even cover their out-of-pocket costs; it was said that these charges didn't cover the cost of the oil used in lubricating the locomotives and car wheels.[3] Under these circumstances one can be sure that the rates charged by the carriers were not uniform to all shippers.

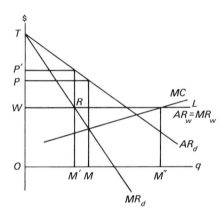

Fig. 10–17

One of the most famous cases of price discrimination in American economic history involves the Standard Oil Company. That company had become so dominant in the petroleum industry by 1885 that it was able to extract from the railroads hauling its traffic a rate of 10¢ a barrel on a particular haul when its competitors were being charged 35¢. And the 25¢ difference was paid to Standard Oil by the railroad![4] Standard Oil was set to make money even if under these conditions its competitors prospered.

We can demonstrate the effect of price discrimination between markets with the use of Figure 10–17. Suppose that a firm enjoys a monopoly position in the domestic market but that its product is sold on the world market under conditions of pure competition. A domestic tariff prohibits the domestic sale

[3] D. Philip Lochlin, *Economics of Transportation*, 4th ed. (Homewood, Ill.: Richard D. Irwin, Inc., 1954), p. 305.

[4] Charles E. Landon, *Transportation: Principles, Practices, and Problems* (New York: William Sloane Associates, Inc., 1951), pp. 268–269.

of imported goods, but the monopolist is free to sell in foreign markets at the world price.

If the firm confined its sales to the domestic market, it would maximize profits by selling OM units at price OP. But if in addition it sold in foreign markets at price OW, its domestic sales would be less than OM and the domestic price would be higher than OP. If the firm sold more than OM' units in the domestic market, its marginal revenue would be less than OW; by selling in foreign markets, the firm need accept no lower marginal revenue than OW. Taking both domestic and foreign markets into account, the firm's marginal revenue curve becomes TRL. Marginal cost equals marginal revenue at an output of OM''; of this, the firm will sell OM' units domestically at price OP' and $M'M''$ units in foreign markets at the world price OW. The effect of price discrimination on domestic buyers in this case is to get fewer units at a higher price than would prevail under conditions of domestic monopoly with no foreign sales.

SELECTED REFERENCES

Bain, Joe S. *Price Theory*. New York: Holt, Rinehart & Winston, Inc., 1952. Chap. 5.

Boulding, Kenneth E. *Economic Analysis*. 4th ed., Vol. I. New York: Harper & Row, Publishers, 1966. Chap. 21.

Colberg, Marshall R., Dascomb R. Forbush, and Gilbert W. Whitaker, Jr. *Business Economics: Principles and Cases*. 3rd ed. Homewood, Ill.: Richard D. Irwin, Inc., 1964. Chap. 8.

Due, John F., and Robert W. Clower. *Intermediate Economic Analysis*. 4th ed. Homewood, Ill.: Richard D. Irwin, Inc., 1961. Chap. 11.

Hicks, J. R. "Annual Survey of Economic Theory: The Theory of Monopoly," *Econometrica*, 3 (1935), 1–20; reprinted in Kenneth E. Boulding and George J. Stigler, eds., *Readings in Price Theory*. Homewood, Ill.: Richard D. Irwin, Inc., 1952. Pp. 361–383.

Leftwich, Richard H. *The Price System and Resource Allocation*. 3rd ed. New York: Holt, Rinehart & Winston, Inc., 1966. Chap. 10.

Levenson, Albert M., and Babette S. Solon, *Outline of Price Theory*. New York: Holt, Rinehart & Winston, Inc., 1964. Chap. 10.

Liebhafsky, H. H. *The Nature of Price Theory*. Homewood, Ill.: The Dorsey Press, Inc., 1963. Chap. 10.

Pigou, A. C. *The Economics of Welfare*. 2nd ed. London: Macmillan & Co., 1924. Chaps. 15 and 16.

Robinson, E. A. G. *Monopoly*. London: Nisbet, 1941.

Robinson, Joan. *The Economics of Imperfect Competition*. London: Macmillan & Co., 1933. Chaps. 3, 11–16.

Stonier, Alfred W., and Douglas C. Hague. *A Textbook of Economic Theory*. 3rd ed. New York: John Wiley & Sons, Inc., 1964. Chap. 8.

Watson, Donald Stevenson. *Price Theory and Its Uses*. Boston: Houghton Mifflin Company, 1963. Chaps. 19 and 20.

Weintraub, Sidney. *Intermediate Price Theory*. Philadelphia: Chilton Co., 1964. Chap. 10.

PROBLEMS

PROBLEM 1

Given: $AR = 8 - x$
$TC = 2x + 5$.

1. What is the equation for the firm's total revenue curve?   .   .   .   . _____

2. What is the equation for the firm's marginal-revenue curve?   .   .   .   . _____

3. What is total revenue at $x = 3$?   .   .   .   .   . _____

4. What is total revenue at $x = 4$?   .   .   .   .   . _____

5. What is total revenue at $x = 5$?   .   .   .   .   . _____

6. What is marginal cost at all outputs?   .   .   .   . _____

7. What is the equation for the average-total-cost curve?   .   .   .   . _____

8. What is the firm's total fixed cost?   .   .   .   . _____

9. What is the firm's average fixed cost at $x = 5$?   .   . _____

10. What is the firm's total variable cost at $x = 4$?   . _____

11. What is the y-intercept of the firm's demand curve?   .   .   .   . _____

12. What are the break-even points?   .   .   .   .   .
    .   .   .   .   .   .$x =$ _____ and _____

13. What is the equation for the firm's total profit?   . _____

14. What is the most profitable output?   .   .   .   . _____

15. At what price can the most profitable output be sold?   .   .   .   . _____

16. What is the elasticity of demand at the most profitable output?   .   .   .   . _____

17. What is marginal revenue at the most profitable output?   .   .   .   . _____

18. What is total revenue at the most profitable output?   .   .   .   . _____

19. What is total variable cost at the most profitable
    output? . . . . ._____

20. What is total cost at the most profitable output? ._____

21. What is total profit at the most profitable output? ._____

22. What is total profit at $x = 3\frac{1}{2}$? . . . . . ._____

23. Does this firm sell in a monopolistic market? . ._____

PROBLEM II

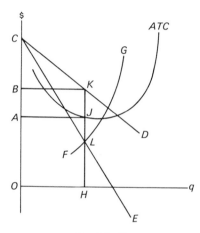

Fig. 10–18

The above figure represents the cost and revenue data for a firm. *ATC* is the
average-total-cost curve, and *CD* is the demand curve.

1. Does this firm sell monopolistically? . . . ._____

2. What is the firm's marginal-cost curve? . . ._____

3. What is the firm's marginal-revenue curve? . ._____

4. What is the profit-maximizing price? . . . ._____

5. What is elasticity of demand at the most profitable
   price? . . . . ._____

6. What is the profit-maximizing output? . . ._____

7. What is marginal revenue at the profit-maximizing
   output? . . . . ._____

8. What is marginal cost at the profit-maximizing
   output? . . . . ._____

9. What is total cost per unit at the profit-maximizing
   output? . . . . ._____

10. What is total cost at the profit-maximizing
output? . . . .————————

11. What is average revenue at the profit-maximizing
output? . . . .————————

12. What is total revenue at the profit-maximizing
output? . . . .————————

13. What is profit per unit at the profit-maximizing
output? . . . .————————

PROBLEM III

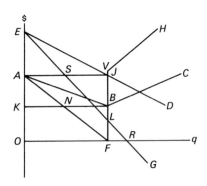

Fig. 10–19

In the above figure costs and revenues are represented by straight-line segments.
ABC is the average-total-cost curve, and *ED* is the demand curve.

1. What is the marginal-cost curve? . . . . .————————

2. What is the marginal-revenue curve? . . . .————————

3. What is the most profitable output? . . . .————————

4. At what price can the most profitable output
be sold? . . . .————————

5. What is elasticity of demand at the most profitable
output? . . . .————————

6. What is marginal revenue at the most profitable
output? . . . .————————

7. Total revenue is at a maximum at what output? .————————

8. What is total revenue at the most profitable
output? . . . .————————

9. What is total cost at the most profitable output? .————————

10. What is total profit at the most profitable output? .————————

11. What is average total cost at the most profitable output? . . . .——————————

12. What is total variable cost at the most profitable output? . . . .——————————

13. What is total fixed cost? . . . . . .——————————

14. What is average fixed cost at the most profitable output? . . . .——————————

PROBLEM IV

A monopolistic seller's demand curve is given by the equation $AR = 8 - x$.

1. On the axes below, draw the firm's total-revenue curve.

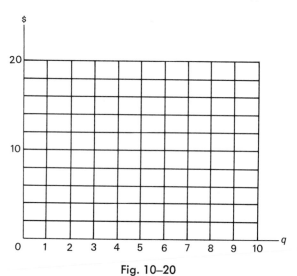

Fig. 10–20

2. If the firm has no costs, what will be the most profitable output? . . . .——————————

3. Assume now that the firm's total cost curve is given by $TC = x + 6$. Plot the total-cost curve on the axes above.

4. What is the firm's total fixed cost? . . . .——————————

5. What are the break-even points? . . . $x =$——————
and $x =$——————

6. What is the equation for total profit? . . .——————————

7. What is the most profitable output? . . . .——————————

8. What is profit at . . . . $x = 4$?——————
$x = 3\frac{1}{2}$?——————
$x = 3$?——————

PROBLEM V

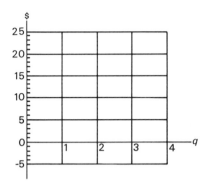

Fig. 10–21

Suppose that it is known that $TC = x^2 + 5$ and $TR = 12x - 2x^2$.

1. Plot the following curves on the chart above: TC, TR, MC, MR, and AR.

2. What is the most profitable output? .   .   .   . ._____

3. What is the most profitable price? .   .   .   . ._____

4. What is the maximum profit the firm can make? ._____

5. What is elasticity of demand at the most profitable price? .   .   .   . ._____

PROBLEM VI

Figure 10–22 represents the cost and revenue data for a monopolist. Assume in the problems below that this is the optimum-size plant and that the economic life of the plant is not affected by high or low rates of operation.

1. At what rate of output would an unregulated profit-maximizing monopolist operate this plant? .   . ._____

2. What price would the unregulated monopolist charge? .   .   .   . ._____

3. Suppose that this industry is declared a public utility and subjected to regulation by a public utility commission. If there are no changes in cost or revenue and if the commission wishes to provide the company with a "fair return" on its investment, at what price should the commission set the rate? ._____

4. How much larger is the rate of output under regulation than under an unregulated monopolist? .   . ._____

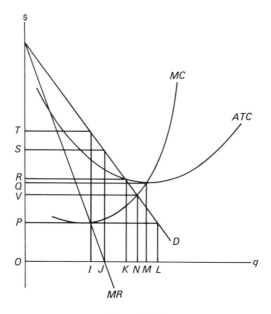

Fig. 10–22

5. If the government owned this public utility and costs were no higher or lower under public management than under private management, at what level should the price be set if resources are to be used to satisfy the wants of consumers best? .   ._____

6. In this instance does the operation of the firm so as to provide the optimum allocation of resources make it possible for the firm to sell at a profit? .   ._____

7. How much larger is the rate of output under public ownership and management under the conditions assumed here than under private management with public regulation? .   .   .   .   ._____

8. How much smaller is the rate of output under public ownership than under private ownership with public regulation if the city which owns this utility decides to maximize profits from the utility in order to eliminate other taxes as a source of revenue to finance its operations? .   .   .   .   ._____

PROBLEM VII

In Figure 10–23, D_a is a monopolist's demand in market A, and D_b is its demand in market B; MC is the firm's marginal-cost curve. Demonstrate geometrically that price discrimination between these markets is not feasible for the profit-maximizing firm. Explain why this is true.

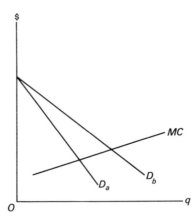

Fig. 10–23

PROBLEM VIII

A new electronic mousetrap is produced under complete patent control by a single manufacturer at a unit cost of $10 for all possible outputs. The demand for this manufacturer is given by $AR = p = 90 - 0.02q$, where p = price in dollars and q = quantity demanded.

1. If the manufacturer maximizes his profits, what output will he produce and sell? . . . . ._____

2. What price will he charge? . . . . . ._____

3. What will be his total profit? . . . . ._____

11

Prices and Output
under
Monopolistic Competition

The theoretical usefulness of the two market types we have been describing, pure competition and pure monopoly, is evidenced by the fact that prior to the 1930s these two models were the only ones available to economists, and they were nonetheless able to say much of significance on matters of economic policy. There is much to be said in favor of dividing all markets into only two categories, but rather into those which are purely competitive and those which are less than purely competitive. Classical and neoclassical economics generally assumed that firms were purely competitive. This assumption, often implicit, must be understood by the contemporary reader if he is to follow the argument of these writers. The classical economists understood full well that monopoly elements existed in many markets, but they considered the competitive model to be the most useful tool for economic analysis, a point of view shared by a number of modern economists.[1]

If what one seeks is descriptive realism, a classification of markets which puts virtually all real-world firms in one category and almost none in the

[1] See, for example, George J. Stigler, *Five Lectures on Economic Problems* (New York: The Macmillan Co., Publishers, 1950), Lecture 2.

other would seem to be quite unsatisfactory. Two works published several years ago, one by an English economist, Joan Robinson,[2] and the other by an American, E. H. Chamberlin,[3] were met with considerable enthusiasm because they were believed to provide market classifications which corresponded more closely with the real world than earlier classifications did, and were therefore believed to provide insights for the solution of real problems. Independently of each other, these two writers worked out analyses of the firms intermediate between pure competition and pure monopoly, and this intermediate category includes most real-world firms. Mrs. Robinson called the intermediate model *imperfect competition* and Professor Chamberlin called it *monopolistic competition*. We shall borrow both terms. The entire category that falls between pure competition and pure monopoly we shall call imperfect competition. We shall then divide imperfect competition into three subcategories: (a) monopolistic competition, which is characterized by a large number of firms, each producing a product somewhat differentiated from those of its competitors; (b) oligopoly, which is a market made up of only a few sellers, usually but not necessarily producing differentiated products; and (c) duopoly, which is a market consisting of only two sellers. The whole spectrum of market types, then, looks like this:

I. Pure competition
II. Imperfect competition
   A. Monopolistic competition
   B. Oligopoly
   C. Duopoly
III. Pure monopoly

It should be noted that this classification is arbitrary, and either fewer or more categories might be identified. Some writers, for example, distinguish between perfect competition and pure competition, on the grounds that pure competition implies only that the number of buyers and sellers be large and that all firms sell homogeneous products, whereas perfect competition implies this plus the assumption that sellers have perfect knowledge, and frictions preventing prompt adjustments to equilibrium price and output are completely absent. In this book we are not making use of this distinction, but the student should be on guard against different uses of the same terminology by different writers.

---

[2] Joan Robinson, *The Economics of Imperfect Competition* (London: Macmillan & Co., 1933).

[3] Edward Hastings Chamberlin, *The Theory of Monopolistic Competition* (Cambridge, Mass.: Harvard University Press, 1933). The term *monopolistic competition* was used in A. C. Pigou, *The Economics of Welfare* (London: Macmillan & Co., 1920), Part II, Chap. 14.

Monopolistic Competition

The term "monopolistic competition" seems on its face to be self-contradictory. How can a market be both monopolistic and competitive at the same time? As the term was used by Professor Chamberlin and as it will be used here, a monopolistically competitive market is similar to a purely competitive market except that in the former the product of one firm is differentiated from those of other firms whereas in the latter it is indistinguishable from them. The wheat farmer is a model of the purely competitive producer. Farmer Jones' wheat differs in no way from Farmer Smith's, and when the wheat is sold it will likely be stored in a grain elevator along with the wheat from dozens of other farms. Wheat is a "homogeneous" product. Under conditions of monopolistic competition, however, each seller has a product which in some way is "differentiated" from the products of other sellers. Differentiation of product may assume a number of forms. The product of one seller may in some particulars actually be different from those of other sellers. Or they may be identical but packaged in different ways or sold under different trade marks. One may, for example, buy baking soda at the drug store, at a relatively high price and under the trade name of a pharmaceutical house, or at a grocery store, at a low price and under the trade name of the grocery chain. The two sodas are identical and in fact may be produced by the same firm. Or products may be differentiated by the sale and credit arrangements under which they are sold. Or the physical conditions under which they are sold may provide differentiation; the same dress may be offered at different prices by the same department store in its elite shop on the fifth floor and in its bargain basement, and many customers may feel that the relative comfort, quiet, and safety of buying in the fifth-floor shop constitute sufficient differentiation of product to justify the higher price. Under conditions of monopolistic competition the product of one firm is a good but not a perfect substitute for the product of another firm. Each firm has a "monopoly" of its own differentiated product; Firm X and only Firm X can produce Brand X cornflakes. But Brand X cornflakes are so similar to Brand Y cornflakes that there is intense competition between them. The competition between these monopolies which produce good substitutes for each other's products is monopolistic competition.

Monopolistic competition, accordingly, is characterized by a large number of sellers, each producing a differentiated product. In the long run, it is generally assumed, the entry of new firms into a monopolistic competition situation is relatively easy. Monopolistic competition is closer to pure competition than it is to pure monopoly. The assumption of differentiation of product gives it the appearance of being more realistic than the purely competitive model, but this is in part an illusion. Actual differentiation of product is a common phenomenon, as a perusal of newspapers, magazines, or television programs will readily attest, but the number of firms selling products which are close substitutes in a given market is usually relatively small, and since in some lines, such as household detergents, a given firm may offer several brands competing with each other as well as with the products of other firms, the number of firms is often even smaller than a superficial view would indicate. Furthermore, if the degree of product differentiation is minute, the pure-competition model may be adequate for economic analysis, and if the degree of product differentiation is great, the pure-monopoly model may serve. This is not to argue that the concept of imperfect competition adds little or nothing to our understanding of price theory. Economics is a complicated subject, and anything which provides us with new insights makes a contribution to our understanding. But these ideas have not constituted a revolution, nor even a significant breakthrough, in economic analysis, as some of their early proponents seemed to expect, and such contributions as they *have* made are not to be explained solely on the grounds that the new theory is more "realistic" than the older one.

Monopolistic Competition as a Theory of the Firm

The theory of monopolistic competition is a theory of the firm rather than a theory of the market or of industry. Since the monopolistically competitive firm has some degree of monopoly power, it can raise its prices without losing all of its sales; that is to say that the firm's demand curve is negatively inclined. And a firm with a negatively inclined demand curve, as we saw in the chapter on monopoly, has no supply curve. At a given price a whole range of quantities may be offered or a given quantity may be offered at a range of prices depending on the shape and position of the demand curve. Since the individual firms in a monopolistically competitive market have no supply curves, there can be no market supply curve. In this respect the monopoly and monopolistic-competition models are similar. But whereas there is a market demand curve for the monopolist, the idea of a market demand in a monopolistically competitive market loses much of its meaning. This is true because the products of the several firms in the monopolistically competitive market are nonhomogeneous. We might be able to draw up separate demand curves for Anacin, Bufferin, and the several brands of aspirin, but it would hardly be feasible to add them together to get a market demand for headache remedies since the units on the x-axis would be heterogeneous. In the analysis of monopolistic competition our attention will be focused on the firm rather than on the industry; the idea of an industry, in fact, becomes vague when all of the firms within the industry produce similar but not identical products.

Since monopolistically competitive firms produce goods which are not perfect substitutes for each other, we may assume that the elasticity of demand for these products is relatively high. If a firm in such a market raises its price, many buyers will shift to a similar product produced by a competitor. A small increase in price by one firm, other firms retaining their old prices, will cause the price-raising firm to lose sales significantly, and the smaller the differentiation of product, the more elastic the demand for the product is likely to be.

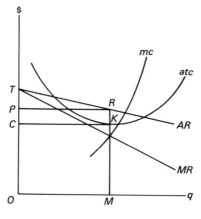

Fig. 11–1

Since the monopolistically competitive firm will have a negatively inclined average-revenue curve, marginal revenue will be less than average revenue at any output. But since the elasticity of demand for the product is great, the difference between average revenue and marginal revenue will be relatively small. This follows from the formula

$$m = \frac{ea}{e-1},$$

where m is marginal revenue, a is average revenue, and e is elasticity of demand expressed as a negative number. If, for example, $e = -1$,

$$m = \frac{-a}{-2} = \tfrac{1}{2}a;$$

but if $e = -4$,

$$m = \frac{-4a}{-5} = \tfrac{4}{5}a.$$

In Figure 11–1, AR and MR are the average-revenue and marginal-revenue curves and atc and mc are the average-total-cost and marginal-cost curves of a monopolistically competitive firm. The curves have the same general shapes as the corresponding curves for a purely monopolistic firm except that we are operating in the range where the elasticity of demand is high. The firm's profits will be maximized where $MR = mc$, which in Figure 11-1 is where output is OM, price is OP, and profit is $CPRK$.

The same rule which determines the most profitable output for the purely competitive seller and for the monopolist holds for the monopolistically competitive seller: produce to the point where $MC = MR$. But there are other decisions which the monopolistically competitive seller must also make. He must decide, first, whether he can increase profits by changing the nature of his product, making it either more or less similar to the products of competing firms. In general, if one firm, say the manufacturer of a soft drink, has been doing well with its product, it is likely that other firms will enter the market with a drink as similar to the old one as possible; that is, the differentiation of product will be slight in order to divert customers away from the first firm, but the advertising for the new product is likely to stress the several ways in which the new drink is different from and superior to the old one! It may be to the advantage of an established firm to increase the differentiation of its product since, with loyal customers, the increased differentiation may serve to reduce the elasticity of demand for the product, making possible a raise in price without a significant loss of sales or a successful holding action against price cutting by its competitors.

Second, the firm must decide how much if anything is to be spent on advertising and other promotional activities in order to maximize its profits. This is a new element in our analysis since neither the purely competitive firm nor the purely monopolistic firm would need to expend funds in this way. Since the purely competitive firm has no control over the price of its product and can sell all that it can produce at the price established in the market, advertising would be to no avail. We do not encounter exhortations to "Buy Farmer Smith's wheat—seven ways better." A monopolist may spend some money on institutional advertising to create good will, or the electric power company may urge women to cook with electricity instead of with gas, since even a monopolist's product may be competitive with the product of other sellers for some uses. But in general, advertising expenditures of monopolists are relatively modest. Monopolistically competitive firms, on the other hand, do resort to advertising and promotional programs, and one of the principal contributions made by the monopolistic-competition model is its analysis of selling costs. (We will henceforth use the term "advertising" to refer to all selling costs.)

Monopolistic Competition and Selling Costs

The monopolistically competitive firm, then, has three profit-maximizing decisions to make, the first two of which the perfectly competitive firm is not concerned with: (1) precisely what kind of product to produce; (2) how much to spend on promotional projects; and (3) how much of the product to produce. We will analyze the equilibrium of the monopolistically competitive firm with reference to each of these profit-maximizing decisions.

Let us begin by assuming that the nature of the product and its price are given, but the amount to be spent on advertising is as yet undetermined. Isolating one of the variables and analyzing it on the assumption that the other elements of the problem are constant makes it possible to treat each of the variables separately. In addition, there is empirical evidence which suggests that firms do, in fact, sometimes operate on the assumption of two absolutely fixed elements and only the third is truly variable. A firm may not consider a change in its price because its price has become traditional; or it may be set by the manufacturer; or the firm may want to avoid price competition which might lead to a "price war." For whatever reason, we are at the moment assuming the price, as well as the product, to be fixed and the amount to be spent on advertising variable.

When a firm undertakes an advertising program, it adds a new set of costs to those we have previously considered. The average-total-cost curve we are familiar with represents production costs, and these arise from the firm's purchases of labor, materials, land, and other fixed and variable factors of production. We now add to these costs the selling costs: advertising, salesmen's commissions, allowances for window displays, free samples, and the like. The effects of these expenditures are twofold: the firm's total costs are increased, and, or so it is hoped, the firm's demand curve is shifted to the right. Whether the advertising adds to the profits of the firm depends upon whether the additional revenue resulting from these expenditures is greater or less than the additional cost. Sales costs may be fixed—for example, the cost of sponsoring a television show for thirteen weeks—or they may be variable—for example, commissions paid to salesmen. But in general it may be assumed that the average-selling-cost curve will be U-shaped; relatively small total advertising expenditures may have little effect on sales, and the average selling cost per unit of output will be high. It is an axiom in many lines of merchandising that small expenditures on advertising are wasted; it appears that the consumer must be beaten over the head repeatedly before the advertising message becomes effective. As total sales expenditures increase, the selling cost per unit of output decreases for a time but eventually will rise again since there is a limit to how much a given firm can sell per time period regardless of how much advertising it does.

In Figure 11–2 the average-sales-cost curve, *asc*, is U-shaped. This curve shows the amount of sales cost per unit of output necessary to achieve any given output; OM units of output may be sold per time period if a total of $OLJM$ dollars, or MJ per unit of output, is spent on advertising. The *apc* curve is the average-production-cost curve, which would be the *atc* curve if there were no sales costs. The average-total-cost curve including the average sales cost will be the sum of *asc* and *apc*, which is atc_s in Figure 11–2. Since the particular nature of the product is assumed to be given and the price is

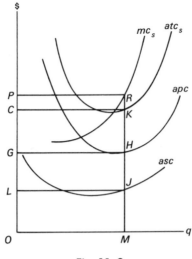

Fig. 11–2

assumed to be OP, the firm will maximize profits when it produces the output where $P = mc_s$. This means that under these assumptions the profit-maximizing output is OM; total cost is $OCKM$, of which $OGHM$ is production cost and $OLJM = GCKH$ is selling cost; and total profit is $CPRK$. No other output sold at price OP will be as profitable as OM units per time period.

Next let us assume that the nature of the product and the advertising budget are fixed, but the price at which the product is sold is variable. Again,

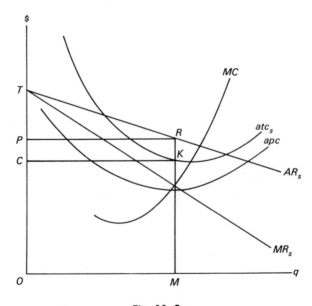

Fig. 11–3

it simplifies the analysis if we can isolate one factor and permit it alone to vary, but also again, this assumption corresponds with some business practices. Many firms allocate a certain figure for advertising in their annual budget. This amount may have been arrived at through their own experience or through the experiences of other firms reported to them through their trade associations, but in any event it is fixed. The effect of the fixed advertising cost is to shift the average-cost curve upward, but if the advertising cost is fixed, the firm's marginal-cost curve will not be affected. The advertising expenditure has the same effect on the firm's cost curves as would an increase in rent or other fixed cost. The important difference is that it is expected that the advertising expenditure will also have the effect of shifting the firm's demand curve to the right. In Figure 11–3, *apc* is the average-production-cost curve, *atc*$_s$ is the average-total-cost curve including fixed sales costs, AR_s and MR_s are the average-revenue and marginal-revenue curves reflecting the effects of the advertising expenditures. The firm's profits will be maximized when $MC = MR_s$; this will come at output OM and price OP, with total profits equal to $CPRK$.

As a third case we may assume that the firm keeps total sales expenses and price constant but may want to consider variations in the product. The procedure would be to prepare charts similar to Figure 11–3 for each "product" under consideration and choose the one which provides the greatest total profit. This, of course, need not be the product for which the *atc*$_s$ curve is lowest or the one for which the AR_s curve is farthest to the right. The profit-maximizing product will simply be the one which at profit-maximizing output and price provides the greatest total profit.

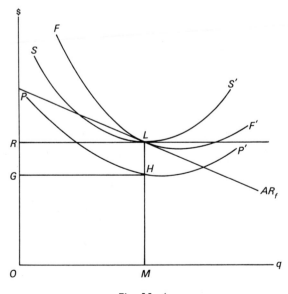

Fig. 11–4

Finally, let us consider a case where only the nature of the product is held constant but price and advertising outlay are both permitted to vary. Our problem is to discover the price and total selling expenditure which will maximize profits for the given product. As a special case let us represent a firm which is just breaking even when it is maximizing its profits. In Figure 11–4 the curve PP' is the average-production-cost curve, which corresponds to apc in Figures 11–2 and 11–3. Curve SS' is the atc_s curve of Figure 11–2; it includes the selling costs necessary to sell any given output when the price of the product is OR. In order to sell OM units of output per time period at price OR, for example, the firm must incur selling costs of $GRLH$. Since the horizontal line RL is drawn tangent to the SS' curve in Figure 11–4, the firm will make just normal profits when price is OR, selling outlay is $GRLH$, and output is OM. Any larger or smaller expenditure on sales promotion would cause the firm to operate at a loss. If price is constant at OR, therefore, the appropriate output is OM, and this will require sales costs totaling $GRLH$.

Now on the same chart let us suppose that total sales outlay is kept constant at $GRLH$ but the price of the product may be varied. The average-total-cost curve is now FF' instead of SS'; the curve FF' is the atc_s curve of Figure 11–3 and reflects the constant advertising outlay of $GRLH$. Since we have seen that when price is OR and selling outlay is $GRLH$, the firm can sell OM units of output per time period, the FF' curve must cut the SS' curve at L. And since at output OM when price was constant at OR the firm was just breaking even, the AR_f curve, which is the firm's average-revenue curve reflecting the effects of the constant sales outlay, must pass through point L and be tangent to FF' at L. If the firm's demand curve is AR_f and its average-total-cost curve is FF', accordingly, the firm will earn normal profits at price OR but would suffer losses at any price either higher or lower than OR. We may conclude, therefore, that OR is the profit-maximizing price; OM is the profit-maximizing output; and $GRLH$ is the profit-maximizing selling outlay.[4]

Monopolistic Competition and Long-Run Equilibrium

The monopolistically competitive firm, like the purely competitive firm or the pure monopolist, will be in short-run equilibrium when it has adjusted its output so that $MC = MR$. Such a firm was represented in Figure 11–1. As drawn in that figure the firm was enjoying supernormal profits, and the short-run equilibrium position could be summarized as follows:

$$P > MR = MC < ATC < P.$$

If the group of firms which are producing products which are good but not

[4] Cf. Chamberlin, *op. cit.*, pp. 140–149.

perfect substitutes for each other are able to keep other firms from entering the market, these greater-than-normal profits may continue in the long run. This might come about if the old firms were so well established that it would be difficult for new firms to attract customers away from them, or if basic patent rights were held by the old firms, or if the fixed costs were so great as to discourage the entry of new firms, or if it were felt by investors that although current profits were more than adequate, there was doubt that favorable conditions would continue indefinitely into the future, or for some

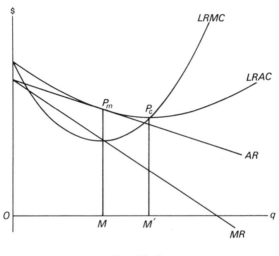

Fig. 11–5

other reason. But more often it is likely true that the entry of new firms in a monopolistically competitive market is relatively easy. If by assumption a monopolistically competitive market includes a large number of firms, it should not be too difficult for still more firms to enter. In the case of easy entry of new firms, the profits of the firm in Figure 11–1 will tend to disappear in the long run. As new firms come in, the demand curve for each firm will tend to shift to the left; prices will fall; and eventually profits will disappear. The long-run equilibrium position of the monopolistically competitive firm with free entry is represented in Figure 11–5, and may be summarized as follows:

$$P > MR = MC < ATC = P.$$

In terms of Figure 11–5, long-run equilibrium output is OM and long-run equilibrium price is MP_m. This may be compared with the purely competitive long-run output and price of OM' and $M'P_c$. Since it is assumed that the elasticity of demand for the monopolistically competitive seller is quite high, long-run output is somewhat less and long-run price is only a little higher than the purely competitive long-run output and price would be.

Because there is a time lag between the decision to build a new plant and the actual operation of the plant, it is possible that so many new firms will be attracted to the market by the short-run profits enjoyed by the monopolistically competitive firms that each firm's demand curve will eventually shift farther to the left than is indicated in Figure 11–5, the result being that each firm operates at a loss. This situation is represented in Figure 11–6. If the average-revenue curve shifts so far to the left that it becomes

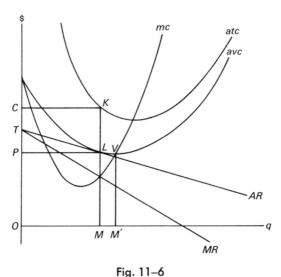

Fig. 11–6

tangent to the firm's average-variable-cost curve, the firm's losses will be equal to its total fixed cost. But if the firm shut down, its total loss would equal its total fixed cost. In terms of Figure 11–6, accordingly, the firm's shut-down output would be OM and its shut-down price would be OP. This can be summarized as:

$$P > MR = MC < AVC = P < ATC.$$

Again it will be noted that the monopolistically competitive firm's shut-down output is less and its shut-down price is somewhat higher than the shut-down output and price of the purely competitive firm, but, also again, if the elasticity of demand of the monopolistically competitive firm is quite high, the differences will not be great.

Monopolistic Competition and Pure Competition Compared

It should be fruitful to compare monopolistic competition as sketched here and pure competition as described earlier. The distinguishing characteristic of monopolistic competition is that the product of each firm is differentiated from the products of other firms with which it competes. This means that the demand curve of the monopolistically competitive firm is negatively inclined instead of being horizontal. And this, in turn, means that there is no supply curve for the monopolistically competitive firm, and hence no market supply curve for the monopolistically competitive industry. Indeed, if an industry is taken to be a group of firms producing homogeneous products, there is no such thing as a monopolistically competitive industry, while if an industry is monopolistically competitive, there is no industry demand curve. The theory of monopolistic competition is, accordingly, a theory of the firm.

If the degree of differentiation is slight, the elasticity of demand for the product of a given firm may be expected to be great; if a firm raises its price above the price of similar goods offered by other sellers, it should expect to lose a significant amount of business to its rivals. If there are many firms in the market, there appears to be no reason to suppose that entry of new firms would be difficult. In the long run, accordingly, profits would tend to disappear, and, as the market is divided among more and more firms, the demand curve for each firm would shift to the left. Long-run equilibrium would be achieved when the firm's average-revenue curve became tangent to its average-total-cost curve. The monopolistically competitive firm, like the purely competitive firm, would make no more than normal profits in the long run, but equilibrium price would be somewhat higher and equilibrium output would be somewhat less than under conditions of pure competition. As the elasticity of demand of the monopolistically competitive firm approaches infinity, the long-run equilibrium position of the firm approaches that of the purely competitive firm.

The profit-maximizing scale of plant for the monopolistically competitive firm may be smaller than the most efficient size plant, and under conditions of long-run equilibrium the firm will operate at less than the most efficient rate of output. This represents some degree of waste of resources, the degree of waste being less as the coefficient of elasticity of demand is greater.

The monopolistically competitive firm is likely to incur selling costs in addition to its production costs, and, as we have just seen, plant size is likely to be smaller than the most efficient size in an engineering sense. Advertising expenditures are likely to cause prices to the consumer to be higher than they would be in the absence of selling costs and almost certainly to be higher than they would be under conditions of pure competition. It may be noted in this connection that whereas, as was pointed out in the chapter on pure monopoly, a market which can be supplied by a single seller with a less-than-optimum size plant operating at less-than-optimum output cannot be compared directly with a purely competitive market where a large number of sellers, each with an optimum-size plant, operates at optimum output, monopolistic competition and pure competition are directly comparable since both include many sellers. It seems clear enough, accordingly, that monopolistically competitive prices will be higher than perfectly competitive prices, and a part of this difference is due to selling costs. To the extent that advertising is informative and makes possible more rational choices by the consumer, the difference in price may work no hardship on him. But to the extent that it is simply persuasive, inducing the consumer to buy the product of one firm instead of the virtually identical product of a competing firm, and especially to the extent that advertising misinforms and deludes the consumer, the general welfare is harmed and the resources devoted to these uses may be properly classified as social waste.

Finally, monopolistic competition increases the variety of commodities available to the consumer and, assuming it results in efforts by sellers to improve their products and otherwise increase their usefulness to consumers rather than merely to provide new trade names or different packages for virtually identical products, improves his economic well-being. Otherwise, the result may be increased consumer confusion and social waste, resulting from the necessity of retailers' finding storage and shelf space and capital investment for several brands of what in fact is the same commodity. On the other hand, since utility and satisfaction are psychological matters as well as economic, perhaps if consumers *believe* that they have choices even where no real choice exists, the higher prices due to selling costs (which may be small in any event) may in fact do little harm to their well-being.

POSTPRANDIUM

The concept of monopolistic competition was introduced in 1933 to provide a model which accorded more closely with the real world than the models at the time being utilized by price theorists. Prior to then economists had developed the models of pure competition and pure monopoly, but it was understood by all that relatively few industries corresponded closely in fact with either of them. As we have noted frequently in earlier chapters, it is not the purpose of price theory to provide an accurate description of the real world, but it is clear nonetheless that a model may lose much of its usefulness even for analytical purposes if its correspondence with real life is remote. The effort to provide a more "realistic" category of markets was, accordingly, generally applauded by economists, and for a time the study of monopolistic competition took on the attributes of an academic fad. Scarcely a respectable economics department in the country failed to offer as part of its graduate curriculum at least one course in the theory of monopolistic competition.

After thirty years a number of economists appear to have retained their enthusiasm for monopolistic competition as a useful tool of analysis, and we would agree that to the extent that it provides new and clearer insights into the complex problems of the theory of the firm, the theory of monopolistic competition serves a useful purpose. But judged on the basis of its "realism," the notion of monopolistic competition proves to be a disappointment.

There appear, in fact, to be relatively few instances of markets characterized by large numbers of firms each selling differentiated products. In such cases as do exist, the degree of product differentiation is so slight that the firms actually have little power to control their prices. The firms' demand curves are so nearly horizontal that the purely competitive model may be employed, since the differences in profit-maximizing price and output are so small under conditions of pure competition and of monopolistic competition that they may be ignored.

On the other hand, if product differentiation is significant, the number of firms in the market is likely to be small, and the appropriate market model in these instances is oligopoly. (Oligopoly is the subject of the next chapter.) Even in retail markets, where it is alleged that instances of monopolistic competition are most frequent, the degree of differentiation of product is likely to be small, and so is the number of firms among which the consumer may effectively choose. Most of the products which the consumer buys are sold under trade names—soap, television sets, bread, automobiles, shoes, canned fruits and vegetables, ham, toothpaste, aluminum foil, motorcycles, cigarettes, gasoline. All of these are differentiated products in today's markets, but in each instance the number of brands available to a given consumer is small. Cases of differentiated products sold by large numbers of firms are extremely rare in the real world, and where they occur they probably represent a transitional stage: in a short time only the fittest will survive, and monopolistic competition will evolve into oligopoly. Judged on the basis of its ability to represent reality, the concept of monopolistic competition appears to be another of what a distinguished English economist described many years ago as empty economic boxes.[5]

SELECTED REFERENCES

Bain, Joe S. *Price Theory*. New York: Holt, Rinehart & Winston, Inc., 1952. Chap. 7.

Carter, W. Harrison, and William P. Snavely. *Intermediate Economic Analysis*. New York: McGraw-Hill Book Co., 1961. Chap. 12.

Chamberlin, Edward Hastings. *The Theory of Monopolistic Competition*. 5th ed. Cambridge, Mass.: Harvard University Press, 1946.

Cohen, Kalman J., and Richard M. Cyert. *The Theory of the Firm*. Englewood Cliffs, N.J.: Prentice-Hall, Inc., 1965. Chap. 12.

[5] J. H. Clapham, "Of Empty Economic Boxes," *The Economic Journal*, 32 (1922), 305–314; reprinted in George J. Stigler and Kenneth E. Boulding, eds., *Readings in Price Theory* (Homewood, Ill.: Richard D. Irwin, Inc., 1952), pp. 119–130.

Leftwich, Richard H. *The Price System and Resource Allocation.* 3rd ed. New York: Holt, Rinehart & Winston, Inc., 1966. Chap. 12.

Machlup, Fritz. *The Economics of Sellers' Competition.* Baltimore: Johns Hopkins Press, 1952. Chaps. 5, 7, 10.

"The Theory of Monopolistic Competition after Thirty Years," *American Economic Review, Papers and Proceedings,* 54 (May 1964), 28–57. (Papers by Joe S. Bain, Robert L. Bishop, and William J. Baumol; discussion by Jesse W. Markham and Peter O. Steiner.)

Triffin, Robert. *Monopolistic Competition and General Equilibrium Theory.* Cambridge, Mass.: Harvard University Press, 1941.

PROBLEMS

PROBLEM I

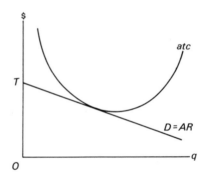

Fig. 11–7

1. In the chart above, draw the firm's marginal-revenue curve, and label it *MR*. Sketch in the marginal-cost curve, and label it *mc*.

2. The most profitable output is *OA*. Locate *A* on the chart.

3. The most profitable price is *OB* or *AC*. Locate *B* and *C*.

4. Total revenue = ...———————————

5. Total cost = ...———————————

6. Total profit = ...———————————

7. Elasticity of demand at the most profitable price = ...———————————

8. If this firm sold in a perfectly competitive market, the long-run equilibrium output would be *OF,* and price would be *OE* or *FG.* Locate *E, F,* and *G.*

9. Under long-run competitive conditions, *TR* would be . . . .———————————

10. Under long-run competitive conditions, TC would
    be .   .   .   .   ._____

11. Under long-run competitive conditions, total profit
    would be .   .   .   .   ._____

PROBLEM II

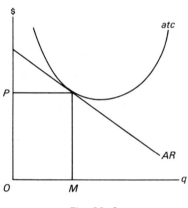

Fig. 11–8

In the figure above, AR is the average revenue curve and atc is the average-total-cost curve of a monopolistically competitive firm in long-run equilibrium. Price is OP and output is OM.

1. Sketch in the firm's marginal-cost and marginal-revenue curves.

2. Now suppose that the firm undertakes the sponsorship of a TV program. The advertising cost may be viewed as an increase in the firm's fixed costs. Draw in the new average-total-cost curve reflecting the increase in fixed costs.

3. Draw new average-revenue and marginal-revenue curves to indicate the new long-run equilibrium situation.

4. On the basis of the chart as you have drawn it, the effects of the promotional expenditure may be summarized as follows: average-total cost has (increased, decreased, remained the same); marginal cost has (increased, decreased, remained the same); demand has (increased, decreased, remained the same); marginal revenue has (increased, decreased, remained the same); output has (increased, decreased, remained the same); price to the consumer has (increased, decreased, remained the same); profit to the firm has (increased, decreased, remained the same).

PROBLEM III

1. Draw on Figure 11–9 the firm's MR curve (p. 270).

2. Indicate the firm's most profitable price as OP and the number of units sold as OM.

3. Assume now that the firm undertakes an advertising program which in-

creases total variable cost and which shifts the *AR* curve to the right. Draw the new *AR′*, *MR′*, and *MC′* curves.

4. Indicate the new price as *OP′* and the new output as *OM′*.

5. The effect of the advertising expenditure has been to cause the price to the consumer (to rise, to fall, not to change).

6. Whether the advertising program has been profitable to the firm depends upon whether increase in _____ exceeds the _____ .

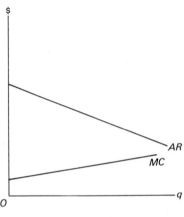

Fig. 11–9

PROBLEM IV

1. Most profitable output = ..._____

2. Total revenue at most profitable output = ..._____

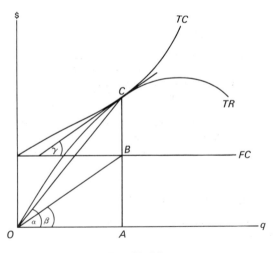

Fig. 11–10

3. Total cost at most profitable output = ..._____

4. Total profit at most profitable output = .   .   ._____

5. Total variable cost at most profitable output = .   ._____

6. Total fixed cost at most profitable output =   .   ._____

7. Average fixed cost at most profitable output = .   ._____

8. Average total cost at most profitable output = .   ._____

9. Average revenue at most profitable output = .   ._____

10. Marginal cost at most profitable output = .   .   ._____

11. Marginal revenue at most profitable output = .   ._____

12. Does this firm sell monopolistically?   .   .   ._____

PROBLEM V

Given: $TC = x^3 - 4x^2 + 6x$
$AR = 5 - 2x$.

1. What is profit-maximizing output? .   .   .   .   ._____

2. What is profit-maximizing price?   .   .   .   ._____

3. What is total cost at the most profitable output? .   ._____

4. What is total revenue at the most profitable output? ._____

5. What is average total cost at the most profitable output?   .   .   .   .   ._____

6. What is average revenue at the most profitable output? .   .   .   .   ._____

7. What is marginal cost at the most profitable output? .   .   .   .   ._____

8. What is marginal revenue at the most profitable output?   .   .   .   .   ._____

9. What is total profit at the most profitable output?   ._____

12

Prices and Output
under Oligopoly

In the last three chapters we discussed prices and output under conditions of pure competition, pure monopoly, and monopolistic competition. For each of these market forms we were able to isolate the forces affecting prices and output and were able to indicate the nature of short-run and long-run equilibrium. As exercises in pure logic, these models have much to commend them. More importantly, they provide significant insights into problems which confront businessmen and into the factors which businessmen must take into account to maximize profits. But on the other hand we know that none of these market forms describes the real world with a high degree of accuracy. Pure competition has something of the quality of a never-never land; there just aren't many market situations where the large number of firms producing homogeneous products makes it impossible for the individual firm to affect the price of its own product. Even in agricultural industries, which provide the economist with most of his illustrations of purely competitive markets, government intervention in the form of price-support programs and quota arrangements has distorted the actual picture. Pure monopoly is also rare. The public utilities are natural monopolies, but they are subject to governmental regulation which largely determines price and output. And if we restrict the term monopolistic competition to those markets where a large number of firms sell differentiated products, we are again considering a model which has few counterparts in real life. The consumer seldom has a choice among products which are good but imperfect substitutes for each other, produced by a large number of sellers; the number of sellers in cases of this sort is usually small.

This brings us to the present chapter. A market of a few sellers is an oligopolistic market. The word *oligopoly* is a term which hasn't yet found its way into many dictionaries but which literally means "few sellers." At long last we are ready to consider the dominant real-world market form. In the United States there are many industries, producing such commodities as automobiles, steel, television sets, aspirin, typewriters, gasoline, electric trains, motorcycles, and detergents, where 50 to 90 percent of the output is produced by a half dozen firms. For most individual consumers, a choice among repairmen, physicians, or housepainters is limited, and the number of grocery stores, clothing shops, and theaters which they might regularly patronize is also small. Products of oligopolists are usually differentiated. A Ford is not just like a Plymouth; Magnavox and Zenith television sets have unique features; Bayer and St. Joseph aspirin are essentially identical but are sold under different trade names, and the higher-priced brand outsells the cheaper one. Products of oligopolists may be homogeneous; industrialists buy metals according to specification; the steel offered by one firm will be identical with that of others. But even here there may be differences in location, credit arrangements, and other conditions surrounding the sale, and to the extent to which this is true, these too are differentiated products. The typical market form is one in which a few sellers produce differentiated products.

Those who have been impatient with market models previously discussed on the ground that they were dissimilar to conditions in the real world are likely to be disappointed again if they feel that in looking at the real business world, they are going to see how it in fact really operates. Predictions about oligopoly price and output will depend upon the assumptions we make about oligopolist behavior. Since the number of assumptions which might be made about the behavior of oligopolists is large, we cannot speak with the same confidence about oligopoly price, output, and equilibrium, as we spoke about the other market situations. As the model becomes more realistic, the theory becomes less determinant.

During the nineteenth century a number of economists turned their attention to the problem of oligopoly price. Their conclusions differed as their assumptions varied. One writer argued that oligopoly price tended to be somewhat higher than competitive price and output somewhat less than competitive output, the discrepancy diminishing as the number of sellers increased. Another writer argued that oligopoly price tended to equal competitive price. Still another thought that oligopoly price and monopoly price tended to be the same. This represents maximum divergence, and the difficulty lies not with the logic of these theorists but with their assumptions about oligopolistic behavior. In fact, oligopolists react one way in one situation and another way in another but similar situation, and not even the cleverest economist can make meaningful generalizations about behavior to which there are no set patterns.[1]

The Cournot Case

The most famous solution to the oligopoly problem is probably the one devised by an early nineteenth century French economist, Augustin Cournot,[2] in his consideration of duopoly, a market consisting of two sellers. Duopoly may be taken as a special case of oligopoly and statements made about it may be extended to any number of sellers. What follows is an adaptation of Cournot's analysis.

Suppose that in a given market there are two sellers offering identical products. To keep the analysis as simple as possible, let us make the unlikely assumption that the product costs nothing to produce. For example, let us suppose that each seller has a mineral spring, and his product is therefore spring water; customers bring their own containers and leave their money in a designated place. Let us further assume that the market demand for the product is linear. In terms of Figure 12–1, the demand function is given by

$$p = b - Q\left(\frac{b}{a}\right),$$

where p is price, Q is the total amount demanded in the market, a is the x-intercept of the demand curve and b the y-intercept. If we let $m = -(b/a) =$ the slope of the demand curve, we may write the demand function as

$$p = b + mQ.$$

If the amount sold by seller I is q_1 and the amount sold by seller II is q_2 we may write the demand function as

$$p = b + m(q_1 + q_2).$$

The unique assumption made by Cournot with regard to oligopolists' behavior is that each seller will assume that the output being produced at any given time by his competitor is the output which he will continue to offer regardless of the first seller's output. Thus, to begin with, if seller II is not yet

[1] For a summary of the several solutions to the oligopoly problem see Edward Hastings Chamberlin, *The Theory of Monopolistic Competition* (Cambridge, Mass.: Harvard University Press, 1946), Chap. 3.

[2] Augustin Cournot, *Researches sur les Principes Mathematiques de la Théorie des Richesses* (Paris: Chez L. Hachette, 1938), Chap. 7. There is an English translation by N. T. Bacon, *Researches into the Mathematical Principles of the Theory of Wealth* (New York: The Macmillan Co., Publishers, 1897).

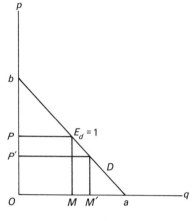

Fig. 12-1

producing any output, seller I will assume, according to Cournot, that he will continue to produce zero output and will make his plans accordingly. Since seller I assumes seller II's output will be zero, the demand for seller I's product will be

$$p = b + mq_1;$$

seller I's total revenue function will on this assumption be

$$TR_1 = pq_1 = bq_1 + mq_1^2,$$

and his marginal revenue function will be

$$MR_1 = \frac{dTR_1}{dq_1} = b + 2mq_1.$$

But since $m = -b/a$,

$$MR_1 = b - 2\left(\frac{b}{a}\right)q_1.$$

Since by assumption spring water costs nothing to produce, marginal cost is zero, and profits will be maximized when marginal revenue equals zero:

$$MR_1 = b - 2\left(\frac{b}{a}\right)q_1 = 0$$

$$2\left(\frac{b}{a}\right)q_1 = b$$

$$q_1 = \frac{a}{2}.$$

This is the pure monopolist's output, which in Figure 12–1 would be OM units per time period, and price would be OP. Since costs are zero, the monopolist would maximize profits by maximizing total revenue, and this would come where the elasticity of demand was equal to -1. Since marginal costs are equal to zero, the purely competitive market supply curve would lie along the x-axis, and competitive price would be zero and competitive output Oa. At this stage of our analysis, when for the moment seller I is a pure monopolist, output is equal to one-half purely competitive output.

Now seller II decides to enter the market. Cournot argues that since seller I is currently producing an output equal to $a/2$, seller II believes that he will continue to produce that output regardless of what seller II decides to do. On this assumption, seller II's demand function will take the form

$$AR_2 = p = b + m(q_1 + q_2),$$

where now $q_1 = a/2$. Total revenue for seller II will be

$$TR_2 = pq_2 = bq_2 + mq_2(q_1 + q_2)$$
$$= bq_2 + mq_2q_1 + mq_2^2,$$

and

$$MR_2 = \frac{dTR_2}{dq_2} = b + mq_1 + 2mq_2,$$

since q_1 is taken to be a constant. But $m = -b/a$ and $q_1 = a/2$, so we may write

$$MR_2 = b - \frac{b}{2} - \frac{2bq_2}{a} = 0$$
$$\frac{2bq_2}{a} = \frac{b}{2}$$
$$q_2 = \frac{a}{4}.$$

Total quantity sold will equal

$$Q = q_1 + q_2 = \frac{a}{2} + \frac{a}{4} = \frac{3a}{4}.$$

Since the market demand is given by

$$p = b + mQ,$$
$$p = b - \frac{b}{a} \cdot \frac{3a}{4} = \frac{b}{4}.$$

But this does not represent the equilibrium price and quantity. According to Cournot's assumptions, seller I will now assume that seller II will sell $a/4$ units of output per time period without regard to what seller I does. In general, as firm I adjusts its output to changes in firm II's output, the demand function for seller I will be

$$AR_1 = p = b + m(q_1 + q_2),$$

where q_2 is a constant. Seller I's total-revenue function will be

$$TR_1 = pq_1 = bq_1 + mq_1(q_1 + q_2) = bq_1 + mq_1^2 + mq_1q_2,$$

and marginal revenue will be

$$MR_1 = \frac{dTR_1}{dq_1} = b + 2mq_1 + mq_2.$$

Similarly it may be shown that the marginal-revenue function for seller II is

$$MR_2 = \frac{dTR_2}{dq_2} = b + 2mq_2 + mq_1.$$

Since when both firms are maximizing profits, $MR_1 = MC = 0$ and $MR_2 = MC = 0$, we may write $MR_1 = MR_2$:

$$b + 2mq_1 + mq_2 = b + 2mq_2 + mq_1$$
$$mq_1 = mq_2$$
$$q_1 = q_2.$$

Substituting q_1 for q_2 in the formula for $MR_1 = 0$, we get

$$b + 2mq_1 + mq_1 = 0$$
$$b + 3mq_1 = 0$$
$$3mq_1 = -b$$
$$q_1 = \frac{-b}{3m}.$$

But $m = -b/a$, so we may write

$$q_1 = \frac{-b}{3} \cdot \frac{-a}{b} = \frac{a}{3} = q_2,$$

and $Q = q_1 + q_2 = 2a/3$. This is output OM' in Figure 12–1. Substituting $2a/3$ for Q in the market demand function, we get

$$p = b - \left(\frac{b}{a}\right)Q$$

$$= b - \left(\frac{b}{a}\right)\left(\frac{2a}{3}\right) = b - \frac{2b}{3} = \frac{b}{3}.$$

Cournot's solution to the duopoly problem is, then, that if each seller takes the current output of his competitor as fixed, the equilibrium output will be two-thirds of the competitive output. In general, if the number of firms is n, the total oligopolist output will be $n/(n + 1)$ times the competitive output. If the number of firms is very large, approaching the purely competitive model, output will approach the competitive output. If the number of firms is small, oligopoly output is less than competitive output but greater than monopoly output; oligopoly price is higher than competitive price but less than monopoly price.

Rival's Price Assumed Constant

We may consider briefly a second solution to the duopoly problem which was presented in 1883 by Joseph Bertrand, a French mathematician, as a refutation of the Cournot solution.[3] Again we may consider two owners of mineral springs who sell mineral water which costs nothing to produce. But this time instead of stipulating that each seller will assume that the current output of his rival is fixed, we will assume that each seller believes that the current price being charged by one seller will not be affected by the activities of the other seller. In terms of Figure 12–2, we assume that TT' is the demand curve for the combined output of both sellers; the total capacity of each seller is $OM = MT'$; and if both sellers were to put their entire daily output on sale, the price would be just equal to zero. Let seller I enter the market first. Since he is at the moment the only seller, he will offer OM units of output for sale at price OP, where the elasticity of demand is equal to -1. Since total cost is by assumption equal to zero, profits will be maximized when total revenue is at a maximum. Now seller II enters the market. Since seller I is selling his entire output at a profit-maximizing price, seller II feels sure that he will not lower his price. Seller II might suppose that the best it can do is to offer MM', which is equal to one-half MT' units, at a price of OP'. But he will soon discover that at a price of OP' the market will take OM' units, of which he can supply an amount equal to only OM. If seller I continues to sell at price OP, seller II can set its price slightly below OP and dispose of virtually all of its daily capacity at this price by taking customers away from seller I. Seller I now assumes that the price set by his rival will remain constant, and he will accordingly cut his price below it. The process of price-cutting may be expected to continue until the price falls to zero and a total combined output of OT' is offered by the two sellers. This is, of course, the same as purely competitive price and output under the assumed conditions. This differs from Cournot's conclusion that duopoly price would be higher than competitive price but lower than monopoly price, and duopoly output less than competitive output but greater than monopoly output. The Bertrand model does not, in fact, constitute a refutation of the Cournot solution, but provides a different answer resulting from differences in basic assumptions. It may seem that the assumption of either constant output or constant price without regard to one's rival's behavior—which is called the assumption of zero conjectural variation—is quite unrealistic, but Professor Baumol[4] has concluded on the basis of his empirical studies that oligopolistic

[3] Chamberlin, *op. cit.*, pp. 34–37.

[4] William J. Baumol, *Business Behavior, Value, and Growth* (New York: The Macmillan Co., Publishers, 1959), Chap. 4.

interdependence plays only a small role in day-to-day decision making. This suggests that what is or is not "realistic" can scarcely be determined by intuition or armchair speculation.

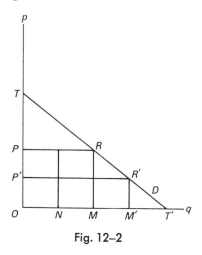

Fig. 12–2

Mutual Dependence Recognized

Most recent writers on oligopoly have assumed that each seller realizes that his rivals will react to any move that he makes and that if he is to maximize his own profit situation he must try to anticipate what counteractions his competitors are likely to make. In this respect these writers believe that the oligopolist reacts in much the same way that a chess player might; any gain which one duopolist enjoys is at the expense of the other, and one's rival is not likely to play a passive role in the contest. (Indeed, a theory of games has been developed, and for a time it was hoped that this analysis might be useful in explaining oligopolist behavior.[5]) For our third model, therefore, we will use what Professor Chamberlin called the case where mutual dependence is recognized, the outcome of which is a price and output equal to pure monopoly price and output.

With reference again to Figure 12–2, if seller I enters the market first, he will offer output *OM* at price *OP,* which are monopoly price and output. The best seller II can now do is to offer output *MM'*, which will cause the price for both sellers to fall to *OP'*. Recalling that total costs are assumed to be zero, the total combined profit of the two firms is now *OP'R'M'*, which is less than *OPRM* enjoyed by seller I before the second firm entered the

[5] John von Neuman and Oskar Morgenstern, *Theory of Games and Economic Behavior,* 2nd ed. (Princeton, N.J.: Princeton University Press, 1947). For a discussion of the use of game theory in economic analysis see William J. Baumol, *Economic Theory and Operations Analysis* (Englewood Cliffs, N.J.: Prentice-Hall, Inc., 1961), chap. xviii. For a very brief discussion of game theory see H. H. Liebhafsky, *The Nature of Price Theory* (Homewood, Ill.: The Dorsey Press, Inc., 1963), pp. 277–81.

market; since the elasticity of demand is -1 at price OP, the rectangle $OPRM$ is the largest that can be inscribed under the demand curve. Since the products of the two firms are assumed to be identical, there is no reason to suppose that seller I can sell more units at price OP' than seller II can, and seller I's profits will accordingly be reduced to one-half of $OP'R'M'$. Both firms will be better off if seller I cuts back his output to $ON = MM'$, which is one-half of OM, the total combined output of both firms. Price will now be OP, which is equal to monopoly price, and combined output of both firms is OM, which is equal to monopoly output. Any departure from this price and output would be detrimental to both sellers, and we may assume therefore that this represents the equilibrium situation. This is, incidentally, the same solution we would reach if we assumed that the several sellers formed a perfect cartel. A cartel is an agreement among sellers designed to reduce or eliminate competition, and this may be accomplished by selling through a common sales organization, by dividing up geographic markets, by agreeing on price and output, or by various other devices. A perfect cartel would attempt to maximize the joint profits of its several members and divide the profits among them equally or according to some agreed plan. The aggregate well-being of the cartel members would be achieved when the combined output of the several firms was equal to monopoly output and the price charged was equal to monopoly price.

The Kinked Demand Curve

Enough has been said to indicate that oligopolist pricing and output policy depends on the assumptions made by the oligopolists, and it is not yet clear from empirical studies which set of assumptions is most representative of oligopolist behavior in general.[6] One concept which may be helpful in understanding oligopolist behavior is the idea of the "kinked" demand curve.[7] This idea also has its detractors,[8] but the approach is sufficiently interesting to justify a brief consideration of it.

Suppose in terms of Figure 12–3 that an oligopolistic seller's current price is OP and his output OM. He is considering a change in his price and, since there are only a few other sellers in his market, assumes that his rivals may react in one way or another to his price policy; that is, we are now

[6] For a more extended treatment of oligopolist pricing and price policy see Joe S. Bain, *Price Theory* (New York: Holt, Rinehart & Winston, Inc., 1952), pp. 267–349.

[7] This analysis was introduced in Paul M. Sweezy, "Demand under Conditions of Oligopoly," *Journal of Political Economy*, 47 (August 1939), 568–573; reprinted in Kenneth E. Boulding and George J. Stigler, eds., *Readings in Price Theory* (Homewood, Ill.: Richard D. Irwin, Inc., 1952), pp. 404–409.

[8] The existence of a kinked demand curve is denied on the basis of a small statistical sample in George J. Stigler, "The Kinky Demand Curve and Rigid Prices," *Journal of Political Economy*, 55 (October 1947), 432–449.

rejecting the assumption of a "zero conjectural variation." In trying to visualize what his firm's demand curve looks like, the oligopolist might reason something like this:

"All I can be sure about at the moment is that I am selling OM units of output per time period at price OP. If I decide to reduce my price and my rivals do not follow my lead, I will be able to increase my sales—first, because at a lower price I can sell more than at a higher price, and, second, because if my competitors do not cut their prices and I do, I will be able to take some of their customers from them. Under these circumstances the demand for my

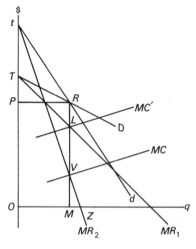

Fig. 12–3

product for prices less than OP should be highly elastic, and my demand should have the general appearance of segment RD in Figure 12–3. On the other hand, if my rivals match my price cut, I will not be able to take customers from them; the demand for my product will be less elastic and should have the general form of segment Rd in Figure 12–3. Since I do not know how my competitors will react to my price cut, to play it safe I had better assume the worst; that is, that if I reduce my price, my rivals will also cut theirs, and my demand curve below price OP will be Rd.

"Now if I should decide to raise my price, I am confronted with the same sort of uncertainty. If I should raise my price and my rivals followed my example and also raised theirs, I would expect to sell somewhat fewer units because the price was higher, but I would not in addition lose customers to my rivals. My demand curve above OP would then take on the form tR. But if my competitors did not raise their prices, my demand would be highly elastic because I would lose sales to other firms. Again, if I am to play it conservatively, I will have to assume that my competitors would not raise their prices if I raised mine, so I had better assume that my demand curve for prices above OP looks something like TR. If I assume that my rivals will cut prices to match mine but will not increase prices to match mine, my demand curve will be kinked: TRd in Figure 12–3.”

The kinked demand curve, it will be noted, is a subjective thing. It indicates the general form which a conservative oligopolist would suppose that the demand curve for his product would take. If the demand curve is TRd, it will be noted that TL is the marginal-revenue curve corresponding to the segment TR of the demand curve; VZ is the marginal-revenue curve corresponding to segment Rd of the demand curve, and at output OM there is a gap in the marginal-revenue curve equal to VL. If the marginal-cost curve should shift anywhere between MC and MC' in Figure 12–3, the intersection of marginal-cost and marginal-revenue curves would come at output OM and price OP. This means, of course, that even though there might be significant changes in cost, the most profitable output and price would not be affected. A commonly noted phenomenon in the real world is that oligopolistic prices frequently tend to be rigid, and competition frequently is of a nonprice sort. The rigidity of oligopolist price might be the result of collusion among sellers, but if the oligopolists visualized their demand curves as kinked, prices might remain constant over long intervals of time in the complete absence of collusive action on the part of the sellers.

Price Leadership

At various times in our history such products as steel, corn, petroleum, and photographic film have been produced by a small number of firms, one of which was dominant in its field and determined prices for the rest of the firms in that field, and there is considerable evidence that in local and national markets some sort of price leadership is still a common phenomenon. The leader may have attained that position by virtue of its size or by aggressive merchandising or tradition, but whatever the reason, when it announced a change in price, other firms would follow suit. The price set by the leader might not be the profit-maximizing price for the other firms, and their outputs might be more or less than their profit-maximizing outputs, but since refusal to go along with the leader might invite retaliation and possibly financial ruin for the noncooperating firms, the latter simply *would* go along.

Figure 12–4 shows the cost and revenue curves for two firms. AR_1, MR_1, and MC_1 are the average-revenue, marginal-revenue, and marginal-cost curves for firm I, which is the price leader. It will be noted that the demand for the product of firm I is greater than the demand for the product of firm II, the follower; the marginal-cost curve for firm I is lower than the marginal-cost curve for firm II; and at any price the elasticity of demand for firm I is less than the elasticity of demand for firm II. Firm I will set price at OP and sell OM units of output per time period at that price. Firm II accepts price OP

and is able to sell *ON* units at that price. But note that this price is higher and the output correspondingly less than its profit-maximizing price and output would be if it were left to itself. At price *OP* firm II is operating in the highly elastic range of its demand curve and could increase sales significantly by a small decrease in price. But in order to avoid a price war with firm I, firm II sells at the higher-than-profit-maximizing price.

Firm I may, it might be added, feel that its position of leadership is

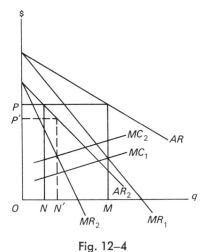

Fig. 12–4

somewhat precarious. Then, instead of determining price solely on the basis of maximizing its own profits, it might try to find the price which would more closely approach the profit-maximizing prices for the other firms in the market. If firm II in Figure 12–4 is representative of the smaller firms in the industry, the price set by firm I might be somewhere between *OP* and *OP'*.

Sales Maximization

We may make one more assumption with respect to possible oligopolist behavior. Professor Baumol[9] has advanced the hypothesis that managers of large companies are likely to be more concerned with increasing sales than with maximizing profits. There is evidence that corporate managers feel their rewards will be greater if they are able to increase sales rather than profits. It is easier to get and retain good dealers and distributors if sales are increasing. (Distributors reason: There may be bandwagon purchasing by consumers. Everyone else is buying this product, so I will try it too.) If sales are increasing, it may be easier to get low-interest bank credit for purposes of expansion. And there may be satisfaction in just being big; Ford might prefer to outsell Chevrolet and realize smaller profits than be No. 2 with larger

[9] Baumol, *Business Behavior, Value and Growth.*

profits. But the effort to maximize sales is subject to the significant constraint that profits, if not maximized, must at least not drop below some acceptable minimum. If profits are too low stockholders will complain even though sales are booming. There will be inadequate funds for investment and growth, and bank credit will be harder to get. Baumol's thesis, then, is rather that the effort of managers of large corporations to maximize sales revenue is subject to the constraint that total profits must be "adequate."

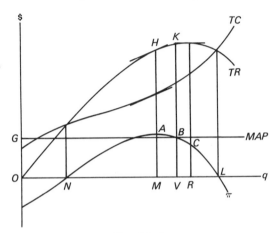

Fig. 12–5

In terms of Figure 12–5, TC and TR are the firm's total-cost and total-revenue curves, and π is the total-profit curve. The profit-maximizing output is OM, where the slope of the TC curve is equal to the slope of the TR curve, and total profit at this output is equal to MA. If, however, the firm prefers to maximize sales revenue, it would produce an output of OR, where the slope of the TR curve is equal to zero. But at output OR profit is only RC, which is less than the minimum acceptable profit, OG. The greatest sales revenue which will provide the minimum acceptable profit is OV, where profits are $VB = OG$. The difference between MA and VB represents the profits which the firm has sacrificed in order to increase output from OM to OV and total revenue from MH to VK.

Evidence of firms actually operating in this fashion, i.e., of not attempting to maximize profits, can only be determined by empirical research, and the findings are not yet conclusive enough to confirm Professor Baumol's hypothesis.

Another consideration relevant to the question of profit maximization is that if the firm's fixed costs increased with no change in variable cost, total profits would be reduced but the profit-maximizing output would not be affected. If a firm were trying to maximize profits, accordingly, an increase in fixed costs would not affect the firm's rate of output. But if a firm behaved in the fashion suggested by Professor Baumol, a reduction in profits due to an increase in fixed cost would cause the output which provided minimum acceptable profits to become smaller, and empirical studies indicate that, in fact, firms usually do respond to an increase in fixed costs by a reduction in output. This, of course, does not confirm Professor Baumol's thesis. Businessmen may reduce output in response to an increase in fixed costs because they do not understand that a change in fixed cost does not affect marginal cost, or their impressions of what their cost and revenue curves actually look like may be so vague that their response to a change in fixed cost is based more on feeling and intuition than on analysis.

Alternative Solution to the Oligopoly Problem

It may be fruitful to consider an alternative solution to the duopoly problem. Let us first consider a case of what might be called perfect duopoly: a given market is made up of two firms; the products of the firms are homogeneous and each firm is of optimum size and their costs, accordingly, identical. In Figure 12–6, D_m is the market demand for the product of the

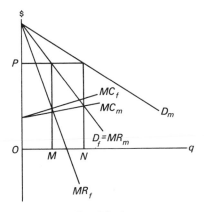

Fig. 12–6

duopolists. Since the products of the firms are homogeneous and we are ruling out any extrinsic special advantages, the presumption is that the demand curve for each firm will be one-half the market demand; each firm's demand is represented in the figure by D_f. Each firm has the same marginal-cost curve, MC_f.

In order to maximize profits, each firm will produce to the point where $MC_f = MR_f$, and, in terms of Figure 12–6, the profit-maximizing output for each firm will be OM and the profit-maximizing price, OP. Since each firm produces OM units per time period, the total output for both firms will be $ON = 2OM$.

Now suppose that the two firms consolidate into a single firm with two plants, each of optimum size and identical costs. The marginal-cost curve of the monopolist will be the horizontal summation of the separate-firm marginal-cost curves; that is, at any given marginal cost, the monopolist can produce an output equal to twice the output produced by either firm at that marginal cost. In the figure, the monopolist's marginal-cost curve is represented by MC_m, and the monopolist's marginal-revenue curve is MR_m, which is the same as D_f. The most profitable output for the monopolist is ON, which is the same as the most profitable outputs of the two firms combined when they were separately owned. Under these conditions, therefore, monopoly price and duopoly price are identical.

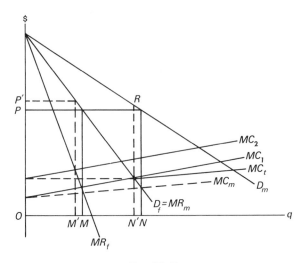

Fig. 12–7

Now suppose we have a market consisting of two firms selling homogeneous products, but this time only one of the firms is of optimum size. The marginal-cost curve of the more efficient firm is MC_1 and the marginal-cost curve for the less efficient firm is MC_2. The profit-maximizing price for firm I, the lower-cost firm, is OP. Firm II would like to sell at price OP' but, since the products are homogeneous, will have to accept firm I's price of OP. At that price each firm will produce OM units per time period, and the total market output will be $ON = 2OM$.

Now suppose as before that these two firms combine into a single monopolistic firm. The monopolist's marginal-cost curve again will be the horizontal summation of the separate-firm marginal-cost curves, but this time it will assume the form of MC_t in Figure 12–7. The most profitable output for the monopolist will be ON', where $MC_t = MR_m$.

It will be noted that when one plant of the monopolistic firm is relatively inefficient, the most profitable output will be somewhat less and price will be somewhat higher than if both plants were of optimum size. If both plants had a marginal-cost curve such as MC_1, the marginal-cost curve of the monopolist would be MC_m, and the most profitable output for the monopolist would be the same as the combined outputs of the two firms when they were separately owned. The effect of the consolidation of the two firms, one of which is not of optimum size, has been to reduce total output and raise price. This is not a surprising conclusion since before the consolidation only one of the firms was able to maximize its profits; the less efficient firm was required to produce more than its profit-maximizing output and sell below its profit-maximizing price.

POSTPRANDIUM

We have indicated that oligopolistic markets are common in contemporary economic society and, although predictions about the behavior of oligopolists are difficult because their reactions to the moves of their competitors are uncertain, we can make assessments of this market form in terms of its efficiency in producing goods to meet consumer wants. For this purpose let us consider a market in which there are few sellers but into which entry is relatively easy. If the firms in the market are enjoying supernormal profits, new firms will be attracted; the demand curve for each firm will shift to the left as its share of total sales diminishes; and long-run equilibrium will be reached when each firm's demand curve becomes tangent to its average-total-cost curve. The profit-maximizing price will be the price where profits are zero, and each firm will of necessity be operating to the left of the lowest point on its average-total-cost curve. This leads to the curious result that this market, which is characterized by a few firms, actually has too many firms; fewer firms, each operating at its most efficient output, could supply the market at lower unit costs. In this case, as in all instances of monopolistic selling, firms will usually operate at less than their technically most efficient outputs and at prices higher than purely competitive prices. But whereas in the case of pure monopoly the firm may enjoy supernormal profits even in the long run, oligopolists where entry is easy will in long-run equilibrium earn no more than normal profits. The higher prices to consumers and the inefficient utilization of plant are in the case of oligopoly not even compensated for by unusual profits to the sellers. The firm is not gaining at the expense of consumers; it would appear that in oligopolistic markets with free entry everyone loses.

Oligopolistic firms are likely to be inefficient not only in that they produce less than their lowest-cost outputs but also in economic terms: they may not produce goods in close accord with consumer preferences. Several years ago in a North Carolina city of about 50,000 population there were some half-dozen local radio stations. This community was reputed to have more radio stations than any other city of its size in the country and all of them played country and Western music most of the day. Now it seems reasonable to suppose that perhaps as many as three-fourths of the potential radio listeners in that community liked country and Western music and were delighted with the fare offered them on the air waves. But the other quarter of the population were less enthusiastic and found this sort of music positively distasteful. It would have seemed sensible for at least one of the radio stations to offer programs which would appeal to the disenchanted one-fourth; 25 percent of the total population would seem to hold more potential than one-sixth of 75 percent (12.5 percent). But each station went after its share of the larger market, and eventually several of them were forced into bankruptcy. A significant fraction of the population found itself without programs suited to their taste and the behavior of the existing firms led to the failure of several of them.

In more recent years the television industry has provided an even more striking example of the failure of oligopolists to respond to the wants of a significant portion of the public. The programming of network television has been described by a former chairman of the Federal Communications Commission as a "vast wasteland"; this has resulted from the unending quest by television officials for higher "ratings," since a wide appeal is necessary to the profitable operation of a network. The ideal from the point of view of the television people would seem to be to have everyone watching his television set 24 hours every day. In order to approach this optimum situation as closely as possible, programming is reduced to the lowest common denominator. And the disenchanted 25 percent remain disenchanted. In the days before television, network radio did provide Sunday afternoon symphony concerts and even an occasional chamber-music recital. On television we rarely see a symphony orchestra.

Under conditions of oligopoly the divergence between the welfare of the firm and the general welfare is particularly marked. The wishes of all consumers might be better served in some instances under pure monopoly. If all three television networks were owned by the same firm, it would seem unlikely that all three channels would carry the same distasteful programs at the same time; more attention might be given to the programs with the greatest popular appeal, but the monopolist would also try to have something which attracted the sizable minority of viewers. This likelihood is borne out by the experience of British radio, which consists of a three-station monopoly. At any given hour the programs offered by the three stations are varied, and there is likely to be something for all tastes. But as long as we have a small number of separately owned television networks, we are likely to have the choice of watching a Western or turning off the set; and if we shift from channel to channel, we are likely to encounter the same "personalities" *ad nauseam*.

SELECTED REFERENCES

Bain, Joe S. *Price Theory.* New York: Holt, Rinehart & Winston, Inc., 1952. Chap. 6.

Baumol, William J. *Business Behavior, Value and Growth.* New York: The Macmillan Co., 1959.

Boulding, Kenneth E. *Economic Analysis.* Vol. I, 4th ed. New York: Harper & Row, Publishers, 1966. Chap. 22.

Colberg, Marshall R., Dascomb R. Forbush, and Gilbert R. Whitaker, Jr. *Business Economics: Principles and Cases.* 3rd ed. Homewood, Ill.: Richard D. Irwin, Inc., 1964. Chap. 6.

Fellner, William J. *Competition among the Few.* New York: Alfred A. Knopf, Inc., 1949.

Leftwich, Richard H. *The Price System and Resource Allocation.* 3rd ed. New York: Holt, Rinehart & Winston, Inc., 1966. Chap. 11.

Levenson, Albert M., and Babette S. Solon. *Outline of Price Theory.* New York: Holt, Rinehart & Winston, Inc., 1964. Chap. 11.

Wilcox, Clair. *Competition and Monopoly in American Industry.* Washington, D.C.: U.S. Government Printing Office, 1940.

PROBLEMS

PROBLEM I

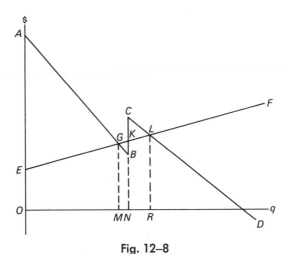

Fig. 12–8

In the above figure, *ABCD* is a firm's marginal-revenue curve, and *EF* its marginal-cost curve. *MR = MC* at points *G, K,* and *L.*

1. Draw the firm's average-revenue curve.

2. At output *OM,* total revenue = ...——————————

3. At output OM, total variable cost $=$ . . . .————————————————

4. At output OM, $TR - VC =$ . . . . . .————————————————

5. At output ON, $TR =$ . . . .————————————————

6. At output ON, $VC =$ . . . .————————————————

7. At output ON, $TR - VC =$ . . . . . .————————————————

8. At output OR, $TR =$ . . . .————————————————

9. At output OR, $VC =$ . . . .————————————————

10. At output OR, $TR - VC =$ . . . . . .————————————————

11. What is the most profitable output? . . . .————————————————

12. Most profitable price is OP; locate P on the figure.

PROBLEM II

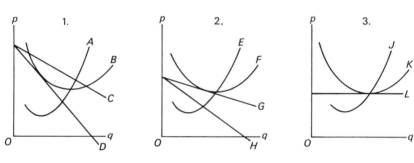

Fig. 12–9

One of the firms whose cost and revenue curves are represented in the figure above sells in a purely competitive market, one is a pure monopolist, and the other is an oligopolist. All are assumed to be in long-run equilibrium. Indicate the most plausible answers to the following questions:

1. Marginal cost under pure competition is represented by curve
   (a) A (b) B (c) C (d) D (e) E
   (f) F (g) G (h) H (j) J (k) K

2. Marginal revenue under pure monopoly is represented by curve
   (a) C (b) F (c) G
   (d) J (e) D (f) L

3. Marginal revenue under pure competition is represented by curve
   (a) A (b) F (c) C
   (d) K (e) G (f) L

4. Average revenue under oligopoly is represented by curve
   (a) C (b) F (c) G
   (d) H (e) K (f) L

5. The curve which shows by itself that many other firms are competing with the one whose graph is shown is
   (a) C   (b) E   (c) F
   (d) G   (e) K   (f) L

6. Firm 2
   (a) makes a profit.
   (b) suffers a loss.
   (c) breaks even.
   (d) will make a profit in the long run.

7. The firm least likely to sponsor a TV program is
   (a) Firm 1   (b) Firm 2   (c) Firm 3

PROBLEM III

A description of the short-run situation for fifteen firms is presented below; no account is taken of long-run adjustments.

(a) $P = MR = MC = ATC$

(b) $P > MR = MC > ATC > P$

(c) $P > MR = MC > ATC < P$

(d) $P > MR = MC < ATC < P$

(e) $P > MR = MC = ATC < P$

(f) $P = MR = MC > ATC$

(g) $P = MR = MC < ATC$

(h) $P = MR > MC < ATC < P$

(i) $P > MR = MC < ATC = P$

(j) $P > MR > MC = ATC < P$

(k) $P = MR > MC = ATC < P$

(l) $P = MR > MC < ATC > P$

(m) $P > MR < MC = ATC < P$

(n) $P = MR < MC > ATC < P$

(o) $P = MR < MC < ATC > P$

1. Which of the firms are competitive?

2. Which of the firms are in short-run equilibrium?

3. Which of the firms are monopolistic?

4. Which of the firms are making positive profits? Which losses? Which are breaking even?

5. Which of the firms could make more profit by expanding output?

6. Which of the firms could make more profit by contracting output?

7. Which of the firms are operating at their lowest-cost output?

8. Which of the firms operating at their lowest-cost output could increase their profit by changing output?

9. Find the one firm in a totally impossible situation.

PROBLEM IV

Represent graphically each of the fifteen situations described in Problem III.

PROBLEM V

Figure 12–10, page 292, includes demand curves *AB, DE, DJB,* and *AJE.*

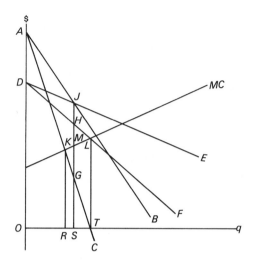

Fig. 12–10

1. The marginal-revenue curve corresponding to *AB*
   is   .   .   .   . ._____

2. The marginal-revenue curve corresponding to *DE*
   is   .   .   .   . ._____

3. The marginal-revenue curve corresponding to *DJB*
   is   .   .   .   . ._____

4. The marginal-revenue curve corresponding to *AJE*
   is   .   .   .   . ._____

Suppose the marginal-cost curve is *MC*:

5. When demand is *AB*, the most profitable output
   is   .   .   .   . ._____

6. When demand is *DE*, the most profitable output
   is   .   .   .   . ._____

7. When demand is *DJB*, the most profitable output
   is   .   .   .   . ._____

8. When demand is *AJE*, the most profitable output
   is   .   .   .   . ._____

13

Average, Total, and
Marginal Product

To this point in our analysis we have been concerned with the firm as a
seller of products, or outputs. We have, of course, taken note of the fact that
the firm is also a buyer of factors of production, or inputs, but the purchase of
inputs has been related to the sale of outputs. The fact that the firm has costs
reflects the fact that the firm is a buyer. We have classified inputs as fixed and
variable and have analyzed fixed and variable costs, but the costs have been
associated with the production of a given output. Total cost, as we have used
the term heretofore, was not the cost of a given number of inputs; it was the
total cost of producing a given output. Average cost was the average cost of
producing a given output. Marginal cost was the additional cost of producing
an increment of output. The short-run equilibrium position of the firm was
identified in terms of its most profitable output. In geometric charts the units
on the x-axis were quantity of output.

In this and the remaining chapters we concentrate on the firm as a buyer
of inputs. The role of the firm may be described as purchasing inputs and
transforming them into outputs. It is assumed that some inputs are fixed in
amount during a given time period, and others are variable. As more and
more units of the variable factors are used in combination with the fixed

factors, the proportions between fixed and variable factors vary, and with each combination of fixed and variable factors a given total product results. The relationship between the various proportions of fixed and variable inputs employed and the resulting total product is known as the production function. If the firm is to maximize profits it will attempt to utilize the least expensive combination of inputs to produce a given output, or, alternatively, to get the maximum output from a given expenditure on inputs. The short-run equilibrium position of the firm can be expressed by input as well as output, and for this purpose units on the x-axis of geometric charts can represent inputs, and in algebraic representations of total, average, and marginal product, x can be used to measure inputs.

The production function may be stated symbolically as

$$TP = f(x, y),$$

where TP is total product, x is the variable factor or combination of variable factors, and y is the fixed factor or combination of fixed factors. The amount of the total product produced during a given time period depends upon several things:

1. The amount of output derived from any combination of inputs depends on the current state of technology. In the long run, new methods of production and new kinds of equipment may result in an increase in total product with a given combination of factors, but in the short run we will assume the proficiency-level of technology as given.

2. The amount of output derived from any combination of inputs depends on the efficiency with which the firm operates. We will assume that the firm utilizes for any cost outlay the most efficient techniques available.

3. The amount of output depends on the scale of production. In the long run, the amount of the fixed factor (y in the production function) can vary, and in general, we should suppose that a greater amount of y in combination with a given amount of x would result in a greater total output. But in the short run the fixed factor is fixed, which is to say that the size of plant is given.

4. The amount of output depends on the proportions in which the factors of production are employed. If a given amount of fixed factor is employed in combination with increasing amounts of the variable factor, the proportion of variable to fixed factor, that is x/y, increases as x increases.

Total, Average, and Marginal Product

The basic mathematical relationships between total, average, and marginal product are the same as the relationships between total, average, and marginal values discussed earlier in the chapters on revenue and cost. The nature of these relationships is indicated in Table 13–1.

TABLE 13–1

(1) Fixed Input	(2) Variable Input	(3) Average Product	(4) Total Product	(5) Marginal Product
1	0	—	0	—
1	1	10	10	10
1	2	13	26	16
1	3	15	45	19
1	4	15	60	15
1	5	14	70	10
1	6	11	66	−4

It will be noted that if the first three columns of Table 13–1 were given, it would be possible to calculate Columns 4 and 5; Column 4 is Column 2 multiplied by Column 3, and Column 5 is the successive increments in Column 4. Or if Columns 1, 2, and 4 were given, one could calculate Columns 3 and 5; Column 3 is Column 4 divided by Column 2. Or if Columns 1, 2, and 5 were given, Columns 3 and 4 could be determined. Column 4 at any row is equal to the sum of Column 5 to that row; for example, total product with 3 units of variable input is equal to $10 + 16 + 19 = 45$.

The basic total-average-marginal relationships may be summarized as follows:

1. As just noted, the sum of the first n marginal products is equal to the total product of n variable inputs.
2. When average product is increasing, marginal product is greater than average product.
3. When average product is decreasing, marginal product is less than average product.
4. When average product is constant, marginal product equals average product.
5. The addition or subtraction of a fixed amount to total product does not affect marginal product. If, for example, each value in the total-product column were increased by 10, the marginal-product column would remain unchanged.[1]

Geometry of Total-Average and Total-Marginal Product

Average product and marginal product bear the same relation to total product that average revenue and marginal revenue bear to total revenue and that average utility and marginal utility bear to total utility. In Figure 13–1 a total-product curve has been drawn with the variable factor measured on the x-axis. When input is OM units per time period, total product is MR. Since

---

[1] The worrisome distinction made in Chapter 7 between discrete and continuous marginal revenue must also be made with reference to marginal product. $MP_c = dTP/dx$, where x is input; $MP_d = \Delta TP/\Delta x = TP_{n+1} - TP_n$. In Table 13–1 discrete marginal product was calculated.

average product is total product divided by input, $TP = MR/OM$. But $MR/OM = \tan \alpha$, and we say, accordingly, that $AP = \tan \alpha$. When ON units of input are employed, total product is NV and average product is $NV/ON = \tan \beta$. Since angle β is larger than angle α, $\tan \beta$ is greater than $\tan \alpha$, and average product is greater at input ON than it is at input OM. Indeed, since OV is tangent to the TP curve, if angle β were any larger, the vector would miss the TP curve entirely. It follows, then, that at input ON average product is at a maximum. If one visualizes vectors drawn from the origin to various points on the TP curve, the angles formed by the vectors and the x-axis would increase in size until we get to point V, and from that point the angles would become smaller. The average-product curve corresponding to TP in Figure 13–1 will, accordingly, begin at the origin, rise until input ON is reached, and then decrease. If the TP curve had been extended until it reached the x-axis, average product would be equal to zero at the input where total product was equal to zero. The average-product curve, then, has an inverted U shape, reaching its maximum value at input ON and having common x-intercepts with the total-product curve.

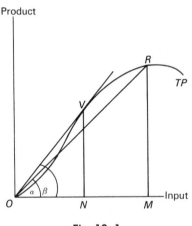

Fig. 13–1

We now turn to an investigation of the geometric relationships between the total-product and marginal-product curves. In Figure 13–2 a total-product curve is drawn, and we begin by determining the value of marginal product at input OM. The basic point in this connection is that the marginal value at any input is equal to the slope of the total curve at that input. At input OM the slope of the TP curve is equal to the slope of the tangent AL, which in turn is equal to $\Delta y/\Delta x = ML/AM = \tan \alpha$. Similarly, the marginal product at input ON is equal to the slope of the tangent $OV = NV/ON = \tan \beta$. But since the tangent OV passes through the origin, $\tan \beta$ is also the value of average product when average product is at a maximum. It follows, accordingly, that when average product is at a maximum, average product and marginal product are equal. For inputs less than *ON*, where average product is increasing as input increases, marginal product is greater than average product. For inputs greater than *ON*, where average product is decreasing, marginal product is less than average product. At input *OR* the slope of the total-product curve is equal to zero, and marginal product is, therefore, equal to zero. For inputs greater than *OR*, the slope of the total-product curve is negative, and marginal product is negative.

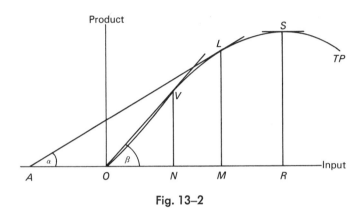

Fig. 13–2

We may summarize the geometry of total-average and total-marginal relationships as follows: To determine the average product corresponding with any point on the total-product curve, draw a vector from the given point on the total curve to the origin; the tangent of the angle formed by the vector and the *x*-axis is the value of average product at the given input. To determine the marginal product corresponding with any point on the total-product curve, draw a tangent to the total curve at the given point and extend the tangent to the *x*-axis (or other convenient horizontal line); the tangent of the angle formed by the tangent to the total curve and the *x*-axis is the value of the marginal product at the given input.

In Figure 13–3 the important total-average and total-marginal relationships are demonstrated. *TP* is the total-product curve, *AP* is the average-product curve, and *MP* is the marginal-product curve. Total product increases until *OL* units of input are used; after that total product decreases as input increases, reaching zero when *OS* units of input are employed per time period.

The average-product curve also increases for a time as input increases, reaches a maximum when *OM* units of input are employed, and equals zero when *TP* equals zero. It will be noted that the maximum average product comes at the input where the vector from the origin is tangent to the *TP* curve; the vector is tangent at *R*, which lies directly above *M*.

The marginal-product curve also assumes the form of an inverted U. As long as average product is increasing as input increases, marginal product is greater than average product. When average product is at a maximum, marginal product equals average product: MR/OM measures both average product and marginal product at input OM. When average product decreases as input increases, marginal product is less than average product. Marginal product is zero when the slope of the total-product curve is zero; this comes at input OL. When the slope of the total-product curve is negative, marginal product is negative. It will be noted that marginal product attains a maximum

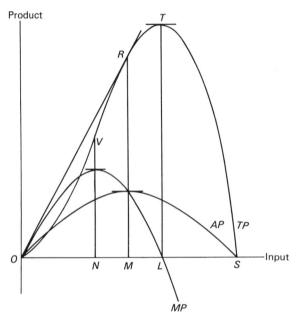

Fig. 13–3

at input ON. This comes at what is called the point of inflection of the total curve, which in Figure 13–3 is at point V. To the left of V the total-product curve is concave from above; this means that total is increasing at an increasing rate as input increases. To the right of V, the total-product curve is concave from below; this means that total product is increasing at a decreasing rate. When total product is increasing at an increasing rate, marginal product is positive and increasing; when total product is increasing at a decreasing rate, marginal product is positive and decreasing. At the point of inflection, the marginal-product curve is at a maximum; that is, $dMP/dx = 0$. If one were to draw a tangent to the TP curve to the left of V, the tangent would lie below the curve except at the point of tangency; a tangent to the TP curve to the right of V, e.g., OR, would lie above the TP curve. If one attempted to draw a tangent to the TP curve at point V, the tangent would lie below the TP curve to the left of V, above the TP curve to the right of V, and would cross the curve at V. The point of inflection of the total curve has no particular economic significance except that it locates the input where the marginal-product curve is at a maximum.

Returns to Scale

Before we return to a consideration of the firm's production function in which one set of factors is assumed to be fixed while the other set is assumed to be variable, a word needs to be said about the nature of changes in total product as all factors are assumed to be variable. If there are no fixed factors of production, it is clear that we are talking about long-run adjustments and are concerned with changes in size of plant.

Suppose that we are considering a firm which is currently using x units of factor X in combination with y units of factor Y, and the resulting output is P. We may write

$$x + y \rightarrow P.$$

Now suppose that the amount of both inputs used is multiplied by the constant a, and the result is that the output is multiplied by the constant b. We may write

$$ax + ay \rightarrow bP.$$

If b is less than a, if, for example, a 100 percent increase in the amounts of factors X and Y employed results in a 50 percent increase in output, the situation is described as one of decreasing returns to scale. If b is greater than a—if, for example, a 50 percent increase in the quantity of inputs employed results in a 100 percent increase in product—the firm enjoys increasing returns to scale. And if b equals a—if, for example, a doubling of the factors employed results in a doubling of output—the case is one of constant returns to scale.

The case of constant returns to scale is a useful one for economic analysis, in part because it is a simple case which lends itself to easy manipulation, in part because there is evidence that in the real world this is not an uncommon case. Linear programming, the broad outlines of which are sketched in the next chapter, assumes that output increases proportionately with changes in inputs, and this device has found many useful applications in the business world. Professor Douglas has found on the basis of statistical studies that total production tends in fact to increase proportionately with increases in the amount of capital and labor employed.[2]

A production function which reflects proportionate changes in inputs

[2] For a discussion of the Cobb-Douglas production function see Paul H. Douglas, "Are There Laws of Production?", *American Economic Review*, 38 (March 1948), 1–41.

and outputs is described as linear and homogeneous or homogeneous of the first degree.[3] The Cobb-Douglas production function was given as

$$P = bL^k C^{1-k},$$

where P is total output, L is the amount of labor employed, C is the amount of capital employed, and b and k are constants ($k < 1$). Suppose now that both inputs are multiplied by the constant a. L^k becomes $(aL)^k$ and C^{1-k} becomes $(aC)^{1-k}$;

$$b(aL)^k(aC)^{1-k} = ba^k L^k a^{1-k} C^{1-k}$$
$$= ba^{k+1-k} L^k C^{1-k}$$
$$= abL^k C^{1-k} = aP.$$

When L and C are multiplied by a, P is also multiplied by a, and the Cobb-Douglas production function is linear and homogeneous; that is, it reflects constant returns to scale.

Law of Variable Proportions

Let us consider a firm which buys inputs and sells outputs in purely competitive markets at fixed prices, a firm whose long-run production function reflects constant returns to scale and whose short-run production function is subject to the law of variable proportions, or, as it is frequently called, the law of diminishing returns. This means that as the firm's scale of plant is increased in the long run, output will increase in proportion to the change in the quantity of factors employed—a doubling of all factors will result in a doubling of output. But in the short run as more and more units of the variable factor are used in combination with the fixed factor, the additional output resulting from the use of an additional unit of the variable factor will after a point become smaller and smaller. That is to say that we are assuming that if

      x men work on y land, the product is z,

and if

      $2x$ men work on $2y$ land, the product is $2z$,

and if

      $2x$ men work on y land, the product is more than z but less than $2z$.

It will simplify the exposition if we assume that the firm's short-run production function is given. Let us assume that when the fixed factor, Y, is equal to one, the firm's product functions are:

---

[3] For a brief discussion of homogeneous functions see Clark Lee Allen, *Elementary Economics of Price Theory* (Belmont, Calif.: Wadsworth Publishing Co., Inc., 1962), pp. 48–52.

$$TP = 6x^2 - x^3$$
$$AP = 6x - x^2$$
$$MP = 12x - 3x^2.$$

The production function is represented in Table 13–2 and Figure 13–4.

TABLE 13–2

X	Y	TP	AP	MP$_c$
0	1	0	0	0
1	1	5	5	9
2	1	16	8	12
3	1	27	9	9
4	1	32	8	0
5	1	25	5	−15
6	1	0	0	−36

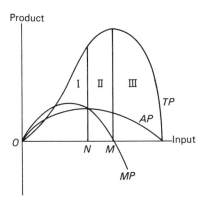

Fig. 13–4

Figure 13–4 has been divided into three stages. Stage I is the phase of increasing average returns to the variable factor. Total product at first increases at an increasing rate and then at a decreasing rate, but throughout this stage total product increases more than proportionately with the increase in the variable factor. Marginal product is positive throughout this phase, reflecting the fact that total product is increasing; marginal product increases for a time and then decreases, reflecting the changing rate of change of the total product; and marginal product is everywhere greater than average product, reflecting the fact that average product is increasing.

Stage II is the phase of diminishing average returns to the variable factor. The total product increases as the variable factor increases, and marginal product is, accordingly, positive, but total product is increasing at a decreasing rate, and marginal product is, therefore, decreasing. Average product is decreasing and at any input is, therefore, greater than marginal product.

Stage III may be described as the phase of negative marginal returns.

Total product is diminishing and marginal product is negative. This means that the use of an additional unit of the variable factor actually reduces total product, and if enough units of the variable factor are employed, total, and hence average, product become zero.

It is clear that even if the variable factors were available to the firm at price zero, the profit-maximizing firm would never use more than OM units of the variable factor. If the marginal product of a factor is negative, total product can be increased by using less of that factor. We may conclude, accordingly, that the profit-maximizing firm would never operate in Stage III.

What is not so apparent on its face is that the profit-maximizing firm would not operate in Stage I. There is, as a matter of fact, a symmetry between Stages I and III. Just as in Stage III we have too little of the fixed factor to make effective use of the variable factor, in Stage I we have too little of the variable factor to make effective use of the fixed factor. In Stage III the marginal product of the variable factor is negative, and in Stage I the marginal product of the fixed factor is negative. This last statement will require brief analysis.

Table 13–2 tells us that if we use 1 of X with 1 of Y, the total product is 5. If we use 2 of X with 1 of Y, the total product is 16. But since we have assumed that the long-run production function is linear and homogeneous, if 1 of X with 1 of Y results in a total product of 5, 2 of X with 2 of Y would result in a total product of 10. If 2 of X with 1 of Y produces 16, and 2 of X with 2 of Y produces 10, the marginal product of Y is

$$MP_y = \frac{\Delta TP}{\Delta y} = \frac{-6}{1} = -6.$$

Similarly, Table 13–2 tells us that 3 of X with 1 of Y produces a total product of 27. If we start with the combination 2 of X and 1 of Y and multiply each factor by 3/2, we get: 3 of X with 3/2 of Y will produce 3/2 times 16, or 24. Again the marginal product of factor Y is

$$MP_y = \frac{\Delta TP}{\Delta y} = \frac{-3}{\frac{1}{2}} = -6.$$

It is not until we get to the next combination in Table 13–2 that the marginal product of factor Y is positive, and this comes at the beginning of Stage II, where marginal product equals average product. The table tells us that if we use 4 of X with 1 of Y, the total product is 32. But if we start with the combination 3 of X with 1 of Y and multiply each factor by 4/3, we get: 4 of X with 4/3 of Y will result in a total product of 4/3 times 27, or 36. The marginal product of Y is

$$MP_y = \frac{\Delta TP}{\Delta y} = \frac{4}{\frac{1}{3}} = 12.$$

Since everywhere in Stage I the marginal product of the fixed factor is negative, the profit-maximizing firm with constant returns to scale will not operate in this stage. The most profitable input will, accordingly, be somewhere between ON and OM in Figure 13–4, the precise point being determined by the prices of inputs which the firm buys and the price of the firm's output. The most profitable input with input and output prices given will be discussed in a later chapter.[4]

The three stages of the short-run production function may be distinguished by the use of the elasticity concept. The elasticity of total product shows the responsiveness of total product to a change in input:

$$E_{tp} = \frac{\dfrac{\Delta y}{y}}{\dfrac{\Delta x}{x}} \, .$$

Note the difference between this and the formula for the elasticity of demand:

$$E_d = \frac{\dfrac{\Delta x}{x}}{\dfrac{\Delta y}{y}} \, .$$

This difference comes about because when we were measuring the elasticity of demand, we were concerned with the responsiveness of the x-value (quantity sold) to a change in the y-value (price); the elasticity of total product is a measure of the responsiveness of the y-value (total product) to a change in the x-value (input).

We may write

$$E_{tp} = \frac{\dfrac{\Delta y}{y}}{\dfrac{\Delta x}{x}} = \frac{\dfrac{\Delta TP}{TP}}{\dfrac{\Delta x}{x}} = \frac{\Delta TP}{TP} \cdot \frac{x}{\Delta x} = \frac{\Delta TP}{\Delta x} \cdot \frac{x}{TP} = \frac{\Delta TP}{\Delta x} \div \frac{TP}{x} \, .$$

But $\Delta TP/\Delta x$ is marginal product, and TP/x is average product, and we may write

$$E_{tp} = \frac{MP}{AP} \, .$$

By referring to Figure 13–4 we may note that in Stage I, marginal product is everywhere greater than average product, and elasticity of total product is, accordingly, greater than one; that is, total product is increasing more than proportionately with increases in input. In Stage II, marginal

---

[4] It should be noted that this analysis has assumed that the firm sells its output and buys its input in purely competitive markets at fixed prices. If the firm buys or sells in less than purely competitive markets, it may find that its most profitable input will come in Stage I. A case of this sort is discussed in Chapter 15.

product is less than average product, and elasticity of total product is less than one but greater than zero; total product is increasing less than proportionately with increases in input. In Stage III, marginal product is negative, and the elasticity of total product is less than zero; as input increases, total product decreases. Since, as we have seen, the profit-maximizing firm operates only in Stage II, the elasticity of total product is positive but less than one in the significant range of the production function.

Production Functions and Cost Functions

As we have seen, the mathematical relationships between average, total, and marginal product are essentially the same as the relationships between average, total, and marginal cost, which were discussed in Chapter 8. There is in addition an obvious relationship between the firm's production function and its cost function. If, as more units of the variable factor are used in combination with the fixed factor, the output per unit of input increases, it follows that the variable cost per unit of output must be decreasing. When the output per unit of variable factor is at a maximum, the variable cost of a unit of output must be at a minimum. And when the output per unit of variable factor decreases as the number of variable factors employed with the fixed factor decreases, the average-variable cost of output must be increasing. The interrelations between the firm's cost and product functions are indicated in Figure 13–5.[5]

If one holds Figure 13–5 so that the line OF is horizontal, this line is the x-axis, and TVC is the total-variable-cost curve with output measured along the x-axis. The vector OL is drawn tangent to the TVC curve at point E. When output is OF, average-variable cost is at a minimum and is equal to tan a. For outputs less than OF, average-variable cost is decreasing, and for outputs greater than OF, average-variable cost is increasing. The point of inflection of the TVC curve comes at G; at output OH, marginal cost is at a minimum. For outputs less than OH, marginal cost is decreasing, and for outputs greater than OH marginal cost is increasing.

If the figure is turned so that the line OB is horizontal, this line is now the x-axis which measures input and is read from right to left. The curve which was formerly the TVC curve is now the total-product curve. The vector OK is tangent to the TP curve at point A, and this locates the input OB where average product is at a maximum and is equal to marginal product, which, in turn is equal to tan β. The point of inflection of the TP curve comes at C, and this determines the input OD where marginal product is at a maximum. For inputs less than OD, marginal product is increasing as input increases; for inputs greater than OD, marginal product is decreasing. For

[5] This figure was suggested to me by my colleague, Mr. Kanji Haitani.

inputs less than *OB*, average product increases as input increases; for inputs greater than *OB*, average product is decreasing. Output *OH*, where marginal cost is at a minimum, corresponds with input *OD*, where marginal product is at a maximum. Output *OF*, where average-variable cost is at a minimum, corresponds with input *OB*, where average product is at a maximum.

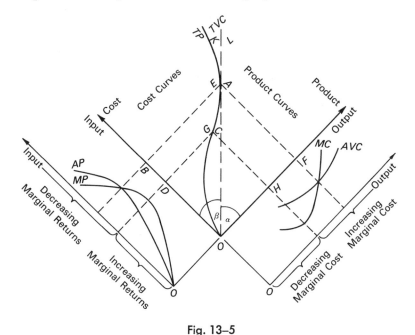

Fig. 13–5

POSTPRANDIUM

The production function involves a minimum of three variables: factors *X* and *Y* and the resulting total product, *Z*. The most direct way to represent such a function is with a three-dimensional figure called the physical-production surface or the production mountain. In Figure 13–6 such a representation is made. The quantity of factor *X* is measured along the *x*-axis; the quantity of factor *Y* is measured along the *y*-axis; and the quantity of the total product is measured along the *z*-axis. Any point on the physical-production surface, such as *A*, *B*, *C*, and *E*, represents a combination of factors *X* and *Y* and the resulting quantity of total product. If we start at point *C*, for example, and drop line *CC′* perpendicular to the base, *C′x′* perpendicular to the *x*-axis, and *C′y′* perpendicular to the *y*-axis, then *C′C* represents the total product when *Ox′* of factor *X* is used in combination with *Oy′* of *Y*.

Suppose now that we make a perpendicular slice of the figure parallel to the x-axis. Such a section is $y''EF$. This gives us the curve along the surface designated as $y''AE$, which is the total-product curve when factor Y is fixed at Oy'' and X is the variable factor. Or we may take a section parallel to the y-axis, such as $x''EF$, and this gives us the curve $x''BE$, which is the total-product curve when factor X is fixed at Ox'' and Y is the variable factor.

Finally, we may take a section parallel to the base plane, such as ABD. This gives us the curve along the surface ACB, and this curve indicates the various combinations of factors X and Y which will produce equal products. Ox of X plus Oy'' of Y will produce a total product of $A'A$; Ox' of X plus Oy' of Y will produce a total product of $C'C$; Ox'' of X plus Oy of Y will produce a total product of $B'B$; and $A'A = C'C = B'B$. ACB is called a contour line of the production surface.

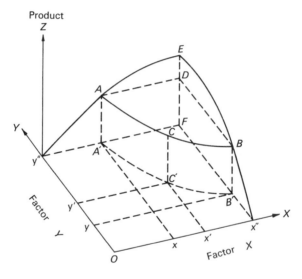

Fig. 13–6

The projection of ACB on the base is the curve $A'C'B'$, which is called an *isoproduct curve* or an *isoquant*. Just as geographers represent in a two-dimensional figure the hills and valleys of a land area with contour lines, it is possible to represent the various combinations of two factors of production which will produce the same total product without resorting to the use of an awkward three-dimensional figure. In terms of Figure 13–6, Ox of X with Oy'' of Y or Ox' of X with Oy' of Y or Ox'' of X with Oy of Y will all produce the same total output. By drawing a family of isoquants, each representing a different total product, the production function with its three variables can be represented in a two-dimensional figure. That is the subject of the next chapter.

SELECTED REFERENCES

Allen, Clark Lee, Robert H. Strotz, and Aurelius Morgner. *Problems in the Theory of Price.* (Englewood Cliffs, N.J.: Prentice-Hall, Inc., 1954.) Pp. 154–168.

Cassels, John M. "On the Law of Variable Proportions," *Explorations in Economics.* New York: McGraw-Hill Book Co., 1936. Pp. 223–236; reprinted in William Fellner and Bernard F. Haley, eds., *Readings in Income Distribution.* Philadelphia: The Blakiston Co., 1946. Pp. 103–118.

Knight, Frank H. *Risk, Uncertainty, and Profit.* Boston: Houghton Mifflin Co., 1921. Chap. 4.

Leftwich, Richard H. *The Price System and Resource Allocation.* 3rd ed. New York: Holt, Rinehart & Winston, Inc., 1966. Chap. 7.

Lerner, Abba P. *The Economics of Control.* New York: The Macmillan Co., 1944. Chaps. 10–13.

Stigler, George J. *The Theory of Price.* Rev. ed. New York: The Macmillan Co., 1952. Pp. 20–30.

PROBLEMS

PROBLEM I

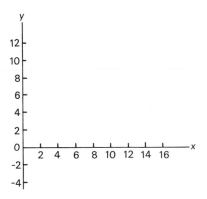

Fig. 13–7

A total curve is made up of two linear segments. From $x = 0$ to $x = 4$, the equation for the total curve is given by $T = 2x$. From $x = 4$ to $x = 12$, the equation for the total curve is $T = 12 - x$.

    1. Plot the total function on the axes above.

    2. What is the equation for the average function from $x = 0$ to $x = 4$? . . . .———————

3. What is the equation for the average function from $x = 4$ to $x = 12$? . . . . . . ._____

4. Plot the average function.

5. What is the equation for the marginal function from $x = 0$ to $x = 4$? . . . . . . ._____

6. What is the equation for the marginal function from $x = 4$ to $x = 12$? . . . . . . ._____

7. Plot the marginal function.

8. All segments of the total, average, and marginal curves are linear except the _____ function from $x = $_____ to $x = $_____.

9. When the total function is increasing at a constant rate as x increases, the average curve has a slope (equal to, less than, greater than) zero; during this range the average value is (equal to, less than, greater than) the marginal value.

10. When the total function is decreasing at a constant rate as x increases, the average curve has a slope (equal to, less than, greater than) zero; during this range the average value is (equal to, less than, greater than) the marginal value.

11. When the average value decreases as x increases, the marginal value is (equal to, less than, greater than) zero.

PROBLEM II

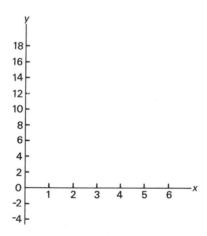

Fig. 13–8

The total function is given as $T = 12x - 2x^2$.

1. Plot the total, average, and marginal curves on the axes above.

2. Draw a tangent to the total curve at $x = 3$.

3. What is the *y*-intercept of the tangent to the total
    curve at *x* = 3?   .   .   .   .——————————

4. What is the slope of the total curve at *x* = 3? .   .——————————

5. What is the marginal value at *x* = 3? .   .   .   .——————————

6. Draw a tangent to the total curve at *x* = 2.

7. What is the *y*-intercept of the tangent to the total
    curve at *x* = 2?   .   .   .   .——————————

8. What is the slope of the total curve at *x* = 2? .   .——————————

9. What is the marginal value at *x* = 2?

10. Draw a tangent to the total curve at *x* = 4.

11. What is the *y*-intercept of the tangent to the total
    curve at *x* = 4?   .   .   .   .——————————

12. What is the slope of the total curve at *x* = 4? .   .——————————

13. What is the marginal value at *x* = 4? .   .   .   .——————————

PROBLEM III

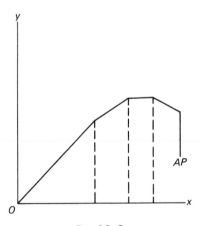

Fig. 13–9

In the above figure, the average-product curve is represented by linear segments.
Determine geometrically the corresponding marginal-product curve.

PROBLEM IV

In Figure 13–10, *TP* is the total-product curve. Sketch in the corresponding
average-product and marginal-product curves.

PROBLEM V

1. When 6 units of input are employed, marginal
    product and average product are both 10. What is

the slope (positive, negative, or zero) of the average-product curve at this point? . . . . . .————————

2. If 8 units of input are employed, marginal product is 0. What is the slope of the total-product curve at this point? . . . .————————

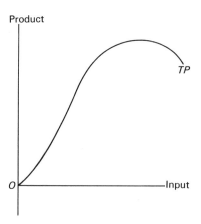

Product

TP

O   Input

Fig. 13–10

3. If 3 variable factors are employed, marginal product is 13 and average product is 4. What is the slope of the average-product curve at this point? . .————————

4. With the use of 10 units of the variable factor, marginal product is −3. What is the slope of the total-product curve at this point? . . . . .————————

PROBLEM VI

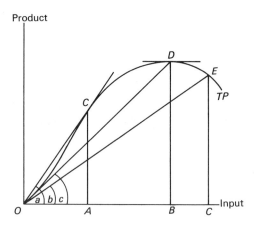

Product

D

E

C

TP

a *b* *c*

O   *A*   *B*   *C*   Input

Fig. 13–11

1. In Figure 13–11, when TP is at a maximum, $AP =$ _____/_____ or tan _____.

2. When OB units of input are employed, $MP =$ _____.

3. When OA units of input are employed, $MP =$ _____/_____ or tan _____.

4. When OA units of input are employed, $AP =$ _____/_____ or tan _____.

5. Average product is at a maximum when _____ units of input are employed.

6. If fewer than OA units of input are employed, MP is (greater than, less than, equal to) AP.

7. If more than OA units of input are employed, AP is (greater than, less than, equal to) MP.

8. If OC units of input are employed, $AP =$ _____/_____ or tan _____ and MP is (positive, negative, zero).

9. MP is at a maximum when (OA, more than OA, fewer than OA) units of input are employed.

14

Isoquants and the Production Function

Clearer insights into a number of topics discussed in the preceding chapter as well as an understanding of additional matters may be obtained with the use of an analysis employing the device called isoquants (see above, p. 306). The word isoquant is derived from the Greek *isos,* meaning equal, and *quant* for quantity. Just as isobars and isotherms are drawn on meteorological charts through points of equal barometric pressure and equal temperature respectively, an isoquant is a line drawn through points representing combinations of factors of production which will produce equal quantities of output per time period. If we consider two inputs, such as labor and capital, the presumption is that a given output, say 20 units per time period, might be produced with a great deal of capital and relatively little labor, or with less capital and more labor. If we assume that the inputs are perfectly divisible, the number of combinations of factors which might produce a given output is infinite. The locus of points representing combinations of inputs which would produce a given output per time period is an isoquant. A larger output would be represented by another isoquant, which would be the locus of points representing combinations of inputs appropriate to that output. An isoquant map or a family of isoquants includes isoquants appropriate for all rates of output, each isoquant, of course, representing a given output. The mechanics of isoquant analysis is quite similar to indifference-curve analysis; in the case of isoquants it is output which is held constant instead of utility.

Marginal Rate of Substitution

Figure 14–1 shows an isoquant representing, say, an output of 20 units per time period. Of the many possible combinations of factors X and Y which might be employed to produce an output of 20, two are indicated—combination R and combination V. Combination R utilizes Ox of factor X plus Oy of

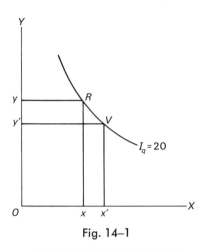

Fig. 14–1

factor Y; combination V produces the same output by using Ox' of X and Oy' of Y. In terms of purely technological considerations, it is a matter of indifference which of these or any other combination lying on this isoquant is used to produce the given output. It will be noted that if we shift from combination R to combination V, we employ xx' more of factor X and yy' less of factor Y; that is, we have substituted xx' of X for yy' of Y, and the ratio of the change in Y to the change in X, $\Delta y/\Delta x$, is called the marginal rate of substitution of X for Y and is abbreviated MRS_{xy}. If the changes in X and Y are taken to be infinitesimally small, the marginal rate of substitution at any point on the isoquant is dy/dx and is equal to the slope of the tangent to the isoquant at that point. (The algebraic sign of the slope of the tangent is ignored as a matter of convenience.)

While it is true in a purely engineering sense that a given output could be produced equally well by any combination of inputs lying on an isoquant, it clearly is not a matter of indifference to the firm which combination it uses. The best combination from the point of view of the firm is the one which will produce the given output at the lowest total cost. And the lowest-cost

combination of factors will depend upon the prices of the factors as well as
the form of the isoquant.

The Isocost Curve

Let us suppose that a firm will spend on factors X and Y a total amount,
measured in dollars, which we may designate as C. Suppose in terms of
Figure 14–2 that if the firm should spend the total amount of C on factor X,
it would be able to buy OA units of X. If, on the other hand, it should spend

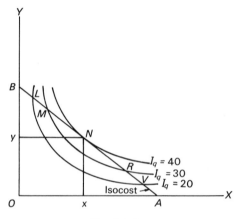

Fig. 14–2

the total amount of C on factor Y, it would be able to buy OB units of Y. It
follows that any combination of X and Y which falls on the curve BA would
also represent a total outlay equal to C, and the line BA, accordingly, is
known as the constant-outlay or isocost curve.

The fact that the isocost curve will be the linear curve BA can be
demonstrated as follows. Let P_x be the price of a unit of X and P_y be the price
of Y. The total amount spent on X will be price times quantity or xP_x, and
the amount spent on factor Y will be yP_y. Since the total amount spent on
both factors is assumed to be C, it follows that

$$xP_x + yP_y = C.$$

Dividing through by C,

$$\frac{xP_x}{C} + \frac{yP_y}{C} = 1.$$

Dividing the numerators and denominators of the first term by P_x and of the
second term by P_y,

$$\frac{x}{\frac{C}{P_x}} + \frac{y}{\frac{C}{P_y}} = 1.$$

But, as we have seen, C divided by the price of X equals OA in Figure 14–2, and C divided by the price of Y equals OB. Hence

$$\frac{x}{OA} + \frac{y}{OB} = 1,$$

and this is the equation for a straight line with an x-intercept at A and a y-intercept at B.

Any combination of factors X and Y lying on the isocost curve BA can therefore be purchased by the firm at the same total outlay of C. Among the many combinations lying on the isocost curve are L and V. Since both of these combinations of inputs lie on $I_q = 20$, either would result in an output of 20 units per time period. But either combination M or R would be better than L or V since these also fall on isocost curve BA and, therefore, represent the same total expenditure on inputs, but, since they lie on $I_q = 30$, the resulting output with either of these combinations would be 30 instead of 20. The best combination clearly is N, where the isocost curve is just tangent to an isoquant. With Ox of X plus Oy of Y, the firm can produce 40 units of output at the same total outlay for factors of C, and there is no way to produce more than this with the given total outlay and the given prices of factors.

The Factor-Price Line

When the firm is employing the optimum combination of factors, the marginal rate of substitution of X for Y is equal to the price of X in terms of the price of Y as the following demonstrates:

$$MRS_{xy} = \frac{\Delta y}{\Delta x} = \frac{OB}{OA} = \frac{C}{P_y} \div \frac{C}{P_x} = \frac{C}{P_y} \cdot \frac{P_x}{C} = \frac{P_x}{P_y}.$$

The slope of BA, accordingly, represents the price of X in terms of the price of Y. If the price of X should fall, for example, while the price of Y remained unchanged, A would move to the right since if C were all spent on X, more than OA of X could be purchased at the lower price, and the slope of BA would be diminished. The optimum combination of factors for producing a given output may be described as being that combination where the marginal rate of substitution of X for Y is equal to the price of X in terms of the price of Y.

It is also true that the slope of the factor-price line is equal to the ratio of the marginal product of factor X to the marginal product of factor Y. At combination N in Figure 14–2, where the optimum quantities of the two inputs are employed, the marginal product of X divided by the price of X is equal to the marginal product of Y divided by the price of Y. This is essentially the same point we encountered in the analysis of marginal utility.

The marginal product of X divided by the price of X is the marginal product per dollar spent on X. If the last dollar spent on X provides more or less additional product than the last dollar spent on Y, we have not yet located the optimum combination of factors; we should buy more of the input which provides the greater marginal return to the dollar and less of the other. When we have attained the equilibrium position, the marginal product of X divided by the price of X will equal the marginal product of Y divided by the price of Y. We may write

$$\frac{MP_x}{P_x} = \frac{MP_y}{P_y}.$$

Multiplying both sides by P_x,

$$MP_x = \frac{MP_y \cdot P_x}{P_y}.$$

Dividing both sides by MP_y,

$$\frac{MP_x}{MP_y} = \frac{P_x}{P_y} = MRS_{xy}.$$

The slope of the factor-price line (BA in Figure 14–2), therefore, indicates (1) the ratio of the marginal product of X to the marginal product of Y, (2) the price of X in terms of the price of Y, and (3) the marginal rate of substitution of X for Y.

Relevant Range of the Isoquant

We noted in the preceding chapter that the profit-maximizing firm with constant returns to scale would operate in only Stage II of its short-run total-product function. We can now demonstrate that there is a restricted range of the firm's isoquant within which it will operate, and outside this range some of either one or both factors would be redundant. The relevant range of the isoquant may be described as lying between the points where the marginal rate of substitution of X for Y is equal to infinity and where MRS_{xy} is zero.

Recalling that

$$MRS_{xy} = \frac{MP_x}{MP_y},$$

the marginal rate of substitution will be infinity when MP_y is equal to zero. The marginal product of Y is zero when the use of an additional quantity of Y with a fixed amount of X results in no change in total output. This comes at the point where the tangent to the isoquant is a vertical line, at point R in Figure 14–3. The MRS_{xy} will equal zero when $MP_x = 0$. The marginal product of X is zero when the use of an additional quantity of X with a fixed amount of Y results in no change in total output. This comes at the point where the tangent to the isoquant is a horizontal line, at point V in Figure 14–3.

It can easily be seen that any part of the isoquant outside the range between point R, where Ox of X is used in combination with Oy of Y, and point V, where Ox' of X is used with Oy' of Y, would involve the use of excessive amounts of inputs. Any point above and to the right of either point R or point V would represent a greater use of both factors, but the total output, since they lie on the same isoquant, would be the same. If the

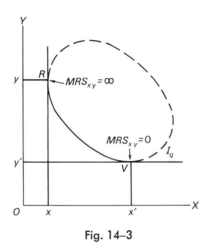

Fig. 14–3

isoquant were elliptical in shape, the point on the isoquant directly to the right of R would represent the same amount of Y in combination with a great deal more of X, and the point on the isoquant directly above V would represent the same amount of X with much more of Y. We may conclude, accordingly, that even when both factors are variable and without regard to returns to scale, there is a restricted segment of an isoquant which is relevant to the profit-maximizing firm. The optimum combination of factors to produce the output represented by a given isoquant will be determined by the point of tangency between the factor-price line and the isoquant somewhere within the significant range of the isoquant.

Suppose now that the marginal rate of substitution of X for Y is everywhere equal to zero; this means that with a fixed amount of Y, additional units of X will not increase total output, and the MP_x is zero. The isoquant will then assume the form of a horizontal line. But suppose in addition that the marginal rate of substitution of Y for X is also zero. This means that the MP_y is zero with a given amount of X, and the portion of the isoquant which reflects $MRS_{yx} = 0$ will be a vertical line. Figure 14–4 represents isoquants reflecting the fact that $MRS_{xy} = 0$, and $MRS_{yx} = 0$.

This figure implies that the factors must be used in fixed proportions. If it takes three men to run a machine, a fourth man with one machine would not increase output per time period, or a second machine with a total of three men would not increase output. Figure 14–4 represents the case of factors in a perfectly complementary relationship to each other.

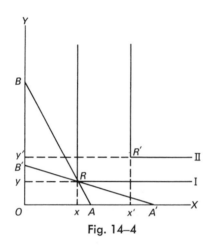

Fig. 14–4

It will be noted that when factors are perfect complements, the relative prices of factors will not affect the proportions in which the factors are used. If the firm in Figure 14–4 is to produce the output indicated by isoquant I and the price of X in terms of the price of Y is very high, as is reflected by the slope of the factor-price line BA, the firm would employ Ox of X and Oy of Y. If now the price of X falls relative to the price of Y, as is represented by the slope of B'A', the appropriate combination of factors remains Ox of X and Oy of Y. If the firm decides to increase its output to that represented by isoquant II, it will use Ox' of X and Oy' of Y regardless of the relative prices of X and Y. In the case of isoquants of the form of those in Figure 14–4, the relevant range of the isoquants is restricted to their corner points.

Let us now consider the special case where $\Delta MRS = 0$ as x changes. Since the marginal rate of substitution is the slope of the isoquant, if the slope is constant, the isoquant must be linear, as is BA in Figure 14–5. If, for example, $OA = OB$, this means that one unit of Y could always be replaced by one unit of X without affecting total output, and X and Y are, therefore, perfect substitutes in a one-to-one ratio. If the factor-price line is also BA, it would be a matter of indifference which combination of X and Y was employed; with any combination of factors the output would be the same and the total cost of inputs would be the same. If, however, the price of X in terms of the price of Y is relatively high, as is indicated by the isocost curve BA', the firm would use none of X and OB of Y. If, on the other hand, the price of Y as compared with the price of X were relatively high, as indicated by the factor-price line $B'A$, the firm would use none of factor Y and OA of X to produce the output represented by isoquant BA.

As was noted in the discussion of indifference curves, the cases of perfect complements and perfect substitutes are probably uncommon in the real world, but they do represent limiting cases. The closer the isoquant comes to being parallel to the axes, the smaller the degree of substitutability between them; the closer the isoquant comes to being linear, the greater the degree of substitutability.[1]

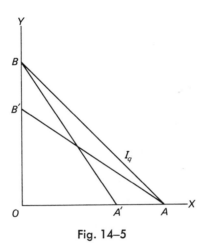

Fig. 14–5

Changes in Factor Prices and Output

Let us now investigate the effect of a change in relative-factor prices on the firm's optimum-factor use. It is clear that to the extent that one factor can be substituted for another, the firm will, as one input becomes relatively less expensive, tend to substitute the cheaper for the dearer factor. In Figure 14–6 we assume the firm to be, initially, in equilibrium at point R, where it is

[1] The concept *elasticity of substitution* is sometimes employed as a measure of the degree of substitution between X and Y. Elasticity of substitution is defined as

$$E_{sn} = \frac{\Delta(X/Y)/(X/Y)}{\dfrac{\Delta MRS}{MRS}}.$$

If MRS is plotted on the y-axis against X/Y on the x-axis, the elasticity of the resulting curve, which is the elasticity of substitution, can be determined in the same way that the elasticity of demand is determined. If E_{sn} is to be determined at the point on the curve having a y-value of OP, for example, draw a tangent to the curve at the given point on the curve and call the y-intercept of the tangent T. The elasticity of substitution at the given point can then be measured as OP/TP. For the development of the E_{sn} formula, see R. G. D. Allen, *Mathematical Analysis for Economists* (London: Macmillan & Co., 1942), pp. 340–343.

using Ox of factor X and Oy of factor Y. Suppose now that the price of X falls relative to the price of Y, a fall represented by a shift from factor-price line BA to BA'. Now BA' at the lower price of X represents the same total outlay as BA at the higher price of X. With no change in total cost, accordingly, the firm now can increase its output over that represented by isoquant I to that represented by isoquant II. If the firm decides to increase its output by this amount, its optimum position will be at point R', where it uses Ox' of X with Oy' of Y.

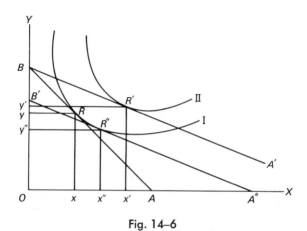

Fig. 14–6

The firm may decide, however, not to increase output. If the decision is to continue the original output, represented by isoquant I, it will do this by substituting some of the cheaper factor for some of the dearer. Since it is the slope of the factor-price line which represents the price of X in terms of the price of Y, we may draw a new isocost curve parallel to BA' and tangent to isoquant I. In Figure 14–6, $B'A''$ is such a line. Isocost curve $B'A''$ represents a lower total outlay than does BA. The original total outlay was equal to the price of Y times OB, but the new total outlay represented by $B'A''$ is equal to the price of Y times OB', and since the price of Y has not changed and OB' is less than OB, the new isocost curve represents a smaller total outlay. But with isocost curve $B'A''$ and isoquant I, the firm will employ combination R'', which is Ox'' of X plus Oy'' of Y. The reduction in the price of factor X has caused the firm to substitute xx'' of X for yy'' of Y and total output is unaffected.

The Expansion Path

Much of the technique of the isoquant analysis is summarized in Figure 14–7. Isoquants representing outputs of 100, 200, and 300 units per time period have been drawn. The curve *OL* has been drawn so that it intersects each isoquant at the point where the tangent to the isoquant would be a vertical line. Since *OL* passes through the isoquants at points of equal slope, it is known as an *isocline*. Curve *OV* is drawn through each of the isoquants at the point where the tangent to the isoquant would be a horizontal line, and *OV* is, accordingly, also an isocline. The portions of the isoquants lying between these isoclines are the only relevant segments of the isoquants; this is the range between the point on each isoquant where $MRS_{xy} = \infty$ and the point where $MRS_{xy} = 0$. Since *OL* and *OV* separate the relevant from the irrelevant areas of the figure, they are known as *ridge lines*.

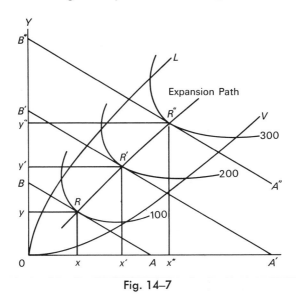

Fig. 14–7

Suppose that the price of factor *X* in terms of the price of factor *Y* is indicated by the slope of the isocost line *BA*, and the firm begins by producing 100 units per time period. This output can be produced at lowest cost by combining *Ox* of factor *X* with *Oy* of factor *Y*. If output is to be increased to 200 with no change in the prices of the factors, the appropriate combination is *R′*, where isocost line *B′A′* is tangent to isoquant 200. Since the prices of the factors have not changed, the slope of *B′A′* is equal to the slope of *BA*. Similarly, the best combination of factors for producing an output of 300 is combination *R″*, where *Ox″* of *X* is used with *Oy″* of *Y*. The curve *RR″*, which passes through the points of tangency between isoquants and parallel factor-price lines, is called the *expansion path*; it indicates the lowest-cost combination of factors for any output which the firm might produce. Since the expansion path cuts the isoquants at points of equal slope, it, too, is an isocline.

Isoquants and the Total Product Curve

The general form of the family of isoquants implied by a given total-product curve can be determined, and this is demonstrated in Figure 14–8. In the lower portion of the figure a total-product curve is drawn; this figure indicates that with a fixed amount of the Y factor and Ox_5 of X, the firm can

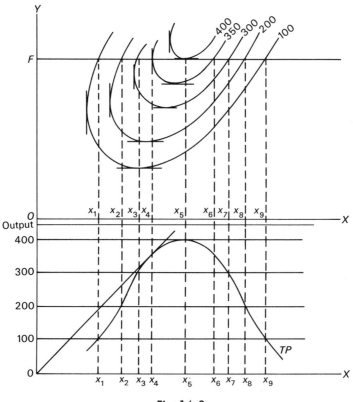

Fig. 14–8

produce a maximum output of 400 units per time period, and average product equals marginal product with Ox_4 units of factor X, where total product is equal to 350 units. As was demonstrated in the preceding chapter, the relevant range of the firm's product function is, therefore, between Ox_4 and Ox_5 units of X and between 350 and 400 units of output; this is Stage II of the firm's production function.

In the upper portion of Figure 14–8 a family of isoquants consistent with the given total-product curve is drawn. Assuming that the firm uses OF of the fixed factor Y, the firm's total product will be 100 units when OF of Y is used with either Ox_1 or Ox_9 of X. But both of these combinations of factors lie outside the relevant range of isoquant 100, just as they lie outside Stage II of the total-product curve. In similar manner, the intersections of the horizontal line from F and isoquants 200 and 300 represent combinations of factors outside the relevant ranges of the isoquants. Combination OF of Y and Ox_4 of X comes at the beginning of the relevant range of isoquant 350, and combination OF of Y with Ox_5 of X comes at the end of the relevant range of isoquant 400. The isoquant map, like the total-product curve below it, indicates that the profit-maximizing output of the firm will be somewhere between 350 and 400 units per time period, and the number of units of factor X employed will be between Ox_4 and Ox_5, the precise profit-maximizing input depending upon the relative prices of the factors.

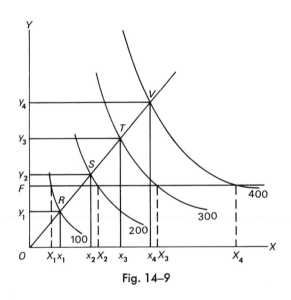

Fig. 14–9

The nature of the law of variable proportions, which was described in the preceding chapter, can also be demonstrated with the use of the isoquant technique. In Figure 14–9 we have drawn isoquants which represent a linear and homogeneous production function; when the amount of factors X and Y is doubled, total output doubles. Along the scale line RV, $RS = ST = TV$, and these isoquants, therefore, represent constant returns to scale. But if we assume that the amount of factor Y is fixed at OF, the amount of factor X required to provide a given increase in output increases in greater proportion than the increase in output; that is, in Figure 14–9, $X_1X_2 < X_2X_3 < X_3X_4$. We may conclude that even a firm with constant returns to scale is subject to the principle of diminishing returns.

POSTPRANDIUM

A technique related to isoquant analysis which has some applications in price theory and extensive uses in the solution of other problems in economics and business is known as linear or mathematical programming.[2] Instead of assuming that factors of production may be used in an infinite number of combinations with a continuous isoquant resulting, the method of linear programming assumes that there are only a relatively few feasible combinations of factors which will produce a given output, and each method of

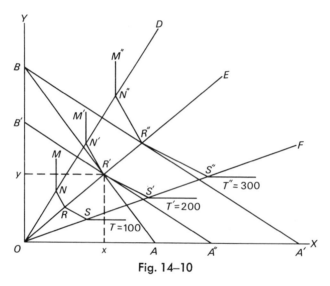

Fig. 14–10

combining inputs is known as a process. Each process may be represented by a scale line, and it is assumed that the production function is linearly homogeneous. It is also assumed that for any given process the proportions between inputs are fixed, as, for example, two men to a machine. These restrictions may seem to be so severe that this technique could have only limited usefulness in the solving of problems in the actual world, but in fact linear programming was devised specifically for dealing with the internal problems of the military forces and other large organizations.

In Figure 14–10 each of the rays, *OD, OE,* and *OF* represents a process by which the factors of production, *X* and *Y,* can be combined to produce a given product. Point *N* on process *OD* represents a combination of factors *X* and *Y* which would produce a given output, say, 100 units per time period. Point *N′,* which represents twice the amount of each factor, would also

[2] For a brief discussion of linear programming, see Clark Lee Allen, *Elementary Mathematics of Price Theory* (Belmont: Wadsworth Publishing Co., Inc., 1962), pp. 110–120. For a more detailed introduction to this subject, see Robert Dorfman, "Mathematical or 'Linear' Programming: A Non-mathematical Exposition," *American Economic Review,* 48 (December 1953), 797–825.

represent twice the product. The fact that $ON = NN' = N'N''$ indicates that the firm enjoys constant returns to scale when using process OD. The firm might also produce an output of 100 by employing either combination R on process OE or combination S on process OF. The line $MNRST$ passes through the combinations on each process line which would produce 100 units of output per time period; this line is known as a contour line or isoproduct curve and is actually a kinked isoquant. The determination of the optimum combination of factors and the best process is made by locating the point of tangency between the isoproduct curve and the isocost line. In Figure 14–10, if the isocost line is given by BA, the best process is OE, and the best combination of inputs for producing an output of 200 units per time period is R', which represents Ox of X plus Oy of Y. If now the price of X in terms of the price of Y should fall, and the isocost line becomes BA', the firm would, if it chose to increase output from 200 to 300, move to combination R'', also on process line OE, and the 50 percent increase in output would be effected by a 50 percent increase in the use of each factor. Or if the firm decided to continue producing at the rate of 200 units per time period even though the price of X had fallen, it would continue to use Ox of X with Oy of Y as determined by the point of tangency between isoproduct curve 100 with the isocost line $B'A''$, which is parallel to BA'. Combination R' would now cost the firm less than it cost before the price of X had fallen; that is, $B'A''$ represents a lower cost than BA.

This use of the linear-programming technique adds little that we do not already know from the more conventional isoquant analysis. The chief difference is that since the number of possible combinations of inputs which will produce a given output is limited, there can be a considerable shift in the relative prices of inputs without affecting the number of each input employed. In Figure 14–10, if the slope of the isocost line should be anywhere between the slope of segment $N'R'$ and the slope of segment $R'S'$, R' will remain the best combination of factors. This is undoubtedly in accord with actual business practice; firms do not, in fact, change the proportions of factors employed every time there is a change in the price of one of them.

A second difference between the conventional isoquant method and the linear-programming method is illustrated in Figure 14–11, where the isoproduct curve ($= 300$) of Figure 14–10 has been reproduced. In addition to the three processes represented by scale lines OD, OE, and OF, we may get additional processes by combining two of the given processes. Suppose, for example, that the firm decided to produce 200 units by process OE and 100 by process OF. If we start at point R' on OE and draw $R'V$ parallel to OF we locate point V on the isoproduct curve, and this locates another combination of factors which could produce 300 units of output per time period. We have in effect established another process, OV. Or, we could produce 200 units by process OF and 100 by process OE, which would establish a fifth process, OV'.

If the slope of the isocost curve were equal to the slope of segment *R"S"* of the isoproduct line, it would be a matter of indifference whether combination *R", V, V'* or *S"* were employed; total cost would be the same, and, of course, total output would be the same. This point was made when we discussed the case of perfect substitutes; if the isoquant is linear and the factor-price line is the same straight line, it would be a matter of indifference

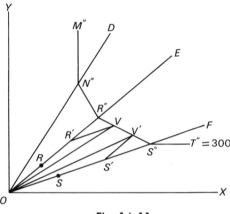

Fig. 14–11

which combination of factors was employed. This means that in terms of Figure 14–11, combinations *V* and *V'* provide no advantage to the firm over combinations *R"* and *S"*. The firm may, accordingly, ignore any combinations of processes and restrict its attention to the corners of the isoproduct curves. When problems of this sort are solved algebraically instead of geometrically, the elimination of combinations of processes lying between the corners of the isoproduct curves reduces the number of equations involved, and with the use of high-speed computers complex problems can be solved promptly.

Two Outputs and Three Inputs

In isoquant analysis usually only one product and two factors of production are assumed. The number of factors might be increased to three if it is assumed that two variable factors, *X* and *Y*, may be used in variable proportions with a fixed factor, *Z*, but a two-dimensional chart restricts the number of variables that can be handled at a time. The linear-programming method makes it possible to consider simultaneously a larger number of variables, and this, of course, broadens its range of usefulness.

To illustrate this aspect of linear programming, let us consider a firm which is trying to maximize its total revenue in a productive operation which involves two products and three factors of production. The firm may produce some of both products or confine its output to either one. It may use all or a part of the amount of each factor available to it during a given time period. We assume that the firm buys inputs and sells outputs in purely competitive markets. Let one product be designated X and the other Y. The price of X, P_x, is \$6 and the price of Y, P_y, is \$2. The inputs are A, of which 100 units are available per time period, B, of which 72 units are available, and C, of which 150 units are available. The objective of the firm is to maximize total revenue. What is known as the *objective equation* may be put in the form

$$xP_x + yP_y = \text{maximum } TR,$$

where x is the amount of X produced, y is the amount of Y, and TR is total revenue. Substituting 6 for P_x and 2 for P_y, the objective equation may be stated as

$$6x + 2y = \text{maximum } TR.$$

The solution of the objective equation is subject to what are called *constraints*. We have noted that the firm may produce both X and Y or only one of them. Since the firm cannot produce negative quantities of either product, we may write

$$x \geq 0$$

and

$$y \geq 0.$$

Suppose that, to produce one unit of X, 20 units of factor A are required and, to produce one unit of Y, 5 units of A are required, and that the firm has available to it 100 units of A. Since it is not required that all of factor A be employed, we may write

$$20x + 5y \leq 100.$$

Assume that it also requires 12 units of B to produce a unit of X and 6 units of B to produce a unit of Y, and a total of 72 units of B are available. The constraint with reference to input B may be written

$$12x + 6y \leq 72.$$

Finally, the production of a unit of X also requires 10 units of factor C, and one unit of Y requires 15 units of C. This constraint takes the form

$$10x + 15y \leq 150.$$

The input-output relationships are summarized in Table 14–1.

TABLE 14–1

Input	Input per Output X	Y	Amount of Input Available
A	20	5	100
B	12	6	72
C	10	15	150

If we ignore for the moment the fact that less than the amount of each factor available may actually be employed, we may set up the following equations:

$$20x + 5y = 100$$
$$12x + 6y = 72$$
$$10x + 15y = 150.$$

In Figure 14–12 each of these functions has been plotted. If in the first of these equations we let $x = 0$, we get $5y = 100$, or $y = 20$; if we let $y = 0$, $20x = 100$, and $x = 5$. AA' in Figure 14–12 has a y-intercept at 20 and an x-intercept at 5. Any point on or below AA' represents a *feasible* combination

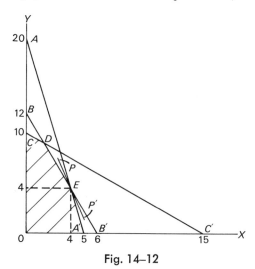

Fig. 14–12

of outputs of X and Y insofar as the limitation on the amount of factor A is concerned; any combination represented by a point on AA' would employ all of factor A, and any point under AA' would use only part of the amount of factor A available to the firm. In similar fashion the other two functions have been plotted as BB' and CC'.

Any point representing a combination of X and Y which does not lie above AA', BB', or CC' is a feasible point with respect to constraints relating to the available supply of all three inputs. The cross-hatched area bounded by $CDEA'$ includes all of the feasible points. If there were more than three inputs, the area of feasible points might be further restricted by lines similar to AA', BB', and CC'.

The problem now resolves itself into finding the *optimal* feasible point. This will depend upon the prices of the products. We have assumed that $P_x = \$6$ and $P_y = \$2$. The price of X in terms of the price of Y is, therefore, $6/2 = 3$. If we draw the factor-price line PP' with a slope of 3 tangent to $CDEA'$, we find that the optimal feasible point is at E, which represents an output of 4 units of X and 4 units of Y. Total revenue with this combination of outputs will be $4 \times \$6 + 4 \times \$2 = \$32$, and this is the greatest total revenue which this firm can make per time period subject to the indicated constraints. And it may be noted in passing that this solution could not be arrived at through the use of the calculus.

Let us see how much of each of the three factors of production we will employ to produce the maximum total revenue. To produce 4 units of X requires $4 \times 20 = 80$ units of factor A, and to produce 4 units of Y requires $4 \times 5 = 20$ units of A, and the entire quantity of 100 units of A available to the firm will be employed. The production of 4 units of X requires $4 \times 12 = 48$ units of factor B, and 4 units of Y requires the use of $4 \times 6 = 24$ units of B, and all 72 units of B are employed. But 4 units of X require $4 \times 10 = 40$ units of factor C, and 4 units of Y require $4 \times 15 = 60$ units of C, so only 100 of the 150 available units of C are used.

Suppose now that the price of X is \$3 and the price of Y is also \$3. The P_x/P_y would then be equal to one, and a factor-price line with a slope of one would be tangent to $CDEA'$ at point D, representing an output of $1\frac{1}{2}$ units of X per time period and 9 units of Y. Total revenue would be $1\frac{1}{2} \times \$3 + 9 \times \$3 = \$31.50$, and this is the greatest total revenue which could be made with these prices. The total amounts of the factors needed are summarized below:

A: $1\frac{1}{2} \times 20 = 30 + 9 \times 5 = 45$. Total: 75 out of 100 available
B: $1\frac{1}{2} \times 12 = 18 + 9 \times 6 = 54$. Total: 72 out of 72
C: $1\frac{1}{2} \times 10 = 15 + 9 \times 15 = 135$. Total: 150 out of 150.

It will usually be found in problems involving two products and three inputs that the optimal feasible combination of products will fully employ two of the factors and use less than the full amount available of the third; point D lies on BB' and CC' but below AA', whereas point E lies on AA' and BB' but below CC'.

SELECTED REFERENCES

Allen, Clark Lee. *Elementary Mathematics of Price Theory.* Belmont, Calif.: Wadsworth Publishing Co., Inc., 1962. Chaps. 20 and 21.

Allen, R. G. D. *Mathematical Economics.* London: Macmillan & Co., 1956, Chap. 16.

Baumol, W. J. "Activity Analysis in One Lesson," *American Economic Review,* 48 (December 1958), 837–873.

Dorfman, Robert. "Mathematical or 'Linear' Programming: A Non-Mathematical Exposition," *American Economic Review,* 43 (December 1953), 797–825.

Leftwich, Richard H. *The Price System and Resource Allocation.* 3rd ed. New York: Holt, Rinehart & Winston, Inc., 1966. Pp. 117–125.

Levenson, Albert M. and Babette S. Solon. *Outline of Price Theory.* New York: Holt, Rinehart & Winston, Inc., 1964. Chap. 7.

Liebhafsky, H. H. *The Nature of Price Theory.* Homewood, Ill.: The Dorsey Press, Inc., 1963. Chap. 6.

McKenna, Joseph P. *Intermediate Economic Theory.* New York: Dryden Press, 1958. Chap. 4.

Watson, Donald Stevenson. *Price Theory and Its Uses.* Boston: Houghton Mifflin Co., 1963. Chap. 12.

Stonier, Alfred W. and Douglas C. Hague. *A Textbook of Economic Theory.* 3rd ed. New York: John Wiley & Sons, Inc., 1964. Chap. 10.

Weintraub, Sidney. *Intermediate Price Theory.* Philadelphia: Chilton Co., 1964. Chap. 3.

PROBLEMS

PROBLEM 1

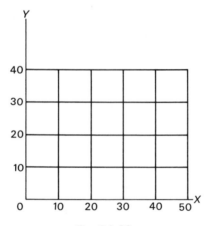

Fig. 14–13

1. A firm spends a total of $1,200 on factors X and Y. The price of X is $40 and the price of Y is $30. Draw the isocost curve = $1,200. Sketch in an isoquant tangent to the isocost curve. Indicate the amount of X used as Ox and the amount of Y as Oy.

2. The price of X now falls to $20, the price of Y remaining unchanged. The firm decides to maintain the original output. Indicate the amount of X now used as Ox′ and the amount of Y as Oy′.

3. As result of the decrease in the price of factor X, if the firm's output remains the same, the firm will employ (more, less, the same) of X and (more, less, the same) of Y; the total cost of the output will be (more, less, the same).

PROBLEM II

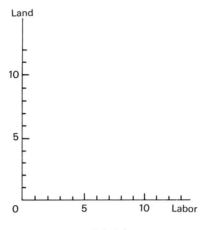

Fig. 14–14

The price of a unit of labor is $4 and the price of a unit of land is $6. A firm uses 6 units of labor and 4 units of land to produce a given output.

    1. Locate the point R on the figure to indicate that the firm employs 6 units of labor and 4 units of land.

    2. Draw the isocost line on which point R falls.

Now assume that the price of labor rises to $8 while the price of land remains at $6. At these prices the firm now employs 4 units of labor and 6 units of land.

    3. Locate R′ on the figure to indicate that the firm employs 4 units of labor and 6 units of land.

    4. Draw the isocost line on which R′ falls.

    5. With the new combination of factors, the firm produces the same output as before. Draw the isoquant.

PROBLEM III

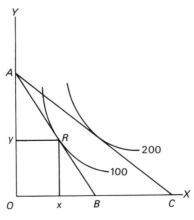

Fig. 14–15

In Figure 14–15 the firm is initially using Ox units of factor X and Oy units of factor Y to produce 100 units of output per time period. Then the isocost curve shifts from AB to AC.

1. The shift from AB to AC represents (an increase, a decrease) in the price of X in terms of the price of Y.

2. Suppose that after the shift of the isocost curve the firm decides to continue to produce at the rate of 100 units of output. Indicate on the figure with the letter S the appropriate combination of factors to produce this output at lowest cost.

3. Suppose that after the change in factor cost the firm decides to operate at the same total cost as before. Indicate on the figure with the letter V the appropriate combination of factors.

PROBLEM IV

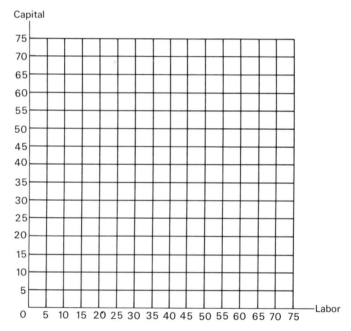

Fig. 14–16

Suppose that a given firm has three processes available to it by which it can produce its product. Each process represents a linear and homogeneous production function. By process A the firm can produce an output of 100 units per time period with 5 units of labor and 20 units of capital; by process B the firm can produce 100 units of output with 10 units of labor and 10 units of capital; by process C the firm can produce an output of 100 with 20 units of labor and 5 units of capital.

1. Draw the isoproduct contours for outputs of 100, 200, and 300.

2. If the price of labor is $5 per unit and the price

of capital is $10 per unit, which is the lowest-cost
process to produce 200 units? .   .   .   .   .   .————————————

3. If the price of labor is $8 per unit and the price
   of capital is $8 per unit, which is the lowest-cost
   process to produce 100 units? .   .   .   .   .   .————————————

4. If the price of labor is $14 per unit and the price
   of capital is $7 per unit, which is the lowest-cost
   process to produce 300 units? .   .   .   .   .   .————————————

15

The Firm as Buyer of
Inputs and Seller of Outputs

What today are known as courses in microeconomics or price theory were known to earlier generations of college students as courses in value and distribution. This final chapter is a generalized theory of distribution. We will not concern ourselves specifically with analyses of wages, interest, rent, and profits, but we will set up a framework for a theory of the prices of these things, which are what the firm buys as factors of production. The prices of factors of production are of the greatest importance to the firm since they determine costs and hence affect profits, and are of the greatest importance to all of society since they determine wages, interest, and rent, which constitute income to various factors of production.

If we define "factors of production" as those things which a firm buys and "products" as those things which a firm sells, the product of one firm is often the factor of production of another. If the price of the first firm's product is determined in its product market, the price of the second firm's factor is determined in the same market, and no special theory of input pricing is required. For some purposes a theory of interest is of great significance, but as modern economics has developed, interest theory has become a part of monetary theory and macroeconomics and will not be developed here. But the role of the firm as buyer does require further attention.

We have seen in earlier chapters that a firm will maximize profits at the output where marginal cost equals marginal revenue, and we have examined profit-maximizing output under conditions of pure competition, pure monopoly, oligopoly, and monopolistic competition. We have also observed that the profit-maximizing firm will produce any given output at the lowest possible cost, which is determined by choosing the combination of factors indicated by the point of tangency between the factor-price line and the isoquant. The total outlay of the firm on factors of production represents the firm's total costs. The difference between the firm's total cost and its total revenue is, of course, its profit, and this is the magnitude which we have assumed the firm is trying to maximize. To this point we have analyzed the activities of the firm as a seller of products separately from its activities as a buyer of factors of production. But since the role of the firm may be described as buying inputs and transforming them into outputs, the buying and selling functions of the firm represent two sides of the same broad process, and it is the purpose of this chapter to set forth more clearly the interrelationships between several matters which have heretofore been considered separately. We will begin with a brief exposition of the marginal-productivity theory of distribution, and then we will consider the matter of determining the profit-maximizing input for the firm under various conditions of monopoly and competition in product and factor markets.

The Determination of Factor Prices

We begin by considering a firm which sells outputs and buys inputs in purely competitive markets. Just as the firm may sell its product in either a competitive or a monopolistic market, it may buy its factors in a competitive or a monopolistic market. When a firm is the only user of a factor, it is called a *monopsonist*, i.e., a monopolist on the buying side; if only a few firms buy a factor, they are known as *oligopsonists*. Later in the chapter we will consider cases of monopsony, but at the moment we consider the simpler case of pure competition in both product and factor markets.

In an earlier chapter we noted that an average-product curve normally assumes an inverted U shape; as long as average product is increasing as input increases, $MP > AP$; when average product is at a maximum, $MP = AP$; and when average product is decreasing as input increases, $MP < AP$. At that time we were concerned with product in physical terms, such as yards, tons, or bushels, so average product was in fact average physical product (APP) and marginal product was marginal physical product (MPP). For our present purposes we need average and marginal product expressed in money terms rather than in physical units in order to get what is called average-revenue product (ARP) and marginal-revenue product (MRP). Since we are now considering the case of the firm which sells its product in a purely competitive market, and since the price of the output is therefore constant regardless of the firm's output, the *ARP* is simply *APP* multiplied by price of the output, and *MRP* is *MPP* multiplied by price. The general shapes of the *ARP* and *MRP* curves are the same as those of the *APP* and *MPP* curves, as represented in Figure 15–1. It should be noted that marginal revenue product is the addition to total revenue resulting from the use of an additional unit of input; that is, *MRP* is marginal revenue when the units on the *x*-axis are input rather than output, and as an equivalent of *MRP* we may use the term marginal input revenue (MR_i).

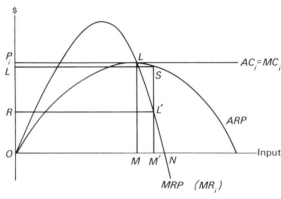

Fig. 15–1

Since it is also assumed that the firm is buying factors in a purely competitive market, the firm can buy as many or as few units of input as it requires without affecting the price of the input. This means that what we may call the average-input-cost curve (AC_i) will be a horizontal line, and if the average-cost curve is horizontal, the corresponding marginal-cost curve (MC_i) will be represented by the same horizontal line.

Suppose now that the input price has been established by the market forces of demand and supply at OP_i, and that the firm uses only one factor of production. We are to determine what the most profitable input will be at that price. The same rule applies here that determines the most profitable output. As long as the hiring of an additional unit of input adds more to the firm's revenue than it adds to its cost, the additional unit of input will add to the firm's total profit; that is, the profit-maximizing firm will employ factors of production until $MC_i = MR_i$. In terms of Figure 15–1, if the price of the input is OP_i, the firm should employ *OM* units of input to maximize its profits. If input price is *OR*, profit-maximizing input will be *OM'*. At any price, the profit-maximizing input is determined by the point of intersection of the MC_i curve and the *MRP* curve; at an input price of zero, the profit-maximizing input would be *ON*, where *MRP* is zero and where total-revenue product is, accordingly, at a maximum. In general, *for the firm which buys factors in a purely competitive market,* the marginal-revenue-product curve is the firm's demand-for-input curve. As we will see later, this is not true of the monopsonistic firm.

In Figure 15–1, when OM units of input are employed, the revenue per unit of input (ARP) is equal to ML, and total revenue is OP_iLM. When OM units of input are employed, cost per unit of input (AC_i) is also ML, and total input cost is OP_iLM. This means that with the price of the input at OP_i and OM units of input employed, the firm is making only normal profits, and the industry is in long-run equilibrium. This is the same situation described in output terms when the firm's average-revenue curve is just tangent to its average-total-cost curve, but since we are assuming that the firm buys only one factor, $atc = avc$. If the price of inputs fell to OR, the firm would hire OM' units of input; total revenue would be $OLSM'$; total payment to the input would be $ORL'M'$, and the firm would make excess profits equal to $RLSL'$. In the long run new firms would be attracted by the high rate of profits; the entry of new firms would cause the price of the product to fall, resulting in a reduction of average- and marginal-revenue product, and possibly raising the price of the input, and long-run equilibrium would be reestablished when the AC_i curve became tangent to the ARP curve. If the price of the input were higher than OP_i in Figure 15–1, the total amount paid out to the input would be greater than the firm's total revenue, and the firm would suffer losses.[1]

The relationship between the analysis of the firm's profit-maximizing output and the firm's profit-maximizing input may be seen with reference to Figure 15–2. In Figure 15–2A, the firm's total-physical-product curve is drawn with input measured on the x-axis and output on the y-axis. Figure 15–2B indicates that the most profitable output is OM', and Figure 15–2C shows that the most profitable input is OM. In Figure 15–2, an output of OM' requires an input of OM.[2]

That the input which maximizes profits will produce the profit-maximizing output may be demonstrated as follows. The additional cost of a unit of output is equal to the additional cost of a unit of input divided by its marginal physical product; for example, if an additional unit of input costs $12 and its marginal physical product is 4, the additional cost per unit of output is $12/4 = $3. This may be written

$$MC_o = \frac{MC_i}{MPP}.$$

---

[1] If more than one input is considered, a distinction must be made between average-gross-revenue product and net-gross-revenue product, which takes into account the productivity of the other factors. Since marginal-revenue-product is not affected in any event, this more complex analysis is not included here. See Alfred W. Stonier and Douglas C. Hague, *A Textbook of Economic Theory* (New York: John Wiley & Sons, Inc., 1964), Chap. 11, for the distinction between $AGRP$ and $ANRP$.

[2] *Cf.* Figure 13–5.

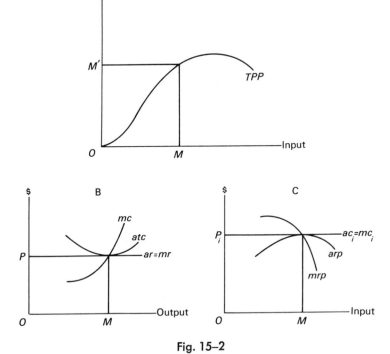

Fig. 15–2

Similarly,

$$MR_o \leftharpoondown \frac{MR_i}{MPP}.$$

If

$$MC_o = MR_o,$$
$$\frac{MC_i}{MPP} = \frac{MR_i}{MPP}$$

and

$$MC_i = MR_i.$$

Input-Output and Cost-Revenue Relationships

Before we turn our attention to the determination of the firm's most profitable input under various combinations of competition and monopoly in product and factor markets, we need to consider certain relationships, some of which are familiar and some of which have not to this point been made explicit. A hypothetical table has been prepared for this purpose. The table is not intended to correspond too closely with the facts of the real world, but it has been kept as simple as possible while still pointing up the important relationships upon which our subsequent analysis is based. We begin by identifying each column.

*Column 1 represents the firm's total fixed cost, which remains constant as variable input and output change. This quantity is assumed as given. (Columns whose figures are given are designated by asterisks.)

*Column 2 indicates the number of units of the variable factor used in combination with the fixed factor of production.

* Column 3 is the total-physical-product column, indicating output with each combination of fixed and variable factors. The units in this column are physical units, e.g., tons, yards, or bushels, rather than money. It is assumed that with zero units of the variable factor, total physical product would be zero.

Column 4 is marginal physical product. This is the first derived column. It represents the increments in Column 3 as we move down Column 2. The units are again physical rather than monetary, and the marginal product indicated here is discrete rather than continuous.

*Column 5 is the price of a unit of input. Since the price of the variable factor is constant as more and more units of input are employed, the firm is assumed to buy factors in a purely competitive market; that is, the firm's purchases of this factor are such a small part of the total market for the factor that changes in purchases by this firm will have no effect on the market price of the factor.

Column 6 is total variable cost. It is the product of the price of a unit of input and the number of inputs employed: Column 6 = Column 5 × Column 2.

Column 7 is total cost: Column 1 + Column 6.

Column 8 is marginal cost measured as output. Since output is given in Column 3 in discontinuous terms, we must resort to interpolation to compute the additional cost of producing an additional unit of output. For this purpose we use the formula

$$MC_o = \frac{P_i}{MPP}.$$

If, for example, the price of the variable factor is $20 and the marginal physical product of the variable factor is 5 bushels, the marginal cost measured in output terms is $4 per bushel: Column 8 = Column 5 ÷ Column 4.

* Column 9 is the price of a unit of output. Since in Table 15–1 output price is constant as output varies, we know that the firm is selling in a purely competitive market; that is, its average-revenue curve is a horizontal line at $P_o = \$2$.

Column 10 is marginal revenue in output terms. Since the firm is selling

TABLE 15–1

(1) FC*	(2) Input*	(3) TPP*	(4) MPP	(5) P_i^*	(6) TVC	(7) TC	(8) MC_o	(9) P_o^*	(10) MR_o	(11) TR	(12) VMP	(13) MR_i	(14) MC_i	(15) π
$100	1	70	70	$35	$ 35	$135	$0.50	$2	$2	$140	$140	$140	$35	$ 5
100	2	105	35	35	70	170	1.00	2	2	210	70	70	35	40
100	3	125	20	35	105	205	1.75	2	2	250	40	40	35	45
100	4	135	10	35	140	240	3.50	2	2	270	20	20	35	30
100	5	140	5	35	175	275	7.00	2	2	280	10	10	35	5

* Given.

in a purely competitive market, marginal revenue is the same as average revenue: Column $10 =$ Column 9.

Column 11 is total revenue and is price of a unit of output multiplied by the output: Column $11 =$ Column $9 \times$ Column 3.

Column 12 is value of the marginal product and is equal to the price of a unit of output multiplied by the marginal physical product: Column $12 =$ Column $9 \times$ Column 4.

Column 13 is marginal revenue in input terms; that is, it is the increment in total revenue resulting from the use of an additional unit of input. This is also known as *marginal-revenue product* since it is measured in money terms in contrast with marginal physical product, which is measured in physical units. The relation between MR_i and MR_o is given in the following formula:

$$MR_o = \frac{MR_i}{MPP}$$

or

$$MR_i = MR_o \times MPP.$$

Column $13 =$ Column $10 \times$ Column 4. We have seen that $VMP = P_o \times MPP$ and in a purely competitive market $P_o = MR_o$, so it follows that in a purely competitive market $VMP = MR_i$: Column $12 =$ Column 13.

Column 14 is marginal cost in input terms; that is, the additional cost of hiring an additional unit of input. Since the firm is buying factors in a purely competitive market, $MC_i = P_i$: Column $14 =$ Column 5.

Column 15 is the profit column and is the difference between total revenue and total cost: Column $15 =$ Column $11 -$ Column 7.

Column 15 reveals that profits are maximized at $45 per time period when the fixed factor is used in combination with 3 units of the variable factor with a resulting output of 125 units. But if only Columns 13 and 14 were available, we could determine the most-profitable-input combination. With 3 units of the variable factor, $MR_i = \$40$ and $MC_i = \$35$. The additional revenue from employing factor 3 is greater than the additional cost of using it, and it should, therefore, be employed. But the fourth variable factor results in an increase in revenue of only $20, which is less than the additional cost of hiring that factor; accordingly, it would not be used. The most profitable combination of factors is three variable inputs with the fixed factor. Or, in output terms, Columns 10 and 8 are sufficient. When output is 125 units per time period, marginal revenue is $2 and marginal cost is only $1.75. But when 135 units are sold, marginal cost is $3.50 and marginal revenue remains at $2. The sale of the last ten units would have the effect of reducing the firm's total profits. The firm's profit-maximizing position may be described in either output or input terms, and, as we have seen, the most profitable input will produce the most profitable output.

Demand for a Factor

In Table 15–1 it was noted that when the price of an input was $35, it paid the firm to hire the third unit of input but not the fourth. In general, the firm should continue to add units of the variable factor as long as MC_i is less than MR_i. For the firm buying inputs in a purely competitive market, the MR_i curve (or, as it is frequently called, the marginal-revenue-product curve) is the firm's demand curve for the variable factor. In terms of Table 15–1, if the price of an input is more than $140, the firm would use no inputs and, of course, produce no output; if the price of an input is less than $140 but more than $70, the firm would hire one unit of input; if the price of an input is anywhere less than $70 and more than $40, two units of input would be used; and so on.

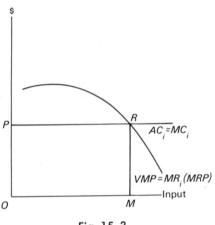

Fig. 15–3

In Figure 15–3 the average-cost, marginal-cost, value-of-marginal-product, and marginal-revenue curves for a firm which buys and sells competitively have been drawn with input measured on the x-axis. Since the firm *buys* in a purely competitive market, AC_i and MC_i are represented by the same horizontal line; since the firm *sells* in a purely competitive market, VMP and MR_i are represented by the same negatively inclined line. The MR_i curve is the firm's demand-for-inputs curve; it indicates the quantity of inputs which the firm would hire at any given price. Since the firm is buying inputs in a purely competitive factor market, the price of inputs will be established by the market forces of demand and supply, and the firm can buy as many or as few as it cares to at that price. In Figure 15–3 the market price of inputs is assumed to be OP. At input price OP, the firm will take OM units of input. The total outlay for the variable input is $OP \times OM$ or $OPRM$. If we assume that the input is labor, OP is the wage and $OPRM$ is called the wage bill. If the wage should be raised above OP by the demand and supply forces of the market, which, of course, might happen, or by labor-union activity, which in a purely competitive industry is unlikely, or by minimum-wage legislation, which is a possibility, the number of workers employed by this firm would decline. Whether the total wage bill increased or decreased would depend upon the elasticity of demand for labor.

When the firm buys inputs and sells outputs in purely competitive markets, the equilibrium position of the firm may be described as follows:

$$VMP = MRP = AC_i = MC_i.$$

Equilibrium with Many Inputs

Suppose that instead of one variable factor used in combination with the fixed factor, the firm employs several inputs, which may be designated as A, B, . . . , N. To achieve equilibrium the profit-maximizing firm must employ each factor in such quantities as to make the marginal return per dollar spent on one factor equal to the marginal return per dollar spent on all other factors. This may be written

$$\frac{MPP_a}{P_a} = \frac{MPP_b}{P_b} = \cdots = \frac{MPP_n}{P_n}.$$

This is equivalent to

$$\frac{P_a}{MPP_a} = \frac{P_b}{MPP_b} = \cdots = \frac{P_n}{MPP_n} = MC_o = P_o;$$

that is, in general,

$$MPP_i \times P_o = P_i$$

or

$$VMP_i = P_i.$$

This means that for each input taken separately the conditions of Figure 15–3 must be met.

It will be noted that the equilibrium input of each factor is the function of three variables: the marginal physical productivity of the input, the price of the output, and the price of the input. If, due to technological advances, the $VMP = MRP$ curve should shift to the right, input and output prices remaining unchanged, the firm would use more units of the input. Or, if the marginal physical productivity of the input remained unchanged but the price of the output increased, the $VMP = MRP$ curve would shift in the same way. And if the horizontal line PR should rise or fall, the profit-maximizing input would change.

Suppose that the price of factor A falls while the prices of the other factors $B, \ldots, N$ remain unchanged. This means that the numerator of the fraction P_a/MPP_a is smaller and the value of the fraction is smaller. This requires that the value of P_b/MPP_b and of all other factor prices divided by their marginal physical products must become smaller. Since by assumption the prices of other factors have not changed, their marginal physical products must increase if the value of the ratios of price to marginal physical product is to fall.

What will happen to cause the marginal physical productivities of factors $B, \ldots, N$ to increase? If the price of factor A falls, the firm will, as we have seen, employ more of factor A. If the firm uses more of factor A, will it use more or less of the other factors? The answer to this question depends upon whether the other factors are substitutes for or complements of factor A. Those factors for which factor A may be substituted will be employed in smaller quantities; the firm will substitute the cheaper for the dearer factors. As fewer of these factors are employed, their marginal physical productivities will increase, since the MPP curve is negatively inclined, and this will restore the equality of the ratio of the prices of these factors to their marginal physical productivities to the new ratio P_a/MPP_a. On the other hand, some factors may be in a complementary relationship with factor A; as more of input A is used, the marginal physical product of the other factors used in conjunction with it will be increased, restoring the ratio of their prices to their marginal physical productivities to the new P_a/MPP_a. To the extent that a fall in the price of factor A resulted in the firm's hiring more of A and also more of other factors, the firm would increase its output. We may say, accordingly, that a decline in the price of factor A will result in an increased employment of A from two causes: even if the firm's total output remains constant, more of factor A will be used because it is now relatively cheaper than other factors; this is the substitution effect. To the extent that the decrease in the price of factor A reduces costs and causes the firm to increase output, more units of factor A will be used from this cause; this is the expansion effect.

The Monopolistic Seller

So far in this chapter we have considered the firm which sells products in a purely competitive product market and buys factors in a purely competitive factor market. Let us now shift our attention to the firm which buys competitively but sells in a monopolistic market. Table 15–2 indicates the revisions in Table 15–1 which this change in assumptions requires.

Since we are using the same basic production function as before and since we continue to assume that the firm is buying the variable factor in a purely competitive factor market, Columns 2, 3, 4, and 5 are reproduced unchanged from Table 15–1. But if the firm is selling monopolistically, it will have to reduce the price of the output in order to increase sales, and the negatively inclined demand curve for the firm's product is indicated in Column 9'. This causes further changes which are reflected in Columns 11', 12', and 13'.

It will be noted that whereas in the case of the purely competitive firm the value of the marginal product (Column 12) was equal to marginal input revenue (Column 13), when the firm sells in a less than purely competitive

TABLE 15–2

(2) Input	(3) TP	(4) MPP	(5) P_i	(9') P_o	(11') TR	(12') VMP	(13') MR_i
1	70	70	$35	$4.00	$280.00	$280.00	$280.00
2	105	35	35	3.50	367.50	122.50	87.50
3	125	20	35	3.20	400.00	64.00	32.50
4	135	10	35	3.00	405.00	30.00	5.00
5	140	5	35	2.75	385.00	13.75	−20.00

product market the marginal input revenue is less than the value of the marginal product. This comes about because for the competitive firm an increase in sales represented an increase in total revenue by the full amount of the value of the additional units sold; for the monopolistic seller, however, it is necessary to reduce the price charged for the original output in order to increase sales, and the increase in total revenue is the value of the marginal product minus the reduced revenue from the original output. The relationship between VMP and MR_i can be demonstrated as follows:

Let p = the original price of the output
   x = the original quantity of output
   p' = the new lower price resulting from the increased output due to the hiring of an additional unit of input
   x' = the new greater output
   Δx = the change in output
   Δp = the change in price.

$$MR_i = p'x' - px$$
$$= p'(x + \Delta x) - x(p' + \Delta p)$$
$$= p'x + p'\Delta x - p'x - \Delta px$$
$$= p'\Delta x - \Delta px.$$

Since $p'\Delta x$ is the value of the marginal product and since if the firm sells in a purely competitive market $\Delta p = 0$, for the purely competitive seller, $MR_i = VMP$. If the firm sells monopolistically, however, marginal input revenue is always less than the value of the marginal product by an amount equal to Δpx.

The most profitable input for a firm buying competitively but selling monopolistically is indicated in Figure 15–4. Since the firm is buying in a

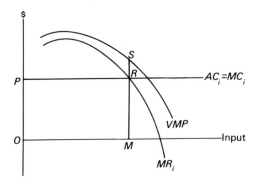

Fig. 15–4

purely competitive factor market, its average- and marginal-revenue curves are represented by a single horizontal line, as in Figure 15–3. But since the firm is selling its product in a monopolistic market, at any input $MR_i < VMP$. The most profitable input is determined at the point where $MR_i = MC_i$, which in Figure 15–4 is with OM units of the variable factor. Equilibrium for the firm which sells monopolistically and buys competitively may be summarized as follows:

$$AC_i = MC_i = MR_i < VMP.$$

The Monopsonistic Buyer

Two more cases remain to be considered: first, where the firm sells its product competitively but buys factors monopsonistically and, second, where the firm sells monopolistically and buys monopsonistically. Instances of monopsonistic buying are sometimes encountered in the real world, particularly in the purchase of inputs of labor. A weaver or loom-fixer in a textile-mill town, for example, may be able to sell his services only to the one textile mill in the community. If there are several buyers of a productive service, the firms are said to be oligopsonists, but this is included under the broad meaning of monopsony. The distinguishing feature of monopsony is that in order for the firm to employ additional units of a factor of production, it must raise the price offered for the input. The AC_i curve is, accordingly, positively inclined and constitutes the supply-of-input curve to the firm. This simply reflects the fact that because the number of firms is so small, increased purchases of the variable input tend to increase the price of the input. The MC_i curve bears the usual marginal-average relationship to the AC_i curve; that is, it has the same y-intercept as the AC_i curve with twice the slope.

The most profitable input for a firm which sells its product in a purely competitive market but buys its factors of production in a monopsonistic market is indicated in Figure 15–5. The VMP and MR_i curves are identical,

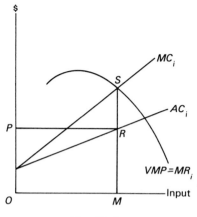

Fig. 15–5

as in Figure 15–3, where the firm was also assumed to be selling in a purely competitive product market. But the AC_i and MC_i curves are positively inclined, indicating that the firm buys monopsonistically. The most profitable input is again determined at the point where $MR_i = MC_i$, which in Figure 15–5 is with OM units of input, which will be available at a price of OP. The equilibrium condition for the firm which sells competitively and buys monopsonistically may be summarized as

$$AC_i < MC_i = MR_i = VMP.$$

Finally, we consider the firm which sells monopolistically and buys monopsonistically. In Figure 15–6 the cost curves of Figure 15–5 are combined with the revenue curves of Figure 15–4. The most profitable input again comes where $MR_i = MC_i$, which is OM in Figure 15–6. The equilibrium for the monopolist-monopsonist may be summarized as

$$AC_i < MC_i = MR_i < VMP.$$

The last case, where the firm sells monopolistically and buys monopsonistically, appears to be a relatively common situation in the real world. Two observations about the monopsonistic buyer are appropriate.

First, there is no demand curve for inputs for the monopsonist. This is analogous to the point made in an earlier chapter that the monopolist has no supply curve. In all four cases described in this chapter, the AC_i curve is the supply-of-inputs curve. In Figure 15–3, which represents a firm buying and selling competitively, AC_i is the supply-of-input curve and MR_i is the demand-for-input curve, and price and quantity are determined by the point of their intersection. In Figure 15–4, where the firm was assumed to be buying competitively and selling monopolistically, MR_i and AC_i are again the demand and supply curves, and the point of their intersection determines price and quantity. But in Figure 15–5 and 15–6, where the firms are assumed to be buying monopsonistically, price is below the point of intersection of the MR_i and AC_i curves. Given the MR_i curves of Figures 15–5 and 15–6, the profit-maximizing input could come at a higher or lower price if the AC_i curves shifted appropriately or the profit-maximizing input price would come at a different quantity if there were an appropriate shift in the AC_i curve. For the firm which sells competitively, the MR_i curve is the demand-for-inputs curve, but for the monopsonist no single curve indicates the quantity that will be bought at any given price.

Second, if one argues that a factor is "exploited" when it receives less than the value of its marginal product,[3] in all instances except when the firm is buying and selling competitively, productive factors are subjected to economic exploitation. This does not necessarily imply any moral disapproval

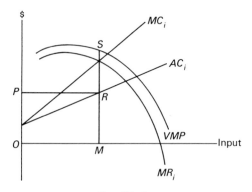

Fig. 15–6

but indicates simply that factors receive in compensation an amount less than the value of their marginal products. The extent of the exploitation is indicated in Figures 15–4, 15–5, and 15–6 as the amount RS. When the firm buys competitively but sells monopolistically, exploitation of factors comes about because MR_i is less than VMP; when the firm sells competitively but buys monopsonistically, exploitation results because AC_i is less than MC_i; when the firm buys monopsonistically and sells monopolistically, exploitation results from both causes.

The Adding-up Problem

The fact that factors often are paid less than the value of their marginal products provides the key to the question: if factors of production are paid on

---

[3] See, for example, Joan Robinson, *The Economics of Imperfect Competition* (London: Macmillan & Co., 1942), p. 283: "We shall say that a group of workers are being exploited when their wage is less than the marginal physical product that they are producing, valued at the price at which it is being sold."

the basis of their marginal productivities, how do we know that the total outlay for factors will just equal the total value of the product? Is it not possible that the total payment to factors might be more or less than the value of the total product? If the value of the marginal product of each factor multiplied by the number of each factor employed exceeds the value of the total output, where do the additional funds required to compensate the factors come from?

We turn again to a consideration of the linear and homogeneous production function. According to a mathematical principle known as Euler's Theorem,[4] if total product is a function of inputs X and Y, i.e.,

$$TP = f(x, y),$$

and if this function is homogeneous of the first degree, the amount of factor X employed multiplied by the marginal product of X plus the amount of Y employed multiplied by the marginal product of Y will just equal total product:

$$TP = x \cdot MP_x + y \cdot MP_y.$$

This means that in the special case of linear and homogeneous production functions, if each of two (or more) inputs is paid the value of its marginal product, the total outlay on factors will just exhaust the total revenue. This can be illustrated with the use of Figure 15–7.

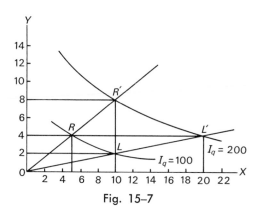

Fig. 15–7

Figure 15–7 shows two isoquants reflecting constant returns to scale. It will be noted that either 5 units of X plus 4 units of Y or 10 units of X plus 2 units of Y will result in an output of 100 units per time period. If the number of inputs is doubled, the total product will be doubled: 200 units of output

[4] For a brief discussion of homogeneous functions and Euler's Theorem, see Clark Lee Allen, *Elementary Mathematics of Price Theory* (Belmont, Calif.: Wadsworth Publishing Co., Inc., 1962), pp. 48–52. For the development of Euler's Theorem, see R. G. D. Allen, *Mathematical Analysis for Economists* (London: Macmillan & Co., 1942), pp. 317–320.

can be produced with either 10 units of X plus 8 units of Y or 20 units of X plus 4 units of Y. The production function represented by these isoquants is, accordingly, homogeneous to the first degree.

If we begin with combination L, which represents an output of 100 produced with 10 units of X and 2 units of Y, and, holding the amount of X constant at 10 and increasing the amount of Y hired to 8, we arrive at combination R' on isoquant = 200. Since

$$MP_y = \frac{\Delta TP}{\Delta y},$$

with the amount of X held constant, the marginal product of Y is equal to

$$MP_y = \frac{200 - 100}{8 - 2} = \tfrac{100}{6} = \tfrac{50}{3}.$$

In similar fashion, the marginal product of X can be determined if we hold the amount of Y employed constant at 4 and let the quantity of X used increase from 5 to 20, moving from point R on isoquant = 100 to point L' on isoquant = 200:

$$MP_x = \frac{200 - 100}{20 - 5} = \tfrac{100}{15} = \tfrac{20}{3}.$$

Applying Euler's Theorem, the total outlay on factors X and Y will be

$$TO = 5 \cdot \tfrac{20}{3} + 4 \cdot \tfrac{50}{3} = \tfrac{100}{3} + \tfrac{200}{3} = 100 = TP.$$

The total payment to factors just exhausts total revenue when the production function is linear and homogeneous.

It will be noted that when a function is homogeneous to the first degree, the average product is constant; if total product increases in proportion to the increase in factors, the output per unit of input remains constant. In general, it may be argued that when an average curve is constant over a range as measured on the x-axis, the corresponding total function through that range is linear and homogeneous. This is the situation with reference to a purely competitive firm in long-run equilibrium, whether that equilibrium position be represented in output or input terms. In Figure 15–8, the long-run equilibrium position of a purely competitive firm is represented both ways. In output terms, the average-total-cost curve at the point of tangency with the average-revenue curve is, at least for an infinitesimal distance, a horizontal line; the ATC curve has stopped decreasing but has not yet begun to increase at point R. Since at output OM the average-cost curve is a horizontal line, the total-cost function at that point is homogeneous of the first degree. The total payment to factors, OPRM, is just equal to total revenue, which is also represented by OPRM. The payment to factors just "adds up" to the total revenue.

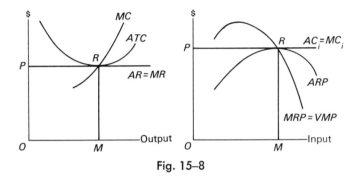

Fig. 15–8

The same point can be made in input terms. At point R on the average-revenue-product curve, the average curve is horizontal, and the total product function must at that point be homogeneous of the first degree. At input OM, marginal revenue product is equal to average revenue product, and again the total payment to factors, $OPRM$, just equals average revenue product multiplied by the number of inputs used, which is also represented by $OPRM$. We may conclude, accordingly, that in the special case of the purely competitive firm in long-run equilibrium, if all factors are paid on the basis of the value of their marginal products, the total outlay on factors will just add up to the amount of the total revenue.

The situation is quite different, however, if the firm is operating under conditions of increasing or decreasing returns, or if it buys inputs monopsonistically. Consider the firm whose cost and revenue data are represented in Figure 15–9. The fact that the AC_i curve is positively inclined indicates that

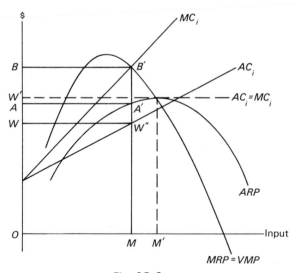

Fig. 15–9

this firm buys inputs monopsonistically, and the fact that $MRP = VMP$ tells us that it sells products competitively. If this firm bought factors competitively, in long-run equilibrium its average input-cost curve would be the dashed line ac_i, and the maximum number of inputs it could hire would be OM' at price OW'. If the price were higher than OW', where MRP is greater than ARP, the firm would be paying out to factors more than its total revenue. Since the firm would not be covering total variable costs, it would shut down. As was pointed out in an earlier chapter, a purely competitive firm would not operate in stage I of its production function, where $MP > AP$. But if the firm is a monopsonist with an average-input-cost curve such as AC_i, it may well choose to operate in stage I. In terms of Figure 15–9, the firm would maximize profits by employing OM units of input. The monopsonistic firm can operate in the stage of increasing average returns because it pays factors less than the value of their marginal products. The price paid to OM units of input in this instance would be OW, which is less than the value of the input's marginal product by an amount equal to WB.[5]

We conclude that there is nothing unusual or "abnormal" about the payment to factors of production an amount less than the value of their marginal product. Profit-maximizing firms which buy or sell in markets less than purely competitive will pay less than the value of their marginal products to productive factors. If the payment of less than the full value of the marginal product to factors of production constitutes moral as well as economic exploitation in the sense that what is taken away from one group is appropriated by another, there are circumstances under which minimum-wage legislation or labor-union activity might provide some relief, and brief attention to these policies will be given in our final postprandium.

POSTPRANDIUM

From time to time the American social conscience is disturbed by the presence of low wage rates and "pockets of poverty" in our affluent society, and efforts of a variety of kinds are enthusiastically undertaken in the "war on poverty." Labor unions have for many years attempted to raise wage rates by collective bargaining. For those workers who do not belong to unions a more direct approach has been urged by many people: if wages are too low,

---

[5] The three stages of the production function may be, and frequently are, defined in marginal rather than in average terms. When this is done, stage I ends at the input where marginal product is at a maximum, and the stages may be identified as (1) the stage of increasing marginal returns, (2) the stage of diminishing marginal returns, and (3) the stage of negative marginal returns. On the basis of this classification, even the monopsonistic firm would not operate in the first stage since at any input in this range it would not cover total variable cost. To delimit the significant range of the production function we may consider the maximum average-product input to mark the beginning of stage II for all firms except those which buy monopsonistically; for monopsonists, stage II begins at the maximum marginal-product input.

they argue, let us pass a law. It would seem that nothing could be simpler than to solve the problem of inadequate wages through the enactment of minimum-wage legislation. But while no one favors poverty, many people oppose legislation of this sort. Some feel that economic problems cannot be permanently solved by legislative fiat. And even if legislation could help the situation, the increasing use of this type of solution to economic problems creates the danger of big government, and it is feared that the cure may be worse than the disease. And then there is the embarrassing question: Where will the additional funds required to pay higher wages come from? Labor union leaders appear to assume that the increased payment to labor will come from profits, which in many instances they feel are excessive. But since profits in the aggregate represent a very small fraction of the national income and wages represent a very large part, even a small percentage increase in wages would wipe out all profits, and long before that happened the economy would be in serious trouble since profits provide the chief incentive for undertaking production. And, it is further argued, if wages are increased either by

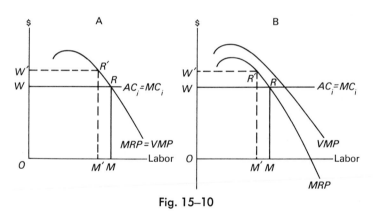

Fig. 15–10

legislation or by union activity at a rate in excess of the increased productivity of labor, either prices will increase, eliminating much if not all of the gain from the higher money wages, or the number of workers employed will diminish. Such gains as would come to some workers as a result of higher wages would be at the expense of other workers who were unemployed as result of the increase in labor costs, at the expense of consumers generally who would have to pay higher prices, and at the expense of entrepreneurs' profits. But in spite of these arguments labor unions continue to press for higher wages, and legal minimum wages are frequently revised upward.

The analysis developed in this chapter can be used to assess the effects of increased wages on the volume of employment, and while this will not in itself provide an answer to the question of whether minimum-wage laws are good or bad, it will supply evidence which needs to be taken into account when policy matters of this sort are under consideration. We may begin by noting that if a firm employs labor in a purely competitive market, the imposition of a legal minimum wage in excess of the equilibrium wage rate will have the short-run effect of reducing the number of laborers employed by the firm. In Figure 15–10, chart A represents a firm which employs labor and sells its product in purely competitive markets; chart B represents a firm which employs labor competitively but sells its product in a monopolistic market. In both instances the equilibrium wage is OW and the number of workers employed is OM. If the wage rate is increased to OW' either as a result of labor-union activity or the passage of a minimum-wage law, the number of laborers employed will fall to OM'. The MRP curve is the firm's demand-for-labor curve, and at the higher wage rate the number of workers demanded will be smaller. But, it is sometimes argued, the workers who do keep their jobs have higher wages than before, and their increased purchasing power will increase demand for goods in general, and the increased demand for goods will eventually increase the number of jobs; the ultimate result will be, according to this view, that as many workers as before will have jobs, and each of them will enjoy higher wages.

But whether the higher wage rate will actually increase the aggregate purchasing power of labor depends upon the elasticity of demand for labor. At the original wage of OW, the wage bill was $OWRM$; at the higher wage, the wage bill is $OW'R'M'$. If the elasticity of demand for labor is greater than one, the wage bill, that is, the "purchasing power" of labor, at the higher wage will be less and not greater than before, and this, we may suppose, would cause further unemployment of labor. Only if the demand for labor were inelastic would the higher wage have job-creating consequences even in the long run. The case for higher wages based on purchasing-power arguments is, accordingly, highly suspect.

The situation is quite different when the firm employs labor in a monopsonistic market. In Figure 15–11, chart A represents a firm which sells its product in a purely competitive market but hires labor in a monopsonistic market; chart B represents a firm which buys labor monopsonistically and sells its product monopolistically. In both instances the profit-maximizing wage rate is OW and the number of workers employed is OM. If a legal minimum wage rate of OW' is imposed, the number of workers employed will increase to OM'. If the law or a union contract requires a minimum wage of OW', the effective average-labor-cost curve for inputs up to OM' is the horizontal line $W'R'$. This time there is no doubt that the purchasing power of labor has been increased. At the original wage of OW, the wage bill was $OWRM$; at wage OW', the wage bill is $OW'R'M'$. The wage rate in either of these cases could be pushed as high as OW'' without reducing the number of workers below OM.

Any federal minimum-wage legislation which covers all firms, or, what seems to be only a bit less inclusive, all firms engaged in interstate commerce, will include some firms which buy labor in purely competitive markets and

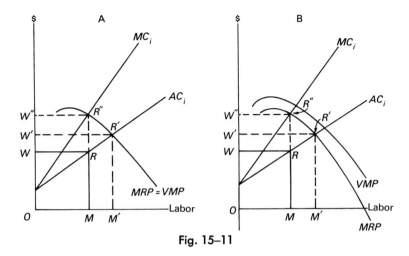

Fig. 15–11

some which buy monopsonistically. Some firms subject to the law will have highly elastic demands for labor, and the demand for labor on the part of other firms will be quite inelastic. The effect of the legislation will not, accordingly, be uniform from firm to firm and from industry to industry. Under these circumstances one may suppose that labor unions will continue to press for higher wages and social reformers will continue to urge higher minimum-wage legislation. This exposes us to the hazards of permitting resource allocation to be determined by politicians who have less than crystal-clear ideas of the issues involved, and this poses the threat of the break-down of private-enterprise capitalism.

SELECTED REFERENCES

Allen, Clark Lee, James M. Buchanan, and Marshall R. Colberg. *Prices, Income, and Public Policy.* 1st ed. New York: McGraw-Hill Book Co., 1954. Pp. 400–407.

Brennan, Michael J. *Theory of Economic Statics.* Englewood Cliffs, N.J.: Prentice-Hall, Inc., 1965. Chaps. 19–20.

Carter, W. Harrison, and William P. Snavely. *Intermediate Economic Analysis.* New York: McGraw-Hill Book Co., 1961. Chap. 15.

Chamberlin, Edward Hastings. *The Theory of Monopolistic Competition.* 5th ed. Cambridge, Mass.: Harvard University Press, 1946. Chap. 8.

Colberg, Marshall R., Dascomb R. Forbush, and Gilbert R. Whitaker, Jr. *Business Economics: Principles and Cases.* 3rd ed. Homewood, Ill.: Richard D. Irwin, Inc., 1964. Chap. 12.

Leftwich, Richard H. *The Price System and Resource Allocation.* 3rd ed. New York: Holt, Rinehart & Winston, Inc., 1966. Chaps. 13 and 14.

Levenson, Albert M., and Babette S. Solon. *Outline of Price Theory.* New York: Holt, Rinehart & Winston, Inc., 1964. Chap. 12.

Liebhafsky, H. H. *The Nature of Price Theory*. Homewood, Ill.: The Dorsey Press, Inc., 1963. Chap. 12.

Marshall, Alfred. *Principles of Economics*. 8th ed. London: Macmillan & Co., 1938. Book VI, Chaps. 1–2.

Robinson, Joan. *The Economics of Imperfect Competition*. London: Macmillan & Co., 1933. Chaps. 17–26.

Ryan, W. J. L. *Price Theory*. London: Macmillan & Co., 1962. Chap. 5.

Stigler, George J. *The Theory of Price*. Rev. ed. New York: The Macmillan Co., Publishers, 1952. Chap. 11.

Stonier, Alfred W., and Douglas C. Hague. *A Textbook of Economic Theory*. 3rd ed. New York: John Wiley & Sons, Inc., 1964. Chap. 11.

Watson, Donald Stevenson. *Price Theory and Its Uses*. Boston: Houghton Mifflin Co., 1963. Chap. 25.

PROBLEMS

PROBLEM I

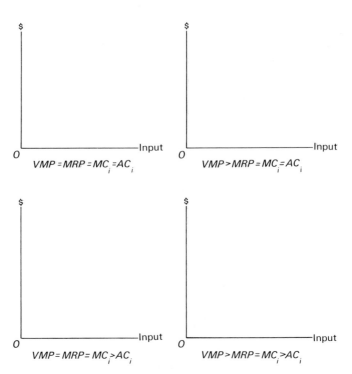

Fig. 15–12

Sketch in value-of-marginal-product, marginal-revenue-product, marginal-input-cost, and average-input-cost curves representing each of the equilibrium conditions described in the four parts of the figure above.

PROBLEM II

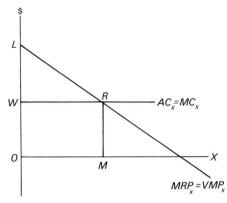

Fig. 15–13

Assume that a firm uses two factors, X and Y. The firm's production function is linear and homogeneous. The cost and revenue curves in terms of factor X are represented in the figure above.

1. Does this firm sell its product in a competitive market? . . . .————————————

2. Does this firm buy factor X in a competitive market? . . . .————————————

3. How many units of factor X will this firm hire to maximize profits? . . . .————————————

4. What price will the firm pay for factor X? . . .————————————

5. What will be the total outlay on factor X? . . .————————————

6. What will be the firm's total revenue? . . .————————————

7. What will be the total outlay on factor Y? . .————————————

PROBLEM III

Assume that 70 identical workers are employed on two grades of farms—A farms and B farms. Wage rates are determined competitively. Workers are perfectly mobile as between A farms and B farms. Land and labor are the only factors of production. Total revenue on A farms is given by $TR_a = 100q - q^2$, where q is the number of workers on A farms. Total revenue on B farms is given by $TR_b = 50x - x^2/2$, where x is the number of workers on B farms.

1. Complete the tables below:

q	TR_a	q	MRP_a	x	TR_b	x	MRP_b
0	————	0	————	0	————	0	————
10	————	10	————	10	————	10	————
20	————	20	————	20	————	20	————
30	————	30	————	30	————	30	————
40	————	40	————	40	————	40	————
50	————	50	————	50	————	50	————

2. How many workers will be employed on the *A* farms? . . . .——————————

3. How many workers will be employed on the *B* farms? . . . .——————————

4. What will be the wage rate on *A* and *B* farms? .——————————

5. What will be the total gross income of the *A* farms? . . . .——————————

6. What will be the total gross income of the *B* farms? . . . .——————————

7. What will be the total wages paid to workers on the *A* farms? . . . .——————————

8. What will be the total wages paid to workers on the *B* farms? . . . .——————————

9. What will be the total rent of the *A* farms? . .——————————

10. What will be the total rent of the *B* farms? . .——————————

PROBLEM IV

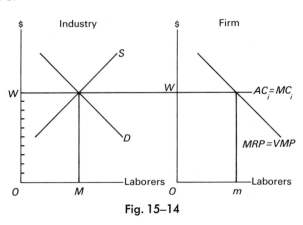

Fig. 15–14

In the above figure the industry demand-and-supply situation for workers is pictured on the left and the cost and revenue curves for a single firm are pictured on the right. The industry employs *OM* workers at wage *OW*; each firm employs *Om* workers. Assume now that the government levies a 10 percent tax on wages, 5 percent to be paid by the employer and 5 percent by the worker. Make the appropriate changes in the demand and supply curves. Indicate the new volume of employment in the industry as *OM'*. Indicate the number of workers employed by each firm as *Om'*. Indicate the net wage (after taxes) to the worker by *OW'*. Indicate the net wage (after taxes) paid by each firm as *OW''*.

PROBLEM V

1. Label the average-input-cost curve for a firm which buys competitively ac_i and the average-input-cost curve for a firm which buys monopsonistically AC_i.

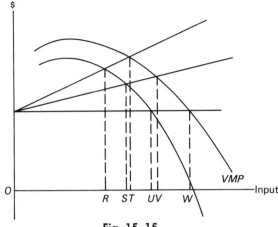

Fig. 15–15

2. Label the marginal-input-cost curve for a firm which buys competitively mc_i and the marginal-input-cost curve for a firm which buys monopsonistically MC_i.

3. Label the marginal-revenue-product curve for a firm which sells competitively mrp and the marginal-revenue-product curve for a firm which sells monopolistically MRP.

4. How many units of input should a profit-maximizing firm employ if it buys and sells competitively? ._____

5. How many units of input should a profit-maximizing firm employ if it buys competitively and sells monopolistically?   .   .   .   .   ._____

6. How many units of input should a profit-maximizing firm employ if it buys monopsonistically and sells competitively?   .   .   .   .   ._____

7. How many units of input should a profit-maximizing firm employ if it buys monopsonistically and sells monopolistically?   .   .   .   .   .   .   ._____

8. If the firm buys and sells competitively, the cost per unit of input is OP. Locate P on the figure.

9. If the firm buys monopsonistically and sells monopolistically, the cost per unit of input is OP'. Locate P'.

PROBLEM VI

In Figure 15–16, page 360, MRP_I is the marginal-revenue-product curve of Country I, and MRP_{II} is the marginal-revenue-product curve of Country II. Firms in both countries hire labor competitively.

1. If ON workers are employed in Country I, total revenue product in

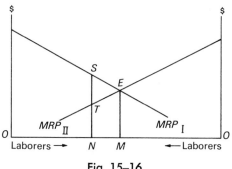

Fig. 15–16

Country I will be _____ and the wage rate will be
_____.

2. If $O'N$ workers are employed in Country II, total revenue product in Country II will be _____ and the wage rate will be
_____.

3. The total revenue product of the two countries taken together will be
_____.

4. To maximize the total combined revenue product of the two countries, workers should migrate from Country _____ to Country
_____. After the appropriate migration has taken place, the number of workers in Country I will be _____, and the wage rate will be _____; the number of workers in Country II will be _____, and the wage rate will be
_____.

5. The total revenue product of the two countries taken together will be
_____; this exceeds the combined total revenue product before migration by _____.

6. Political opposition to the migration of workers might be expected to come from what group? _____

PROBLEM VII

Assume a simple economy consisting of only two factors: land and labor. Labor consists of 25 workers, identical in all respects and all willing to work at any wage above zero. The total revenue product of labor is given by $TRP = 100x - x^2$, where x is the number of workers.

1. Plot the demand-for-labor and the supply-of-labor curves on the axes below.

2. What will be the wage rate? . . . . . ._____

3. What is the elasticity of demand for labor at this wage? . . . . ._____

4. What is the elasticity of supply of labor at this wage? . . . . ._____

5. What is the total amount paid to labor? . . ._____

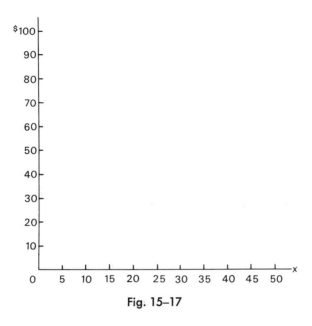

Fig. 15–17

6. What is the value of the total output of this economy? . . . .—————————

7. What is the total rent received by land? . .—————————

Now assume that a minimum wage of $60 is established by law.

8. What is the elasticity of demand for labor at this wage? . . . .—————————

9. How many unemployed workers will result from the minimum-wage law? . . . . . .—————————

10. What is the total amount now paid to labor? . .—————————

11. What is the value of the total output of the economy? . . . .—————————

12. What is the total rent received by land? . .—————————

13. The minimum-wage law has (increased, decreased) the economy's total wage payments by .—————————

14. The minimum-wage law has (increased, decreased) the economy's total income by . . .—————————

15. The minimum-wage law has (increased, decreased) the economy's total rental income by . .—————————

16. In general, a minimum-wage law will (increase, decrease) the economy's total income; it will (increase, decrease) the return to land; and whether it increases or decreases the total payment to labor depends upon . . . .—————————

16

Post-postprandium

Economic theory, as developed by contemporary writers, is divided into two major divisions. *Microeconomics* is the economics of small units and is concerned in large part with the *firm* as the basic economic unit. The heart of microeconomics is *price theory*. *Macroeconomics* is the economics of large units and is concerned with *aggregates*. The essence of macroeconomics is *national-income analysis*. Since of the two major divisions microeconomics is the older, it is not surprising that much of the vocabulary of micro-theory has been incorporated into or adapted for macroeconomics. It should be fruitful, accordingly, to refresh our memories about some of the concepts employed in price theory, and before we close the book on our survey of micro-theory we may do well to see how the application of price theory constitutes much of the subject matter of other areas in economics.

The fundamental problem with which microeconomics is concerned is the *allocation of resources*. Man's *wants* are virtually unlimited, but the *means* available for satisfying his wants are limited. This creates the problem of *scarcity* and means that somehow it must be decided *what* will be produced, *how* it will be produced, and *for whom* it will be produced: in some way, choices must be made. There are essentially two methods by which resources may be allocated: either by force through the state, or possibly through tradition and precedent, or through the operation of the *pricing system*. The latter is the method of a *private-enterprise* economy. If resources are allocated through the pricing system, goods are produced in accordance with the principle of *consumer sovereignty*. Interferences with the allocation of resources by government or by *monopoly* change the allocation of resources and *distribution of income* from what they would have been under conditions of *pure competition*. The *economic welfare* of the people may be increased or decreased by governmental interference with resource allocation and income distribution, and one of the current economic and political issues turns on the question of how many of our resources should be used in the *public sector* of the economy in the form of such things as schools, highways, and parks, and how many should be used in the *private sector* to produce goods which will be bought directly by consumers. But in a private-enterprise economy such efforts at reallocation of resources as are undertaken usually assume the form of indirect controls, such as *monetary* and *fiscal policy*, and prices continue to be used as allocators of resources. Even communist economies appear to be placing more and more reliance on prices for allocating their resources, and the Russians seem to be making limited use of the *profit motive* to stimulate production.

Prices in a private-enterprise economy constitute signalling devices to indicate to firms which goods need to be produced in larger quantities and which in smaller. If a decrease in demand for a commodity causes a reduction in its price, *producers* will reduce their rates of *output*. If prices are bid up by *consumers*, this constitutes a signal to producers to expand output. In this way in a *free-market* economy, goods are produced in accordance with the wants of consumers.

It has been said that if a parrot could be taught to answer "demand and supply" to any question, the parrot would be an economist. These terms are indeed important enough in economic analysis to justify the witticism, but it is rather the noneconomist than the economist who parrots the terms without understanding their meaning, at least as economists use them. Demand is distinguished from *quantity demanded,* and supply is not the same as *quantity supplied.* Demand and supply are *functional* concepts; the demand for commodity X is a function of the price of X, the prices of other goods, *consumer income,* and *tastes.* Goods are often in a *complementary* or *substitutable* relationship to each other, and a measure of interdependence of this sort is given by the coefficient of *cross-elasticity;* if two goods are substitutes for each other, their coefficient of cross-elasticity is positive; if they are complements, their coefficient of cross-elasticity is negative. The basic elasticity concept is a useful one in economic theory and has a number of applications. The *point price elasticity of demand* is measured by the formula $e = dq/q \div dp/p$ and indicates the responsiveness of the demand to a change in price. Several formulas are available for measuring *arc* price elasticity of demand, which measures the elasticity of demand between two points on the *demand curve*. The responsiveness of the demand to a change in income is measured by the *income elasticity* of demand. The *price elasticity of supply* provides a measure of the responsiveness of supply to a change in price.

But as important as the concepts of demand and supply are, it is only in purely competitive markets that prices are determined strictly by demand and supply as these terms are defined by the economist. For a seller enjoying some degree of monopoly power, there is no unique combination of price and quantity supplied; for the monopolist the amount supplied depends not only on his *marginal-cost curve* but also on the shape and position of his *marginal-revenue curve*.

In a private-enterprise economy *profits* are the principal motivating force for production. Total profit is *total revenue* minus *total cost*. To the typical businessman, cost consists of expenses. But a more fundamental view of cost is *opportunity cost*. Part of the cost of owning one's own home is the loss of *interest income* that one could get from government securities which one could have bought if he had not invested his funds in a house. *Inputs* have prices because they have *alternative uses,* and to get them a firm has to bid them away from others who would like to use them. There is sometimes a difference between *private* and *social* costs. The pollution of streams and the air by industrial firms illustrates costs which are borne by society rather than by the firm itself.

The assumption is usually made that firms attempt to *maximize* their profits. Although this is an imperfect picture of the actual behavior of businessmen, and other motives often affect decisions as to how much to produce, profit maximization seems to be the best single assumption that can be made to explain conduct of businesses. Other things being equal, firms will usually prefer more to less profits. And the assumption that businessmen want to maximize something makes possible a much more precise analysis of their behavior.

It is the function of the firm to *transform inputs* or *factors of production* into *outputs* or *products*. Factors of production may be variously classified. The traditional classification identifies *land, labor, capital,* and *entrepreneur* as factors. For some purposes it is convenient to classify all factors into two categories: labor and capital. And at other times it is helpful to consider anything which the firm buys as an input and anything which it sells as an output.

Each of the factors of production receives its *distributive share* of the total product. If we use the traditional classification of factors, the distributive shares are *rent, wages, interest,* and *profits*. The term *economic rent* has come to have a broader meaning than that part of the national income going to land; economic rent is that part of the payment to a factor in excess of the minimum amount necessary to keep the factor in its present use—the difference between the income of the factor in its present use and in its next-best use. If the supply of a factor is perfectly elastic, no part of the compensation of that factor is rent, but if the supply is less than perfectly elastic, a part of the payment to the factor is described as economic rent. *Interest* is also a term with more than one meaning. When we speak of *capital* as a factor of production, we mean *capital goods*. But interest is also defined to mean the return realized on *capital funds*, and in this sense interest theory is an important part of macroeconomics.

In the analysis of economic phenomena it is often true that what is significant is what happens *at the margin. Marginal utility, marginal cost, marginal revenue, marginal product,* and the *marginal rate of substitution* are terms which are frequently encountered in price theory. This makes an understanding of the relationships between *marginal, average,* and *total values* critical to a comprehension of contemporary price theory. And these relationships are also important in macroeconomics; the *marginal propensities to save, to consume,* and *to import* are basic tools of national-income theory.

Price theory is concerned with *equilibrium conditions*. It may be that the economy never reaches equilibrium because, before the equilibrium position has been attained, conditions may change and equilibrium conditions will accordingly change. But it is assumed that the market at any given moment of time either is at or is approaching equilibrium. The *consumer* is in equilibrium when he has budgeted his income so that he has maximized his *total satisfaction* with his tastes, income, and the prices of commodities given. The equilibrium condition may be described in marginal-utility terms by saying that the consumer is in equilibrium when the marginal utility of any commodity divided by the price of that commodity is equal to the marginal utilities of all other commodities divided by their prices. Or, in terms of the newer *indifference-curve* analysis, the consumer has maximized his satisfaction in the purchase of commodities X and Y when the *marginal rate of substitution* of X for Y is equal to the price of X in terms of the price of Y; i.e., where the *price line* is tangent to an indifference curve. A purely competitive *market* is in equilibrium at the price and quantity determined by the intersection of the market demand and supply curves. A *firm* is in *short-run equilibrium* when it is maximizing profits by producing to the point where marginal cost equals marginal revenue. A perfectly competitive firm is in *long-run equilibrium* when average revenue = marginal revenue = marginal cost = average total cost = long-run average cost. Viewed as a buyer of inputs, the firm is in equilibrium when it is producing the profit-maximizing output with the *lowest-cost combination* of inputs. In terms of *marginal-productivity* analysis, the firm will buy factors in such quantities that the marginal product of any one of them divided by its price is equal to the marginal product of any other factor divided by its price. In terms of *isoquants,* the equilibrium position of the firm comes where the marginal rate of substitution of factor X for factor Y is equal to the price of X in terms of the price of $Y,$ or where the *factor-price line* is tangent to an isoquant.

All of economics, and price theory in particular, is concerned with the *efficient use* of resources. By *technological efficiency* is meant the production of the greatest output with given resources, or what is essentially the same thing, the production of a given output with the fewest resources. When a firm is producing at the lowest point on its *average-total-cost curve,* it is producing at its technologically most efficient output, which, of course, may or may not be the most profitable output. Questions of technological efficiency for the most part lie outside the scope of economics. But economists are concerned with *economic efficiency,* which may be defined as producing goods in conformity with the wishes of consumers. This involves the proper allocation of resources among industries, correctly combining factors of production, and producing goods in the right amounts and in the proper proportions. The purely competitive model, which provides a poor description of reality, rates high marks as the norm for economic efficiency.

Economics has been defined as the "science of *wealth,*" or the "study of mankind in the ordinary business of life." While either of these statements may be true in a very broad sense, neither gives much hint as to the nature of matters which concern contemporary economists. Economics has become a highly technical study, and the first step in its mastery is an understanding of the principal techniques employed by its partisans.

Price Theory and Other Areas of Economics

To a considerable degree other areas of economics constitute applications of the methods of price theory to specific problems. *Distribution theory* is the study of the pricing of factors of production, and in many curricula it is combined with price theory in courses in *value and distribution theory.* Courses in *wage theory, labor economics, interest theory, land economics,* and *production theory* have at their base price theory and to some degree constitute extensions of matters developed in this text. The *normative* aspect of price theory is known as *welfare economics,* which is concerned with the well-being of consumers and producers and methods by which their economic welfare might be improved. The application of the methods of price theory to some of the problems confronted by businessmen is known as *managerial economics,* and this course is often a basic part of the curriculum in programs in schools of business. Much of *agricultural economics* is an application of price theory. *Macroeconomics,* in addition to borrowing much of the vocabulary of price theory, concerns itself with average prices as measured by *price indexes,* methods of preventing and correcting *inflation* and *deflation,* and analyzing national income into *wages, rent, interest,* and *profits.* Much of *econometrics* is a development of the methods of price theory. And *international economics* views economic phenomena from the broadest possible base and concerns itself with matters pertaining to both micro- and macro-theory;

exchange rates, for example, are prices, and *tariffs* and *quotas* are significant because they affect prices of imports and the allocation of resources.

It is clear that a course in price theory cannot explore at length the numerous "applications" of the theory; to do so would result in covering much of what we call economics and would violate one of the important concepts of economics—*the division of labor.* It is hoped that for those students for whom this is the terminal course in economics some understanding has been imparted of the sort of problems which interest economists, the kinds of tools which they use, and how they go about seeking solutions. For those who will pursue further study in economics, this course should provide a base for analyzing problems in a variety of applied fields. And it should be clear to all that this is a text in *intermediate* price theory; there is much more to be said on virtually all of the topics discussed here; we have attempted to provide no more than the *framework* for price theory. And although price theory is one of the older branches of economics and all economists have done some work in this area, there is much that needs to be done in developing better theories.

Some months ago a congressman from a Midwestern state said in a television speech that he considered himself something of an economist since as an undergraduate 30 years ago he had majored in Economics at the state university. It may be comforting to economists to learn that practical politicians would like to be identified as their brothers in the Fraternity of Economics. It has not always been so. But if all of the economics that the congressman knows is what he remembers from courses taken three decades ago and probably imperfectly understood at the time, he may come closer to qualifying as an economic illiterate than as an economist by contemporary standards. Much of what students are learning in college courses at the present time will undoubtedly be considered obsolete or irrelevant in another generation. But by a concentration on essentials it is hoped that the rate of obsolescence of the information provided in this text will be minimized. Such concepts as that of elasticity of demand and average-total-marginal relationships come about as close to eternal verities as the science of economics has yet produced.

INDEX

Adding-up problem, 348–352
Advertising, 258–262
Agents of production, 6
Alternative cost, 170, 364
Allen, Clark Lee, 77n, 242n, 300n, 324n, 349n
Allen, R. G. D., 319n
Allocation of resources, 8–10, 212, 362
Arc elasticity, 68–81, 363
  and total expenditure, 71–74
Average costs, long-run, 209–211, 226–229
Average-input cost, 336
Average-marginal relationships, 148–151, 159–160, 180–181, 295–299
Average-physical product, 335
Average-revenue product, 335
Average-total relationships, 156–158, 159–160, 172–177, 295–299

Bacon, N. T., 274n
Bain, Joe S., 280n
Basing-point system, 243
Baumol, William J., 137n, 278, 279n, 283
Bertrand, Joseph, 278
Blanket freight rates, 243
Boulding, Kenneth E., 11n, 267n, 280n
Buchanan, James M., 242n

Capital, 6, 364
Capital goods, 5
Ceteris paribus, 31–32
Chamberlin, Edward Hastings, 254, 262n, 274n, 278n, 279
Clapham, J. H., 267n
Cobb-Douglas production function, 299–300
Colberg, Marshall R., 242n

Collective bargaining, 352
Comparative statics, 11
Competition
  cutthroat, 228, 243–244
  monopolistic, 13, 253–267
  and monopoly contrasted, 238–241
  perfect, 12
  pure, 12, 21–32, 193–213
Competitive supply, 82
Complements, 81, 120, 318
Constant-cost industry, 203
Constant returns to scale, 325
Constraints, 327
Consumer
  equilibrium, 95–97, 117–118
  sovereignty, 9, 363
  subsidy, 127–128
  surplus, 103–105
Consumption, 6
Contour line, 325
Cost, 170–186
  alternative, 170, 364
  and production functions, 304–305
  average-total-marginal, 170–186
  fixed, 171
  imputed, 171
  long-run, 209–211, 226–229
  opportunity, 170–364
  selling, 258–262
  total, 171
  variable, 171
Cournot, Augustin, 274n
Cournot case, 274–278
Cross elasticity, 74–77, 363
Cutthroat competition, 228, 243–244

Decreasing-cost industry, 208–209
Demand, 21–25
  curve, 24
  curves from indifference curves, 123
  effective, 22
  elasticity of, 45–60, 101–103, 363

Demand (continued)
　for factors, 342–343
　potential, 22
　schedule, 23
Derivative of a function, 99
Differentiated products, 13, 255–256
Discounts, quantity, 242
Discrimination, price, 234–237
Distribution, 7, 334, 363
Distributive share, 7
Division of labor, 367
Dorfman, Robert, 324n
Douglas, Paul H., 299
Duopoly, 274–278

Econometrics, 366
Economically optimum vs. engi-
　neering optimum, 228
Economic
　dynamics, 11
　efficiency, 212, 366
　goods, 3
　policy, 212
　rent, 364
　welfare, 363
Economics, 1
Efficiency, economic, 212
Elasticity and slope, 55–59
Elasticity average-marginal relation-
　ships, 160–162
Elasticity of demand, 45–60, 101–103,
　363
　and average and marginal revenue,
　　160–162
　cross, 74–77, 363
　income, 76–77, 130–132
　and mark-ups, 162–163
　and total expenditure, 46–48
Elasticity
　of substitution, 319n
　of supply, 77–79, 199–200, 364
　of total product, 303–304
Engel curve, 122n
Entrepreneur, 6, 364
Equilibrium, 11, 262–264, 365
　consumer, 95–97, 117–118
　market and firm, 203–208, 365
　price, 27–30, 201–202
　with many inputs, 343–344
Euler's theorem, 349, 350
Excess profits, 230
Exchange, 8

Excise tax vs. income tax, 133–135
Expansion path, 320–321

Factor, demand for, 342–343
Factor-price line, 315–316
Factor prices, 335–338
Factors of production, 6, 334, 364
Fair price, 232
Fair return on fair investment, 232
Feasible combinations, 328
Firm, 10, 256–258, 334–355
Fixed cost, 171
Form utility, 6
Franchise tax, 230
Free-market economy, 363
Friedman, Milton, 32n

Games, theory of, 279
General linear equations, 33–39
Giffen effect, 129
Goods, 2–3
　inferior, 128
Googol, 61
Government, 8

Hague, Douglas C., 337n
Haitani, Kanji, 304n
Henderson, Hubert D., 11n
Hickman, C. Addison, 14n
Homogeneous products, 13

Ideal price, 233
Imputed cost, 171
Income-consumption curve, 122
Income effect, 124–126
　negative, 128–129
Income elasticity of demand, 76–77,
　130–132
Income tax vs. excise tax, 133–135
Indifference curves, 111–133, 365
　and elasticity of demand, 130–133
　linear, 118–119
　properties, 113–115
Inferior goods, 128
Infinity, 61–62
Input-output relationships, 338–341
Interest, 8, 364
Isocost curve, 314–316, 325
Isoproduct curve, 306, 325
Isoquants, 306, 312–329
　and total-product curve, 322–323
　relevant range of, 316–319

Joint demand, 81
Joint supply, 82

Kasner, Edward, 61n
Keynes, John Maynard, 11n
Kinked demand curve, 280–282
Kuhn, Manford H., 14n

Labor, 6, 364
Land, 6, 364
Landon, Charles E., 244n
Liebhafsky, H. H., 279n
Linear-cost functions, 182–186
Linear programming, 324–329
Lochlin, D. Philip, 244n
Long-run costs, 209–211, 226–229
Long-run supply 202–203

Macroeconomics, 10
Marginal-average relationships, 148–
    151, 159–160, 180–181,
    295–299
Marginal cost and supply, 198
Marginal-input cost, 337
Marginal rate of substitution,
    313–314, 316
Marginal revenue, 153–156, 335
Marginal-revenue product, 335, 341
Marginal-total relationships, 158–159,
    159–160, 178–180
Marginal utility 88–98
    and demand curves, 92–93
    of expenditure, 93–95
Marginal values, continuous vs. dis-
    crete measures of, 153–156
Market place, 10
Markets classified, 11–14, 254
Mark-ups and elasticity of demand,
    162–163
Marshall, Alfred, 1, 18, 103, 129n
Mathematical programming, 324–329
Microeconomics, 10
Mikesell, Raymond F., 60n
Minimum profits, 197
Minimum-wage laws, 353–355
Model building, 19
Models, 19
Monopolies, taxation of, 230–232
Monopolistic competition, 13, 253–
    267
    and pure competition compared,
    264–266

Monopoly
    legal, 228
    natural, 228
    pure, 13
Monopoly and competition contrasted,
    238–241
Monopoly firm and supply curve, 240–
    241
Monopsonist and demand for inputs,
    347–348
Monopsony, 13, 335, 346–348
Morgenstern, Oskar, 279n
Multiple outputs and inputs,
    326–329
Mund, Vernon A., 243

Natural monopolies, 228
    regulation of, 232–234
Newman, James, 61n
Normal profit, 171
Normative science, 18

Objective equation, 327
Oligopoly, 13, 272–288
Oligopsony, 13, 335
Opportunity cost, 170, 364
Optimal feasible point, 328
Optimum-size plant, 210, 226–228

Perfect competition, 12
Pigou, A. C., 254n
Pittsburgh-plus system, 243
Place utility, 6
Policy, economic, 212
Positive science, 18
Potential demand, 22
Price
    equilibrium, 27–30, 201–202
    fair, 232
    ideal, 233
    leadership, 282–283
    line, 115–117
    mechanism, 9
Price as a signalling device, 212–213
Price-consumption line, 122
Price discrimination, 234–237
    spatial, 243–245
Price effect, negative, 129–130
Price theory, 11, 362
Prices, factor, 335–338
Private and social costs, 364
Private-enterprise economy, 363
Process, 324

Product, 7
  average, total, and marginal, 293–306
Production, 6
  and cost functions, 304–305
  factors of, 6, 334, 364
  function, Cobb-Douglas, 299–300
  function, linear and homogeneous, 299–300, 349–352
  functions, 294–295, 305, 312–329
Products
  differentiated, 13, 255–256
  homogeneous, 13
Profit, 8, 364
  function, 197
  maximization, 14–15, 135–137, 194, 364
  motive, 363, 364
Profits
  excess, 230
  minimum, 197
  normal, 171
  supernormal, 204
Programming, linear or mathematical, 324–329
Public finance, 8
Public interest, businesses affected with, 228
Public utilities, 228, 232–234
Pure competition, 12, 21–32, 193–213
Pure and monopolistic competition compared, 264–266
Pure competition, evaluation of, 211–213
Pure monopoly, 13, 220–241

Quantity discounts, 242

Regulation of natural monopolies, 232–234
Relevant range of isoquant, 316–319
Rent, 7, 364–365
Reservation price, 26
Resources, 2, 4
  allocation of, 8–10, 212, 362
Returns to scale, 299–300, 325, 349
Revenue, average-total-marginal, 145–163
Robbins, Lionel, 8
Robinson, Joan, 254, 348n

Sales maximization, 283–285
Say, Jean Baptiste, 5

Scale line, 324
Scale, returns to, 299–300
Scarcity, 3, 362
Scientific method, 18
Selling costs, 258–262
Shortages, 39–40
Smith, Adam, 6n
Specific taxes, 230
Statics, comparative, 11
Stigler, George J., 253n, 267n, 280n
Stonier, Alfred W., 337n
Substitutes, 81, 119, 319
Substitution effect, 124–126
Substitution, elasticity of, 319n
  marginal rate of, 313–314, 316
Supernormal profits, 204
Supply curve and monopoly firm, 240–241
Supply
  elasticity of, 199–200
  long-run, 202–203
  and marginal cost, 198
  schedule, 26
  short-run, 198, 202–203
  very-short-run, 202
Surpluses, 39–40
Sweezy, Paul M., 280n

Taxation of monopolies, 230–232
Taxes, 8
  franchise, 230
  lump-sum, 230–232
  specific, 230
Time utility, 6
Total-average relationships, 156–158, 159–160, 172–177, 259–299
Total-marginal relationships, 158–159, 159–160, 178–180, 295–299
Total-product curve and isoquants, 322–323
Total product, elasticity of, 303–304
Transportation, 7

Utility, 6, 89
  cardinal measures of, 111
  ordinal measures of, 111

Variable cost, 171
Variable proportions, law of, 300–304
Von Neuman, John, 279n

Wages, 7, 364
Wants, 2, 362
Weintraub, Sidney, 30n
Welfare, 8n, 363
Welfare economics, 366

Welfare of firms vs. general welfare, 288

Zero conjectural variation, 278